Testimonials from I

"I am convinced that without the intervention of Dr. Coral and the Coral Method®, Skye would still be struggling. She would still be effectively mute. [But now she] is working *above* grade level in all of her classes. She is articulate. She is meeting her potential. She is, finally, herself." – *Mother of student with dyslexia and speech impairment*

"I saw improvement quickly in just a couple of months in Dysolve, like changes in his reading. We weren't working on reading directly at the beginning of his Dysolve program, but still he could see his mistakes and stop and correct them and read a little longer." – *Mother of student with dyslexia and ADHD*

"When Patience continued to remain on the Honor roll for the 2nd and 3rd quarters of the school year, we knew that this was for real. I am truly confident in saying that Patience will no longer be limited by her ability, but only by her motivation." – *Father of student with dyslexia, dyscalculia and speech impairment*

"One of the great things is, Dr. Coral gets him. She's not put off by his temper tantrums. He got an 85—in English. Before, he hated to write; he hated to read. I was correcting every other word he read. He's actually quite articulate in his writing now. He hasn't had any anger outburst or any meltdown since the beginning of 7th grade. He had been studying for tests alone since the last quarter in 6th grade. Definitely, he's moving in the right direction." – *Mother of student with dyslexia, autism, ADHD and ODD*

"It's hard to think of her as that little girl who was defeated when I first met her. But not now, not anymore. She's going to go out and grab the world by storm." – *Teacher of student with dyslexia and speech impairment*

"By the eighth month in Dysolve, Will was thriving at school. He had an 86% overall average that quarter. Will left 7th grade with…the Most Improved Student [Award]… Dysolve retrained the brain and helped Will create the correct ways to read. Dysolve is so different from any other program. It is so individualized that they can focus on his strengths while dealing with his "weak" spots. – *Mother of student with dyslexia and auditory processing deficits*

"He's done relatively quickly. He very rarely has questions about homework. That's one of the best things we've seen with Dysolve, because it was such a struggle to get him to do his homework." – *Father of student with dyslexia, ADHD and processing speed difficulties*

"Her growth was fast in Dysolve. After four months of Dysolve, Bella's speech cleared up and her stuttering dissipated. Before, even with my help, she got 60s and 70s in her spelling tests. Now she consistently gets 100s on spelling tests. Now she thinks she's great at spelling and wants to spell. There's a new confidence about her. Bella went up three reading levels within four months of Dysolve. Bella didn't read before. Now she's more apt to read. With the AIS at school, the improvement was slow. But since Bella started Dysolve, she skyrocketed." – *Mother of student with ADHD, dyslexia and speech impairment*

"Buster was never diagnosed with a learning disability. Until he used Dysolve, he showed slow progress but not enough to reach grade level. Buster was reading at grade-level expectations less than half a year after starting the Dysolve Program. Not only was he a reader, he was a motivated learner on the path for scholastic success...Given the relatively low cost of Dysolve as well as the short amount of time one needs to dedicate each day to the method, school administrators should consider using such a program to complement traditional reading instruction. Dysolve's targeted activities can benefit learners on the margins and pull them into grade-level performance in a precise and efficient way" – *College Professor and father of student with dyslexia*

"Dr. Coral said, 'I can fix this problem.' That gave me and my wife the confidence we were needing in a program to help our son. They're great coaches. They encourage and really want to see their students succeed. While their students succeed, it brings them pleasure and joy. I would love to see parents do that for their children academically because I think the tools that you'll give them in a program like Dysolve will really help them way beyond high school...It's going to help them with their future." – *Father of student with dyslexia and auditory processing deficits*

Dyslexia Dissolved

Successful Cases with Learning Disabilities, ADHD and Language Disorders

With
Artificial Intelligence and
Computational Microlinguistics

Coral P.S. Hoh, PhD
Evan Y. Haruta

AI 2018

Alpha Infonational™

© Coral P.S. Hoh and Evan Y. Haruta 2018

This publication is in copyright. All rights reserved. No part of this publication may be reproduced in any form. For queries, contact Permissions Department, Alpha Infonational, 4328 Albany Post Road, Suite 6, Hyde Park, NY 12538, USA.

Limit of Liability/Disclaimer of Warranty: This publication is intended to educate the public on the subjects addressed within. The advice and strategies contained in this publication may not be suitable for your situation. Consult with a professional where appropriate. The authors and publisher specifically disclaim all responsibility for any liability, loss or risk, personal or otherwise, which is incurred as a consequence, directly or indirectly, of the use and application of any of the contents of this book. Nothing in the book guarantees, or predicts, any results of or for anyone using the Dysolve Program or any ancillary services provided by any entity affiliated with the authors or other parties engaged or involved with the provision of the Dysolve Program; results vary from person to person and we make no claim with regard to expected results for any person, in any circumstance, whatsoever. Use of the Dysolve Program is governed by the terms of use and the terms of service on the Dysolve.com platform.

Names of cases and their families have been changed. Case studies follow the protocol for human subjects research and informed consent.

First published 2018
Cover design by KBH
Manufactured in the United States of America

Library of Congress Control Number: 2018911322

ISBN 978-1-7327886-0-2

Dedicated to our children

Brief Contents

Preface
About the Authors
Introduction

Part 1 – Past Cases
1 Patience – *Math Disability*
2 Duke – *Processing Speed*
3 Skye – *Dyslexia*
4 Storm – *Autism*
5 Will – *Auditory Processing*
6 Prince – *ADHD*
7 Grace – *Dyslexic or Poor Readers*
8 Uno – *First Subject of AI System*
9 User2 – *Second Subject of AI System*
10 Max – *Writing Disability*
11 Lessons Learned

Part 2 – Present and Future
12 The True Cost of Dyslexia
13 State of the Science
14 Computational Microlinguistics
15 Responsive Intelligence Technology
16 Responsible Education
17 Our Answers to Your Questions
18 An Ideal World

References
Index
Acknowledgments

Contents

Preface	vii
About the Authors	x
Introduction	xii

Part 1 – Past Cases

1 Patience – Math Disability   **3**
    Father's Story–*Limited by Motivation*   7
    Mother's Story–*I Did Everything Right*   18
    Dr. Coral's Story–*The Math-Language Connection*   26
    Patience's Story–*The Grades in between were Wasted*   42
    Key Takeaways   46

2 Duke – Processing Speed   **47**
    Dr. Coral's Story–*Twice-Exceptionality*   51
    Father's Story–*One of the Dumbest Things*   68
    Mother's Story–*You're Talking about Someone Else*   78
    Duke's Story–*Something Good is Going to Happen*   87
    Key Takeaways   91

3 Skye – Dyslexia   **93**
    Mother's Story–*You should All be Ashamed*   97
    Dr. Coral's Story–*Root Cause of Her Dyslexia*   122
    Teacher's Story–*Grab the World by Storm*   134
    Skye's Story–*I Became Numb to the World*   139
    Key Takeaways   150

4 Storm – Autism   **151**
    Mother's Story–*The Cost of Amputation*   155
    Dr. Coral's Story–*Language-Processing Deficits*   179
    Instructor's Story–*Chameleon*   194
    Teachers' Stories–*Spiral of Self-Loathing*   199
    Storm's Story–*Pulled Apart*   203
    Key Takeaways   210

5 Will – Auditory Processing — 211
- Mother's Story–*She Knew Things before I Told Her* — 215
- Father's Story–*I can Fix this Problem* — 229
- Dr. Coral's Story–*Motivation* — 235
- Will's Story–*Nothing's Going to Hold You Back* — 250
- **Key Takeaways** — 255

6 Prince – ADHD — 257
- Dr. Coral's Story–*Language-Related ADHD* — 261
- Mother's Story–*A Place that Focused on Language* — 281
- Instructor's Story–*Be Alarmed* — 289
- Prince's Story–*You Push through the Headaches* — 293
- **Key Takeaways** — 296

7 Grace – Dyslexic or Poor Readers — 297
- Dr. Coral's Story–*Dialect vs. Deficit* — 301
- Principal's Story–*Create New Pathways* — 313
- Founder's Story–*Not-For-Profit* — 327
- **Key Takeaways** — 331

8 Uno – First Subject of AI System — 333
- Dr. Coral's Story–*Artificial Intelligence* — 337
- Professor's Story–*Buster v. Puffy the Vampire Fish* — 345
- **Key Takeaways** — 355

9 User2 – Second Subject of AI System — 357
- Engineer's Story–*Problem Resolution* — 361
- Mother's Story–*She Skyrocketed* — 371
- **Key Takeaways** — 377

10 Max – Writing Disability — 379
- Dr. Coral's Story–*Early Childhood Deprivation* — 382

11 Lessons Learned — 386
- *The Ones who Walked Away* — 386
- *The Ones who Failed in Society* — 387
- *Chances are, It's Dyslexia* — 389
- *Dyslexia can be Corrected* — 390
- *You should be in Crisis Mode* — 390

Trust Yourself	393
Don't Settle for Less	394

Part 2 – Present and Future

12 The True Cost of Dyslexia — **401**
We all Pay for Dyslexia — 401
Why is Special Ed so Expensive? — 403
What does It Buy Us? — 404
Cost Comparisons — 405
Individual Toll — 407
Societal Cost — 409
Key Takeaways — 414

13 State of the Science — **415**
The State We Inherited — 415
The Solution — 423
Dyslexia-Free Life — 424
Define the Deficit, Not Dyslexia — 425
New Science — 431
Correct, Not Compensate — 431
Functional, Not Physical Brain — 432
Key Takeaways — 440

14 Computational Microlinguistics — **441**
The Challenge — 441
Structure-Complex — 441
Problem-Complex — 446
Computational Problem — 450
Computational Microlinguistics — 453
Key Takeaways — 458

15 Responsive Intelligence Technology — **459**
System and Human Requirements — 459
Computer Expert System — 460
Responsive Intelligence Technology^{TM} — 463
Individuated Programs — 465
Advantages of Responsive Intelligence — 466
Implications for Dyslexia Intervention — 468

Dyslexia Dissolved	470
Key Takeaways	476

16 Responsible Education — **477**
Anger	477
Owning the Problem	479
Saving a Life	480
Key Takeaways	486

17 Our Answers to Your Questions — **487**
Context	487
Questions from the Public	489
Questions from Schools	493
Questions from Families	501
Questions from Doctors	506
Questions from Researchers	509

18 An Ideal World — **515**
Full Circle	515
Transformation	517
Dissemination	518
Dysolve Dyslexia	519

References	523
Index	537
Acknowledgments	552

Preface

When a child has a learning condition, the adults in her orbit—her parents, relatives, teachers, doctors and specialists—feel the weight of this problem. As the parent, it is particularly distressing to hear that your child has a learning or reading disability, that she could be dyslexic. And that she is way behind her peers at school. To compound matters, her behavior may continue to perplex despite all attempts to help her. You suspect other additional issues (perhaps ADHD) are preventing her from responding positively to your efforts. You are most fearful, as are most parents, when your child's predicament appears beyond your control.

Every story in Part 1 of this book begins with this fear. The families here got out of their predicament. They were the early participants of a new program, Dysolve, that corrected their children's conditions. We use specific cases here to illustrate how learning and reading disabilities, dyslexia and coexisting ADHD, speech impairment, auditory processing disorder, dyscalculia, dysgraphia and other problems with no name are interrelated through a common source. This source is the complex of language-processing deficits affecting each person.

The cases here show how language-processing deficits can create far-reaching effects on the behavioral, psychosocial and even physical. One case alone experienced a slew of disorders—dyslexia, ASD, ADHD and ODD. Cases such as this one prove that it is possible to remove language difficulties through corrective training *and* lose the debilitating effects of coexisting conditions at the same time. These stories offer hope to other families facing a multiplicity of such challenging issues.

Each problem is reflected through the eyes of the parents, instructors, the expert, and the child. The parents and children speak in their own voices through their own writing or interviews. The frustration of the parents is palpable and understandable given their long, hard struggle to find a solution. Their stories are balanced by those of teachers and a principal, who illuminate the difficult position that schools were placed in when resources were limited and no solution was available (until now).

Names, of course, have been changed to ensure anonymity, even though the children and their families are enormously proud of what they have been able to accomplish. The chapters in Part 1 are modular and can be read in any order.

While Part 1 gives a closeup of these conditions and their resolution, Part 2 takes a broader perspective to discuss why a solution was not invented before Dysolve. In its absence, compensatory methods kept dyslexia chronic while placing a huge drain on education budgets.

The complexity of dyslexia and its coexisting conditions required a computational and technological solution. The computational solution came from a new science we founded, Computational Microlinguistics. The solution was delivered through a new type of artificial intelligence system that corrects language-based conditions, of which Dysolve® is a prototype.

Solving the problem of learning and reading disabilities changes the state of education. We discuss the implications on education and answer questions that various stakeholders may have about this new solution, science, and technology. We end the book with our vision of a new world that the solution to dyslexia promises.

Preface

This is a story with a happy ending. Another parent, caretaker, teacher, doctor or counselor facing a child who has not responded to every intervention attempted may not think that such an outcome is possible in their case. For such cases, we say, read this book. The cases here are but a small sample of the variety of experiences encountered by the many affected by dyslexia and its related conditions. If the condition continues to defy all explanation, ask us.

Coral P.S. Hoh and Evan Y. Haruta
Dysolve.com
f Dysolve Dyslexia

CORAL P.S. HOH, PhD, works in the rare specialty of exceptional languages and twice-exceptionality. She is one of a few experts on the language processes of exceptional populations across the spectrum. She is a referee for academic journals owing to her pioneering studies. Her research received funding from the National Science Foundation, and she served on an editorial advisory board for the National Association for Gifted Children. She is the author of a book and research articles on Linguistics, language and cognition. Through her fieldwork on language disorders and dyslexia for over two decades, Dr. Coral developed the Coral Method® for their evaluation and correction. She cofounded tech company EduNational, which built the artificial intelligence system for dyslexia, Dysolve®. She is the co-inventor of this patented computing technology for language disorders. The AI system launched on Valentine's Day in 2017 on the Dysolve.com and SolveDyslexia.com platform.

EVAN Y. HARUTA, MS, specializes in problem evaluation of large-scale computing environments and has resolved problems with parallel sysplex systems worldwide for nearly 30 years. As a Senior Software Engineer for IBM, he is a regular presenter at technology conventions for global companies in education, healthcare, finance, energy, transportation, retail, and service industries as well as federal agencies. He is a lead developer of an international software workshop series and a contributing author to a tech magazine. He serves on a patent review board. With a Master's in Mathematical Engineering, Evan volunteered as a MathCounts coach for many years and later trained high school students as coaches. He founded the not-for-profit IDLWorld in 2017 to support the academic needs of gifted and twice-exceptional students.

Coral and Evan have two grown children. Together, they volunteer to help immigrant families and children with special needs in the Mid-Hudson Valley in New York.

Introduction

It is 2018. Self-driving cars are traversing America's roadways. Over 100 years of innovation have enabled the automotive industry to build autonomous machines that can perform like humans. In automotive plants, robots with artificial intelligence assemble machines alongside human workers.

At about the time the first automobile was built, the problem of dyslexia first gained recognition. Yet over this span of 100 years, reading instruction did not encounter similar breakthrough technologies.

So in this year, as in the years before it, nearly two-thirds of American children fail to meet reading standards in elementary and middle school. And about the same number will continue to fail in high school. For about 20% of them, graduating from high school is difficult and attending college is challenging if not impossible. Many of them contend with related conditions such as ADHD and various language disorders.

Reading experts set up special clinics and propose best evidence-based practices, but a significant number of the 10 million struggling learners in the US remain "resistant to intervention." Experts say more expertise is needed. Meanwhile, overburdened schools try to manage as many of such students as their budgets allow. But their budgets allow services for less than half of them. So complicated is their reading problem, so costly the methods to help them cope year after year. Some students see no progress; some see a little but not enough to get them to grade level. Close to three-quarters of these students stay in reading remediation throughout school.

At a school meeting once, Directors of Special Education told us privately that the parents of such students were angry by middle school. But Special Ed had no new solution to offer—just the same methods they had been using since elementary grades.

The learning environment morphed into a battleground for support services, with families and school staff as adversaries. *What families did not realize was that schools did not have a solution to offer.* The problem of dyslexia was too complex for existing fields of study and practice.

A series of critical breakthroughs had to happen before a solution was available. It started with a small group of parents who refused to accept that their children's reading disability could not be corrected. It led to a new science and new technology that offer the solution to dyslexia for students everywhere.

This is the story.

Dyslexia Dissolved

PART 1

Past Cases

Dyslexia Dissolved

1

Patience

Math Disability

Patience

Dysolve Finding:
Language-processing deficits leading to dyslexia, speech impairment, ADHD symptoms[1, 2]

School Classification:
Learning disability, speech/language impairment, math disability

School Services:
Early intervention for speech/language, speech therapy, Academic Intervention Services (AIS)

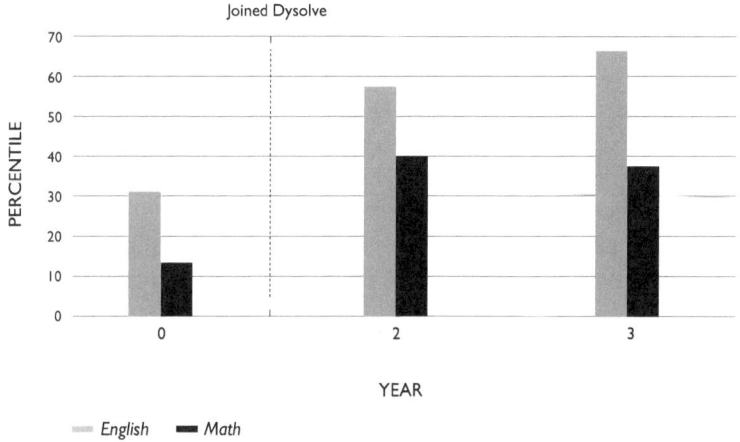

FIGURE 1
Patience - State Scores for English and Math before and in Year 2-3 in Dysolve[3]

NOTES

1. By *language-processing deficits*, we mean deficiencies in the processes involved in executing the language functions of speaking, listening, reading or writing.
2. *ADHD* refers to Attention Deficit/Hyperactivity Disorder. It is also referred to as *ADD* as well as other labels that have been updated over the years. The core components of this condition are inattention, hyperactivity and impulsivity. See Chapter 6 for further discussion.
3. State percentiles refer to student's ranking among peers in the state of New York. Scores for Year 1 were unavailable.

Father's Story

Limited by Motivation
Charles

Authors' note: This story illustrates the difficult position both the family and school are placed in when support services are limited due to the cost of present compensatory methods. See Chapter 12.

Emergency

"You'll have to wait outside, Sir!"

"Wait—outside, you'll have to wait—"

About 10 feet before the Labor and Delivery Room, the doctors stopped me. I was not going to be able to go in with my wife, Faye. She went through the operating room doors out of my sight and I was left in the hallway, half-dressed in scrubs, wondering what the hell just happened!

I only knew that it wasn't good. The waiting room lights seemed deafening. My parents, and then my in-laws, came in. I recounted the turn of events. Faye, who was seven months pregnant at the time, called me at about 10:30 PM to say that her coworkers in the evening shift thought she looked a little pale, and she was going to go over to Labor and Delivery to get checked out. She thought she was just a little dehydrated. I asked her if she wanted me to come to the hospital and she said "no." Well, I went anyway. Like a good husband, I brought the "to-go" pregnancy bag just in case. When I got up to Labor and Delivery, I noticed a lot of commotion.

The nurses at the front desk took me right to Faye. She was in a lot of pain. Her platelet cell count had dropped dangerously low. The doctors said she needed an emergency C-section, for she could no longer carry the baby. My wife was later diagnosed with a rare form of pre-eclampsia called *HELLP Syndrome*.

HELP. In the waiting room, I waited to respond to my in-laws. I just needed more details. I'd know how to respond if I had more details. Faye's parents, shaken with worry, held each other. I did not tell them how serious the situation was because I didn't want to get them upset on what was supposed to be a happy moment. This was going to be their first grandchild.

About a half hour later, a nurse brought our baby, Patience, to us in the waiting room. The nurse nodded, "She's gonna be okay." The lights flushed another filter of color over the room.

"But your wife is in critical condition..."

I've heard this too many times as a police officer. I saw shadows from the next hallway moving quickly. There seemed to be a lot of people in the hospital. I just needed more details. I'd know how to respond if I had more details. The doctors told me that my wife had a 50/50 chance of survival. It was a wait-and-see game at this point. I held Patience in my arms. She was so tiny, just 4 ½ pounds, but she was very strong and did not need to go to NICU. I remember holding our baby and thinking that I might be a single parent.

By the grace of God and the great medical staff at the hospital, my wife made a full recovery. After two days in the Intensive Care Unit and five more days in Labor and Delivery, I was so happy to bring them both home together.

And that's how we brought our first child into this world five weeks early to save my wife's life. Little did we know that we would spend the next 12 years trying to save our child's.[1]

Good Enough

Patience's first months seemed typical to us. When Patience was about 20 months old, we went on a cruise. Patience was not happy about being on the ship and made it known. By the third day, she had had enough! She pounded on the closet door. I opened the closet. She pointed at our luggage. She pulled out her little suitcase. She was telling us that she wanted to go home. My first thought was, "Wow! This kid is smart! She was able to associate the luggage with going home."

Still, Patience was behind in her development in various ways since she was born premature. Throughout most of her primary grades, Patience struggled with school, receiving *1*s and *2*s in all of her classes on a 4-point rating system. In the beginning and after all of the school's testing, the district's special education staff told us that Patience would classify for multiple services. They believed that, despite her premature birth and developmental delays, Patience would catch up and not need any services by 6th grade.

Patience had co-teaching classes, one-on-one aides, speech therapy sessions, and extra time to complete tests and classwork.[2] But over the course of her five years in elementary school, the district tried to withdraw services one by one. The administrators said that she was improving, but my wife and I didn't see it. Every night, we helped her with homework, which was usually a 2-3 hour ordeal. And that was just in the primary grades. It was obvious to us that something was wrong.

We had independent experts test her to confirm what we suspected. Even Patience's teachers offered their opinion that these services and her special education status should not be removed. All of this did not seem to matter. According to the school's testing, Patience was "good enough."[3] She was receiving mostly 2s in her classes, which was just below average. The school only had a limited amount of time and resources, and there were kids who were worse off than Patience because they had behavior issues.[4] And there were also students who didn't even speak English. Patience was always well-behaved.

Just Going to Get by

My wife would end up in tears at some of these special ed meetings. Faye and I faced challenges on the job with the right tools and skills. Our daughter had to confront hers with her bare innocence. She was growing up fast, which made her challenges harder and harder to manage.

We had become extremely frustrated that we had not seen any improvement in Patience by the 5th grade—especially when we were told by the Special Education Department and school staff that, according to their diagnoses, Patience should have caught up by then.

Reluctantly, I had started to come to the realization that Patience was just going to get by in life. I felt that if Faye and I could keep Patience from dropping out of school and she got her high school diploma, we would be winners in my book. Faye and I both have Bachelor's degrees and I am proud to say that I graduated Magna Cum Laude.

Part of my career involved being a school resource officer and I had a lot of exposure to different kinds of students and the inner workings of a school district on all levels. As a school resource officer, I observed children like Patience who were good kids behavior-wise and were very bright, but somehow they would end up dropping out of school.[5] A few years later, I would end up arresting some of these kids.[6] The system failed them. That's the future for Patience that I hoped to avoid. *It was very unsettling to me that Patience would be limited in life by her ability and not by her motivation.*

Then one day in 5th grade, her teacher, Ms. White, sent home a sticky note in her homework folder with the word "Dyslexia?"

My wife and I were pretty upset. Patience had been in school for six years, and no one caught this. We later learned that school staff was not supposed to diagnose students with this condition; it was not tested for and there was no program in the school to help children with dyslexia. We discussed the issue with our pediatrician, who recommended Dr. Coral.

Fighting Chance

We brought a mountain of Patience's school and medical records to Dr. Coral. After Dr. Coral's testing, we were told that Patience was highly intelligent but faced language issues that led to the dyslexia.

To be honest, although I was happy to hear this, I was also very skeptical. I honestly didn't see the high intelligence. From living with Patience, I had been frustrated with how she had a tough time following our instructions.[7] I would tell her to do A, B, and C, but usually she would do only A and forget about everything else.[8] I would ask her to pick up her shoes and place them by the door on the mat. She would pick up her shoes and wander around the house with them until she found something else that looked more interesting. Or I would ask her to throw out a piece of paper in the kitchen garbage. She would pick up the paper, leave the room with the intention of throwing it out in the kitchen, but I would usually find the paper near the garbage on the floor while she played in another room.

We would hear from her teachers that when a story was read in class, Patience would not be able to recall or answer questions about specific facts. But she would answer correctly questions about the deeper meaning of the story.[9] The teachers would say to us that this was a very advanced skill and kids her age were not supposed to be able to do that. Although my father, my wife and I would see flashes of brilliance from Patience on occasion, there were too many nights where it would take me three hours a night just to get through 2nd, 3rd and 4th grade homework.[10] She was so smart in some regards but so far behind in others. However, I was happy to at least have a definite finding from Dr. Coral.

Next Dr. Coral explained the process to correct Patience's condition and the commitment it would take from my wife and me. We had to help Patience with her Dysolve program at home even with other younger kids in the house.[11] Then there was the fact that there was no guarantee that the corrective training would work! In spite of all of this, Faye and I were determined to do whatever it took to give Patience a fighting chance. We knew that we were going to have to make sacrifices to make this work, but that's what any parent would do for their kids. There just wasn't any other option in our minds. The idea that we could give Patience a fighting chance in the world was all the inspiration we needed.

So over the next year for usually five nights a week, either Faye or I would struggle through several hours of Patience's homework and then when that was all done, we would do Dysolve. I wish I could say Patience enjoyed it but she did not. We battled with her every single night for a long time. We would always feel guilty about making Patience do all of this work. She did not get a lot of free time to herself to just play and be a kid. There were weeks where we would only do three nights of Dysolve because we wanted to balance out and reward her hard work with play. However those weeks we cut short her training, there was a noticeable difference in her sessions with Dr. Coral.

Report Card Shocker

A year went by and Patience exceeded our expectations. We started seeing improvement at the end of 5th grade. While this was going on, we continued to battle with the district over services. I remember the last special ed meeting we had with the district. I told them that their testing was archaic and they should advance it into the 21st century.[12] I did all of this politely of course and with respect, but I wanted to be honest with how I felt. They did not really respond. My wife and I thanked everyone for their time and we walked out.

We continued the drills at the direction of Dr. Coral almost every day over the summer and into the spring. The 1st quarter's report card in 6th grade was a shocker for us. Patience made the Honor roll in the 1st marking period, which required a grade point average of 90 or higher. When Patience continued to remain on the Honor roll for the 2nd and 3rd quarters of the school year, we knew that this was for real. Now Patience continues to work to maintain these grades and to catch up on what she missed in the early grades. Her teachers are so impressed with her work ethic and tell me every time that they wish they had a class full of Patiences.

I am so proud of Patience and so grateful for Dr. Coral, her husband and her children, who tutored Patience in math and language. We are also grateful to her teacher, Ms. White, who slipped us that note that started our journey. I look back and can now say it was worth every long night, all the sacrifices and every battle we had with Patience. I believe this experience has given Patience confidence in her ability to overcome any obstacle.

I am just happy that we found Dr. Coral when we did. I am truly confident in saying that Patience will no longer be limited by her ability, but only by her motivation. I don't think a parent could ask for anything more.

MY MESSAGE TO PARENTS

My advice for parents out there is to never take "no" for an answer. If one door closes on you, kick open another! If you feel something is not right with your child, keep on fighting until you get the answers you need and the services your child requires to give them a chance for greatness. I look back and think about how trusting we were in the school district's ability to assess Patience's needs. I think if Patience was our second or third child, we may have found Dr. Coral a little sooner. Since Patience was our firstborn, and no one in our family had a kid with learning disabilities, we had blind faith in the district.

Authors' note: We sympathize with the parent here, at the same time that we recognize the limited resources and the absence of an effective solution previously for schools to offer to students like Patience.

NOTES

1. About 13% of children are born prematurely in the US. Many studies report that even those born late preterm (32-36 weeks) face language and reading deficits. Patience in this chapter was born in the 35th week. See Feldman, H.M., Lee, E.S., Yeatman, J.D., & Yeom, K.W. (2012). Language and reading skills in school-aged children and adolescents born preterm are associated with white matter properties on diffusion tensor imaging. *Neuropsychologia, 50*, 3348-3362. Retrieved from https://doi.org/10.1016/j.neuropsychologia.2012.10.014
2. Co-teaching classes contain at least two teachers. Often, one teacher covers the material for the whole class while the second is a special education teacher who attends to students with special needs.
3. See the Engineer's Story in Chapter 9 on the problem with standardized testing or assessments in dyslexia diagnosis. Chapter 14 on the complexity of the problem of dyslexia explains why cookie-cutter testing kits are ineffective.
4. See the Principal's Story in Chapter 7 and Chapter 12 *The True Cost of Dyslexia*.
5. Students with learning disabilities drop out of high school at three times the typical rate. See Chapter 12.
6. Those incarcerated have low literacy rates. See National Center for Education Statistics. (1994). *Literacy behind prison walls*. US Department of Education, Office of Educational Research and Improvement. See also Snowling, M. J., Adams, J. W., Bowyer-Crane, C., & Tobin, V. (2000). Levels of literacy among juvenile offenders: The incidence of specific reading difficulties. *Criminal Behaviour and Mental Health, 10*(4), 229-241.
7. Language-processing deficits obviously affect the ability to process and hence follow verbal instructions. This effect is common. See other cases in Chapters 3, 4 and 6.
8. In this chapter, we use a case study to present up close how language-processing deficits affect short-term and working memory. Short-term memory is the passive storage of infor-

mation for a brief period. Working memory covers both the passive storage and processing of information. While our focus here is on the causal effect of language-processing deficits on memory, research on dyslexia has generally examined the reverse relationship. This research in other studies on how memory affects language has yielded confusing results: "A sound and consensual understanding of the precise nature of the relationship between short-term and working memory and reading disability has proven difficult to achieve" - Elliott, J.G., & Grigorenko, E.L. (2014). *The dyslexia debate*. New York: Cambridge University Press, pp. 57-58.

9. As with Patience in this chapter, our case studies in Chapters 2 and 5 show high levels of text comprehension despite their reading problems. However, research by others tend to focus on deficits in reading comprehension among the population with reading disabilities. See Kida, A.S.B., de Ávila, C.R.B., & Capellini, S.A. (2016). Reading comprehension assessment through retelling: Performance profiles of children with dyslexia and language-based learning disability. *Frontiers in Psychology, 7*, 787. doi:10.3389/fpsyg.2016.00787
Research in this field is still preliminary and occupied with issues of classification. See for example Werfel, K.L., & Krimm, H. (2017). A preliminary comparison of reading subtypes in a clinical sample of children with specific language impairment. *Journal of Speech, Language and Hearing Research, 60*, 2680-2686. See our critique of this focus on classification in the Engineer's Story in Chapter 9.

10. Many of our students and their families spend hours on homework every night before their language deficits were resolved. See our cases in Chapters 2, 3, 5, 6 and 9.

11. Patience joined Dysolve before the program was fully automated.

12. See Chapters 14 and 15 for the computational and technological solution to dyslexia testing.

Mother's Story

I Did Everything Right
Faye

A Sticky Note

The night of the first parent-teacher conference in 5th grade, Patience came home with a sticky note from her teacher.

"My teacher thinks I might have this."

The word "Dyslexia" was written on the note. The one thing I had asked other teachers if Patience had but was always told "no." The one thing most parents fear their children might have. Even though this word *Dyslexia* was upsetting at first, I was relieved that someone had a hunch, something that I could actually use to help Patience with. To this day, I am so thankful this teacher was assigned to Patience as she changed our lives for the better.

By that time, my husband and I have had more responsibilities than most as parents. Since Patience was born premature, she needed more care, including for a weak sucking reflex. When she said few words at 18 months, we enrolled her in sign language classes. This created another problem when she signed instead of speaking. By three, she was in an Early Intervention Program. At the same time, we also enrolled her at a private preschool to give her exposure to children without disabilities.

As Patience's parents, we did our best to help her become successful in life. We felt bad that she started life with disadvantages, so we fought for her for longer. Starting as early as six months old, Patience went to Music Together classes for two years. We would sing along with the numerous songs we brought back, in our home or in our car. We signed her up for swim classes for infants. We took her to reading groups at the public library every week. I thought I did everything right.

But when Patience entered kindergarten, we were surprised at how much kids of this age group had to know or quickly pick up. Patience didn't know all of her alphabet. Some kids already knew how to read. I never thought of holding Patience back in preschool, but I now thought that it was a mistake. Patience was always tall for her age and had good social interactions with peers, so I never thought about how much emphasis was placed on academics, even in kindergarten. Patience continued to receive speech therapy services as part of her IEP (Individualized Education Program).[1]

Losing Services

In 2nd grade, Patience continued to fall behind. We asked at a parent-teacher meeting, "Should we hold her back a year?"

"No, absolutely not. It's not recommended."

The support of a co-teaching classroom with an extra teacher would continue to help Patience, they said. Second grade was also the year that Patience had to get retested for special education services.[2] For the first time, both Charles and I were frustrated at our annual meeting.

"According to our evaluation, Patience is only one year behind in reading. In order to qualify for speech therapy services, she has to be *two* years behind in reading."

So this was how the school would remove her speech therapy services. Our annual meeting took over an hour because I tried to fight my hardest to keep speech therapy services for our daughter.[3]

"I'm sorry, but her speech articulation problems aren't affecting her reading enough," said one administrator.[4]

"Her grades aren't bad enough to justify speech therapy services," echoed another.

I tried to bring up our entire journey of trying to provide support for Patience since she was a baby, but nothing worked.

Then the school psychologist suggested, "Well, I'm looking at the math…there're two numbers I'm concerned with…We can classify her for…a disability in math?"

And that was how Patience lost speech therapy and gained a math disability. It was the consolation prize. But math support meant a small table in the back of the regular classroom, where the special ed teacher helped children who had IEPs.

Did we consider private school? Yes, we did. We toured a local Catholic school, but when I asked how the school would provide extra help, there was no concrete answer or plan. And since the tuition for Patience plus my other children would be so expensive, we decided not to change schools.

How Much Worse can It Get?

One time, Charles scolded Patience for making too much noise while he was trying to get some sleep after his night shift. I came home to find the living room plastered with yellow sticky notes. They had the word "sorry" spelled every which way except correctly. How could her school not *see* her problem?

By the time Patience joined Dysolve in 5th grade, she was already two grades behind in reading.[5] We were scared and at the same time so hopeful that Dr. Coral would be our answer to Patience's school struggles. Thankfully I have a very supportive husband, so he helped with Patience's schoolwork and Dysolve exercises.[6]

A few months into Dysolve, Dr. Coral voiced concerns over Patience's vision. Patience once had vision therapy, and retesting showed that she needed more. Dr. Coral was also concerned about Patience's speech problems. We got Patience qualified for speech therapy services at a local hospital. So for a while, we shuttled Patience to all three services every week. Financially too, paying for the services made it hard for us to set money aside for home repairs or college saving accounts.

Throughout, both Charles and I worked fulltime, me during the evening shift and him at night. We were often tired and drained. My three-year-old often got impatient and did not understand why I had to spend so much more time at the kitchen table with Patience. But as new parents, I think we expected to be tired and knew this was all worth it for Patience. Many times, Patience would forget to bring home something that she needed to do her homework.[7] So before I could sit down with her to tackle the work, I had to drive her back to school to get it.

So Good at Your Job

For the 5th grade meeting with the special ed team, I got an experienced parent advocate because I felt the rules had failed Patience in the past.[8] We fought for Patience to get a reading evaluation, and when the results came back, it supported Dr. Coral's conclusion that Patience was having issues with reading. But the school could provide no support services for her reading problem. We fought for a technology evaluation so Patience would have the option to type in class. No matter how hard we fought, it didn't seem to matter.

I looked at the administrator: she sounded sure of herself, prepared. Did she say the same thing to every parent?

I tried unsuccessfully to speak up: "You can't say that…Before you go into that next, may I—"

Charles joined in, "We're doing everything we can. I can't give anymore. Look, we have all this evidence that she needs help. We're not getting *anything* back!"

But the administrator just said, "In conclusion—"
She didn't display any emotion. I thought, "You are so good at your job." Nothing was going to make her deviate from her set goals. I tried to argue from my perspective as a hospital administrator: insurance companies set criteria for eligibility, but they would allow deviations if necessary, based on the evidence. But Patience's school would not consider any at all.

The Fire to Do Her Best

Having lost school services, we worked with Dr. Coral and Dysolve exclusively to clear Patience's problems in 5th grade. Things started coming together for Patience in the 3rd quarter.

By the time she got to 6th grade, Patience's grandfather no longer had to help her much with homework before my husband and I got home from work. "She's doing pretty good now," he said.

Patience's writing got better. The misspelled words were no longer obvious in 6th grade, compared to 5th grade, when I couldn't understand what she wrote. The *b/d* letter flops ended in 5th grade. For the first time, Patience wrote an essay on her own in 6th grade—her writing was better, and her words were fine and did not stand out with crazy errors.

Life for us is less stressful now. Patience does homework on her own. Before this, Patience was quieter than the other girls her age and did less. "She's young for her age," her teachers would say. The other girls talked more and seemed spunkier. But by 7th grade, Patience was on par with them. Socialwise, you can't tell Patience apart from the other girls now. She's still anxious about doing well at school, but her head doesn't hurt anymore.[9]

It has been all worth it as we see such a difference in Patience's abilities now. Why did we sign Patience up for Dysolve? It was our only chance. The program all made sense. The tutoring options offered elsewhere wasn't what Patience needed. It was crucial at her age to correct the problem head-on. As her grades improved, Patience wanted to do even better. Now it's in her—Patience now has the fire to do her best.

Authors' note: We sympathize with the parent here, at the same time that we recognize the limited resources and the absence of an effective solution previously for schools to offer to students like Patience.

NOTES

1. An IEP is an Individualized Education Program (or Plan) for students with special needs to receive support services in public schools. *IEP* also refers to the legal document that charts the student's needs, evaluative and support services, and targeted goals. IEPs are covered by the Individuals with Disabilities Education Act (IDEA).
2. When a student in public school has an Individualized Education Program (IEP), parents and other members of the IEP committee or Committee on Special Education (CSE) meet at least once a year to review the plan in place. At least once every three years, a reevaluation is conducted.
3. See how schools deal with limited resources in the Principal's Story in Chapter 7 and Chapter 12 *The True Cost of Dyslexia*.
4. Difficulties with the production of speech sounds (speech sound disorder) combined with other language-processing deficits often lead to reading problems. See Lewis, B.A., Avrich, A.A., Freebairn, L.A., Hansen, A.J., Sucheston, L.E., Lara, E. et al. (2011). Literacy outcomes of children with early childhood speech sound disorders: Impact of endophenotypes. *Journal of Speech, Language and Hearing Research, 54*, 1628-1643.
5. Most of our students were two grades behind in reading when they first joined Dysolve. See Chapters 2-9.
6. Patience joined Dysolve before the program was fully automated. Moreover, some of her language-processing deficits had to be addressed in person due to their severity.
7. This forgetfulness is common. See Note 7 in the Father's Story in this chapter.
8. A parent advocate or special education advocate helps parents navigate through the school system to obtain appropriate resources to meet their children's education needs. The services of an advocate may be provided free of charge in some regions.
9. See the reference to recurrent headaches in Note 7 at the end of Dr. Coral's Story in this chapter.

Dr. Coral's Story

The Math-Language Connection

Can't Count

"What is 6 + 4?"

Patience, in 5th grade, blinked, paused, and fumbled the answer. By the time she was done with her math session, her math tutor and I looked at each other in despair. How could a 5th grader not know how to count up to 10?

"Go ahead, use your fingers," we prompted. But Patience didn't even know *how* to count with her fingers. Her school classified her as having a math disability.[1]

What does a math disability entail? Generally, such a student may not understand foundational concepts or struggle to recall math facts and hence cannot apply them fast enough to compute.[2] However, studies show that interventions to improve conceptual knowledge have yielded negligible effects.[3]

We decided to give Patience the benefit of the doubt, as we do with all the students we see. Our own evaluation showed that she had severe language-processing deficits. How much of her math learning was affected by her language problems?[4] After all, she had to understand her math teachers' verbal instructions. What if she missed the foundational work in math in her early primary years as she sat quietly in the corner, understanding little of the lessons?

At first, my son, who tutored math, volunteered to train Patience. At their first session, he showed her how to use fingers to count. But she did not keep to a set method, like counting from left to right, and so was often confused as to what the fingers she held up were supposed to represent. My son patiently demonstrated for her each addition problem up to 20, yet she kept tripping in her counting even when she was just imitating each step he did with his hands. When she left, my son asked, "How is she going to manage in 6th grade?"

I wondered that myself. I arranged to meet both of Patience's parents.

Calm in Crises

Charles and Faye are tall, strong people—the kind who can build a house with their own hands or shoulder any burden that life throws at them. And indeed, they were asked to shoulder more than their fair share at this point in their lives. As we went down this path to confront Patience's "disabilities" directly, we uncovered more and more problems that needed attention.

Language, math, vision, speech. Charles and Faye did not hesitate for a moment to jump right in to tackle each problem, on top of taking care of other young children.

At my first meeting with Faye and Charles, I laid out very candidly the breadth and severity of Patience's problems and the commitment required of her parents to address them. I told them I had seen the same scope and depth of processing deficits in other children, but these other students were labeled with cognitive impairment by their schools.[5] Yet, Patience was functioning at school, albeit poorly. Her parents' support at home and her natural intelligence had bridged that gap.

Both Charles and Faye took in the news of their firstborn's severe problems calmly. In fact, they seemed surprisingly calm despite hearing for the first time that their daughter had dyslexia plus a bewildering number of other deficits. From this point of discovery onwards, they faced a steep, uphill climb. Charles and Faye were trained professionally to deal with crises in life-and-death situations. They had learned to hold emotions in check and direct all their energy to solving the problem at hand.

At the end of our candid meeting, I assured them that their child would be fine in the end. How did I know that? Because her parents would not rest until everything possible was done to take care of her. It was rare for me to see both parents equally committed to doing that. Charles and Faye would assure their daughter's success, no matter what.

Too Much of a Good Thing

Patience received training in math and language with us simultaneously. When my son left for college soon after, his younger sister took over. And when she too left for college a year later, my husband, Evan, who has a Master's in Mathematical Engineering, stepped in. We formed this tight unit of language and math teachers so that we could observe, analyze and innovate to tackle a particularly difficult case.

For the first few months, Patience's math tutors felt they were going round and round in circles—nothing seemed to stick. Patience even had trouble pronouncing numbers like "three" and "four."

The biggest obstacle loomed in front of us and would not budge until we faced it squarely. Despite the severity of her academic problems, Patience did not feel the urgency to resolve them. So mighty were her parents' efforts that she was shielded somewhat from the full brunt of her academic issues. They took hours each night to go through homework with her, but it was always completed to turn in the next day.

Faye and Charles were the kind of parents who went all out for their children. They didn't just throw birthday parties; Patience had a slumber party under the stars with a large, sturdy tent for comfort. They didn't just organize party games; Charles wrote clever clues and tucked them all over the house for treasure hunts. They didn't just hang out with their children; they built cars for derbies on weekends.

But there can be too much of a good thing. Faye brought Patience's book bag, opened her notebooks, closed them and put them away, and toted the bag home. Patience only needed to show up for our sessions. She had not learned to be responsible for her own learning.

Taking Charge

I decided to have a talk with them. I told them that Patience had to empower herself as a learner. It was up to her to know why she was doing a certain activity with us and what to do at home. And if she didn't know what or why, she should ask us, not her mother. Faye tried to shield her daughter: How much time should a 6th grader really spend on homework? When does Patience get to be a child?

I refrained from telling Faye that, knowing what I did know as a practitioner, Patience should be operating in crisis mode. If she failed to turn things around in the next year, she might never be able to live independently as an adult. In the grand scheme of things, *I had always thought that working your hardest for a year or two to secure an easier future was a good bargain.*

Things improved a little after my lecture. Patience started taking care of her own notes and bag, and under her mother's prompting, followed up on what she needed to do as practice before she left. Still, we were concerned that her rate of progress was too slow, given how much she had to catch up on at school. To hit the knee of the curve in the trajectory of her progress, Patience had to find that inner drive to motivate herself. Given how far behind she was, Patience's progress could not fall short of spectacular.

I had another talk with Patience and Faye. This time, I talked to each one separately. I told Faye that it was time to let Patience go. At 10 years of age, Patience had to know what she was actually capable of, free of the assured support of her parents and grandparents. If she succeeded, she would shape the confidence to aim even higher. If she failed, she would build the resilience to try even harder.

"Patience," I said, holding up one of her school tests, "How much of this do you think you can do right now?"

"85%?" Patience ventured.

"Take a good look. How much of this do you understand?"

"50%?" she hazarded.

I led her down this line of inquiry—if she didn't understand, she couldn't have done it, and if she couldn't do it, how could she pass?

"What do you need to do?" I asked.

"Work very hard."

I told her about the MathCounts kids. These were students who already excelled in math. Yet, day in and day out, for several hours a week, they kept practicing computation, to the point that before the adults even finished reading a problem, the MathCounts kids had the answer. I hoped that it sunk in—what it took to excel.

I asked Patience to gauge where she was in her academic abilities, where she needed to be to pass, where she wanted to be to reach her life's goals, to be a vet. There was no hiding from the truth—Patience was smart enough to realize that she would have to work her hardest that year to even have a fighting chance of turning things around.

From that day on, we worked exclusively with Patience. Now, Patience had no choice but to take the responsibility for her own learning. If she failed, her parents and grandparents could no longer help her: they did not know what she was supposed to do.

Upward Trajectory

Patience's adjustment was seemingly instantaneous. She monitored herself, and we exchanged notes on the problems she encountered. Where she needed help from her parents, she was the one who directed what was asked of them. She started working independently at home. As her language improved, so did her math. In three months, her school performance turned around. She received grades that used to be out of her reach—that added the boost she needed to propel further into this upward trajectory.

She now was the model student, and classmates asked *her* for help instead of the other way around.[6] She worked even harder to protect her new reputation. She became ambitious—she wanted to get into Honors. Her school report card went up on the fridge door. Her grandparents and teachers were rooting for her. When you have so many people you care about rooting for you, you couldn't let them down.

For years, Patience had been suffering from headaches at school.[7] Her headaches cleared in the spring of 7th grade. I knew they were gone because her demeanor changed—her face opened up. She stood up straight. She was now confident enough to speak openly on what she needed to fix when she fell short. She asked me to help her reduce the time it took her to study for a Social Studies test. We worked side-by-side as partners on her study techniques. She came back with a smile and 100 for her quiz.

My mind returned to a fall day the year before. I looked at the sun shining on Patience's hair, and her face, fresh, innocent, and apologetic for admitting that my drills hurt her head. I remembered the other girls I had known in more than two decades of working with students like her. I thought of the rows and rows of Patiences sitting quietly and nicely in their classrooms, day after day, year after year, struggling to do their best even as their heads hurt as the school day wore on, bearing the indignity of constant failure, wearing the shame of having their classmates and teachers define them that way.[8] Then getting up the next morning to go over all this again for yet another day.

THE PROBLEM

The school viewed Patience through the lens of the services they had available for her. Even if she had received all their services, would they have resolved her problems satisfactorily? Probably not. Each support service tackled that piece of her problem in isolation.[9] But Patience had difficulty coordinating the various subprocesses of language.

For example, to understand her teacher's sentence, Patience would have to process the sounds (phonemes) that make up her teacher's words, assemble the sounds together to produce her teacher's words, retrieve words she had learned to match to her assembled words, break the words into their morphological (word structure) units to get parts of their meaning (e.g., *-ed*), assemble the words into phrasal units, retrieve the word meanings and phrasal meanings, analyze the order of the phrasal units to get their syntactic (sentence structure) relations, analyze the syntactic relations to get the meaning of the sentence, confirm that the sentence meaning matches the context. And that is just a cursory description without going into the nuts and bolts of sentence parsing.[10]

Because Patience could not coordinate these subprocesses efficiently, she often failed to understand what was told to her, leading others to perceive her as very forgetful. She could not follow lessons in class because her teachers' words were, as she said, "all jumbled up."

Since her problem was not understood in totality, her behavior seemed contradictory. This affected not just language reception (listening comprehension) but also language production (speech).[11] Patience could not coordinate these linguistic subprocesses especially when she got excited, at which point she usually stuttered.[12] She had a serious stuttering problem, particularly with the hard plosives /p, t, k/. Thus, she had difficulty saying something as simple as "Can I?" while she could generate a lot of creative ideas. The same teacher who failed Patience in a reading quiz commented: "Patience is able to understand higher-level concepts, such as author's purpose."[13]

OUR SOLUTION

Given the host of problems Patience faced, her intervention program had to be holistic and comprehensive. We have to see the student as a whole person, a functioning being who needs to speak, understand, remember, and compute.[14] In the case of Patience, that meant identifying her language-processing deficits and training her to perform and coordinate the subprocesses involved efficiently.[15]

Her schoolwork in 5th grade contained what her Mom called "crazy errors" that stood out: *Amacan (American), rail *roud staion (railroad station), *hepls (helps), *poele* (*people*), *invirent* (*environment*), *aratucle* (*article*), *learen* (*learn*), *rihgt* (*write*). These errors compromised the intelligibility of her writing because many of them involved the wrong number of syllables and metathesis (switching the positions of sounds/letters).[16]

By the beginning of 7th grade, Patience captured the number of syllables correctly in her spelling in 77.48% of the time, as in *meliceler jenetisist* (*molecular geneticist*), *regeneritive medicine* (*regenerative medicine*), *indoginus* (*endogeneous*), *anticoagulent* (*anticoagulant*), *nuralagicle disorders* (*neurological disorders*), *microsefily* (*microcephaly*), *distrophy* (*dystrophy*), *entomoligist* (*entomologist*).[17] We lengthened the new words she had to learn to five syllables or more. At the same time, she continued to work on acquiring the orthographic (spelling) forms of simpler, common words she missed in the earlier grades.

Patience was now able to syllabify (break words into syllables) correctly: ex|clu|sio|na|ry; a|llo|ca|tion; pro|longed; pre|me|di|ta|tion; phe|no|me|non; *a|no|ni|ma|ty (*anonymity*); *a|se|sa|bi|la|ty (*accessibility*). Her spelling errors in 30.53% of instances involved using the correct letters for unstressed vowels, which also confound typically developing learners, as in *anonymity* and *accessibility*. That is, when they occurred, Patience's spelling errors were now typical of those produced by the rest of the population: *refirential* (*referential*), *representitive* (*representative*), *enormaty* (*enormity*). You can see from these word examples that we did not dumb down the program for her. Rather, Patience had to rise up to the demands of linguistic development that would match her grade level and intellectual ability.

From there on, Patience worked on English spelling patterns to accelerate her spelling acquisition. She used our *Dysolve® Sounds and Spelling Manual*, which streamlines spelling rules by simplifying the patterns and exceptions to memorize.

BREAKTHROUGH

Patience was not diagnosed with ADHD, but some typical symptoms appeared regularly during our exercises besides incidents of forgetfulness reported by her parents.[18] Her feet would tap restlessly during training.[19] As her upbringing had taught her to control her impulses, she would stay put in her chair and push through the exercise, even when she felt her head throbbing from the exertion.

At the end of 5th grade, when Patience was still new in Dysolve, her head hurt often during our exercises. Her headaches gradually declined in the course of the program, but returned once in December of 6th grade while doing a school assignment.[20] After a session at Dysolve to address this problem, she was able to complete the assignment without any further head discomfort.

By the end of 6th grade, Patience's head no longer hurt from schoolwork or our exercises, even as the work became progressively harder. In 7th grade, her headaches did not recur except once at Dysolve and at school.

Throughout much of 6th grade, working on math problems also used to induce head pressure for Patience at school. But by the end of that year, this too dissipated. She was able to speak up more, to answer questions in class. Because she was getting better at math, she was no longer as shy. Her math teacher moved her to the back of the class, as the front rows were reserved for those who were struggling and needed more attention.

Within two years after she joined Dysolve, Patience overcame the impediments created by her premature birth to become an independent, motivated learner in the top quarter of her class. She remained there in the following years (Figure 2).

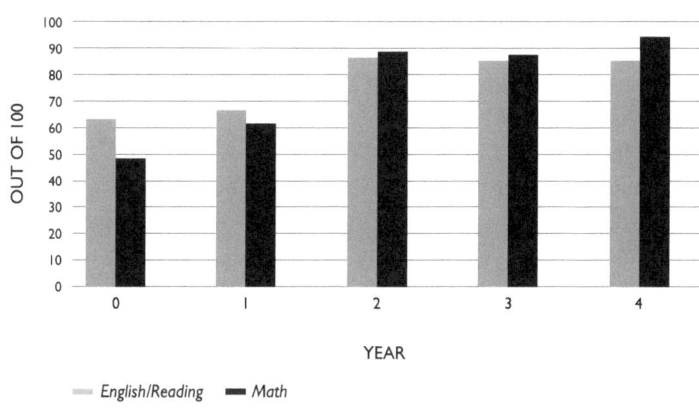

FIGURE 2

*Patience - School Grades
in Years before and after Joining Dysolve[21]*

NOTES

1. Math disability or dyscalculia involves difficulty with math-related tasks such as understanding numerical concepts, performing arithmetic operations and recalling math facts. It is less researched than dyslexia. Math and reading disabilities are known to coexist (comorbid), but studies report differing rates of co-occurrence (comorbidity). Research tends to focus on one disability separate from the other, but mathematical and reading tasks do activate some general brain networks in common, with impairments shown in both types of disabilities. See Ashkenazi, S., Black, J.M., Abrams, D.A., Hoeft, F., & Menon, V. (2013). Neurobiological underpinnings of math and reading learning disabilities. *Journal of Learning Disabilities, 46*(6) 549–569. doi:10.1177/0022219413483174
2. See National Mathematics Advisory Panel (NMAP). (2008). *Foundations for success: Final report of the national math advisory panel.* Washington, DC: US Department of Education. See also Geary, D.C. (2013). Learning disabilities in mathematics: Recent advances. In H.L. Swanson, K.R. Harris, & S. Graham (Eds.), *Handbook of learning disabilities* (2nd ed., pp. 239–255). New York: Guilford Press.
3. See Baker, S., Gersten, R., & Lee, D. S. (2002). A synthesis of empirical research on teaching mathematics to low-achieving students. *Elementary School Journal, 103*, 51–73.
4. About 5-8% of schoolchildren have some form of math disability. The computational deficit most consistently associated with math disability is difficulty with retrieving basic math facts from memory. Children with this particular math deficit also often have phonological processing deficits that define dyslexia. This suggests the role of language in retrieval deficits and partly explains the relationship between math and reading disabilities. In this view, math disability (MD) or math learning disability (MLD) is a heterogeneous disorder with varied versions. See Geary, D. C. (1993). Mathematical disabilities: Cognitive, neuropsychological, and genetic components. *Psychological Bulletin, 114*(2), 345–362. See also

Chong, S. L., & Siegel, L. S. (2008). Stability of computational deficits in math learning disability from second through fifth grades. *Developmental Neuropsychology, 33*(3), 300-317.
5. Cognitive impairment occurs when the person affected has difficulty with thinking functions such as remembering, learning, concentrating or making decisions about daily life.
6. Skye in Chapter 3 also became a model student to her classmates.
7. The association between recurrent headaches and dyslexia (and ADHD) has not received much research interest. Recent studies do show a higher incidence of recurrent headaches among children with dyslexia, ADHD, and both conditions. Yet the explanations put forth remain controversial. One hypothesis uses overlapping brain mechanisms to account for the associations. A second hypothesis suggests that learning disabilities and ADHD create stresses that induce headaches. A third speculates that frequent headaches hinder learning and cause ADHD behaviors. A fourth proposes a common disorder underlying headaches and ADHD. Which is the cause? Which is the effect? Depending on the hypothesis, headaches can be either. For a review of studies, see Genizi, J., Gordon, S., Kerem, N.C., Srugo, I., Shahar, E., & Ravid, S. (2013). Primary headaches, attention deficit disorder and learning disabilities in children and adolescents. *Journal of Headache Pain, 14*(1), 54. doi:10.1186/1129-2377-14-54
Our own fieldwork shows that headaches are common among students with dyslexia and co-occur with ADHD. Headaches or head pressure often occur when processing load increases. See also our blogs on this kind of headaches in Dysolve Dyslexia on Facebook.
8. Fewer girls than boys are referred to intervention services for dyslexia because they do not display behavioral problems as often. See Pennington, B.F. (2009). *Diagnosing learning disorders: A neurological framework* (2nd ed.). New York: Guilford Press.
9. Researchers have begun to recognize the importance of investigating related (comorbid) disorders together because current instruction to address dyslexia solely has failed to help

25-40% of students with learning disabilities. See Fuchs, D., Compton, D.L., Fuchs, L.S., Bryant, V.J., Hamlett, C.L., & Lambert, W. (2012). First-grade cognitive abilities as longterm predictors of reading comprehension and disability status. *Journal of Learning Disabilities, 45*(3), 217–231. doi:10.1177/0022219412442154

10. Sentence parsing involves breaking a sentence down into its structural (phrasal and lexical) units in order to derive its meaning.
11. Children with speech disorders, which are different from mere speech delay, often also have difficulty with recognizing the sounds and sound patterns of language (phonological awareness). Followup studies show that they continue to face literacy problems at 12 years old, especially if they have other language impairment. See Holm, A., Farrier, F., & Dodd, B. (2008). Phonological awareness, reading accuracy and spelling ability of children with inconsistent phonological disorder. *International Journal of Language and Communication Disorders, 43*, 300–322. See also Hulme, C., Nash, H.M., Gooch, D., Lervåg, A., & Snowling, M.J. (2015). The foundations of literacy development in children at familial risk of dyslexia. *Psychological Science, 26*, 1877–1886.
12. Stuttering may involve repetitions of words or syllables, lengthening (prolongation) of sounds and blocking or hesitation before word completion. Research into the relationship between stuttering and dyslexia has only just begun. But two out of the 10 cases in this book have a stuttering problem. See Chapter 9 *User2*. See also Chen, H., Xu, J., Zhou, Y., Gao, Y., Wang, G., Xia, J. et al. (2015). Association study of stuttering candidate genes GNPTAB, GNPTG and NAGPA with dyslexia in Chinese population. *BMC Genetics, 16*, 1-7. doi:10.1186/s12863-015-0172-5
13. See Note 9 in the Father's Story in this chapter.
14. See Note 9 above.
15. Processing speed has often been mentioned as a core component of the deficits underlying dyslexia. However, its role and relationship to other components are still unclear in the research literature. See Elliott, J.G., & Grigorenko, E.L. (2014). *The dyslexia debate.* New York: Cambridge University Press.

16. Error patterns differ between spellers with dyslexia and those without. Studies found that spellers with dyslexia tend to commit more errors related to their difficulty with segmentation (breaking words into single sounds) and phoneme identification (recognizing sounds in words). For example, they reduce consonant clusters (*str→st*) and substitute consonants. They omit vowels and substitute vowels that are not even phonetically similar. They often leave out word endings (*-s, -ed*). In contrast, writers without dyslexia produce words that sound like the target words (phonetically accurate) even when they are not spelled correctly (orthographically inaccurate). Thus, they may substitute same-sounding words (homophones: *buy→by*), use the incorrect letters for unstressed vowels (*attitude → attatude*), and overgeneralize the silent *–e* rule (*plan→plane*). Spelling instruction is needed for students with dyslexia, but research shows that it is more effective before 4th grade. See Bernstein, S.E. (2009). Phonology, decoding, and lexical compensation in vowel spelling errors made by children with dyslexia, *Reading and Writing, 22*(3), 307-331.
17. Now Patience's misspellings are of the type found among writers without dyslexia—see Note 16 above. With this set of errors, the next step involved learning common word stems and affixes, as in *molecule, -lar, endo-, -neous, neuro-, -cal* (morphological instruction).
18. See Note 8 in the Father's Story in this chapter.
19. See Chapter 6 on ADHD.
20. See Note 7 above.
21. Scores in the lower grades (Year 0 before Dysolve and Year 1 in Dysolve) were converted from a 1-4 rating scale (i.e., 4 = 100). Patience graduated from our intensive program in Year 3 and only engaged with Dysolve games sporadically thereafter.

Patience's Story

The Grades in between were Wasted

I had to Deal with this Pain

In the beginning, I remember I was the kid who was "out" of the class. I felt left out, the only one who has this problem. I was always behind the work. I looked at other kids like they were better than me, smarter. I didn't know a lot of answers, and the other kids did. I felt dumb.

When a teacher tried to explain something to me, she had to say it again.[1] It didn't come to me fast enough. My Dad would sit with me a lot for homework and show me visually. After an hour, I still couldn't get it. In 3rd grade, I had an assistant teacher who broke it down, step by step. It helped a little bit, but it wasn't enough. Looking back, I think I didn't get it because I didn't know how to break down what they were saying. One step at a time. All the words were jumbled together, all mixed up. I couldn't focus, couldn't tell what was important.

I would read and read when I couldn't understand. The headaches would come and distract me.[2] I thought it was normal to have them.[3] When the reading got hard, there was this feeling in my brain. And when I got excited, I had to move around; I had to move some part of my body.[4]

They're always there for me, my parents. But I had to deal with this pain by myself. I wanted to be a vet, but my parents said I needed math and science. I wasn't good in them. Sometimes, I felt like a small fish in a big pond—you can't do anything about it. But when you find somebody who can help you, you can grow into a big fish. It was weird that somebody had to teach me how to count with my fingers in 5th grade.[5] I didn't know how to count systematically. I didn't know that I couldn't do it.[6]

The Choice to Do a Harder Problem

When I got my math problems right [after joining Dysolve], the teachers noticed.

Now I think I can do it. Through this experience, I learned about myself. At the beginning, I thought I wasn't able to do things. I thought that was the way it was going to be. Now I know I can do anything. Now I know I have the potential. I feel good. Nothing can stop me.[7] Now I can get good grades. Now, when I have the choice to do a harder problem, I take it. Now I challenge myself.[8] I know I can do it.

I always needed a teacher beside me in the early grades. But now I figure out the problems by myself. I don't need the teacher to give me extra help to be on the Honor roll. Other kids are now looking up to me, asking for my help.[9]

MY MESSAGE TO TEACHERS

In every grade, they always put me in an easier reading level. Sometimes, it was too easy. *I wish they had raised me up more to see how much I could do.*[10] I didn't realize at that time that it wasn't helping me to keep things too easy for me. With math, they pushed me down. I always got the easier problems.

If a kid is having trouble in class, maybe she should stay back a year. Help the kid more. Try to figure out why the kid is acting this way and help her get through it.[11] I couldn't understand what my teachers were saying from kindergarten on, but I was only diagnosed with dyslexia in 5th. All the grades in between were wasted. Teachers should learn from specialists about dyslexia and autism. Some teachers saw I tried my best, but they still didn't know what to do. Other teachers thought I was trouble, not paying atention on purpose. I was upset about this every year.

NOTES

1. Skye in Chapter 3 also struggled with listening comprehension.
2. See Note 7 in Dr. Coral's Story in this chapter.
3. Most of the children who come to us experience recurrent headaches, yet many do not tell adults about them. Some do not recognize them as headaches because these have become so much a part of their daily state. As Patience said, "I thought it was normal to have them." See Dr. Coral's blog *Their Heads Actually Hurt* in Dysolve Dyslexia on Facebook and child and parent blogs on the same topic.
4. Hyperactivity in this regard is caused by cognitive overload, when the brain is overwhelmed by the input it has to process. See the ADHD case in Chapter 6.
5. See the beginning of Dr. Coral's Story in this chapter.
6. School curriculum and testing leave such gaps—what students do not know or cannot do.
7. This statement is echoed by Will in Chapter 5.
8. Academic success requires our students to navigate from the old path of defeatism to the new one of self-challenge. The cases in Chapters 1-9 managed to change course.
9. Skye in Chapter 3 also became a role model to her classmates.
10. This position is echoed in the Principal's Story in Chapter 7.
11. The majority of teachers in the US are not trained to deal with learning disabilities. See the Principal's Story in Chapter 7.

Key Takeaways

Evaluate learners with math disabilities for language issues.

Select a program that analyzes learning problems in totality so that they can be resolved.

Empower children to take charge of their education.

2

Duke

Processing Speed

Duke

Dysolve Finding:
Deficits in language processing and processing speed leading to dyslexia, ADHD symptoms[1]

School Classification:
None

School Services:
Academic Intervention Services for English, resource room

Doctor's Diagnosis:
ADHD[2]

Processing Speed

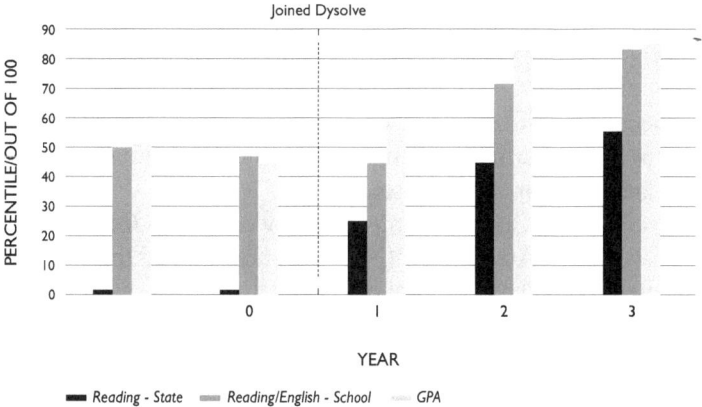

FIGURE 3
*Duke – State and School Grades
before and after Joining Dysolve[3]*

NOTES

1. By *language-processing deficits*, we mean deficiencies in the processes involved in executing the language functions of speaking, listening, reading or writing.
2. *ADHD* refers to Attention Deficit/Hyperactivity Disorder. It is also referred to as *ADD* as well as other labels that have been updated over the years. The core components of this condition are inattention, hyperactivity and impulsivity. See Chapter 6 for further discussion.
3. New York State reading scores were from the Northwest Evaluation Association (NWEA) standardized tests administered by the student's school.

Processing Speed

Dr. Coral's Story

Twice-Exceptionality[1]

Race against the Clock

"All along we thought the other kids were picking on him. Now we learn he's the one who throws the first punch at times," said Conny about her son, Duke, who had been coming to our Dysolve Center for a year.

Conny brushed back a lock of hair escaping from behind her ear, her hair pulled back tight into a neat pony tail. A no-nonsense person. She and I huddled at the corner of our conference room table, conferring on what to do with an 11-year-old who was letting his anger get the better of him. Lately, we seemed to be doing that all too frequently with Duke. Complaints from school about his talking back, locking horns with teachers, scuffles with classmates.[2]

Duke had come to us in the middle of 5th grade with several intractable problems related to language processing. Our program was working as fast as it could to resolve them, in a race against the clock. Now in 6th grade, Duke was beginning to accumulate school reprimands for his behavior towards his peers. As a martial arts black-belt holder, he wasn't supposed to use his hands, or even respond when provoked.

Were we going to lose Duke? In all the years of pulling students up, we had never lost that fight. But preteen boys come to a fork in the road, and they can go on the right or the wrong path.³ Duke was starting to veer off track. Within a year, he would experience phenomenal physical growth. When he towers over his Mom, would he still listen to her?

Gifted

"Your son is exceptional," I had told Duke's parents after our evaluation at the beginning of his Dysolve program.⁴

"Nobody ever said that about him."

Conny and Ken sounded wary, unsure of what to make of the direction of our discussion.⁵ They had expected me to discuss all the ways their son came up short. They did not expect me to talk about how exceptionally intelligent he was.

During our testing, Duke handled mentally challenging tasks effortlessly. With a shrug of his shoulders, he'd transform a straightforward answer into a witticism with ease. Knowledge transformation and witticisms—two hallmarks of a gifted child.⁶

He listened to the poem "Homework" read to him for the first time.⁷

"What do you think the poem means?" I asked.

"A kid that hates homework," Duke answered without missing a beat. Many other children we tried this poem on missed that inference.

Duke queried not only the tests but the instructions for the tests and at times changed the nature of the assignment to fit his abilities.[8] Before he carried out an activity, he considered alternative methods. He thought outside the box instead of doing blindly as he was told. A flexible thinker. He was also metacognitively aware—knowing what and how he was thinking himself.[9]

Suburb. He defined the word and commented, "I'm probably the only one in my 5th grade class who knows what that means." He also used words that *I* didn't know, like *impact gun*. He relished the mental challenge of creating humor, a typical trait of gifted children. His gift was obvious—so long as he did not have to read or write.

I explained twice-exceptionality and giftedness to Conny and Ken at our second meeting.[10] Duke fell into the exceptional end of the spectrum in at least two ways—being intellectually gifted and having a learning disability.[11] While in 5th grade, he performed above a 12th grade equivalent in listening comprehension in a standardized test but only at a 2nd grade equivalent in reading comprehension.[12] Conny started researching twice-exceptionality and I gave her parenting literature on giftedness. The adults first had to understand the child. There were gifted programs like the Johns Hopkins Center for Talented Youth, but Duke did not qualify for these programs because he registered at a low 2nd percentile in state reading tests before Dysolve.

Stoic

"I don't know how he does it. He doesn't miss a day of class. Just goes in and takes it day after day. I wouldn't have been able to myself." Conny was marveling over what Duke had to put up with each day he went to school—the failures, the teasing and bullying, the embarrassment of being singled out for extra help.

"If I didn't go, my Mom would've thrown me under the bus," Duke said dryly.

One time, he showed up with his little finger heavily bandaged. He had fractured it that morning. It was throbbing, but he shrugged it off and wrote with his injured hand. He showed up for our sessions on time, no excuses, no complaints. He did as he was told, even when he failed over and over again.[13] He did as he was expected. His parents expected it.

During our first evaluation, he fidgeted incessantly.[14] These were Duke's symptoms that his brain was overwhelmed. He said he was often tired at the end of the school day, with a slight head pressure.[15]

Yet Duke never complained.

"Does your head hurt?" I asked.

It must have, because our tasks were more cognitively taxing for him than his schoolwork. He was stretched to the limit. But he just shrugged and continued. He didn't quit. When he couldn't execute a task on the 10th try, I learned to read his cue. He would look away, suck in his stomach, exhale, and face again the challenge, ready to take the next blow. Over and over again in our games, he got beat. Stoic.

With a child like Duke, you give him less because he doesn't demand. Because he didn't demand, I thought he didn't require as much. In all the weeks he'd been to our center, only once in two years did he seem down.

"What's the matter, Duke?" I tried to get him to open up. I felt for him. An 11-year-old with the mental age of a 16-year-old, who could not do schoolwork meant for an average child.

"Nothing." He sat silent, immovable. In a few minutes, he brushed it aside. He sucked in his stomach, exhaled, and went back to the mental pummel.

And things would have gone on in this way at our Dysolve Center had his mother not brought the problems at school to our attention. His behavioral problems at school worsened by the week in 6th grade.

Expected

Discipline. Much was given to Duke by his family, and much was expected.[16] Every few weeks, he'd model some new gift he'd received—a pair of Timberland boots, a fancy hairstyle, the biggest paint gun I'd ever seen. Or a vacation at an indoor water park in the dead of winter. In return, his parents expected that he would do as he was told—complete routine chores both paid and unpaid, chop firewood, and help around the house. His hardworking parents were strict yet generous in providing for his needs and wants. Duke's upbringing was reflected in his obedience to authority and rules, his friendliness to all, and his good manners. Even while on vacation, he was expected to continue with our Dysolve training every week, and he brought back his work to show us.[17]

So the Duke that his school was seeing was not the Duke we had come to know at Dysolve. Some of his teachers also saw this side of Duke and were sympathetic. Even though he read haltingly, he still volunteered to read aloud in class—for his teacher's sake.

"It made Mrs. James *so* happy to see me read." Duke had this effect on people.

Latent

What did Duke want? What did he want in return for all this hard work? What did he want in life?[18] At first, he just shrugged. Finally, he opened up. His eyes brightened and he smiled.

"Robotics. I want to build robots." He and his Dad were already assembling and disassembling all sorts of equipment at home in their spare time.[19] This wasn't beyond him—except for his school grades.

We took little steps to get him invested in his future. I showed him videos of life-size robots that could navigate rocky terrain and get up each time they're knocked down. My son in college showed Duke a kinetic contraption operated by sensors that he had built. Duke was hooked. He slung on a Carnegie Mellon School of Computer Science bag and beamed, "I'm going to wear this college bag to school on Monday. I want to go to MIT."

I appealed to Duke's familiarity with the laws of physics. Conservation of energy—he should be expending his energy on reaching his lofty goals. Why was he wasting it on a pesky kid taunting him in the hallway? Why was he handicapping his Mom with school complaints about his behavior? Why not let her save her energy on finding gifted programs for him?[20]

By the middle of 6th grade, he grew noticeably. His legs lengthened; the chubbiness of childhood disappeared. "I don't want them to watch over me." Duke complained about his parents' close supervision of his schoolwork.

I said, "You can tell them that. You have to let them know that you're ready. They're worried. Parents also have to learn when to take the next step, to let go. Prove to them that you're ready to go it alone. Reason with them. They need to see that you can talk to them at their level. Use your words, negotiate."[21]

Conny was anxious. She and Ken had spent all of their son's school years propping him up with test preparations and homework. When Duke forgot to bring home the material to study for a vocabulary quiz, Conny spent over an hour searching online for the likely test words and made up the quiz herself to prep Duke.[22] Letting Duke handle homework alone was alien to them. Was he ready? What if he stumbled, or fell into the same troubles as at the beginning of the year?

I assured Conny. Duke had grown since our conferences on his troubles at school at the beginning of 6th grade. Now in the middle of that grade, he was mature enough to redirect his energies to constructive elements in his life. He had goals and big dreams. The needling at school from the other kids were now mere annoyances to be ignored. More importantly, our internal measures at Dysolve showed that he was tracking upward, even though this progress was still latent and was not reflected in his school grades yet.[23]

For example, we monitored Duke's ability to identify the structure of words (lexical structure). At the most basic level, students need to recognize the number of syllables in a word.[24] If the number of syllables is correct, the word is usually still recognizable in spite of misspellings. If the number of syllables is wrong, misspellings may mangle the word too much for it to be recognizable. For instance, Duke misspelled "influence" as *inflouence* while retaining its syllable structure. On the other hand, his misspelling of "literally" as *litorly* is harder to decipher because he omitted an entire syllable.[25] Progress with lexical structure at Dysolve preceded his improvement in his English grades at school in the 3rd and 4th quarters of 6th Grade (Figure 4).

The internal measurements at Dysolve showed that he was close to breaking through in the middle of 6th grade. His improvement was still latent at school until his school grades shot up in the 4th quarter. He received an achievement award at school—the first time for him, and his family.[26] He received an 85 for English. I wanted to give him a hug. He didn't like hugs.

"My Dad expects my grades next year to be in the 90s," he grinned.

Last year, that would have been impossible. This year, it's expected.

Processing Speed

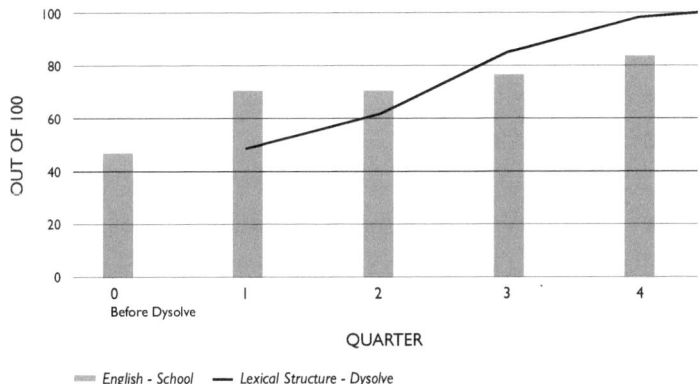

FIGURE 4
*Duke – School Grades and Dysolve Index
in 4 Quarters of 6th Grade*

THE PROBLEM

"You don't need high grades to do sports."

Duke had heard this said often to students like him who were struggling academically.[27] That reassured Duke because he was still struggling at the beginning of 6th grade. Cs would do, he was told.

He still needed his Dad to revise his homework for him every night. With the jump in demands from elementary to middle school, Duke started making up excuses not to go to school, not to do his homework or study.[28] By the fifth period at school—during his dreaded English subject—he was feeling drained mentally.

No matter how much time he put in, he could not nudge his grades up. So why even try? Right answer but wrong spelling—no credit. Knew the definitions but not the answer options—no credit. Understood the passage but could not find the information—no credit. By Mother's Day in 6th grade, Duke missed classes often, and when he was there, he was getting into trouble.

If it were just the language part we had to deal with, Duke would have proceeded uneventfully through Dysolve until he was done. But there was the giftedness we had to contend with as well. A supercharged brain is often also a supersensitive one.[29] As his Mom said, he "wore his heart on his sleeve." Every little slight, look, mean word was magnified for him. It hurt him to the core of his being, even though most of the time, he kept a tough façade.

To their credit, Conny and Ken educated themselves on this aspect of his giftedness to help him work through his issues. Duke had to learn how his psyche worked, to learn to manage his emotions and reactions.

OUR SOLUTION

Duke had severe problems with processing speed in many language functions.[30] During our initial evaluation, his responses were delayed by as much as 50.3% on some tests. He read short, grade-appropriate passages with errors on every line. He misread common, simple words such as *one*, *about* and *around*. He substituted words with non-words such as **aported* and **eventing*. In 5th grade, he had not even mastered the sound-letter (phoneme-grapheme) correspondences in English required in kindergarten. By then, he was two grades behind in reading.[31]

At Dysolve, Duke was in a hybrid program, with one-on-one conferencing an hour per week and online games. The automated part of his Dysolve program tracked his language-processing deficits and set about correcting them methodically as he played with its interactive games for about 15 minutes a day.

About five months into the program at the end of 5th grade, Duke's reading was no longer as disfluent. He was no longer misreading every line, and his occasional mistakes did not render the sentences he read incomprehensible, unlike before.

BREAKTHROUGH

After a year, Dysolve had built enough of the foundation to enable Duke to fulfill the demands of schoolwork. His resilience strengthened; his attitude changed.[32, 33] He was now coming to class every day eager to work. His grades in the 3rd quarter of 6th grade trended generally in the 70s-80s and in the 80s-90s in the 4th. In the summer of that year, he set out to master the spelling of words in the *Dysolve® Word Frequency List*—100 words a day, 3,000 a month.[34] For his New York State standardized reading test for 6th grade, he scored 200% higher than projected.

In the 1st quarter of 7th grade, Duke made the Academic Achievement List at school for the first time. At Dysolve, his processing speed registered at 70 WPM (Words Per Minute) in some modalities—still considerably lower than our target but good enough for him to excel at school.

Imagine what he can do when he hits the target speed.[35]

NOTES

1. Children who are gifted/talented and have a disability are considered twice-exceptional. Since gifted children comprise a tiny fraction of the student population, giftedness education is a comparatively small area of research and the subfield of twice-exceptionality is even smaller and is still in its infancy. For an overview of giftedness research, see Plucker, J., & Callahan, C. (Eds.). (2013). *Critical issues and practices in gifted education: What the research says.* Waco, TX: Prufrock. For resources, go to www.nagc.org.
2. Very little research has been conducted on the relation between bullying and learning disabilities such as dyslexia. The scant research to date suggests that children with these disabilities are more likely to be bullied (peer victimization) than bully others. See Mishna, F. (2003). Learning disabilities and bullying: Double jeopardy. *Journal of Learning Disabilities, 36*(4), 336-47.
3. The case study here had moderating factors that minimized the risk of delinquency such as a positive home environment and self-resilience. In contrast, for other individuals, research shows that childhood physical aggression and opposition are robust predictors of problem behaviors at older ages. In one study, 8- to 10-year-old boys who showed signs of high impulsivity, inattention and restlessness (ADHD symptoms) displayed heightened levels of aggression in adolescence and were more likely to be convicted of a violent crime by age 32. In another study, youth who fought and bullied during early adolescence were more likely to be arrested by age 16. See the research overview in Staff, J., Whichard, C., Siennick, S.E., & Maggs, J. (2015). Early life risks, antisocial tendencies, and preteen delinquency. *Criminology, 53*(4), 677-701. doi:10.1111/1745-9125.12093
4. "Exceptional" refers to those who are outside the typical, at either end of the spectrum. Thus, one can be exceptional for having gifts or deficits. That is why those with both are called *twice-exceptional.*

5. Even parents can fail to recognize the level of intelligence in their own children when language-processing deficits suppress certain traits. The uncertainty shown by Duke's parents over their son's intelligence is echoed by Patience's parents in Chapter 1 and Will's in Chapter 5.
6. See Hoh, P.-S. (2008). Cognitive characteristics of the gifted. In J. Plucker & C. Callahan (Eds.), *Critical issues and practices in gifted education: What the research says* (pp. 57-83). Austin, TX: Prufrock.
7. "Homework" by Russell Hoban.
8. See the Mother's Story in this chapter about how Duke tried to change another test to get the results he wanted.
9. Metacognitive awareness involves knowing one's own mental processes and abilities as a learner, thinker and problem-solver. We help Dysolve learners develop metacognitive awareness to empower them to help themselves.
10. The term *gifted* is used in the field to suggest that the exceptional ability simply presents itself. It usually implies intellectual giftedness.
11. Unlike in Duke's case, intellectual giftedness can mask a learning disability such that the student's performance is still at or above proficiency. If the disability is corrected, the student's performance will then rise to his actual high potential. We have seen such students with dyslexia who were able to keep their school grades in the average range.
12. Wechsler Individual Achievement Test – 3rd Ed. (WIAT-III).
13. This tenacity is needed for success and is also reported in the cases in Chapters 5 and 8.
14. Similar symptoms were found in the cases in Chapters 4-6 and 10.
15. The association between recurrent headaches and dyslexia (and ADHD) has not received much research interest. Recent studies do show a higher incidence of recurrent headaches among children with dyslexia, ADHD, and both conditions. Yet the explanations put forth remain controversial. One hypothesis uses overlapping brain mechanisms to account for the associations. A second hypothesis suggests that learning disabilities and ADHD create stresses that induce headaches. A third speculates that frequent headaches hinder learning and

cause ADHD behaviors. A fourth proposes a common disorder underlying headaches and ADHD. Which is the cause? Which is the effect? Depending on the hypothesis, headaches can be either. See our ADHD case study in Chapter 6. For a review of studies, see Genizi, J., Gordon, S., Kerem, N.C., Srugo, I., Shahar, E., & Ravid, S. (2013). Primary headaches, attention deficit disorder and learning disabilities in children and adolescents. *Journal of Headache Pain, 14*(1), 54. doi: 10.1186/1129-2377-14-54

Our own fieldwork shows that headaches are common among students with dyslexia and co-occur with ADHD. Headaches or head pressure often occur when processing load increases. See also our blogs on this kind of headaches in Dysolve Dyslexia on Facebook.

16. Clear expectations and self-discipline are key factors for excellent performance and success in our program. These factors are dependent on parents and caretakers.
17. Duke was in a hybrid program with one-on-one consultations and online games due to the severity of his processing problems.
18. Motivation is a key factor for success in Dysolve. To correct a processing deficit, our program has to expand the student's abilities beyond his current limit. This can be physically, mentally and psychologically challenging, as described by Will in Chapter 5.
19. Many of our students have strong interests in designing, creating or building structures and machinery. This interest was found among the students in Chapters 1-7.
20. We encourage gifted students to join gifted programs. Summer programs are offered by universities across the US. This allows gifted students to meet intellectual peers they may not encounter at school due to their small number.
21. Dysolve students typically seek independence in their learning around 6th grade when they enter junior high.
22. Patience's parents in Chapter 1 also put in extra work when she forgot to take home her homework.
23. Dysolve indices track improvements at the micro level while school grades measure global skills. See Chapter 14 *Computational Microlinguistics*.

24. Research has documented extensively the relation between reading disability and lack of awareness of the sounds of one's language (phonemic awareness). The focus has primarily centered on the segmental or single sound level. However, newer studies seem to suggest problems at the syllable level as well for those with reading impairment. See for example Johnson, P.E., Pennington, B.F., Lowenstein, J.H., Nittrouer, S. (2011). Sensitivity to structure in the speech signal by children with speech sound disorder and reading disability. *Journal of Communication Disorders, 44*(3), 294-314. Retrieved from https://doi.org/10.1016/j.jcomdis.2011.01.001
25. Error patterns differ between spellers with dyslexia and those without. Studies found that spellers with dyslexia tend to commit more errors related to their difficulty with segmentation (breaking words into single sounds) and phoneme identification (recognizing sounds in words). For example, they reduce consonant clusters (*str→st*), and substitute consonants. They omit vowels and substitute vowels that are not even phonetically similar. They often leave out word endings (*-s, -ed*). In contrast, writers without dyslexia produce words that sound like the target words (phonetically accurate) even when they are not spelled correctly (orthographically inaccurate). Thus, they may substitute same-sounding words (homophones: *buy→by*), use the incorrect letters for unstressed vowels (*attitude → attatude*), and overgeneralize the silent *–e* rule (*plan→plane*). Spelling instruction is needed for students with dyslexia, but research shows that it is more effective before 4th grade. See Bernstein, S.E. (2009). Phonology, decoding, and lexical compensation in vowel spelling errors made by children with dyslexia, *Reading and Writing, 22*(3), 307-331.
26. The students in Chapters 1, 3 and 5 received awards from their schools for academic achievement in the 1st year of Dysolve. Duke also received an award for improved conduct.
27. This runs counter to our philosophy of raising expectations for all students so that even struggling learners can exceed expectations, as the cases did in this book. See the Principal's Story in Chapter 7.

28. This avoidance behavior was reported for all cases in this book except Grace in Chapter 7. Grace was exceptionally compliant.
29. Perceptual sensitivity is a known characteristic of gifted children. See Hoh, P.-S. (2008). Cognitive characteristics of the gifted. In J. Plucker & C. Callahan (Eds.), *Critical issues and practices in gifted education: What the research says* (pp. 57-83). Austin, TX: Prufrock.
30. Processing speed has often been mentioned as a core component of the deficits underlying dyslexia. However, its role and relation to other components are still unclear in the research literature. See Elliott, J.G., & Grigorenko, E.L. (2014). *The dyslexia debate*. New York: Cambridge University Press.
31. Most of our students were two grades behind in reading when they first joined Dysolve. See Chapters 1-9.
32. Resilience comprises character strengths that enable one to cope, adapt and thrive in the face of adversity. Rather than view resilience as a static, intrinsic trait of one's personality, it may be more productively treated as a learned aptitude developed through experiences of adversity.
33. This change in attitude is common among Dysolve students as they progress in the program. See the cases in Chapters 1-9 (except 7, who was compliant throughout).
34. Following resolution of their processing problems, students need to catch up on the acquisition of written vocabulary, especially if they had lagged behind their classmates for years.
35. For example, orthographic (spelling) processing may occur at 100-200 milliseconds (ms), phonological (sound) and semantic (meaning) processing at 200-500 ms, and syntactic (sentence) processing at 600 ms. For a review of studies, see Landi, N., & Perfetti, C.A. (2007). An electrophysiological investigation of semantic and phonological processing in skilled and less-skilled comprehenders. *Brain and Language, 102*, 30–45. doi:10.1016/j.bandl.2006.11.001

Father's Story

One of the Dumbest Things
Ken

Authors' note: The responsibility of diagnosing dyslexia was relegated to the medical field for historical reasons. The concept of dyslexia is still under debate in reading research. Our solution comes instead from the new field of Computational Microlinguistics. See Chapters 13 and 14.

No Clue

"I have no clue about dyslexia." Our son's doctor shrugged. "What do you need me to do? Do you need me to put on the letter that Duke has dyslexia so the school will help him?"

"Yes, that's what we need," I replied.

"Ok."

Our son, Duke, was in 5th grade when his teacher said we should have him evaluated for dyslexia. One of the dumbest things about the whole entire thing is that you have to go to your medical doctor to have them diagnose it when it's not medical-related whatsoever.[1] Not something you can fix with medication or operation or anything. So the fact you have to involve a medical person at all is ridiculous. It's in the wrong field.[2]

Teachers should be able to point you in the right direction on these types of things, but they're not allowed to.[3] Luckily, Duke's pediatrician knew about Dr. Coral and gave us her contact information.

Made No Sense

Duke would read things wrong throughout a book. But when you ask questions about it, he would know all the answers, which made no sense.[4] As he was reading it, he wasn't reading the words on the page, so how could he even understand what the book was saying? We weren't really sure what to do with *that*.

My wife and I saw that he was struggling in 2nd grade and continued to fall further and further behind every year. His school was using the Orton or Norton Gillingham thing.[5] I don't think anyone explained to us what actually the Norton Gillingham thing was, really.[6] It didn't even get him up to grade-level reading.[7]

You go in at the beginning of the year and the teachers say, "We try to not give more than half an hour's worth of homework every night. If the homework is taking more than half an hour, let us know."

But Duke would be doing homework for an hour-and-a-half. We would have to sit there with him to get him through it because he would be struggling so badly that he'd walk away and not do it if given the chance.[8] It was a daily struggle and he would get upset because it was difficult. He'd write *anything* down, whether it made sense or not. We'd go over his homework with him, and the answers he wrote down made absolutely no sense. I'd read the questions to him and his responses, and he'd have this look on his face like, that doesn't make any sense. He just didn't understand the question the way it was written. His verbal skills had always vastly outweighed his natural ability to read.

Something to Blame It on

He wanted something to blame his problem on. He wanted to release it. He didn't want it to be, because he was stupid or something. That he couldn't do it because he wasn't capable. He wanted a reason. He wasn't satisfied with the fact that it was just something he couldn't do.

There were behavioral issues at points too at school. Not any type of real trouble—kind of him doing things just to draw attention or go to the nurse's office. To get out of class, he would just say he didn't feel good so he didn't have to do it. Or just acting out. Some of it I think was to deflect away from the schoolwork.[9]

In 5th grade, when we tried to go through the process of getting him services at school, it was just his classroom teacher reporting on his struggle. But in 6th grade, the reading teacher in his middle school was very adamant that he needed the assistance. The school psychologist was also insisting on his needing additional services, to get an IEP instead of a 504.[10] There were so many people in the school that were on his side by then, pushing for what he needed that there wasn't any way to go except to recommend for the IEP.

Ridiculous Memory

Duke has these struggles at school, but he's got a ridiculous memory.[11] He'd say, "Remember that one time when such and such happened?"

My wife and I would look at each other. "Do you have any idea what he's talking about?"

"No, do you?"

And he'd go on and describe it and describe it. Sometimes we'd remember it after a while, and sometimes we still couldn't remember. But Duke remembers things vividly.

He's always been observant and watch what you do. He can figure out how you do things just by seeing it done. I've always learned that way better too. One time, Dr. Coral gave him an old radio to pull apart to figure out why it wasn't working.

"Do you think it could be the speakers, Dad?" Duke asked.

"I don't know." Before I finished talking, he was already unbolting the cover.

We couldn't find anything wrong with the speakers. He checked the wires connected to the circuit boards.

"Maybe the circuit board isn't sending the signals right," he said.

We started taking it apart, and while he was touching the circuit board with the screwdriver—KKKRRRRKKK. A loud screeching noise.

"Oops, I guess that was bad," Duke said. It fried the whole entire thing.

Duke was laughing. He enjoys taking things apart, seeing how they work. He's always enjoyed science. He's good at pretty much anything physical or mechanical. He's always been very able to do things that had to do with sports too.[12]

90 is Very Easy

Duke joined Dysolve in the middle of 5th grade. The first three quarters of the school year were rough in 6th grade. But things started to turn around in the last quarter. Now in 7th grade, he comes home from school, gets a snack, sits down, does his homework.[13] He's done relatively quickly. It's not something he's struggling with anymore. Now, if he has a question on something, he'll ask. He very rarely has questions about homework. You don't have to harp on him about it, or remind him six times he needs to do his homework. He doesn't go try do eight other things instead of his homework.

That's one of the best things we've seen with Dysolve, because it was such a struggle to get him to do his homework. Before, if we left him by himself, he'd start to do something else.

I just want him to get past the frustration that he has, and for it to be as easy as it should be for him. The frustration part is the biggest hindrance for him still. It's not as bad as it used to be, but he's still frustrated from time to time. When he gets to that point when he's that frustrated, he feels that there's nothing he can do that is going to make what he's doing work.[14] I just want him to be able to get through that. Once he gets through that, he'll basically be able to do whatever he sets as his goal.

I told him at the end of 6th grade: "If your GPA is 85.7 now though you struggled for most of the year, then a 90 is very easy for you next year."

MY MESSAGE TO PARENTS

Don't take "no" for an answer. You really have to stick with it. You can't give up because if you give up, no one is going to do it for you.[15] No one is going to do it for *your* kid. The kid can't do it for themselves.

Listen to what's going on with your kid. It can help a lot just knowing what they're thinking, what they're feeling. Of course there are some lazy kids out there who don't *want* to do the work. It's one thing not to want to do it and another thing to be struggling through it and getting frustrated because you can't get through it no matter how hard you try, because there's something standing in your way.

If teachers are telling you, "Oh, they'll grow out of it," that's true to a point.[16] When you go to school, and you see other kids' projects on the wall, you can see that kids will eventually grow out of certain behaviors as they learn. When you look at a *d* and you look at a *b*, it's essentially the same symbol flipped backwards.[17] It's going to be one of those things that people get backwards. But there's things you can look for that will help you figure out that there's definitely something more going on, like not being able to read one single line when he's reading a text. Duke would jump around and just pick random words and random parts of words.[18] It kind of pointed to there being more than just getting things backwards. There was definitely more to it.

NOTES

1. Contrary to what the layperson might think, dyslexia currently requires a clinical diagnosis. Dyslexia is folded into the broad category of specific learning disorder (SLD) in the *Diagnostic and Statistical Manual of Mental Disorders – 5th Edition* (DSM-5) published by the American Psychiatric Association. For a history of how the problem of dyslexia diagnosis ended up in the medical field, see Chapter 13 *State of the Science*.
2. See Note 1 above. Dyslexia falls under "specific learning disorder" for clinical diagnosis but under "specific learning *disability*" for intervention. Ken in this story rightly points out that this disjunction is problematic—that it is diagnosed in the medical field but treated in the educational.
3. See Note 1 above. See also the Principal's Story in Chapter 7 about unfunded mandates and the Individuals with Disabilities Education Act (IDEA).
4. Reading accuracy mainly involves word-level decoding but reading comprehension can rely on global skills to get the gist of a passage. It is obvious when a reader cannot sound out a word to read it (decoding). But even with these gaps, he can still rely on prior knowledge and contextual cues to understand the passage.
5. Orton-Gillingham is an instructional approach for reading remediation developed in the 1930s. This compensatory approach is meant to help struggling readers cope with dyslexia. Orton-Gillingham is *not* designed to remove dyslexia as a chronic condition. It is commonly used in schools in some parts of the US. Despite such methods, school statistics on students with learning disabilities are grim, with poor prospects for readers still struggling in middle school. See the research review in Elliott, J.G., & Grigorenko, E.L. (2014). *The dyslexia debate.* New York: Cambridge University Press. See also Chapter 12 *The True Cost of Dyslexia* and Chapter 13 *State of the Science*.
6. Besides Ken, the parents in Chapters 3, 6 and 9 also voiced that they did not know what the intervention services actually did.

7. The cases in Chapters 2, 3, 6 and 8 used Orton-Gillingham-based methods popular in some schools and continued to fail reading proficiency tests until they joined Dysolve. The other cases in this book did not disclose their schools' reading methods or did not use any.
8. All the families in this book spent an inordinate amount of time on homework before the language-processing problems involved were resolved in Dysolve.
9. Behaviors to deflect attention away from schoolwork were also reported in Chapters 4-10 except 7. Interestingly, the cases that did not were all girls.
10. An IEP is an Individualized Education Program (or Plan) for students with special needs to receive support services in public schools. *IEP* also refers to the legal document that charts the student's needs, evaluative and support services, and targeted goals. IEPs are covered by the Individuals with Disabilities Education Act (IDEA). A 504 plan is a formal plan developed by the school to prevent discrimination and protect the rights of children with disabilities. 504 plans are covered under Section 504 of the Rehabilitation Act, which is a federal civil rights law to stop discrimination against people with disabilities. 504 plans are not part of special education and generally do not impose the strict requirements on schools that IEPs do. To learn more, go to https://www.americanboard.org/blog/a-new-teachers-introduction-to-ieps-and-504s/
11. Superior memory is one of the traits of giftedness. Memory is viewed in research as a composite of many subprocesses. Superior memory may be domain-specific, such as the linguistic, mathematical, visual, spatial, and kinesthetic (body). See Hoh, P.-S. (2008). Cognitive characteristics of the gifted. In J. Plucker & C. Callahan (Eds.), *Critical issues and practices in gifted education: What the research says* (pp. 57-83). Austin, TX: Prufrock.
12. Precocious physical development is a prerequisite for gifted performance in many domains, such as fine arts. That is, gifted children tend to walk and talk early. However, in the twice-exceptional case in this chapter, speech was delayed. For giftedness traits, see Hoh, P.-S. (2008). Cognitive charac-

teristics of the gifted. In J. Plucker & C. Callahan (Eds.), *Critical issues and practices in gifted education: What the research says* (pp. 57-83). Austin, TX: Prufrock.
13. Independent reading and learning are two of the early signs that underlying processing issues are dissipating. This is reported in Chapters 1-9.
14. The children in the other chapters were also reported to display the same feelings of defeatism.
15. This is the recurring message from the parents of these successful cases and the theme of this book: You can't give up.
16. Our students typically come to us in 4th-5th grade, after being told for years to wait before taking any action. See the parents' messages advising against this delay in Chapters 1-6.
17. Switching *b* and *d* is indeed common among students with reading disabilities, contrary to the view in some quarters that this is a myth. This occurred with the cases in Chapters 1, 4-7 and 9. This is explained at Dysolve.com, which provides informational materials on other warning signs of dyslexia.
18. Patterns of errors in misreadings vary among those with dyslexia, leading researchers to propose different subtypes of dyslexia. However, studies on this topic are still scant. See for example Valdois, S., Bosse, M.-L., Ans, B., Carbonnel, S., Zorman, M., David, D., & Pellat, J. (2003). Phonological and visual processing deficits can dissociate in developmental dyslexia: Evidence from two case studies. *Reading and Writing: An Interdisciplinary Journal, 16*, 541–572.

Mother's Story

You're Talking about Someone Else
Conny

Disciplinary Meeting

"Duke was the one who instigated the fight."

My husband, Ken, and I were called in to a disciplinary meeting with our son's 6th grade team after an "incident."

"Oh no, Duke told me the other boy had been picking on him and picking on him for well over a year. Duke had had enough. He just got annoyed. Nobody saw what actually happened. That's not the whole story." I tried to speak for our son, Duke, who wasn't at the meeting to defend himself.

Even if he was there, he wouldn't have defended himself. Though he was bullied early on, he wasn't sharing that with Ken and me. We knew of a couple of kids that picked on him over the years.[1] It always seemed to be the same couple of kids over and over again. I don't think the school classified their actions as bullying because Duke was looked at as the bully on occasion.

They'd go back to the earliest report of his behavior issues in 3rd grade. "He was picking on a sweet, docile girl," his 3rd grade teacher told me. I don't think there were sweet, docile girls in 3rd grade.

But this disciplinary meeting in 6th grade was getting serious. Just diagnosed with dyslexia and ADHD, Duke had a tough transition to middle school.[2] He wasn't making friends. He wasn't in classes with people he was friendly with. A lot of anger built up inside him that year. He just wasn't worried about the consequences at the time. I don't know if it's a combination with the struggle, the hormones. I don't even know what was going on in that intelligent head of his. Everything kind of snowballed.[3] The amount of trouble seemed to get worse, one on top of the other. He just didn't know when to keep his mouth shut, when to keep his hands to himself.

Talking to Squirrels

Duke did not start talking until he was three. His delayed talking did not worry us initially.[4] My sister, who's a teacher, was the one who kept saying, "You really need to have that checked."

And we'd say, "Eh, he'll start talking when he's ready." He "eh-eh-ehed" as he pointed, so we knew what he wanted.[5]

We were always told that his aunt didn't talk either until she was much older. She only talked to squirrels. My mother would talk for her. My aunt is a highly intelligent person and now works for a university. So it wasn't like it was a huge concern that Duke wasn't talking much as a baby.

When Duke was two, we looked into a free speech therapy program from the county. Somebody would come to the house once a week, sit there and kind of do their thing with the kid. After about six months of that, Duke started talking and hasn't stopped since. He went from no talking to a vocabulary larger than mine.[6] It's not words I use, so I'm not even sure where he picks them up. Not from the dictionary, that's for sure.

Gaming the System

Duke struggled in 2nd grade, when difficulty reading and the backward letters were supposed to be normal. Then he went through the next couple of years without his school noticing that it should have been corrected at that point and getting further and further behind in reading.[7] We tried to get him help at school but were not successful. The vision specialist didn't find anything that we didn't already know (very expensive waste of time). And the methods she thought would fix his problem, the school was already doing. We knew he had smarts in there but he just didn't know how to get them out. You think you can teach a kid to read, but he just wasn't grasping any of the tools or methods.[8]

My husband and I used to have to watch over Duke to get his homework done. He'd come up with excuses not to do it.

"I have to go to the bathroom."

"I need a tissue."

"I need a drink of water." Or he'd just be sitting there doodling on paper. Or erasing half the page.[9] Or sitting there staring at a blank wall. Lots of tears.

Duke always wanted to go to the eye doctor. We went for the eye test multiple times because Duke complained that he couldn't see and that things were blurry. Just to try to find any answer to the problem.

At the end of 4th grade, we had his hearing tested. The audio tracking person giving the test could tell that Duke was giving false answers.[10] Duke was smart enough to try to fool this person so that this would be the solution to his problem. He would score poorly and it would be something to fix.

Duke was frustrated with his problem. I felt that if he thought he was not good at school, he was not going to work at it. With anything, I think most people would feel that way. Even today, he still doesn't think that he has the smarts. Whenever he does something wrong, his first response is, "Because I'm stupid."[11]

Twice-Exceptional

"Your son is exceptional,"[12] Dr. Coral told us after her evaluation of Duke.

I thought to myself, "You're talking about someone else. You mixed up your notes." Nope, not our Duke.[13] She mixed up the paperwork. She had the wrong folder.

At that time, I wasn't intelligent enough to understand what she was telling us (clearly the genes didn't come from me). But then Dr. Coral told me to look up "twice-exceptional" and gave me some materials written for parents. When I started reading what it meant, I understood how Duke fit into that category. (Now, because of it, I won't let him play football and he hates me.)

Duke is a perfectionist, that's one of the things I found when I looked into the twice-exceptional thing.[14] It put some perspective into it because now I understood why he did certain things before. It clarified things for me. He puts a lot of pressure on himself with succeeding. I don't know where he got it from. We were never "You need to get 90s. You need to get *A*s. You need to win first place in everything." We've never been that kind of parents. We've always instilled in him that as long as he did the best he could, it didn't matter what the outcome was. We're not grounding you because you got a 60. But Duke totally does it to himself on his own.[15] If he doesn't win first place, he sucks. That's what he thinks.

His memory is awesome though.[16] When he was four or five, sitting in the bathtub playing, he'd send me to his bedroom to get a toy.

"Go in my room and get my car. It's in the toy bin next to my dresser in the middle."

He'd be in the bathtub telling me exactly where the toy was in his bedroom, even though his room was a disaster. Disorganized chaos—there's things everywhere and nothing was organized. But he knew exactly where the particular car with the red hood was or whatever. And he was always correct. He remembers cars, what type of cars, what kind of motors, horsepower, torque. I don't know those things myself. Even now, he remembers everything, especially when you promise him something.

Just from watching his Dad start the snowblower in the driveway, Duke was able to explain to my mother step by step how to use one when he'd never actually done it. We'd gotten my mom a snowblower for Christmas, and she had no idea what to do with it. That was when Duke was eight, the winter when it didn't snow.

He taught his grandma. "Turn the throttle up to the rabbit and turn the gas to the ON position. Flip the ignition switch and turn the key. Pull the rope handle. Pull down this handle and this handle and go!! Or if you can't pull the rope, you plug it in here."

Guardian Angel

Now in 7th grade, Duke has a resource teacher who got his back.[17] She saw him in the counselor's office and she told me right away, "I saw him in there, and I just want to make sure everything's ok. Anything you need, please let me know."

It's almost as if he's got a guardian angel now that he didn't have before. And having somebody to talk to at school helps, if it's something he can't talk to us about or doesn't want to talk to us about. He's got someone he can vent to. I think that definitely made a difference.[18]

He said, "She doesn't make me do my work. She makes me *want* to do my work."

He's so all over the place when it comes to what he wants to do in the future. He has those conversations with Dr. Coral, but he doesn't have those conversations with us. There's a lot of intelligence in his relatives. One of his uncles got a free ride in college. Another is getting his PhD. Maybe Duke has their genes. The one who talked to squirrels.

He definitely got people around who aren't going to let him fail.[19] His grades are good now. Everything's starting to come together.

MY MESSAGE TO PARENTS

If the first thing doesn't work, you try something else. If you have to find another way, or a second opinion, or a different approach, go for it. If it doesn't work out with one person, go to the next one.

Sometimes, it's the teacher who is saying, "Your child needs this." But the parents are saying, "No, no, he's fine."[20] You know what? To hell with the stigma! Why would you not help your kid?

My message to other parents? I'll keep thinking about it at midnight or 3 AM in the morning…

NOTES

1. See Note 2 in Dr. Coral's Story in this chapter about peer victimization among those with learning disabilities. The cases in Chapters 2-4 reported being bullied at school.
2. Duke did not receive special services in elementary school despite scoring at the 2nd percentile in state reading tests. His problems with dyslexia were identified at Dysolve.
3. What was originally a linguistic problem can quickly snowball to harm other areas such as the academic and psychosocial. This is why we strongly encourage parents and caretakers to address language-processing deficits immediately before these create other less manageable problems.
4. Parents and caretakers need to be aware of linguistic milestones to realize whether a developmental delay is cause for concern. Information on these milestones is available upon request at Dysolve.com and Dysolve Dyslexia on Facebook.
5. The cases in Chapters 1-3 did not speak in early childhood.
6. The cases in Chapters 4-6 and 9-10 showed distinct discrepancies between their oral and written vocabularies. Most were highly expressive in speech.
7. Information on workshops on the signs of dyslexia is available via Dysolve.com and Dysolve Dyslexia on Facebook.
8. Reading remediation has little effect when underlying processing problems remain unaddressed, as in Duke's case. Nearly two-thirds of 4th and 8th graders across the US were reading below proficiency in 2015, according to the Nation's Report Card on reading assessment
(https://www.nationsreportcard.gov/).
If current methods cannot even help raise performance for those without reading disabilities, what chance do those with dyslexia have? Authorities in the field acknowledge that they do not know how to teach reading to those who do not respond to intervention. See Fuchs, D., Compton, D.L., Fuchs, L.S., Bryant, V.J., Hamlett, C.L., & Lambert, W. (2012). First-grade cognitive abilities as long-term predictors of reading

comprehension and disability status. *Journal of Learning Disabilities, 45*(3) 217–231.
9. Prince in Chapter 6 also erased his homework regularly. All cases in this book struggled with homework even with parental help before Dysolve.
10. The Dysolve Program is designed to detect false answers through data analytics.
11. The students in Chapters 1, 4, 6, 9 and 10 echoed this sentiment before joining Dysolve.
12. See Note 4 in Dr. Coral's Story in this chapter for the definition of "exceptional."
13. The parents in Chapters 1 and 5 also underestimated their children's high intelligence before Dysolve.
14. See Note 1 in Dr. Coral's Story in this chapter for the definition of "twice-exceptionality."
15. Perfectionism is a common personality trait of gifted individuals. However, perfectionism in the presence of a learning disability can exacerbate psychosocial issues, as in this case.
16. See Note 11 about superior memory in the Father's Story in this chapter.
17. The resource teacher in this case helped the student manage his schoolwork and homework.
18. Academic success depends on psychosocial wellbeing. That is why we monitor for each learner the Dysolve ecosystem in which the child in the center is supported by the family, the Dysolve team, school faculty, doctors, counselors and tutors if any.
19. The success of each case in this book is a testament to the adults' determination to fight for him or her.
20. In our experience, sometimes parents do not act on teachers' and doctors' recommendations. Chapter 12 *The True Cost of Dyslexia* conveys some of the dire consequences of delaying action. See also Chapter 16 *Responsible Education*.

Duke's Story

Something Good is Going to Happen

Fighting Back

My name is Duke. I am 12 years old. Last year I was in 6th grade. I was getting into trouble a lot mostly because other kids were bullying me and I started to get hit by them. Eventually I had had enough and I fought back. Though I won the fight, it only put me in the principal's office. And to add to that, I was barely passing my classes one year before. I had gotten bullied pretty much since kindergarten.[1] I was not good at anything but sports.

Last year in Art a kid named Ted who I had known for a very long time punched me in the stomach and then we just kept bickering. Then one day he said, "I feel sorry for your sister if she ends up as dumb and ugly as you are."

I regretted every day that I did not set that kid straight, as in hitting him so hard he'd have to go to the hospital for weeks. I felt like it was the only thing I could do to get other kids that had not felt my fist to back off, but it did not work out that well for me.

And all these people were saying, "Oh, you are going to be very popular or famous in some sort of way."[2] I didn't believe them. Then my parents told me that all the most famous singers and actors all were bullied and struggled in school. I'm like, that's my life! That was pretty much what was happening to me.

But now I don't get bullied pretty much ever and I think that is because I have a lot more friends on my side.[3]

Something Very Good is Going to Happen

In 5th grade, my parents brought me to see Dr. Coral and at first I thought it was useless. Before, it would take me two hours to do homework that was supposed to be for 15 minutes, even when my Mom helped me. I used to make excuses like I had to go to the bathroom or I had to make something to eat. I am very active, but because of the homework, I would not have time to go outside or play video games.[4]

But at about near the end of 6th grade, I went up 20 points in Reading, which was huge for me.[5] Now I can do homework in 20 minutes. Now it is with no help. Now I am in 7th grade and am doing so good that all of my teachers are so proud of me. It also helps if you like your teachers, and I didn't last year. But this year I do.

I got my progress report not too long ago and now I am getting 80+, 90. My parents are very proud of me and so is my grandma. It is great to see how much better I can do and will do in the future. Now I feel something very good is going to happen in my life.[6]

MY MESSAGE TO DYSOLVE STUDENTS

Always remember there is one other way that you have not tried yet. After a couple of weeks in the program, don't say, "This isn't working" and quit. I did not notice any change for like a year in Dysolve, but finally I did.[7] I am sure that you will succeed in this program.

NOTES

1. See Note 2 in Dr. Coral's Story in this chapter about peer victimization among those with learning disabilities. They are more likely to be bullied than bully others. The cases in Chapters 2-4 reported being bullied at school.
2. The adults in Duke's life told him about his giftedness and twice-exceptionality. We believe in age-appropriate honest discussions with children so as to empower them to address these issues with our support.
3. Duke's relations with peers improved as his academic performance improved.
4. Freeing students' homework time improves the quality of life for all involved in the family. This is echoed by Will in Chapter 5 and by almost all the parents in this book.
5. This was about a year-and-a-half into Dysolve.
6. This attitude change from defeatism to optimism is echoed by the students in Chapters 1, 2, 5 and 6 in their own stories.
7. See Dr. Coral's Story in this chapter about latent changes in Dysolve that surface much later in the form of improved school grades. There is a time lag because Dysolve corrects underlying deficits at the micro level. These indepth changes are not assessed directly through school tests and assignments.

Key Takeaways

Instill discipline to build resilience.

Be patient: Improvements may remain latent for some time.

Consider whether twice-exceptionality may account for some behaviors.

Dyslexia Dissolved

3

Skye

Dyslexia

Skye

Dysolve Finding:
Language-processing deficits leading to dyslexia, speech impairment[1]

School Classification:
Learning disability, speech/language impairment

School Services:
Resource room

Private Services:
Speech therapy, Orton-Gillingham tutoring[2]

Private Testing:
Neuropsychological evaluation[3] – Not used in Dysolve
Phonological disorder, dyslexia, mixed expressive and receptive language disorder[4]

Dyslexia

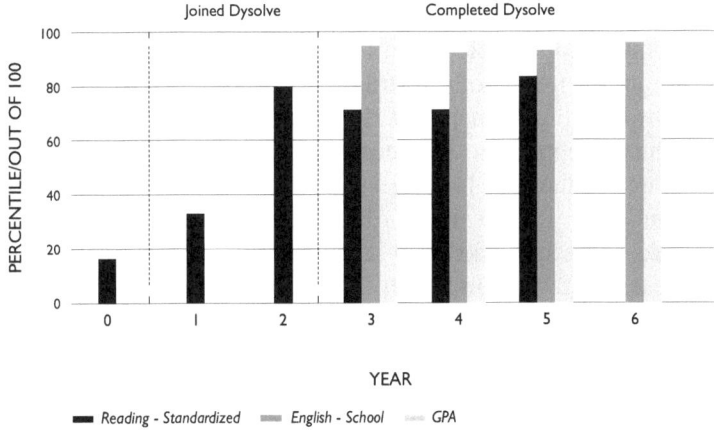

FIGURE 5
Skye – Standardized Reading and School Grades before and after Dysolve[5]

NOTES

1. By *language-processing deficits*, we mean deficiencies in the processes involved in executing the language functions of speaking, listening, reading or writing.
2. Orton-Gillingham is an instructional approach for reading remediation developed in the 1930s. This compensatory approach is meant to help struggling readers cope with dyslexia. Orton-Gillingham is *not* designed to remove dyslexia as a chronic condition. It is commonly used in schools in some parts of the US. Despite such methods, school statistics on students with learning disabilities are grim, with poor prospects for readers still struggling in middle school. See the research review in Elliott, J.G., & Grigorenko, E.L. (2014). *The dyslexia debate*. New York: Cambridge University Press. See also Chapter 12 *The True Cost of Dyslexia*.
3. Dysolve does not use external tests to build students' evaluative and corrective programs. This includes neuropsychological evaluations. See the Engineer's Story in Chapter 9 on the problem with standardized testing or assessments in dyslexia diagnosis. Chapter 14 on the complexity of the problem of dyslexia explains why cookie-cutter test kits are ineffective.
4. See our critique of classification labels in the Engineer's Story in Chapter 9, and Chapter 13.
5. Skye's scores were from standardized tests administered by her public school in New York.

Mother's Story

You should All be Ashamed
Frances

Authors' note: This story illustrates a parent's frustration over her inability to find a solution for her child's condition. If your child cannot speak, read, write and understand language, to what lengths would you go? Later, this mother used the knowledge she gained from her painful journey to help other families.

Apple Juice

"Bags out kids... Skye, what do you want to drink for breakfast?" I turned to look at my 11-year-old daughter.

She whipped her arching eyes at me, then cut to her brother to waste no more time, and with a small squeeze of her hand, placed her juice order.

"Apple juice." Her brother responded obediently.

I popped up my surprised but avenging eyebrows to protest. One deep, short breath: "Skye sweetie, lemonade, grape juice, apple...What do you want to drink?"

Her face sank, as everyone prepared their endurance for this one. It's not a big deal. She just had to speak for herself. Just an ordinary phrase. I couldn't just give in. *She* couldn't just give up.

She began, "Alop su-"

I moved closer to her, not understanding the words she's trying to put together. "Huh, what sweetheart?"

"Apple," Michael chimed, "juice."

"Michael!" I was riled. "I asked SKYE the question. She can answer for HERSELF! Let your sister respond! Juice is for EVERYONE and ordering is for EVERYONE!! GO pull the granola bars out..." Stern as I could ever say "granola."

"C'mon now baby, let's try again, what juice do you want?" I tried to keep it level and casual, while the clock ticked-ticked-ticked away before the school bus showed up at our door.

"Al—A—"

"Mom! I wanted the blueberry ones! I told you last time!" Michael interrupted.

"Michael!"

"And Skye wants apple juice, for the millionth time!"

"And Skye—Michael, use a napkin!—I want you to practice 'apple juice.' Honey, you have to ask for what you want, okay?"

Her tiny face gave in to despair. Her brother's showed disappointment at our still-unresolved communication system. And so it went, morning after morning before they rushed off to school and I rushed off to work—the cycle of frustration that existed in our house for a long, long time.

Not Talking

Michael and Skye had worked out a sort of sign language between them, and Michael was his younger sister's translator. Every evening, I spent at least an hour before bedtime reading to them. Michael loved all the books that I read, from Dr. Seuss to nonfiction. Since small, Michael loved to repeat the words that he heard, pointing to phrases he had memorized. By the time Michael entered kindergarten, he was reading chapter books like *The Magic Tree House* and the *A to Z Mysteries*. He even loved reading to his younger siblings, when they sat still long enough for him to do so.

I mention Michael to illustrate how kids growing up in the same household can be so different.[1] Skye was well over two years old before she started uttering words. And when she did, she was really hard to understand.[2] She spoke little. I would ask her a question at the dinner table and she would stare at me for a very long time. Sometimes she would respond, but many times she wouldn't. It wasn't until years later that I understood that she wasn't being rude. She was having so much trouble processing the language around her that she was overwhelmed.[3] She was missing so much of what was being said that she had to use her natural intelligence to interpret what was being asked of her. That took time, so it appeared as if she wasn't listening. Actually she was listening so intently that it took all of her energy to do so.

In preschool, Skye rarely talked to her teachers. She would stare at them when they asked her a question and there would be a huge delay in her response, if any. Her preschool teachers suggested that I keep her back another year.[4] They didn't think she was socially ready to go to kindergarten since she rarely spoke to anyone, teachers and students alike. But I chose to have Skye start kindergarten because I thought a new set of teachers would be good for her.

Warning Signs

By this time, Skye was showing warning signs of language problems, but I was not educated in recognizing them.[5] There was the delayed speech, the trouble with articulation, and the processing delays in hearing and responding to speech. More signs were to come in kindergarten and 1st grade.

Skye didn't speak to her kindergarten teachers for the first six months of school. She loved the early math but struggled with the reading and writing. However, she didn't shy away from writing because in kindergarten she had to draw a picture along with any writing that she did. She loved to draw. In fact it was her drawing that helped the people around her to understand what she wanted to say. If we didn't understand what she was saying, we would ask her to draw a picture. She became really adept at drawing.[6]

I volunteered to read to Skye's kindergarten class. The first thing I noticed in the classroom was that most of the kids were lounging, slouching, listening to the teacher and taking breaks to chat with one another. Unlike them, Skye was sitting ramrod straight in her chair, completely focused on the teacher and not talking at all with anyone. When the teacher stopped talking, Skye continued to stare at her for a while longer before looking down to do her work.

She didn't take a break to talk with the kids at her table. She focused intently on her work. Her posture remained very stiff. She smiled and looked happy to see me when I walked in, but she still wasn't as relaxed as her peers.

At the time, I didn't know what to make of Skye's behavior. But as the years passed, and later through Dysolve, I became more educated on the signs of language-processing deficits. I began to realize that Skye was struggling so hard to keep up with what people were saying that she had to tune out much of what was going on around her. She had to tune out her friends, she had to tune out the chatter to concentrate on what the teacher was saying.[7] Even with all this concentration, she was still missing much of it.

As kindergarten continued, Skye excelled in anything to do with math but was steadily falling behind in anything to do with language.[8] Her reading was not improving and her spelling was unintelligible.[9]

When I voiced my concern, her school assured me, "She just needs more time."

Skye was placed in a combined kindergarten-1st grade classroom the following year so she could do 1st grade math and kindergarten-level language work. It sounded good.

Raddit

Skye again did not speak for the first six months of 1st grade. I asked Skye's school for a speech evaluation.

They refused.

I asked again.

They refused.

I insisted.

"Well, Mrs. Johnson, we have the evaluation results. Skye doesn't qualify for speech therapy."

"I can't understand my daughter's speech. My parents can't understand my daughter's speech. But her school doesn't think she has a speech problem? Oh, right, she didn't talk at school!"

I asked to see the results from Skye's evaluation. They said there wasn't anything that they could send. I said, "Alright, I will come in tomorrow and you can show me how you evaluated Skye."

The speech teacher at school showed me a flip book with different pictures. One of the pictures had a rabbit. The student being evaluated was supposed to say out loud what she saw in the picture. They were looking for the sound /r/ at the beginning of the word *rabbit*.

I asked the speech teacher, "If Skye had said 'raddit' instead of 'rabbit,' would you have marked that as the wrong answer?"

"No, we're only checking her for the /r/ sound in that question."

"Now, this picture of a snake. So you'd mark it as correct if Skye said 'sake'?"

"Correct."

One after the other, the teacher told me Skye's responses, which were uttered incorrectly, but according to their standard, she still passed since she was able to say the single sound they were looking for in each question.

Flying bads. Bunny raddits. How is this right? How is it just? At this point, I yelled at the whole bunch of them,

"You should all be ashamed of yourselves! Here's a child who can't say words correctly and yet you determine that she passed these standardized tests!"[10]

I decided to pay for speech therapy out of school. The speech therapist determined that indeed Skye had trouble forming many of the consonant and vowel sounds. Even though Skye had speech therapy for much of 1st grade, she continued to struggle in school.[11]

But her school continued to say, "She just needs more time."

At that time, Skye's Dad and I were getting a divorce. I agreed with her teachers to give her more time and kept her in 1st grade for another year.

She Just Needs More Time

First Grade, Take 2, began. Skye already knew the material. But even with this advantage, she struggled to meet 1st grade standards. No matter how much work we put into homework every night, Skye still floundered. I asked her school what testing could be done, because now I was sure that something was not right. No kid should be struggling like she was.

Her school once again assured me, "She just needs more time."[12]

Since Skye already knew the material and got good enough grades in subjects other than English, they moved her on to 2nd grade. She was not reading at grade level, her spelling was random, her speech was still garbled, yet she was moving forward to the next grade.[13]

Skye's pediatrician recommended a neuropsychological evaluation in 2nd grade.[14] This was the first time that I had heard that a test existed that would help with diagnosing learning disorders and language problems.[15] So, with $5,000 out of pocket, I had a diagnosis of dyslexia and delay in phonological processing.[16] I also learned that my dear daughter, who could barely speak, had a high IQ.[17]

I arranged for a meeting with the school's special education staff and Skye's teacher immediately and insisted that the principal be there too.

I told them, "You've got a flaw in the way you diagnose language learning difficulties.[18] My daughter doesn't just need more time. She needs actual intervention."

They said, "She needs an IEP."[19]

"IEP?" I asked. As confusing as the issue was, we were narrowing in.

"Individualized Education Program. It's required for the school to move forward with a student's, in this case Skye's, changing needs."

My furnaced expression signaled that there was clearly more that the administrator in front of me needed to explain, and quickly.

"The IEP must be put together by the Special Education Coordinator, the special ed teachers, and Skye's current 2nd grade teacher."

"I see. Well, if this is how it works, we'll have to get it started right away. And the resource room, my daughter needs to be in there."[20]

"Unfortunately," the administrator cleared her throat, "it's too late in the year to make that change."

"It's too late *not* to," I corrected.

"As unfavorable as it may be, we'll have to wait until the new academic year."

"We're not waiting for anything! Not a minute longer!" This gave my anger wings. "Oh no, she's going into the special ed program right now. I'm not leaving until you write up her IEP. I will meet with her special ed teacher every week until the end of the school year. We will monitor the action plan together and Skye's progress."

I continued, "And I hope you find me good company, because I'm NOT leaving this office until that IEP is completed for her."

I took off my jacket and laid out my things and stationed myself deeper into the room, refusing to leave. I sat across from a small bottle of alop su. I knew the steps I had to take were all against the norm—for my daughter, who was, against all statistics, outside the norm.[21]

I thought their heads were going to explode when I then asked, "Now what are you going to do for Skye during the 10 weeks of summer vacation?"

Special Camp

The school didn't offer any services during the summer months.[22] I found a six-week camp at a private school that specialized in dyslexia.

This school was amazing. It had large open fields, horseback riding, and a whole building for art projects. The school based its methodology for helping kids with dyslexia on the Orton-Gillingham (OG) method.[23] The OG method is rooted in using all of the senses to teach language.[24] All the teachers at this school were trained in OG and they tutored each student individually for a period of time each day.[25] The summer program involved testing, intensive tutoring for part of the day while the rest of the day was filled with arts and crafts, wood-working, horseback riding, water sports, etc. I was thrilled. Skye was excited. So, $7500 later, I had her enrolled in the summer program.

This was my life that summer: Drive an hour to summer camp and 45 minutes to work each way. Work full-time 9-5, arrange day care, drive to doctors' appointments, transport my kids to their activities, coordinate visitation with their Dad and run a household. But Skye blossomed at the camp. She realized that she wasn't the only kid with this language problem. At the end of camp, Skye had made some improvement although she still wasn't reading at grade level.

I inquired about the cost of sending Skye fulltime to this private school. It would cost around $40,000 a year. Ugh, this was way out of my financial league. I researched the OG method over the summer. I purchased *The Gillingham Manual* and read it from cover to cover.[26]

Skye felt confident going into 3rd grade. She embraced her diagnosis of dyslexia. Since the public school didn't offer individualized tutoring, the special education activities were drawn out as they tried to get the entire group on the same page of the training on the OG method.[27] Skye soon became bored since they weren't teaching her anything new that she hadn't learned at summer camp. By the end of 3rd grade, Skye was making little to no improvement in her reading level or fluency. She still struggled to say words. Her speech was still difficult to understand. Frustration was setting in again. I signed Skye up for another summer session at the private school.

The summer camp followed the same format as the year before.[28] When I received the report at the end of the summer, I was disappointed. It didn't show any great improvement in reading or writing at all. Skye was still reading well below grade level.[29] Since the school offered classes for teachers to learn the OG method, I asked if I could sign up for the classes so that I could tutor my daughter myself.

"Parents don't make good tutors," they said.[30] Since I wasn't a school teacher, I wasn't allowed to sign up for any of the classes offered. I was angry: No matter how hard I tried, I wasn't able to help Skye.

Root Cause

Actually, I was beyond angry at this point. My child with an exceptional IQ was getting the support that the school offered, yet she was still struggling a lot in 4th grade.[31] It took her hours and hours each night to complete her homework.[32] She needed help with anything related to reading or writing. I had to proofread everything she wrote. Skye was getting frustrated also because I had her rewrite the assignments I corrected. She was sad that she made so many mistakes. She was cranky. She had headaches.[33] She was not a happy girl.

I was venting to a colleague at work about what was going on when she suggested an expert who helped children with language issues, Dr. Coral. Dr. Coral's initial screening showed that Skye had dyslexia. Dr. Coral said that she would need to do a more indepth evaluation to get to the root cause.[34]

Root cause? Wow, no one ever said that they would get to the root cause of Skye's problems.

What Dr. Coral found was astounding. She described the difficulties that Skye had in a way I could understand. I listened to Skye's speech and understood why she was forming words the way she did. I now understood how much of Skye's mind was preoccupied with processing the language around her.

We signed up for what was later to become the Dysolve Program.[35] We worked with Dr. Coral every week for an hour and then we worked at home every night for 10-20 minutes. Dr. Coral taught me to be Skye's tutor.[36] I now had the resources I needed to help my daughter.

I took Dr. Coral's evaluation to the school to see if they could tailor Skye's IEP to work on the areas that Dr. Coral suggested.

The school administrator said, "This is not a standardized evaluation. We aren't required to make any changes to her IEP."[37]

"So what standardized evaluation would you use to test for phonological issues?"

They said there was a CTOPP test (Comprehensive Testing of Phonological Processing) that existed.[38]

Lo and behold, when the CTOPP results came back, they agreed with Dr. Coral's evaluation. It was not until the beginning of 5th grade that Skye's IEP was updated to reflect this new information from the CTOPP test.[39]

As much as I was frustrated with the school's resources at this point, I was thrilled with the progress Skye made with Dr. Coral's training. Within three months of weekly drills, Skye stopped having headaches.[40] Within six months of training with the Coral Method®, Skye's speech started to clear up. Skye's grandparents even commented on how they could finally understand Skye when she talked to them. Within nine months, Skye's teachers were commenting on the dramatic change they saw.[41] Skye was able to talk with her friends *and* complete the work in the classroom. I was secretly happy when she got a reprimand from her teacher for talking to her friends during class.

Within a year of Dr. Coral's training, Skye was taking an interest in reading by herself.[42] She even asked her grandparents for books for Christmas, something she had never done before. Skye received the President's Honor Award for most improved student in 5th grade.[43]

Skye thrived during that summer before 6th grade while we continued to work with Dr. Coral.

When Skye entered 6th grade, the only support services from school consisted of study techniques and organizational skills—things that Skye did not need any help with.[44] By the middle of 6th grade, Skye was reading at grade level and was excelling in all of her subjects. It was a dramatic change from a year ago when she was below proficiency in the state reading test.

We stopped meeting weekly with Dr. Coral and focused mainly on having Skye read books to increase her vocabulary.[45] She was declassified from special education at the end of 6th grade. She devoured books during the summer before 7th grade.[46]

Amazing Transition

Seventh grade was an amazing transition grade for Skye. She was placed in Honors Math and English classes. She was taking Spanish as a foreign language although her elementary school had said that she would not be able to learn a second language.[47] She was confident and independent. Now when she took her time to complete her homework, it was mainly because she's a perfectionist and wanted to provide a lot of detail. Only occasionally would she ask me to help her to proofread her homework.[48] Our evenings were finally not so hectic.

Skye was on the High Honor roll each semester. This meant that her overall average was above a 95 out of a possible 100 points. Once she made it on the High Honor roll, she made it her goal to stay on the High Honor roll.[49] Her classmates were now beginning to see Skye as a role model and a leader in the classroom.[50] She was being sought after as a partner for projects. Her friends were calling her to check on answers on *their* homework. It was such a dramatic change from the lost child in elementary school.

Eighth grade was much like 7th grade. Skye was in Honors English and Honors Math and taking 9th-grade Science. She was reading everything that she could get her hands on. She loved reading the books that were assigned in English that year including *To Kill a Mocking Bird* and *Macbeth*. Skye has always been my "deep thinker." She would see details in people, stories and her surroundings that others would miss. Her teachers and classmates were now able to see this part of Skye's thoughtfulness and insightfulness. She participated more in classroom activities. This was the year that she blossomed into an incredible young woman.

I am convinced that without the intervention of Dr. Coral and the Coral Method®, Skye would still be struggling. She would still be having headaches. She would still be effectively mute. Angry and frustrated, she would have shut down and not engaged with the world around her. She would have had a very limited future.[51]

As I write this, Skye is in the summer before 9th grade. She is reading every day. She is looking forward to starting high school where she will again be in Honors English and Math. She will be taking college-level Biology as a high school freshman, and best of all she will be taking many Art classes. Her future is bright. I see nothing that will stand in her way. She is well-adjusted, self-confident, bright, friendly and chatty. She is working *above* grade level in all of her classes.

She is articulate. She is passionate about the world. She is full of life. She is meeting her potential.

She is, finally, herself.

MY MESSAGE TO TEACHERS AND ADMINISTRATORS

When a teacher knows of something that will help a student but is discouraged from providing that information to a parent (due to school policy, cost, etc.), it affects the credibility of the school. There are so many parents who are struggling with understanding what their children are going through, are ill-informed as to their rights and school procedures and encounter road blocks in getting a diagnosis.[52] After a diagnosis, they continue to struggle to get services needed to help their children.[53] The school districts should take a closer look at how children with disabilities and the parents of those children feel they are being treated.

MY MESSAGE TO PARENTS

You are not alone.[54] You are the best advocate for your child. Don't give up. You have more rights than you think you do with regards to your child's education.[55] Getting to the root cause of your child's language problems is the key to success. Learn from the stories in this book so that your child can live up to their potential.

MY MESSAGE TO DR. CORAL

Thank you for treating both my daughter and me with dignity. Thank you for working so diligently to create solutions to dyslexia. And thank you for having the vision to create the automated program, Dysolve®, as it will help so many children in this world.

NOTES

1. Researchers widely recognize that dyslexia runs in families. However, genetic studies on dyslexia are still in the first stage of discovery and have not yet determined the specific causal connection(s). Our own fieldwork underscores the complexity of the heritability question. Familial profiles of our students run the gamut, from those with next of kin with dyslexia and those without. Causal factors are difficult to identify because parents with language disorders may create environments that are less conducive to language and reading acquisition. Therefore it is not easy to tease out the genetic (nature) from the environmental (nurture). For the genetic basis of dyslexia, see Pennington, B.F., & Olson, R.K. (2005). Genetics of dyslexia. In M.J. Snowling & C. Hulme (Eds.), *The science of reading: A handbook* (pp. 453–472). Oxford: Blackwell. For an overview of the research, see Snowling, M.J., Melby-Lervåg, M. (2016). Oral language deficits in familial dyslexia: A meta-analysis and review. *Psychological Bulletin, 142*, 498-545.
2. Difficulties with the production of speech sounds (speech sound disorder) combined with other language deficits often lead to reading problems. See Lewis, B.A., Avrich, A.A., Freebairn, L.A., Hansen, A.J., Sucheston, L.E., Lara, E. et al. (2011). Literacy outcomes of children with early childhood speech sound disorders: Impact of endophenotypes. *Journal of Speech, Language and Hearing Research, 54*, 1628-1643.
3. The relationship between auditory processing deficits and reading disabilities is unclear at this stage of research in the field. The percentage of children with dyslexia who also have auditory processing deficits range wildly in the literature, hovering around a third of this population. Various hypotheses have been proposed for the role of auditory processing in reading development, but interventions based on these hypotheses have yielded mixed results. This has led some scholars to consider lately that we are dealing with a multi-dimensional disorder here. For an overview of this research,

see Elliott, J.G., & Grigorenko, E.L. (2014). *The dyslexia debate.* New York: Cambridge University Press.
4. Retention in the same grade for another year was also considered for the cases in Chapters 1, 4 and 5.
5. Warning signs for dyslexia often appear even before schooling begins because of related or underlying problems. Educational materials and information on workshops on this topic are available upon request at Dysolve.com and Dysolve Dyslexia on Facebook.
6. Do people with dyslexia have visual talents? Research on this question is inconclusive, although those with dyslexia have been found to gravitate towards fields requiring visuo-spatial strengths. Studies on visual abilities can only investigate some aspects of this talent. Our own experience with this population reinforces the view that they do have strong preferences for the visuo-spatial. The cases in this book tend to gravitate towards art, architecture and engineering fields. See Skye's explanation for her highly developed visual ability in her story at the end of this chapter. For a recent study on this topic, see Duranovic, M., Dedeic, M., & Gavric, M. (2015). Dyslexia and visual-spatial talents. *Current Psychology, 34*(2), 207-222.
7. Some language-processing deficits make it difficult to process verbal input, which is why more mental effort (concentration) is needed. Distractions in the environment including noise compound the processing challenge.
8. Although math and reading disabilities are known to be related in research, many of our students with dyslexia excel in math except where word problems are involved. In addition to Skye, the cases in Chapters 2, 5 and 6 are strong in math.
9. Although dyslexia implies problems with spelling as well, spelling impairment is not studied as much. While some studies find that spelling errors between those with and without dyslexia are similar, other studies report characteristic differences. Error patterns differ between spellers with dyslexia and those without. Studies found that spellers with dyslexia tend to commit more errors related to their difficulty with segmentation (breaking words into single sounds) and phoneme identification (recognizing sounds in words). For

example, they reduce consonant clusters (*str*→*st*), and substitute consonants. They omit vowels and substitute vowels that are not even phonetically similar. They often leave out word endings (*-s, -ed*). In contrast, writers without dyslexia produce spelling forms that sound like the target words (phonetically accurate) even when they are not spelled correctly (orthographically inaccurate). Thus, they may substitute same-sounding words (homophones: *buy*→*by*), use the incorrect letters for unstressed vowels (*attitude* → **attatude*), and overgeneralize the silent *–e* rule (*plan*→ *plane*). Spelling instruction is needed for students with dyslexia, but research shows that it is more effective before 4th grade. See Bernstein, S.E. (2009). Phonology, decoding, and lexical compensation in vowel spelling errors made by children with dyslexia. *Reading and Writing, 22*(3), 307-331.
10. See Dysolve's advances over standardized testing instruments in Chapter 15 *Responsive Intelligence Technology*.
11. Speech therapy can only deal with some aspects of the production side of the condition. There is also the reception side—listening, reading.
12. Our students typically come to us in 4th-5th grade, after being told for years to wait before taking any action. See the parents' messages advising against this delay in Chapters 1-6.
13. Students typically advance to the next grade in the US even when they are performing below grade level. The 2017 NAEP (National Assessment of Educational Progress) report shows that the percentage of students performing at or above proficiency in reading did not improve from 4th to 8th grade. The number stayed constant at 35% through the grades for public schools nationwide. This means that the 65% who performed below proficiency in 4th grade likely remained so through the years. The reading score for 12th grade only improved by 1%. Go to https://www.nationsreportcard.gov/
14. Pediatricians often recommend neuropsychological evaluations to obtain a diagnosis of dyslexia. As mentioned in this story, such evaluations cost each patient thousands of dollars. They typically involve a battery of standardized tests. The latest 2013 update to the clinical reference, the *Diagnostic and Statistical Manual of Mental Disorders – 5th Edition* (DSM-

5), now suggests dispensing with lengthy and costly neuropsychological assessment of cognitive processing skills for a diagnosis. See our critique in the Engineer's Story in Chapter 9.
15. Skye's neuropsychological evaluation failed to identify her specific deficits. Diagnoses from neuropsychological evaluations are not sufficiently specific to enable correction of the underlying deficits. This is why Dysolve does not use the results of these evaluations and does not require students to obtain these diagnoses before they enroll in our intervention program. See Chapter 15.
16. The diagnoses from Skye's neuropsychological evaluation were inaccurate. This evaluation from a certified psychologist missed her language-processing deficits. Even if they were accurate, traditional neuropsychological evaluations provide diagnosis only. Researchers repeatedly complain that evaluations should link with remediation. See the critique in Elliott, J.G., & Grigorenko, E.L. (2014). *The dyslexia debate.* New York: Cambridge University Press.
17. Traditionally, a discrepancy between high IQ and low reading achievement was used to diagnose dyslexia. This is no longer considered a legitimate criterion by authorities in the field. Nevertheless, neuropsychological evaluations often still include IQ tests, as do schools' evaluations. See Rose, J. (2009). *Identifying and teaching children and young people with dyslexia and literacy difficulties. (The Rose Report).* Nottingham, UK: DCSF Publications.
18. At present, no school or provider has the expertise and capability to identify language-processing deficits at the individual-specific level for everyone except Dysolve.
19. An IEP is an Individualized Education Program (or Plan) for students with special needs to receive support services in public schools. *IEP* also refers to the legal document that charts the student's needs, evaluative and support services, and targeted goals. IEPs are covered by the Individuals with Disabilities Education Act (IDEA).
20. A resource room is a place set aside for a special education teacher to support students with special needs. The type of support varies by school and district.

21. Frances took a confrontational stance to fight for her daughter's right to an appropriate education. See the parents' messages in Chapters 1-4 recommending an aggressive approach.
22. Students with dyslexia often do not improve substantially in summer reading programs—unless their underlying deficits are corrected first.
23. Orton-Gillingham is an instructional approach for reading remediation developed in the 1930s. This compensatory approach is meant to help struggling readers cope with dyslexia. Orton-Gillingham is *not* designed to remove dyslexia as a chronic condition. It is commonly used in schools in some parts of the US. Despite such methods, school statistics on students with learning disabilities are grim, with poor prospects for readers still struggling in middle school. See research review in Elliott, J.G., & Grigorenko, E.L. (2014). *The dyslexia debate.* New York: Cambridge University Press. See also Chapter 12 *The True Cost of Dyslexia.*
24. Multisensory instruction is predicated on the assumption that children, especially struggling readers, learn best when more than one sense is used. Multisensory instruction is often incorporated into reading programs based on Orton-Gillingham, which pioneered it. But note that a comprehensive review of the research to date concludes that "Despite the enthusiasm for multisensory approaches held by many specialist dyslexia teachers...the theoretical grounds and scientific rationale for their use are questionable"— Elliott, J.G., & Grigorenko, E.L. (2014). *The dyslexia debate.* New York: Cambridge University Press, p. 150.
25. See the Principal's Story in Chapter 7 on limited resources at public schools and the cost of these intervention programs.
26. The manual mainly covers spelling patterns in English. Gillingham, A., & Stillman, B.W. (1997). *The Gillingham Manual: Remedial training for children with specific disability in reading, spelling, and penmanship* (8th ed.). Cambridge, MA: Educators Publishing Service.
27. See Note 23 above.
28. Special reading camps and schools, regardless of their tuition costs, typically use compensatory approaches such as Orton-Gillingham. See Notes 23 and 24 above.

29. In addition to Skye, the students in Chapters 2, 6 and 8 also received OG-based remediation but did not reach grade-level reading before Dysolve. See Chapter 12 *State of the Science*.
30. Besides Frances, the parents in Chapters 2, 6 and 9 also voiced that they did not know what the intervention services actually did. Dysolve engages parents as partners in their children's programs because we believe parents are the first and often the most committed and passionate teachers for their children. Their stories in this book testify to this.
31. Students with high IQ and dyslexia are considered to be twice-exceptional (gifted + disability). See Chapter 2 on twice-exceptionality.
32. The families in all the chapters spent hours on homework every night before Dysolve. The one exception may be Uno in Chapter 8, who advanced through the automated program without human intervention from Dysolve. His learning environment at home is thus not known to us.
33. The association between recurrent headaches and dyslexia (and ADHD) has not received much research interest. Recent studies do show a higher incidence of recurrent headaches among children with dyslexia, ADHD, and both conditions. Yet the explanations put forth remain controversial. One hypothesis uses overlapping brain mechanisms to account for the associations. A second hypothesis suggests that learning disabilities and ADHD create stresses that induce headaches. A third speculates that frequent headaches hinder learning and cause ADHD behaviors. A fourth proposes a common disorder underlying headaches and ADHD. Which is the cause? Which is the effect? Depending on the hypothesis, headaches can be either. See our ADHD case study in Chapter 6. For a review of studies, see Genizi, J., Gordon, S., Kerem, N.C., Srugo, I., Shahar, E., & Ravid, S. (2013). Primary headaches, attention deficit disorder and learning disabilities in children and adolescents. *Journal of Headache Pain, 14*(1): 54. doi: 10.1186/1129-2377-14-54
34. To resolve a problem, we need to get to the root cause. In Skye's case, we needed to identify her language-processing deficits.

35. The Coral Method® was developed by Dr. Coral to identify and correct language-processing deficits at the individual-specific level. The Coral Method® can be used in person or in software. The Coral Method® was applied to the program for dyslexia, Dysolve®.
36. Skye joined our program before it was automated.
37. Standardized evaluations cannot identify individual-specific language-processing deficits. See the end of Chapter 15 *Responsive Intelligence Technology*.
38. The Comprehensive Test of Phonological Processing (CTOPP) was published in 1999 and uses normed measures based on 1900 individuals. The latest version is the 2nd edition CTOPP-2. The test kit includes items asking the testee to isolate individual sounds (segments) within words (phoneme isolation), blend nonwords (nonsensical words) together to form new nonwords (blending), and say numbers rapidly (rapid digit naming). Such test kits only use a small number of questions to sample the testee's ability in each category. The test yields normative scores—the testee's results when compared with those of the 1900 base. Normative measures are unnecessary when we can define each person's specific language-processing deficits comprehensively in micro detail with current technology. See Chapter 15 *Responsive Intelligence Technology*.
39. The families in Chapters 1-4, 6, 7 and 10 came to Dysolve in 4th-5th grades after fighting unsuccessfully for years for services at school. This is typical for the students we see.
40. The cases in Chapters 1-6 mentioned the occurrence of headaches before they joined Dysolve and their cessation during our program.
41. Skye's academic progress showed a striking change. This sharp knee-of-the-curve trajectory is typical of our students' progress because they can achieve their true (high) potential once the underlying issues are resolved. See the other cases in this book.
42. Independent reading and learning are two of the early signs that underlying processing issues are dissipating. This is reported in Chapters 1-9.

43. The students in Chapters 1, 3 and 5 received special awards from their schools for academic achievement in the 1st year of Dysolve.
44. See Chapter 12 on limited resources at school due to cost.
45. Following problem resolution, students with dyslexia have to accelerate vocabulary acquisition to catch up with their classmates.
46. Intensive reading of nonfiction is required to accelerate the acquisition of conventional terms and sentence patterns (syntax) for relaying factual information. Intensive reading of fiction is required to accelerate the acquisition of vocabulary and creative phrasing.
47. Some students with dyslexia are told that they will not be able to learn a second language. However, after resolving their language-processing deficits, the students in Chapters 1-4 took foreign language classes and performed generally in the 90-100 grade range.
48. This progress to independent learning is reported in Chapters 1-7.
49. This motivation to stay on the Honor roll is echoed in Dr. Coral's Story about Patience in Chapter 1.
50. Patience in Chapter 1 also became a role model for her classmates.
51. The parent's worry about the child's limited future is echoed in Chapters 1, 4, 5 and 7.
52. Typically, each parent fights alone for her child through the school system. We set up Dysolve Dyslexia on Facebook and a support group, *Ask Dr. Coral*, to address families' concerns. Our tripartite blogs—written from the perspectives of the expert, parent, and child—help families see that the problems they face have been encountered by others who have gone further ahead on their journey. These blogs are at Dysolve Dyslexia on Facebook.
53. The parents in Chapters 1-6, 9 and 10 appealed to their schools unsuccessfully to try to get appropriate services for their children.
54. Our blogs on this theme and others at Dysolve Dyslexia on Facebook offer guidance to parents and caretakers.

55. Most parents are not fully aware of their rights in the decision-making process affecting their children's educational needs under the Individuals with Disabilities Education Act (IDEA). See whether such information is posted on your school's website under the department responsible for special education. Also some government agencies and not-for-profits provide the free services of a parent advocate to guide families through the process of obtaining support services.

Dr. Coral's Story

Root Cause of Her Dyslexia

Glow

Frances's face glowed in the light of the study lamp on my desk. She and I were both beaming because I just explained to her the root cause of her daughter's dyslexia. Frances was overjoyed and relieved, although we had only discovered the source of the problem, not resolved it. But Frances was the kind of person who would somehow find a way to tackle the problem, so long as she knew what she was up against. Naming the problem was the first step. The logical step. That appealed to a programmer.

It was a dark, cold winter evening when we went over the breadth and depth of her daughter's problem, but we both felt giddily optimistic. At that second meeting, we had already sized each other up—that the other person would hold up her end of the bargain to do what it took to attack the problem for Skye, Frances's daughter.

So for the next 20 months, Frances would bring Skye to my practice, first trudging through snow, then soft earth, fallen leaves, and snow again.[1] They stayed long after the root problem had been resolved, to help Skye make up for the lost years.[2]

I noted early on that Skye did not speak much, and when she did, they were short responses.[3] As a linguist, I could understand Skye's speech, but she spoke as if she had a strong foreign accent even though English was her native tongue.

"What should I do next? What should I do next?" Frances always asked, eager to forge ahead. She made no excuses about not completing any practice or taking off for the summer. She just kept going and going week after week. At that time, our program had not been automated yet, so Frances had to do all the practices at home manually. When Skye needed to learn the sounds of English, Frances taught herself English Phonetics. Frances kept a detailed log to show me at each appointment—date, time, duration, etc. And she kept a reward system at home. Strawberry lollipop this time, watermelon lollipop next.

Skye would usually draw as Frances and I conferred, or even while we had her do the practices at my office. It was her mother who had to keep it going. Only an adult could appreciate what was at stake.

Labyrinth of Her Mind

Frances and I worked as partners, both invested in lifting this beautiful girl out of the chasm she was in. We laughed a lot during those sessions, applauding Skye's progress and Frances's ingenious execution. We moved as methodically as we could through the labyrinth of Skye's mind. There were times when we beat back the brushes easily and never looked back. And there were times when I buried my head in my hands, for I just found another big gaping hole for us to fill in the journey of Skye's development.

I never doubted that Skye was intelligent.[4] When I first met her, she was quiet but controlled. Her nails were always painted neatly in some shade of pink. Her eyes gave away the depth of her thinking. I could tell that no one escaped her scrutiny, even though she was only 11.[5] Later, as she opened up and talked, she revealed her critical judgment of those around her. A sharp intellect.[6]

Lexical retrieval. Skye described a little guy running from aisle to aisle in the recesses of her mind, frantically opening and slamming filing drawers, looking for the word she wanted. She drew the picture for us, complete with drawer handles and file labels.[7]

Her mother and I looked on, marveling at the capable mind trapped inside. The three of us worked in tandem, each one with strengths that the other two could lean on to pull the whole team through to the next level. Skye's story in Dysolve is one of methodical climbing of step after step until we reached the summit. No drama. There were few setbacks to make her story more exciting, and none of the interruptions in training that often delayed progress in other students.[8] Frances guaranteed that. I came to expect that a 2nd grader who scored below the 20th percentile in standardized reading tests would eventually earn GPAs in the high 90s in high school.[9]

Only now, upon reading Skye's own story in the following pages—proudly written by herself—did I realize the other effects of her temporary disability in the early grades. I only saw the poised, intelligent person who held her own opinions about things in the world. I did not know about the timid child who was pinched, bullied and shunned at school.

We resolved her processing problems years ago. But the emotional effects will take a little longer to fade.

THE PROBLEM

"I was yelling at them so loudly that the teachers next door came running to see what was going on," said Frances about one of her meetings at her daughter's school.[10]

Frances expended a lot of her scant time and energy battling the school for services. She was not the only parent I had met who felt compelled to raise her voice at her child's school. But even when the parent is successful in getting the school to test her child or provide services, the results often still come up short.[11] The standardized tests used to evaluate Skye's speech and language misrepresented her articulation errors as "developmental" and her ability as "at or above criterion."[12] Nevermind that her teachers reported that she did not speak in the 1st term at school and spelled words randomly with many errors.

Even when well-meaning teachers try to put in extra effort to help the struggling student, the results are often still meager. To help Skye, her 2nd grade teacher used the Orton-Gillingham approach to reading, which covers phonetics, spelling, and penmanship.[13] But her teacher's extra efforts produced little result since the source of Skye's problem was never identified.[14] In a standardized reading test at the end of 2nd grade, Skye scored below the 20th percentile, well below the 25th percentile threshold often used to determine that a student has dyslexia.[15]

Frances willingly paid $5,000 for a neuropsychological evaluation from a certified psychologist.[16] The evaluation concluded that Skye had dyslexia. But to resolve the condition, we needed to know the root cause. What was *causing* Skye's dyslexia? Her problem wasn't just dyslexia, a reading disability. Why couldn't she speak and understand speech as well?[17] Without this answer, we could not correct her problem. Thus, evaluations that stop short at just a diagnosis of dyslexia are unhelpful for corrective intervention.[18]

Frances paid out another $15,000 for summer reading camps run by an established school renowned for specializing in dyslexia.[19] Still, the camps, which used the Orton-Gillingham approach, were not able to nudge Skye's reading scores above the 20th percentile.[20]

Students like Skye can go through years of remediation with a popular approach such as Orton-Gillingham and still have little to show for their efforts. *Close to three-quarters of students classified with a reading disability in 3rd grade stay classified throughout school.*[21] Skye memorized the spelling rules in *The Gillingham Manual* as rote because such material makes little sense to someone who has difficulty processing language.[22] Skye conscientiously learned all the spelling rules taught by her teachers. She recited the rabbit rule (doubling of middle consonants), the tiger rule (dividing syllables), and the floss rule (doubling of *f, l, s*). She even recreated the mnemonic diagram her teacher taught her for the *ie/ei* rules.

Yet she could not apply them to spell.

OUR SOLUTION

The rules of language that are quickly and effortlessly internalized by most of us may not make sense to students with processing deficits. To correct the problem, we have to identify the complex of underlying deficits unique to each student. Until the deeper issue is addressed, remediation merely adds more rules for the already-overwhelmed student with dyslexia to store, access, retrieve, and apply. For such students, learning a new word can take many more operations than required typically. For instance, to learn the word *yield*, Skye had to create an image of a person yelling and a field of grass. Then she took the first sound of *yell* (*y*), dropped the first sound in *field* (= *ield*), and blended the two parts together (*y* + *ield* = *yield*). That is, Skye had to go into the internal structure of the words to operate on them consciously. To retrieve the word *yield* later, Skye had to go through the same cumbersome operations again consciously. Clearly, this was a highly inefficient way to store and retrieve words.[23]

Therefore, we designed an intervention program at Dysolve that enabled Skye to acquire and access words the way we do. We store words by associating them to their phonetic (sound), orthographic (spelling), morphological (word), semantic (meaning), and syntactic (sentence) forms, together with other aspects tied to the history of our encounters with each word.[24] We can retrieve newly acquired words easily later by calling upon any or some of these associations. A major problem with students like Skye is that their phonetic (and consequently their orthographic) representations of new words are weak because of their lack of phonemic and phonological awareness.[25] *Phonological awareness* refers to the ability to detect and manipulate the sounds and sound patterns of one's language. The other term commonly used, *phonemic awareness*, covers only the sounds of one's language.

The total time Skye spent on our Coral Method® at home was just over an hour a week on average. But in the process, Skye relearned how to acquire new words by dispensing with her old habit of using multiple visual- and quasi-semantic-based operations.

We set the goal for her to reach a reading speed of 0.3 second per word (or 200 CWPM – Correct Words Per Minute) so as to approach fluent reading. Measurable outcomes in the form of such quantified scores allowed Skye and her mother, Frances, to chart progress. When improvements are incremental, numeric scores become all the more important: the student needs to *see* that she is indeed advancing. She needs the reward of tangible successes, the incentive to try even harder.

BREAKTHROUGH

Three months into our intervention program in 4th grade, Skye could read small, common words correctly. Five months later, Skye entered 5th grade with strong enough spelling skills to take the full list of weekly spelling items assigned to her regular classroom for the first time. She received scores in the 90s-100 on her spelling tests. She was able to spell correctly words with *–able* suffixes (*huggable,* *kickable, doable*, etc.) and even coined some new words on her own (*shoppable*). Her speech problems dissipated.

Even so, Skye still faced lexical gaps in 5th grade. For instance, she spelled *policeman* as **plocesman*. A student such as Skye who had fallen behind in reading for five years will inevitably struggle to catch up in written word acquisition. That is why improved word decoding does not automatically lead to reading fluency.[26] Consequently and paradoxically, Skye had trouble recognizing simple words that she had missed in the earlier grades, such as *group*, but she could read more advanced, new words such as *wordsmith* and *indirection*.

From there on, Skye and I worked specifically on filling this lexical gap and enhancing orthographic memory so that she could dispense with her old habit of on-the-spot hypothesizing. That is, Skye used to try out the spelling of "your" as *yor, yur, yore* in addition to the correct form. On-the-spot hypothesizing to spell a word is too slow, preventing fluent reading and efficient drafting.[27]

By the beginning of 6th grade, Skye's reading speed arrived consistently at an average of 0.3 second per word (or 200 CWPM – Correct Words Per Minute), as shown in Figure 6. Whereas she was two grades behind in reading in 5th grade at the beginning of our program, her 1st term report in 6th grade registered an unweighted GPA of 97.00, with 95 for English and Reading. In the spring of 6th Grade, her school determined that she no longer needed special support services. She has since maintained her GPA in the high 90s in junior high school and high school.

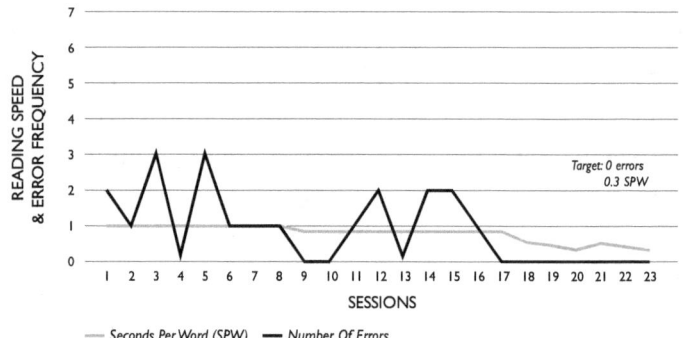

FIGURE 6
*Skye - Reached Reading Targets
in Year 2 in Dysolve*

NOTES

1. Skye had weekly in-person sessions because our program was not automated yet at that point. Moreover, her language problems were particularly severe since she could not even speak clearly or understand other speakers.
2. Skye was in our program from part of 4th-6th grade. Students generally graduate from Dysolve in 1-2 years on average, with the second half being devoted primarily to catching up with written vocabulary acquisition and grade-level language competency.
3. In addition to Skye, Grace in Chapter 7 also did not speak much at the beginning of our program.
4. Language-processing deficits often make those affected seem less intelligent because their responses are delayed or not forthcoming. Unfortunately, some may be misdiagnosed as having cognitive impairment.
5. Skye's own story in this chapter reveals the perceptiveness of children like her.
6. Many of the children we see in Dysolve are twice-exceptional. See Chapter 2.
7. Which came first: that visual skills expanded to compensate for verbal deficits or at the expense of verbal development? See also Note 6 on visuo-spatial talents in the Mother's Story in this chapter.
8. Consistent, uninterrupted practice in our program enabled Skye to progress quickly despite her severe language-processing deficits initially. Unlike Skye, most other cases experienced interruptions in their training due to parents' or caretakers' other obligations. This was one of the reasons why we developed an automated program, to remove this dependence on adult assistance.
9. Our pedagogical philosophy is to set high expectations for *all* students and support everyone in meeting them. The stories in this book are testament to the potential of all students to exceed expectations. See also the Principal's Story in Chapter 7.

10. Should a parent push aggressively at school to obtain support services or hold back to maintain goodwill? This is a tough decision for every parent, considering that the child still has to face the school staff every day after that. Nevertheless, the parents in Chapters 1-4, 6, 9 and 10 advised others to fight hard for their children, based on their own experience.
11. Nearly two-thirds of 8th graders across the US were reading below proficiency in 2015, according to the Nation's Report Card on reading assessment (https://www.nationsreportcard.gov/). The figures do not change much from year to year. Authorities in the field conclude that "we know from recent research on responsiveness-to-instruction (RTI) that many students' poor reading performance is <u>unaffected by the best and most intensive instruction</u> researchers can deliver in their field-based studies and university clinics" and acknowledge that researchers and teachers still do "not yet know how to teach reading to all students in this country" [our underline] - Fuchs, D., Compton, D.L., Fuchs, L.S., Bryant, V.J., Hamlett, C.L., & Lambert, W. (2012). First-grade cognitive abilities as long-term predictors of reading comprehension and disability status. *Journal of Learning Disabilities, 45*(3) 217–231, p. 217.
12. Based on the Clinical Evaluation of Language Fundamentals - 4th Ed. (CELF-4).
13. See Note 23 in the Mother's Story in this chapter for a brief explanation of Orton-Gillingham.
14. No standardized or school test could have identified Skye's specific language-processing deficits. Only the Coral Method®, and now Dysolve®, can.
15. Snowling, M.J. (2000). *Dyslexia*. Oxford, UK: Blackwell.
16. See Notes 14 and 15 in the Mother's Story in this chapter for our critique of neuropsychological evaluations.
17. To understand the interrelationships among Skye's language deficits, we had to first understand her condition as multidimensional.
18. See the Engineer's critique in Chapter 9.
19. In spite of their high tuition costs, special reading camps and dyslexia schools do not remove reading disabilities because they primarily use compensatory methods to help students

cope. Students typically graduate from these programs with their chronic conditions still.
20. The cases in Chapters 2, 3, 6 and 8 used Orton-Gillingham-based methods popular in schools and continued to fail reading proficiency tests until they joined Dysolve. The other cases in this book did not disclose their schools' reading methods or did not use any.
21. Gunning, T. (2003). The role of readability in today's classroom. *Topics in Language Disorders, 23*(3), 175-185.
22. Teachers cover the prescribed curriculum but this population cannot learn spelling rules because of their underlying language-processing deficits. Incorporating multisensory instruction—popular among compensatory methods—is not fully effective when processing deficits remain uncorrected.
23. Lexical storage (learning words) and lexical retrieval (recalling words) are usually subconscious operations. When they are performed as conscious operations, as in Skye's case, they can easily overwhelm mental capacity, causing cognitive overload. At that point, the brain cannot process all the input to perform required tasks. See further elaboration of this example in Chapter 14.
24. See Berninger, V.W., & Richards, T.L. (2002). *Brain literacy for educators and psychologists*. Amsterdam: Academic.
25. See Snowling, M.J. (2000). *Dyslexia*. Oxford, UK: Blackwell. See also Shaywitz, S.E. (2003). *Overcoming dyslexia*. New York: Knopf.
26. See Torgesen, J.K., Alexander, A.W., Wagner, R.K., Rashotte, C.A., et al. (2001). Intensive remedial instruction for children with severe reading disabilities: Immediate and long-term outcomes from two instructional approaches. *Journal of Learning Disabilities, 34*(1), 33-58.
27. For writing issues, see Bereiter, C., & Scardamalia, M. (1983). Does learning to write have to be so difficult? In A. Freedman, I. Pringle, & J. Yalden (Eds.), *Learning to write: First language/second language* (pp. 20-33). London: Longman.

Teacher's Story

Grab the World by Storm
Pauline

She Tried to Make Herself Invisible

When I first met Skye, she was in a combined 1st grade-kindergarten classroom. She tried as hard as she could to make herself invisible. Very rarely did she speak up. Very rarely did she talk even with her friends. She was so quiet, shy and reserved. She walked with her shoulders hunched over as if she was defeated.[1]

Towards the end of 3rd grade, I gave the class a math game to fill up the time before the students boarded their buses home.

"9 + 12 − 4..." I would start the computation orally and had the students follow along with the calculations in their heads.

"Times 7 + 5..." I would continue at a quick pace.

"Divided by 2 equals?" By which time I knew only three students could still keep up to get the answer.

One of them was Skye.[2] She jumped up from her seat, barreled her way up to the board, elbowing and pushing the boys out of the way. She got her answer on the board first. I realized then that she was smart.

Comfortable in Her Skin

I tried to engage Skye. I asked her to teach us how to sign as she knew sign language. I tried to get her more involved in class by having her do something she had success in. But she felt more comfortable staying invisible.

Then in 5th grade, suddenly, she came out of her shell.[3] She was volunteering answers in class, which was something new.[4] She was comfortable in her skin.

To see her now, I'm floored. She's still quiet but now she speaks out and is very thoughtful in what she says. It's hard to think of her as that little girl who was defeated when I first met her. She's quite a confident young woman now. I sat in a meeting with her and watched her come up with these great ideas.[5] She's thoughtful and insightful and thinks things through.

Seeing how she was in 1st grade, I would have expected her at this point probably to be in an area where she wouldn't be working with people because she so avoided it in elementary school.[6] She would have had a solitary career. But not now, not anymore. She's going to go out and grab the world by storm.[7]

She's going to do something creativish.

She'll be out in the open, saying, "Look at me! This is what I can do!"[8]

MY MESSAGE TO PARENTS

If your child is struggling and you're concerned about her, know that teachers can only fight so far in a class of 20+ students to deal with all at the same time. Teachers can't give them the one-on-one that you as the parent can give your child.

Teachers care no matter what. It's just that they may be limited in their resources and so many hours in a day, with so many who need the service.[9] If you're worried about your child, ask the questions, fight the fight. Find out what else you can do.[10]

As a parent, you need to be reading and working and socializing with your child every day. Letting your child be absorbed by other outside sources takes something away from your relationship with your child. As a parent, you are the best source of information for your child.

NOTES

1. The children in Chapters 2-7 and 10 were reported to display these feelings of defeatism.
2. Skye continued to excel in math in high school, scoring in the 90s in Honors math. The cases in Chapters 2, 5 and 6 were also strong in math. Studies on the population with dyslexia have not been able to establish a spatial advantage. Spatial talent is helpful in some areas of math. Dyslexia research has focused more on weaknesses in math. See Gilger, J.W., Allen, K., & Castillo, A. (2016). Reading disability and enhanced dynamic spatial reasoning: A review of the literature. *Brain and Cognition, 105,* 55–65.
3. This was when Skye's language-processing problems cleared in our program.
4. Patience in Chapter 1 also started volunteering to answer questions in the classroom as her processing problems were resolved in Dysolve.
5. Are dyslexia and creativity related? Research to date has yielded inconsistent results. The problem may be due partly to how creativity is measured. If there is a connection, one hypothesis views creativity as an effect of dyslexia—that struggling readers developed alternative processes and strategies to enable text comprehension. The other hypothesis views dyslexia as a neurological condition that favors holistic thinking, a creativity trait. See the review in Cancer, A., Manzoli, S., & Antonietti, A. (2016). The alleged link between creativity and dyslexia: Identifying the specific process in which dyslexic students excel. *Cogent Psychology, 3*: 1190309. Retrieved from
http://dx.doi.org/10.1080/23311908.2016.1190309
6. See Skye's story at the end of this chapter.
7. This newfound can-do spirit was expressed by the cases in Chapters 1-3 and 5.
8. Profound changes in personality were seen in the cases in Chapters 1-6, 8 and 9 after problem resolution in Dysolve.
9. See the Principal's Story in Chapter 7 about limited resources in school and Chapter 12.

10. Dysolve Dyslexia on Facebook as well as Dysolve.com all serve to educate parents and the public about dyslexia and related conditions. See also Chapter 17 *Our Answers to Your Questions*.

Dyslexia

Skye's Story

I Became Numb to the World

Authors' note: In publishing this story, we reveal the inner turmoil of children whose language difficulties prevent them from engaging with the world. After Dysolve, this student used what she learned from her earlier ordeal to mentor younger students, with deep empathy and insight.

I Remember

I remember a lot that happened in preschool. The cool kids ate colorful playdough and didn't get caught. I spent most of the time in the bathroom pretending that magical dragons were flying around talking to me. The world was filled with so many bright colors, and if someone was talking to me, I would just wait until my brother relayed what they said through his actions.

I also remember the kindergarten teacher reading us a story on the rug and this one girl trying to talk to me. I was trying to focus all my energy on the story and kept moving away from her. But she kept following me and talking. We ended up having to switch our green cards to yellow (meaning we did something bad). When I tried to explain to the teacher what actually happened, she looked at me weird and shook her head.

School ended and I remember my Mom taking me to this place for speech therapy. This lady with hairy arms took me into this little room and I colored pictures and listened to her nice voice. I had no idea what she was saying; I just repeated the sounds she made when she waited for a response.[1] When I was brought back to my Mom, it was pitch black outside and she looked tired.

First grade was when the headaches started.[2] Every morning the teachers would write something on this huge pad of paper and have us sit on the rug. We had to find the mistakes on it. To me, it seemed perfectly fine with no mistakes. And when I was called on to fix a part, I would put a period somewhere in the middle or at the end. We also had to use certain words in sentences that we made up. I could not figure out how to do that. I would stare at the pad of paper. I would use all of my power, both mental and physical, to focus on the teachers' instructions so I could perform the task given. This only helped for short instructions, like "Take out your math binder," but if they started talking about what page numbers and what problems to do, I was lost. Since I did not like my classmates and was very shy, I didn't ask the kids around me what the teacher said.

I was stuck in this constant confusing circle, of devoting all my energy on simple comprehension tasks. It was like being dropped off in a foreign country where they spoke a completely different language and everyone just expected you to know it. I spoke with visuals and learned with visuals, not by reading and listening. But as I got older, they stopped giving pictures for the new words to learn. It was exhausting and tiring: *I was lost in this foreign world where I couldn't even understand the maps that were there to help me get out.* I was trapped.

Pity

Whenever we had playtime I would play with the same toys, the kind that you got out of a McDonald's happy meal. I found no need to say the dialogue because no one was playing with me. On the bus, a girl, Sarah, would pinch my arm and pull my hair and I would wait until the bus got to my stop before jumping out of the seat, away from her. A couple weeks later I told my Mom (I did tell her before but she hadn't understood me) and she immediately called the school.[3] The next day me and Sarah had to pinky-promise never to do it again. I did not know why I had to promise— I was not the one pinching her, but I could not tell the teacher that because then she would look at me pitifully.

Then near the end of 1st grade, the teachers had each student in my class assigned to one kid in the oncoming class. When I got paired up with my classmate Sarah, I knew something was wrong. Sarah showed me the tables and the shelf where we kept our work. I kept telling her I knew this already: I was here for a year. She dismissed it and kept on showing me around, with the teachers beaming.

Sometimes I felt trapped in my own mind, not able to express my thoughts to the world. The teachers had commanded that I get paired up with my fellow classmate of two years to be shown a room I knew. Did they think that I had no brain activity whatsoever, that I didn't notice a room I had been in for a whole year in which I was tortured with the English language?

I had noticed too much. I knew there was a plastic dinosaur shoved behind the bookcase since early October. I knew there was still a pencil with throw-up on it under a cabinet near the rug, from when a kid had too many fruit snacks. I knew all these things that had happened. I knew the endless hours of repeating what the teacher had said. And hours working in workbooks and practicing handwriting. And yet I was classified as a child who was slow and didn't understand, one that received the special treatment of pitiful looks and not acknowledgment, a child that just because of these problems with understanding English, could not possibly understand human reactions to tell what they were saying. Certainly, a child classified as such could not have noticed the classroom she was in for a year. After that day, I decided that I would not waste my time to try to understand pitiful people who only looked at grades and numbers to determine what went on inside one's head.

Angry Seven-Year-Old

It was a new school year, same teachers, same room but new kids. I guessed that they believed that I was new to the school or something because they never asked about my past. Being shy does have its perks when you are little—people don't know that much about you so they tend to stay away and not bug you. You hear all of this gossip and everyone just assumes that if you are quiet, you won't eavesdrop.

I found out that my beloved friend, David, was held back in kindergarten, so other kids made fun of him for it and later in the year he moved. By this time I had already sworn off caring about teachers that just looked at grades and not at the kids. I resented receiving pity for everything that happened in my life. I was confused about my future because my whole plan of doing homework and painting pictures on my favorite desk left in a moving truck with my Dad. I was annoyed that people could not understand me when I tried to talk to them, and now I absolutely despised children my own age for being cruel to the one person who understood my world. By now I was an angry little seven-year-old who disliked everyone and the whole world. In all the pictures that were taken of me in those years, I always had a scowl on my face.[4] When family members tried to hug me, I would just stand there and look off into the distance, and they would say I was off in my head.

Noticing Small, Little Things

When I moved onto 2nd grade, this new perspective I had on the world did not go well for making friends. But now I had Arts class. In this world that I had found to be pitch black with no purpose besides the occasional dog or cat, now had a small spark of something. Perhaps it was hope, maybe determination, but it was a way for me to express my creativity.[5] All of the things I would think up in my imagination when people would say I had a far-off look, there was now a way to express them. The skill of noticing small, little things that helped me understand people was now being used for something better. In this dark world, there was now a little bit of light.

    This light was put to the test that year because I was the target of bullying once more. With my Dad gone and my Mom having to work more, I went to daycare after school. The "cool" kids there created the rules for the games we played. They either disliked me because I refused to play with them or because I found many holes in their plot and no real purpose to it. Or maybe they didn't like me because I was quiet and they found me to be a good source for a cheap laugh. So they took over any equipment that I was using, made sure to accidentally hit me with balls or trip me. I did not care, being I already deemed them as a waste of my time and effort. But when they started to try to get this one girl to pinch me, it furthered my despise for children my age, and my disgust for adults who were blind and could not see what was really happening if one looked close enough.

Resource Room

In 3rd grade, I made friends with some other special needs kids in the resource room.[6] This was the first year that I hung out with the "bad" kids who actually understood me more than the "normal" kids. Two of them had anger issues, another had an attention span problem, and then there was me who had a learning disability. For much of my elementary years I was the kid who kept the others in the resource room from punching teachers and flipping desks. My friend Sid said he was mad and wanted to hurt the kids that wouldn't let him play with them. We started talking because they didn't let me play with them either. Resource room was viewed as a mental institution by kids in our class, while we viewed it as a prison in which we were trapped by our disabilities.

"Why are you in here?"

"I got held back."

"Dang, I only flipped a desk over."

When we lined up near the door to leave for the resource room to take a test with pencils in hand, the whole class would treat us like we were prisoners being taken to jail. I loved some parts of resource room, though. I was with other kids who were misunderstood; we would play games, do homework, draw, and do multiplication problems.

Fourth grade in a one-word description would be "ugh." My 4th grade teacher did things the "cookie-cutter" way. She would teach the average kids just fine with the preset lessons and goals. She would ignore the kids behind since there were only three of us in a class of 30. She would pull down the kids ahead and force them to do things by the book even if they could do it better, faster than the "mandatory" lessons.

This year I sort of became numb to the world and time stopped counting. This mixed with Sid getting expelled (he started flipping desks again), a teacher who really didn't care about kids who weren't considered "normal," some fun friend and family drama, and you go from a person who didn't understand the world, to a person who hated the world, eventually to a person who was numb to the world.

Looking Deeper than What Meets the Eye

The first time my Mom met Dr. Coral, I was left at a table in the waiting area with a stack of paper. So I drew and drew and drew for what felt like hours. When Dr. Coral came out and talked to me, I was actually treated like I was understood and I was finally noticed for something other than my disabilities. I was treated like I was a smart kid who had a learning problem that did not make me any less smart and intelligent.[7] The light in my world that was only fueled by my artwork now had another spark in it. And to think all it took was understanding and looking deeper than what meets the eye.

My 5th grade teacher too was just as caring and awesome as my 3rd grade teacher. But by this time, my Mom was running out of options with the school because it was a constant battle on my classification. The resource room was not really helping me in the areas I needed it most, although the dyslexic part of me was getting better through Dysolve (shameless advertising).

Fifth grade was when I started to actually understand literature. During independent reading in class, for once I actually understood the words on the page and did not have to just rely on the pictures. Also during reading time, my teacher had the class read books out loud in different groups. I could actually understand what my classmates were reading. My teacher caught me eavesdropping on the other groups' reading, but he just smiled at me. When the resource room put on a play in front of the class from one of the scenes from the book we were reading, I actually spoke my lines loud and clear. PEOPLE UNDERSTOOD ME!!!!! When my Grandma gave me a small book about a tiger and I sat down and read the whole thing, she was nearly in tears.

With Dysolve, my eavesdropping skills improved because I could understand more. With my previous knowledge of reading people's emotions through their actions and facial expressions, mixed with this newfound communication, I could now read people's intentions. I was like a small Sherlock Holmes but with less impressive cheekbones. I learned that people could not read emotions as easily as I could, and they could not see what I was going through by looking into my eyes. The books I started to enjoy reading had characters that could tell what others felt by the emotion in their eyes, but that was only in fiction.

Middle School will now be referred to as the Dark Ages. I don't know exactly when I started thinking of myself as smart…There were some wellknown smart kids in 7th Grade, but when these smart kids were put in groups with me, they would comment on how smart I was. For the first time, people my own age acknowledged that I was smart.

In 8th grade English, we had one side of the room agree that a statement was right, the other side saying that it was wrong, and the middle be undecided. One of the topics was, "It's not okay to hate a person." For this topic, most of the kids were on the agree and undecided side, while I was the only one on the disagree side. The arguments that the students put out weren't good and mainly said that it's wrong to hate. My teacher asked if there was any further arguments, to which I raised my hand.

I said in the loudest voice I could, "It's okay to hate people as long as you don't let that hate take over your life."

At that moment I realized that I did dislike and hate some people but I was no longer going to let it control me and make me bitter and vengeful against this world. I also realized that I just spoke out loudly and proudly to my whole class, and when I looked up, almost all the kids moved over to the side I was on, and the others who were left looked like they were debating what to do. From that day on, I started sharing my ideas in small groups in all my classes.

MY MESSAGE TO SHY KIDS

First days of school are the worst for a shy, awkward kid—having to guess whether or not the seats are alphabetical, waiting in the hallways for your friends to arrive so you can choose a place to sit, and if you take an AP class freshman year, it's finding the friendliest-looking senior and asking if you can sit next to them, only to have the teacher already have a seating chart.

My word of advice is to listen to your favorite song on the bus, repeat to yourself that someone is going to have a worse day than you, and if you know no one in your class, either ask a friendly or another shy-looking person if you can sit next to them and give them a compliment, or sit off to the side and make yourself look as non-threatening as possible so some other shy kid will sit next to you. When the teachers make the class do icebreakers to get to know everyone, remember to breathe because in 1st grade I almost passed out from not breathing because I was trying so hard to form coherent sentences.

NOTES

1. When speech therapy is conducted in isolation from the other language difficulties facing the student, it may not be effective. See similar problems with Patience in Chapter 1 and User2 in Chapter 9.
2. See Note 33 about headaches in the Mother's Story in this chapter.
3. Duke in Chapter 2 was also bullied for years in school but did not tell his parents. This population may not communicate their problems to friends even. See Sanger, D., Moore-Brown, B.J., Montgomery, J., Rezac, C., & Keller, H. (2003). Female incarcerated adolescents with language problems talk about their own communication behaviours and learning. *Journal of Communication Disorders, 36*, 465–486.
4. Storm in Chapter 4 also wore a perpetual scowl before his language-processing deficits were resolved.
5. See Note 5 about creativity in the Teacher's Story in this chapter.
6. A resource room is a place set aside for a special education teacher to support students with special needs. The type of support varies by school and district.
7. The Coral Method® is predicated on the assumption that the individual's demonstrated level of intelligence can be depressed substantially by language-processing deficits.

Key Takeaways

Standardized evaluations do not identify each person's specific language-processing deficits.

Without locating this root cause of dyslexia, present methods cannot remove reading disabilities.

Dysolve corrects dyslexia by locating each person's language-processing deficits.

4

Storm

Autism

Storm

Dysolve Finding:
Language-processing deficits leading to dyslexia, ADHD symptoms[1]

School Classification:
Autism, ADHD[2]

School Services:
Academic Intervention Services, psychological counseling, resource room[3]

Doctor's Diagnosis:
ADHD, autism spectrum disorder, oppositional defiant disorder[4, 5]

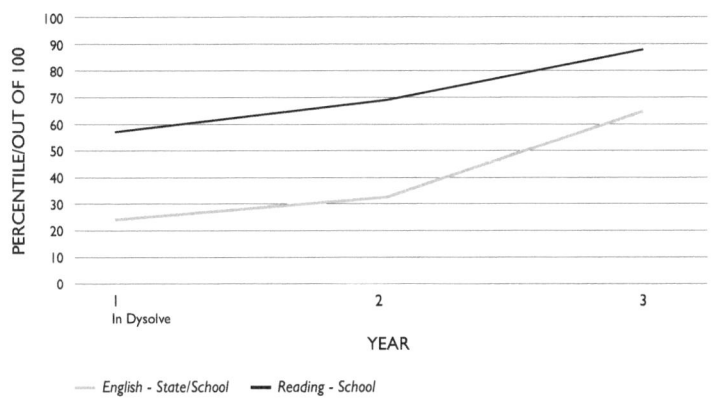

FIGURE 7
Storm – State and School English and Reading Scores in Year 1-3 in Dysolve[6]

NOTES

1. By *language-processing deficits*, we mean deficiencies in the processes involved in executing the language functions of speaking, listening, reading or writing.
2. *ADHD* refers to Attention Deficit/Hyperactivity Disorder. It is also referred to as *ADD* as well as other labels that have been updated over the years. The core components of this condition are inattention, hyperactivity and impulsivity. See Chapter 6 for further discussion.
3. A resource room is a place set aside for a special education teacher to support students with special needs. The type of support varies by school and district.
4. Autism spectrum disorder(s) or ASD are characterized by developmental deficits in socialization and communication and the presence of repetitive behaviors.
5. Oppositional defiant disorder (ODD) is characterized by frequent anger, argumentative behavior and vindictiveness.
6. New York State English tests were administered by Storm's school.

Autism

Mother's Story

The Cost of Amputation
Helen

Authors' note: This story highlights the challenges a family faces when a child has a host of disorders that are beyond the capability of any school or provider to resolve. Our solution demonstrates what is needed to resolve such cases.

Dreading What was Going to Happen Next

"Bob! Bob! Wake up!" I shook my husband's sleeping body, trying to rouse him from deep sleep. It was three o'clock in the morning.

"Huh? Huh?" He stirred, still half asleep.

"SHHHH! I hear noises downstairs!" I tried to keep it to a whisper.

Bob sat up. "Uh…Get me a bat."

He was still not fully awake. We don't have a baseball bat. No guns, no switchblades, nothing. In fact, nothing that can even remotely be used as a weapon.

Bob grabbed the *Oxford Dictionary* sitting on my shelf. It was the biggest and hardest thing he could lay his hands on in the dark. "Wait! Wait for me!" I whispered after him, slipping on my slippers and throwing on my robe.

I grabbed my phone, in case we had to call 911. I stayed close behind him as we tiptoed downstairs.

Nothing in the hallway. At least nobody blocked our path.

Front door seemed locked still.

Living room silent in the dead of night. Dining room as we had left it—all chairs empty. Still the noises had to come from somewhere in the house…

Quick peek in the kitchen. Nobody.

Bob opened the door down to the basement family room. I grabbed a knife from the kitchen along the way. "Here! Here!" I tried to shove a knife into his hands. He ignored me. He had gone too far ahead.

I followed him down the stairs as quietly as I could. A few steps creaked. I winced.

The family room was dark except for the light flickering from the TV screen. The TV was on.

The light from the TV lit up our son's sleeping face. Storm was curled up on the couch in front of the TV, in fetal position. He must be cold without a blanket.

Bob let out a deep sigh. "He must have sneaked down after midnight. I went to bed at 12."

"What do you want to do?" I asked. Our nine-year-old was giving us yet another dilemma.

"It's too late. Let's talk about it in the morning." Bob let out another sigh. He put down the dictionary and replaced it with Storm. Storm wasn't heavier by much.

Bob carried Storm upstairs and into his bed. Our son did not wake up through it all. For us, his parents, it was another matter. We stayed up running through in our heads what we were going to say to him, what the punishment was going to be this time, how he was going to react. And dreading what was going to happen next.

Meltdown

We kept Storm home from school the next morning. He wasn't going to wake up anyway, after staying up all night watching TV. I woke him up at 11 AM so he wouldn't miss breakfast. At his weight, he couldn't afford to skip any meal. His ADHD meds suppressed his appetite; it was hard enough getting him to take enough calories.[1]

Well-rested, well-fed, he should be ready for our talk. Or so we hoped.

Bob started. He cleared his throat. "Well, Storm, what were you doing last night?"

Storm put on his most innocent, surprised look. "Nothing."

"What were you doing downstairs last night?" Bob tried again.

"I don't know." Still the innocent look.

"Let me ask again. What were you doing downstairs in the family room?"

"I don't know." Storm shrugged, pulling his hoodie over his head.

"Storm! Why was the TV on at three o'clock in the morning!" I could not hold it in any longer. He was not going to confess himself.

The cowering look again. Storm always looked like that when we confronted him. "I—I don't know…I couldn't sleep. So I went downstairs…"

"Did you fall asleep earlier? When did you go to bed? Nine? Did you wake up again? Was that what happened?" Bob was investigating. Perhaps Storm's meds were causing his insomnia again?[2]

A part of me followed Bob's line of reasoning, but another part of me cried, Enough! How many times did we have to make excuses for Storm?

"You sneaked down to watch TV because you wanted to!" There, I said it. There was no point in trying to reason with him when he wouldn't admit to anything. How do you reason with somebody who had to get his fix, no matter what?[3]

Storm knew it was coming. Now he looked pained, helpless. "I—I told you I couldn't sleep. I—I just needed a little TV. That's all."

"What did we say about watching TV past bedtime? What did we agree—" Bob was still trying to remind Storm of the rules.

I cut in. "Let's face it, Storm, you're addicted to the TV! So you sneaked down after Daddy went to bed! You knew you shouldn't, but you still did it! EVERY SINGLE TIME!"

"Stop yelling at me! It's not my fault!" He slid down onto the floor, melting before our eyes.

"Storm, you can't get up to watch TV. This is the rule, you know that." Bob tried to stay calm.

"I don't know anything! I'm stupid! I'm worthless! I wish I was dead!"[4] There we go again. Storm crying and rocking on the floor. On to full-scale meltdown.[5]

My husband and I looked on helplessly as our nine-year-old's meltdown ran its course. I caught a glimpse of our older daughter's back as she grabbed a snack from the fridge and scooted into her room, away from the pandemonium. I didn't realize that it was already 3 PM, and Caitlyn had come back from school. Our "talk" with Storm had taken a full three hours.

Way beyond Toddlerhood

When Storm was into the terrible twos, he of course wouldn't behave. Back then, it was hard to separate normal toddler behavior from I-think-he's-got-a-problem. Eventually it dawned on me, this is going WAY beyond toddlerhood.[6]

Storm struggled from the beginning of preschool when the other kids were learning how to write letters. At the end of kindergarten, he was way below grade level. We had a conversation with the teacher, Are you going to keep him back?[7]

And the school actually said to us, No, because there're other kids worse than him.

Storm should have been held back or should have gone into a bridge program to help him transition into 1st grade.[8] Unfortunately the bridge program wasn't available to him so they moved him to 1st grade.

And again he had problems in class. In the fall of 1st grade, we finally had him diagnosed with ADHD with our doctor. I didn't know much about ADHD, but I knew I didn't want medication.[9] Still, with all the problems he was facing, we had to do something. It took a while to get the right medicines and the right dose. For a while, it improved his behavior.

At that point, Bob and I tried to get his academics under control. His school would say, Oh, he'll be fine, he'll be fine, give it time.[10]

But he struggled in 1st grade.
He struggled in 2nd grade.
He struggled in 3rd grade.

We kept trying to figure out what to do. I tried to get him evaluated, but Storm had little, little bits of progress, so we thought, Ok maybe we can wait; maybe it's starting to change.[11]

But once you have the diagnosis from the doctor, you can have a 504, which is accommodations the school will make.[12] When I asked to have him evaluated for special ed, they said, "Well, let's try the accommodations first."[13] That meant giving Storm extra time on certain activities, steps broken down into little pieces and preferential seating with the teacher. Each time we had a meeting, another accommodation was added.

Finally, I've had had enough. Apparently, if you write the school a letter, they have 30 days to test him.[14] So I submitted the letter. It asked for evaluation of his cognitive abilities to see if he was eligible for special ed services. But at that point, he was already in the middle of 5th grade. We'd been fighting for him since 1st grade.[15]

Later, Storm was diagnosed with autism as well. He's always had something in his mouth; he's always chewing on something. That's a classic sign of autism.[16] He's high functioning, but some of the signs were definitely there.

The Problems are Back

I asked the school to show me the results of Storm's test.[17] They'd ask him to write a sentence with simple words like *red* and *ball*. And he wrote a simple sentence like *"The red ball bounced."* He scored Low Average on things like math, which presumably was not low enough to qualify for special education services. But he could not do double-digit subtraction in 5th grade at that point. That wasn't bad enough according to the school's standards.[18]

The school gave him Academic Intervention Services instead, which was like having an in-class tutor. Storm worked in a group with a tutor in addition to his classroom teacher. It was a table with him and five other kids. It's 20 minutes. So the tutor barely had four minutes with each kid. While it helped, it was not enough of a solution. What Storm really needed was more individual attention.

Fifth grade was also horrible because of the teacher. I knew from the beginning she was not the right match for my son. She was very strict, not the warm and fuzzy kind of teacher.

I kept asking the Principal, "I don't think Mrs. Green is the right match."

"Oh, but EVERYBODY loves Mrs. Green!" The Principal was insistent about that.

So Storm was stuck in a class with a teacher who he thought disliked him.[19] Mrs. Green was not sensitive to his needs, and in my opinion picked on him a bit.[20] One time when we came back from vacation, where he'd missed three or four days of school, Mrs. Green said, "Oh, Storm, it was SO quiet when you were gone. Now the problems are back."

Oppositional Defiant

Storm has many issues—lack of focus and concentration, oppositional defiant disorder (butts heads with authority such as his parents), ADHD, anger management issues, autism spectrum issues, and dyslexia.[21]

We see the doctor every three months for a med check to see if his medicine is adjusting properly. As he grows, he needs to change the dose. At some point, the body gets used to the stimulants and they become less effective.

So you have to change medicines to get back to the results you once had. His pediatrician chats with him to decide what to do next. It's a lot of, How is this going? The medication does deter his appetite. That was a problem for a while. They're always checking to see if he's gaining weight and not losing weight, to try to get the dose dialed in to the right amount.[22]

We give him the medicine all the time because we need our home life to be more calm.[23] If he's not medicated, it's a whole bunch of fooling around, and we're yelling at him, and we're stressed out. That's no good for anybody.

Over the years, his norm has been that we yell at him all the time.[24] He's got a complex about it. It hurts his self-esteem. He keeps thinking he's no good. He gets angry, mad at himself, mad at the world, mad at everything. He has temper tantrums and meltdowns.[25] He wants to change and doesn't understand why he can't. It's just very complex for him.

There's a point where you can't push the issue too much because he gets so upset over it. Then he degrades into the I'm-stupid, I'm-worthless sort of thing. You don't want him to be suicidal.[26] It's a fine line. You want to correct him because you don't want him to think that this behavior is acceptable, but when he suffers the consequences, you don't want to push him to a suicidal point either.[27] It's difficult to hold him to the same standard I hold my daughter to.

I noticed my daughter at a certain point withdrawing from the family because of all the drama with Storm.[28] When we're yelling at Storm, she doesn't want any part of that. She would go to her room to avoid the drama. She very rarely sits in the living room when he's around.

Another facet of Storm's issue is that he's addicted to the screen.[29] He wants to watch TV and YouTube constantly in his spare time. Getting him off the computer is hard. It got so bad we put a timer on the TV so he couldn't watch in the middle of the night. He switched to YouTube on the computer. We put passwords on our computers; he found one that wasn't password-protected. We put a password on our router; he got on our neighbor's unsecured network.

Having the computer is a double-edged sword for Storm. It helps him do his work, but it's the thing he has trouble controlling.

It's hard to overcome the impulsivity. He couldn't resist the urge to fool around. I'd ask him to repeat back to me the rules at home. "No more throwing candy wrappers behind the couch." Then the next day, I'd find candy wrappers behind the couch again. When I asked him, he seemed surprised.

"I forgot." His go-to line.

A 90s Student If

His pediatrician recommended Dysolve to us. Storm has been in Dysolve for two years now since 5th grade. I was hoping he would improve, but I actually didn't think he ever would. That's when I was really frustrated with the school. I thought, "I don't know if this would help, but I'll try anything at this point!" For a while, I was worried that he'd end up living in our basement as a 40-year-old.[30]

I was surprised when Storm did improve at Dysolve. At the beginning, I wouldn't see the progress, but then at the Dysolve Center, Dr. Coral would show me his spelling of words I didn't think he could spell, like *flamboyant*.[31]

One of the great things is, Dr. Coral gets him.[32] She's not put off by his behavior. She's not put off by his temper tantrums. She's not put off when he says, "My head hurts. I can't do anymore." That's the great thing, she gets him in a way others don't.[33]

He got an 85—in English. Before, he hated to write; he hated to read.[34] He would give up trying to read at home. I was correcting every other word he read; he had no flow. It's amazing. He's actually quite articulate in his writing now.[35] He just couldn't get it on the paper before. What surprises me is that occasionally now, he'd say something astute in his writing. With the Dysolve exercises, he sees that he can be successful. That's a big plus for him.

He behaves much better at the Dysolve Center. At home, even in 5th grade, he was very resistant and fought a lot of the efforts we had to help him. For a while, he'd have meltdowns at home when we criticized him, even when it's constructive criticism like, "Ok, Storm, you didn't get that done. You need to get that done. You need to learn this. It's important."

You try to be logical and present it in a positive light. But he just saw criticism as negative and he'd go into a tailspin. He would curl up on the floor and cry. There was a period of time when he'd have a meltdown every time you confronted him with something, every day or every other day. It was like, "We talked about it yesterday. And here we are again! You didn't do your homework. Da-da-da-da—"

There was this ebb and flow for a while. He did still have a couple of meltdowns in 6th grade. Recently though, he's been doing very well. He hasn't had any anger outburst or any meltdown since the beginning of 7th grade.[36]

The change in him wasn't smooth. It was sort of like, he'd make progress and he'd backslide.[37] Then he'd make progress in a different area, and he'd backslide. It was very slow at the beginning. Sometimes you don't see the progress even though it's happening. It's hard because it's a combination of things. There's so much that factor into this—the personality of the child at this age, the peers at school, how his teacher relates to him, what he's working on in particular. It's very complex and different from time to time. Sometimes, certain things gel together better, and other times they don't.

Then at the beginning of 6th grade, he started doing his homework on his own and reading on his own and not resisting as much.[38] The 1st quarter in 6th grade was great, but in the 2nd quarter, Storm's grades dropped dramatically.[39] He started to fail things. Part of his problem was that he didn't write down what he needed to do in his planner because writing was his difficulty. He was not doing his homework and lying about it. You want to give him some rope to get him more independent, but then you don't want him to hang himself with it.

We had meetings with the teachers and we had him reevaluated to get him extra help. I asked his teachers to let me know what he had to do every day so I could check off his homework. Storm still failed the 3rd quarter in 6th grade but he managed to pull it off in the last quarter. He had been studying for tests alone since the last quarter in 6th grade.

You have to figure out how to get buy-in from the child, and that's been a very hard part of Storm.[40] It was hard to get him interested in the schoolwork. We tried different things with Storm, but he wouldn't take to much. We tried reading the *National Geographic*; we tried crossword puzzles but that was spelling and he just got frustrated. We got him more bought into the grades. We told him, "Storm, you want to be paid for your grades." If Storm attains grades 70+

and higher, my husband pays him $10 per good grade. The 1st quarter of 7th grade he did well, and he got five classes' worth of payment. But in the 2nd quarter, he went down and got only three classes paid.

But really, Storm just wants computer time—that's the only reward he cares about. Now he gets his screen time *after* he does his work. Recently, he's been more interested in the schoolwork. Now in his classes, the topics are getting more interesting in science, and he likes history. He's interested in the school play.

Definitely, he's moving in the right direction. His grades are improving. His teachers are essentially happy with him, except for the turning-in-the-homework part.

Storm used to look at the Honor roll and say, "I'll never get on the Honor roll" because you have to be 85 or higher in all your classes. He just thought that was an unattainable goal. He's not there yet, but I think he can get on the Honor roll because all of his teachers say his grades would have been higher if he turned in the homework.

He had an 85 in Social Studies. His Social Studies teacher said, "He can be a 90s student if he turned in his homework consistently."

His Math teacher said, "His grades would have been higher except he doesn't answer all the questions."

His English teacher said, "Storm knows his stuff and is vocal in class, but he still doesn't do his homework."

"His grade should have been in the 90s, except he missed his science labs." His Science teacher was surprised that his grade was low, since he likes science and participates in class.

Are You Going to Get Fired?

Storm is a little more outgoing now. For a lot of time in elementary school and early middle school, there was a lot of teasing and bullying going on.[41] But this year, we're hearing a lot less of it. We've worked on getting him separated from kids that are a bad mix for him.

At least lately he hasn't been complaining about kids at school bugging him or distracting him. One teacher said that Storm has requested to sit by himself during some activities. That's maturity on his part. He's learned that "I can't sit with these kids and do my work because it distracts me, so I'd rather sit by myself and spread out my papers and do my own thing."

Storm is kind of the weird kid. He thinks he's funny a lot; he tries to be the comedian. Some of the time he's funny, but half of the time he's just annoying. Part of the autism is that he can't read the room. He can't tell when he's starting to annoy his peers. There was a new kid in his class, and some of the other kids went up to him and said, "Don't hang out with Storm." Storm was very upset about it.

Sometimes, it's not even a matter of teasing or bullying. The other kids are distracting him. It's the whole focus thing. Blocking out something is very hard for him because of the ADHD and autism.[42] If there's a kid doing something as innocuous as tapping his pencil on the table, that will drive Storm nuts. He'd yell, "Don't do that! You're driving me crazy!" The other kids don't understand that. So the social aspects are really difficult for him.

Storm is talkative, long-winded. You ask him, "What did you have for lunch?"

He'd say, "Well, Jimmy in my math class has a sister going to cheerleading this weekend—" There's this long, rambling explanation you're trying to follow. The way he thinks is not a straight line, unlike the way a lot of us think. Other kids too find it difficult to interact with him. But to him, it makes perfect sense when he's telling you the story.

Storm is doing much better now. We're not totally there yet because he still craves that computer and we have to find a way to limit that. We keep trying to interest him in other things so he won't gravitate towards the computer. For a while he loved his Lego bricks. So he had lots of legos, and he built his legos, and that was satisfying for him. But then he grew out of the legos.

There's a lack of focus and he doesn't pick up the social cues. You try to give him an outlet for the social, like soccer, but he didn't contribute to the team effort. The soccer got more competitive, and he's really not a competitive kind of a kid. If he missed a ball, some of the kids would go, "Oh! Why did you miss that!" He switched to taekwondo, and that's a much better fit for him because it's an individual sport. He's not letting the team down if he messes up.

We put him in Boy Scouts, but he would just do the bare minimum. He had to do a presentation to his troop, but he didn't like rehearsing for it. It was work to him.

Storm doesn't seem to aspire to anything. Everything is work for him. He doesn't get the sense of satisfaction from accomplishing something.

He's starting now to take things apart, so I'm hoping that some sort of engineering might interest him, like mechanical engineering, where he's building things and taking things apart and putting them together maybe. We haven't really figured out what is the career path for Storm. That's still difficult to say. He hasn't really excelled in anything. He still has an attitude.

"You can't talk to your boss that way," we keep telling him. These behavior issues trouble us.

"How are you going to get a job?"

"Are you going to get fired?"

MY MESSAGE TO PARENTS

The earlier you get help, the better. Don't give up.[43] If the first thing doesn't work, keep looking for something else, keep trying something different. If ABCD doesn't work, try XYZ. You need to treat each kid as an individual case.[44] If what your doctor or teacher recommends doesn't help, then look for something else. You just have to keep going to find that thing that works for your own child.

Once Storm was diagnosed with ADHD, I began to notice the same thing in other kids. The more you are familiar with the condition, the more you will recognize the signs in the kids.[45]

You really have to learn about your child's condition. Learn A LOT about it. *Each kid is different, so you need a lot of knowledge.*[46] It's not like one label fits all. Storm has a couple of different labels.[47] He has lots of issues. Sometimes the things you do for one area are not constructive for the other area.

It's hard and it's frustrating. I can't count the number of people who say, "Why can't he be quiet?"

Well, he can't. Don't feel guilty about why your child can't behave. Don't worry about questions like, What's wrong with your parenting skills? Brush that off—just do what's best for your child.

It seems it's always a fight with the schools.[48] You feel guilty, as if you're taking more than you should. That was why it took me so long to act. I didn't want to be that nasty parent. I didn't want to be demanding, to make a scene. Because that's not who I am. But that's who you have to be unfortunately sometimes.[49] I really wished I had pushed harder in 3rd and 4th grade.[50] But I liked his teachers in 3rd and 4th grades, so you think, Maybe we're ok. Until you're not.

MY MESSAGE TO TEACHERS AND ADMINISTRATORS

If you've never had an ADHD student, or an autism student, then you think the student is just misbehaving, which was the problem with my son's 5th grade teacher.[51] She thought he was doing things on purpose when he really wasn't. Teachers have to understand.[52]

When we first came to see Dr. Coral, I took her evaluation report to the school and tried to get them to provide services to my son.

His school said, "We don't know how to interpret this. This is not one of our standard tests."

I was thinking, "Of course she used non-standard tests—because yours don't work."[53]

You can give examples of problems with your child, but they still say, he came Low Average in the test, and that's not bad. It's not logical. Their test didn't pick up on the problem. Their tests don't necessarily give you a good predictor of the issues because some parts are too easy so the child scores higher than he should have.[54]

It's like, you go to the emergency room and you tell them, "I have a cut on the finger. Treat my finger now."

But they don't. My cut gets infected later. Then I need my finger amputated. They'd rather deal with the cost of amputation instead of the cost of a bandaid.[55]

Authors' note: We sympathize with the parent here, at the same time that we recognize that the school is not equipped to deal with the severe challenges that her son poses. See Chapters 13 and 14.

NOTES

1. Studies have linked stimulant medication used to treat ADHD with decreases in weight and height. The long-term effects of stimulant medication on young patients are not yet well documented. See Ibrahim, K., & Donyai, P. (2015). Drug holidays from ADHD medication: International experience over the past four decades. *Journal of Attention Disorders, 19*(7), 551-568. doi:10.1177/1087054714548035
2. Research shows that children with ADHD are prone to sleep disturbances. Certain medications used to treat ADHD may exacerbate sleep disturbances as well. Sleep disturbances adversely affect learning. This cycle of adverse effects is still not fully understood in the field. See Ramnaraine, L.D., Rahmani, M., Khurshid, K.A. (2016). Sleep problems and disorders in children and adolescents with attention-deficit/hyperactivity disorder. *Psychiatric Annals, 46*(7), 401-407.
3. In addition to TV watching, Storm seemed to seek screen time from other sources as well, at the expense of most other activities. This kind of obsession has barely been investigated. Internet "addiction" or excessive Internet use has begun to receive some attention in isolated studies in several countries. High co-occurrence (comorbidity) of this type of obsessive use and ADHD has been reported. See Weinstein, A., & Lejoyeux, M. (2010). Internet addiction or excessive Internet use. *The American Journal of Drug and Alcohol Abuse, 36*, 277–283. doi:10.3109/00952990.2010.491880
4. ADHD symptoms are significantly associated with suicidal thoughts (suicide ideation). Scholars in the field are only just beginning to hypothesize on the causal relationship. Studies tend to start with the age group older than Storm's, i.e., late teens to young adults. See Yeguez, C.E., Hill, R.M., Buitron, V., & Pettit, J.W. (2018). Stress accounts for the association between ADHD symptoms and suicide ideation when stress-reactive rumination is high. *Cognitive Therapy and Research, 42*(4), 461–467. Retrieved from https://doi.org/10.1007/s10608-018-9910-0

5. "Meltdowns" associated with autism spectrum disorder are more intense and protracted than temper tantrums in younger children. Typical behaviors include kicking, screaming, withdrawing and destruction of property. Research suggests that meltdowns can be understood as a cycle of predisposing, precipitating and perpetuating factors. Predisposing factors can involve heightened sensitivity to sensory stimulation and social anxiety. Precipitating factors can be frustration from parental criticism. Perpetuating factors can be caregivers' anger over the repetitive behaviors. Storm's case in this chapter illustrate all these factors. Despite its significance, there is surprisingly little research on emotion regulation in people with autism. See Mazefsky, C.A., Pelphrey, K.A., & Dahl, R.E. (2012). The need for a broader approach to emotion regulation research in autism. *Child Development Perspectives, 6*(1), 92-97.
doi:10.1111/j.1750-8606.2011.00229.x
6. Given the prevalence of language and developmental disorders, parents should be informed of developmental milestones. Information on this topic is available upon request from Dysolve.com and Dysolve Dyslexia on Facebook. The children in this book experienced delays in development that turned out to be significant.
7. Skye in Chapter 3 was retained in the same grade for a year. It still did not help her achieve grade-level performance until her dyslexia was corrected in Dysolve. Grade retention was also considered for the cases in Chapters 1 and 5.
8. A bridge program helps students transition from one grade to the next by supporting them in mastering the skills and knowledge of the former before they are fully placed in the higher level.
9. Most of the parents we have met voiced this reservation about medicating their children, regardless of whether they eventually agreed to have their physicians do so or otherwise.
10. Our students typically come to us in 4th-5th grade, after being told for years to wait before taking any action. See the parents' messages advising against this delay in Chapters 1-6.
11. The parents in this book delayed taking drastic measures even though their children were falling further and further behind

each year because they saw small improvements resulting from the schools' efforts. However, these improvements were not sufficient to get their children to grade-level proficiency. Furthermore, these improvements were negligible when we consider that their children's classmates were making far greater advances.

12. A 504 plan is a formal plan developed by the school to prevent discrimination and protect the rights of children with disabilities. 504 plans are covered under Section 504 of the Rehabilitation Act, which is a federal civil rights law to stop discrimination against people with disabilities. 504 plans are not part of special education. To see the difference between 504 plans and IEPs, go to
https://www.americanboard.org/blog/a-new-teachers-introduction-to-ieps-and-504s/
13. Helen was requesting a plan that was more involved than a 504. The plan, called an *IEP*, involves special education services. An IEP is an Individualized Education Program (or Plan) for students with special needs to receive support services in public schools. *IEP* also refers to the legal document that charts the student's needs, evaluative and support services, and targeted goals. IEPs are covered by the Individuals with Disabilities Education Act (IDEA).
14. Part B of the Individuals with Disabilities Education Act (IDEA) sets forth requirements on school districts in providing support services. Part B also includes parents in the decision-making process. See the guidance at
https://sites.ed.gov/idea/files/modelform_Procedural_Safeguards_June_2009.pdf
15. See Note 10 above.
16. See for example Acquarone, S. (2018). *Signs of autism in infants: Recognition and early intervention.* New York: Routledge.
17. The parents in Chapters 1-6 said that their schools' evaluations placed their children out of services despite their special needs. Their exceptionally low state and school scores in reading attest to their learning difficulties.
18. The mother in Chapter 3 also asked to see the school's tests and was equally critical of the evaluation.

19. See the Principal's Story in Chapter 7 on the lack of teacher preparation in dealing with children with disabilities.
20. Duke in Chapter 2 and Storm in this chapter experienced tense relations with their teachers at some point.
21. Research has linked ADHD, reading problems and oppositional defiant disorder for some time. These coexisting (comorbid) conditions may point to a shared underlying dysfunction. The hypothesized link between ADHD and autistic traits, however, is still controversial. For a research overview, see Rommelse, N.N.J., Altink, M.E., Fliers, E.A., Martin, N.C., Buschgens, C.J.M.,...Oosterlaan, J. (2009). Comorbid problems in ADHD: Degree of association, shared endophenotypes, and formation of distinct subtypes. Implications for a future *DSM. Journal of Abnormal Child Psychology, 37,* 793-804.
22. See Note 1 above.
23. Parents of children with autism have reported higher levels of stress compared to those with other developmental disabilities. Factors have included the children's maladaptive behaviors and sleeping problems—the stressors reported in this chapter. (Maladaptive behaviors refer to behaviors that inhibit a person's ability to adjust to certain situations.) See Valicenti-McDermott, M., Lawson, K., Hottinger, K., Seijo, R., Schechtman, M.,... Shinnar, S. (2015). Parental stress in families of children with autism and other developmental disabilities. *Journal of Child Neurology, 30,* 1728-1735. doi: 10.1177/0883073815579705
24. Because a child with language-processing deficits is easily overwhelmed by language input, raising one's voice when addressing him is likely to exacerbate the situation.
25. Which is the trigger in each meltdown incident—autism, ADHD, or language difficulty? Any or all are possible answers.
26. See Note 4 above.
27. The challenge with this case was the multidimensional nature of Storm's conditions, which required a multimodal, multipronged approach. See Dr. Coral's Story in this chapter.
28. Clinical and preliminary research suggests that individuals with autism and their siblings may have impaired rela-

tionships. This topic is still understudied to date. See Smith, L.O., & Elder, J.H. (2010). Siblings and family environments of persons with autism spectrum disorder: A review of the literature. *Journal of Child and Adolescent Psychiatric Nursing, 23*(3), 189-195.
29. See Note 3 above.
30. The parents in Chapters 1 and 3 also voiced the fear that their children would struggle to manage as adults.
31. See Dr. Coral's Story in Chapter 2 about latent changes in Dysolve that surface much later in the form of improved school grades. There is a time lag because Dysolve corrects underlying deficits. These indepth changes are not assessed directly through school tests and assignments.
32. For most of the time, Storm's problem behaviors at our center were caused by cognitive overload during task performance, which also resulted in head pressure. See Dr. Coral's Story in this chapter.
33. See the Principal's Story in Chapter 7 about the lack of teacher preparation in special education.
34. When a child says that he hates reading or writing, we first determine whether his aversion is due to difficulty in this area.
35. Storm wrote his own story at the end of this chapter.
36. The disappearance of Storm's meltdowns paralleled the resolution of his language-processing deficits as well as the improvement in his school grades.
37. Storm's case presented a highly complex picture due to the multidimensionality of his conditions, latent progress in Dysolve, and a multitude of psychosocial issues.
38. Storm's progress to independent work within a year in Dysolve is similar to that of our other students.
39. The fluctuations in Storm's rate of academic progress were unique to his case and due primarily to psychological issues. The other students in this book exhibited a linear upward trajectory instead.
40. See Chapter 5 on motivation.
41. Very little research has been conducted on the relation between bullying and learning disabilities such as dyslexia. The scant research to date suggests that children with these disabilities are more likely to be bullied (peer victimization)

than bully others. See Mishna, F. (2003). Learning disabilities and bullying: Double jeopardy. *Journal of Learning Disabilities, 36*(4), 336-47.
42. ADHD and autism have been linked to distractibility in research. The language-processing problems underlying dyslexia can also cause the affected person to *seem* distracted. See the cases in Chapters 1 and 3.
43. The parents' messages in this book preponderantly tell other parents not to give up, considering the stakes involved in failing to correct the situation as well as the reward awaiting those who succeed.
44. We agree with Helen that each child presents a unique case. The individual nature of each condition makes its resolution difficult and warrants the use of artificial intelligence. See Chapter 14 *Computational Microlinguistics* and Chapter 15 *Responsive Intelligence Technology*.
45. See Chapter 6 on ADHD.
46. Helen rightly points out that vast expertise is required to resolve the problem for each person because of the wide spectrum of language-processing deficits found in affected individuals. See Chapters 13 and 14 for further discussion.
47. See the Engineer's Story in Chapter 9 on the problem of classification.
48. The tussle between parents and schools over support services is discussed in Chapter 12 on the economics of dyslexia.
49. Unlike Helen, the mother in Chapter 3 fought aggressively for support services. Yet the other case still did not get the kind of support needed because schools primarily use compensatory methods, not corrective ones.
50. The parents in Chapters 1-4 and 6 voiced regret over not pushing their schools earlier and/or harder for special services. But see Chapter 12 on limited resources.
51. See the Principal's Story in Chapter 7 on the lack of teacher preparation on special education.
52. Teachers' reactions may unknowingly escalate or perpetuate students' problem behaviors. See Storm's story at the end of this chapter.

53. Dysolve's individuated evaluations, which locate each person's specific language-processing deficits, supersede standardized evaluations that cannot do so.
54. See Note 18 above.
55. See Chapter 12 *The True Cost of Dyslexia*.

Dr. Coral's Story

Language-Processing Deficits

Going to Explode

"I want to rip off my head and throw it into the ocean."

I could see why he wanted a new head. His didn't work too well. He had awful headaches and things flitted in and out in his head, just out of consciousness, so he couldn't peer at them and point, "There, there's the culprit!"

Storm wore a perpetual scowl, shoulders hunched, hoodie up. He was thin—bone thin—with dark circles under his eyes. I kept him at arm's length, not sure what he might do on impulse. After all, his mind, as he said, had a mind of its own.

I asked him to read a page of *True Stories of Heroes*.[1] A few halting words and then—"ACCIDENT?!!! ACCIDENT?!!!" Storm screamed, out of control. He pulled his dark hoodie over his head, flailing jerkily, tugging against invisible demons.[2]

We stopped the reading to let his brain calm down. I popped my head out the door to assure his Dad in the waiting room.

"Not to worry. He's just reading." Storm's Dad, Bob, looked up and nodded. He did not seem particularly alarmed. Used to it at home.

In his school's evaluations, his 5th grade teacher reported that Storm had a temper and exhibited "inappropriate behaviors" including blurting out comments out of turn. When frustrated, he would "bang his hands on the side of his head."[3] His teacher said he "reported hearing voices" and expressed that he was going to "explode." Both parent and teacher gave him highly elevated scores for ADHD symptoms, which included poor control of anger and aggression.[4]

I shuddered to think of Storm as an adult. We had no choice but to help him. And I may add, reluctantly at first.

Taste of Success

"This exercise is so stupid! This game is so stupid!"

Everything was so stupid to Storm at the beginning of our program.[5] He slumped and scowled through every session. Moping was what he did best.

"When was the last time Storm won anything?" I asked his Mom. That caught Helen off guard. It had been so long since Storm won any award or achieved any recognition. Considering the number of certificates and badges and stars and trophies distributed by teachers, clubs and even party hosts, it's unusual for a nine-year-old boy in America not to have caught one of those.

Regardless of the severity the problems of the children who came to us, almost all of them wanted to do well and most had celebrated accomplishments in various arenas in some way. So they wanted to do better and accomplish more.[6] Not Storm—he didn't know what that felt like, the taste of success.

Although Storm could not spell even basic words like *one* (*wone*) in 5th grade, he was verbally articulate.

"You're going to compose an essay today," I told him when he came in for our consultation.

"But I can't write."

"You'll dictate to me. I'll type for you." I got ready at the keyboard and he fired away. He wanted to send a message to his teacher about how he felt. He rattled off fluently, with good use of rhetorical devices, tone, parallelism and even some strong metaphors at the end—no editing necessary. (See his message at the end of this chapter.)

"There, I feel better. I got it off my chest." His message apparently had a therapeutic effect on him. The A+ and gold star I pinned to his essay was just a secondary bonus.

Five Years of Anger

"Focus. Focus. What's the matter?" I asked at our weekly session. Storm couldn't attend to our exercise. He was hungry. He didn't have a regular diet or meal schedule—his ADHD drugs had thrown them out of whack.[7] I felt guilty giving him snickers and Doritos from our office kitchen. That's not lunch. But he was happily chomping away. His Mom was happy he was meeting his daily caloric intake.

"Look, look." He lifted up his shirt. His ribs stuck out as defined as open venetian blinds. His emaciated body looked like it was from a developing country facing famine, not from the land of all-you-can-eat.

We gave Storm a bigger role next.

"You know, you complain a lot about your teacher, Mrs. Green. Now's your chance to tell all the Mrs. Greens out there what students like you go through." We arranged to videotape Storm for our colleagues' presentation at the New Jersey Education Association annual convention.[8]

Storm dressed up in a neat polo for the videotaping. He spoke straight into the camera to address teachers directly, unscripted. He poured his heart out, at times cocky, angry, sad, frank, exposed.

It was all impromptu but his words rolled off his tongue without a hitch. "Remember when you were a kid and you forgot about stuff all the time? You just got home from school and you wanted to watch TV but your Dad said, 'Load the dishwasher.' Then five minutes later, 'Load the dishwasher.' And then again, 'Did you load the dishwasher?' And you said, 'Oh, sorry, I forgot!' And your Dad gets mad. If you're a normal kid, it's kinda like that. But if you have forgetting problems—I mean, you have problems that make you forget stuff—[the teacher] needs to be considerate of that.[9] And also be very, very, very nice to those people."

Storm got up and paced the room. "Don't pick on students only when they don't seem to be paying attention. Sometimes, they may be tired or something. Do not—and I caution: DO NOT—pick on a student who doesn't seem to be following directions. They probably have a problem, like me, and you've got to figure out why they're doing it like that and fix it."

He continued, "If we forget to bring in a paper, unless it's the 100th time, don't make it seem as if we're a big disappointment."

He went up close to the camera. "I'm going to talk about people's feelings. Yes, kids have those too, you know. With me, when I get under pressure with schoolwork, which is a lot, my head starts hurting. People who have that—well, you just have to accept that. When you yell at them a lot, they just start feeling bad and they may not like you. Trust me, *the one thing you do not want is to have a kid hate you.*"

"In 5th grade, I had a teacher who I thought hated me. Do you want your kids to think that about you? Do you really want them to think, 'Oh, that teacher hates me, and I hate them back.'" His voice broke.

Pause. "Yeah."

Cut.

"There, I got five years of anger out of my system!" He brightened up.

For the next several weeks, he held his head high. He felt important.

The Language of Shakespeare

Tackling Storm's tangled web of issues was not unlike home construction. We had to sequence the order of tasks to complete carefully so we could progress on several fronts simultaneously without being held back at some point later because we forgot to install the wiring before putting up the sheetrock. And we had to make sure we didn't forget the studs and headers for the doors so that the roof joists don't collapse on top of our heads.

The indepth, detailed work was managed autonomously by Dysolve's computer expert system, which pulled data from Storm's game responses. Continuous feedback from computer analytics on his performance and progress guided the decision-making for his corrective training in the intelligent program and in person.

He went for one minute, then four minutes of reading without screaming. He read a full page. No cries.

I popped my head out the door to interrupt his Dad reading in the waiting room: "See, no cries." Bob was surprised that a full 10 minutes had passed uneventfully.

For a person with so many language-processing problems, Storm had a love of language. He was spellbound by speakers with accents and loved imitating them. The jester.

"Cumpoolsyon! I'm acting on cumpoolsyon!" he jested.

"What? You want to try Shakespeare's English?" Here's a way to get this kid bought into the language, I thought. I gave him *A Midsummer Night's Dream* and *Much Ado about Nothing* for his 11th birthday.

I flipped open to one of the scenes: "O Lord, he will hang upon him like a disease: he is sooner caught than the pestilence, and the taker runs presently mad." Storm listened, entranced.

"Where is that? Where is that?" He wanted to see the lines on the page himself.

"Well, Storm, if you can get to reading two pages straight through any book, I'll give you a treat." I knew his treat wouldn't be food of any kind.

"What treat?" He was curious.

I promised to teach him Old English.

The next week, he did get through two pages without an episode.

"Where's my thingamajiggy?"

"What? Oh, Old English. It's not thingamajiggy," I laughed.

He smiled. He was becoming a typical kid. Actually, a charming boy.

And witty: "For a great Halloween, you need great candy, great decorations, and great parents."

And opinionated: "Getting $200 shoes is stupid because they are just fabric with a checkmark on them."

Dr. Jekyll and Mr. Hyde

Just as I thought we reached a clearing in the forest, the forest moved, like some surreal scene from *Macbeth*.

Storm got *F*s in English and Social Studies in the 2nd quarter of 6th grade. He had skipped doing his homework.

He and I conversed about his problem. Here was a highly intelligent, astute, very perceptive young man, fully aware of his actions. Controlling them was another matter.[10]

"I decided not to do homework. It could have been a little thing like read this and write two sentences about it. I didn't do it. I thought I could do it just before I handed it in."

He hit his lowest in the 3rd quarter of 6th grade. There was talk of keeping him back if he couldn't pass. The fear of being retained in 6th grade finally spurred him to do his work. He pulled through.

At the beginning of 7th grade, I asked Storm to type his own story for this book. He sat down and typed for a full 15 minutes straight. One page done! No headaches, no screaming.

Storm finally got up from his seat and walked out to chat with my husband, Evan, in the lobby. A tall, lanky kid, still with an angular frame because of his ADHD meds killing his appetite. But his hoodie was pulled back, and he stood straight and looked Evan directly in the eye. Storm enunciated his words crisply. There was a lilting melody to his voice. Perhaps he should go into acting.

At the Dysolve Center, we only saw the new Storm. But at home, the old Storm still lurked. His mother, Helen, reported that he'd do one homework assignment when she asked him. But he'd lie about the others and skipped them. One time, he did not do his math homework for a whole week.

Helen put new procedures in place at home. Storm would spend an hour on homework at night. He would do it independently first, and she would check each one after. Storm prepped for a Social Studies test on his own. He received an 80 on it. Since the beginning of 7th grade, 18 months into Dysolve, the temper fits had stopped at home as well.

"Now I do it when I'm told to do it. I'm forcing myself to do it. I'm really paranoid about what happened last year." Fear kept him going in 7th grade. When he felt it strongly enough, he did his homework. At other times, the darker forces won.

I gave him *The Strange Case of Dr. Jekyll and Mr. Hyde* for Christmas.

Zigzag

Our work was done. We got Storm to reach the 90s in his school grades. Whether he will continue to zigzag through life was now up to him.[11]

THE PROBLEM AND OUR SOLUTION

Sometimes you get a child who does not have long-term goals to drive himself. The child has to *want* to change, to improve.[12]

"What is your goal this year?" I asked Storm at the beginning of 6th grade.

"Just passing."

"Don't you want to get on the Honor roll?"

"Nah, then everybody expects you to work hard."

Just considering the possibility of getting on the Honor roll was a big step for Storm. At his first evaluation at Dysolve, Storm forgot test items immediately after they were presented to him. He used sophisticated words like "*insanity*" and "*dysfunction*" yet could not get past the second page of a grade-level story. He said he had headaches at school, twice every day except for field trips.[13]

Storm had been taking a cocktail of ADHD medications since 1st grade. They did not remove his concentration issues or meltdowns. He could not spell personal pronouns (*their* = *thir; *they* = *thay) and simple digits (*two* = *to; *four* = *fore) in 5th grade.

Storm joined Dysolve in the middle of 5th grade. The complexity of Storm's problems required a multimodal approach. His custombuilt program at Dysolve tackled his *problem-complex* on many fronts simultaneously.[14] The support of a whole team of practitioners, educators and researchers at Dysolve—plus an artificial intelligence system—was needed to lift Storm out of his current state.

He still had so much difficulty writing that he did not take notes at all in 6th grade. He did not write down in his planner what he was supposed to do for homework each day.

As he could not explain to his Mom what he was supposed to do, she could not help him much with homework.

At this time, Storm's mother reported that he was down to just one anger episode a day. His recurrent headaches declined at the beginning of 6th grade but came roaring back in the middle of the school year when the work got a lot harder. Storm was again facing cognitive overload, until we intervened. By the middle of 6th grade, Storm earned an 88 on a vocabulary test, a novelty for someone who used to get 40s in such tests. But his overall grades continued to suffer because he was skipping his homework.

At the end of 6th grade, his Progress Report for his Individualized Education Program (IEP) noted that his writing was "Progressing Gradually," meaning that he was making less than anticipated progress but may still achieve the targeted goal. We gave him our *Dysolve® Sounds and Spelling Manual* to start acquiring the spelling rules he missed in his early grades.

I told him, "Storm, you have to start taking ownership of this. Look at some of the grades you got this year! Did you ever think before you could be an 80s student? You can be a 90s student if you want it!"

But did he want it? He still had not acquired the correct forms for the most common words in the English language: *whare* (*where*), *thay* (*they*), *eney* (*any*), *moather* (*mother*), *hear* (*here*), *thir* (*their*), *theas* (*these*), *thoas* (*those*). We set his summer goals: Learn 100 sight words a day, 3,000 a month from our *Dysolve® Word Frequency List*.

In the middle of 7th grade, Storm's IEP Progress Report documented that his Reading was "Progressing Gradually" while his Study Skills were "Progressing Inconsistently," meaning that he might not achieve the targeted goal. His teachers now recognized that he was smart but noted that he was bringing his grades down by missing assignments. He was at risk of failing Science, having received a "0" for homework. He had missed four assignments in a row.

His mother met with his teachers to put new procedures in place. Helen and his subject teachers would communicate weekly so that they could doublecheck his assignments at both ends.

At Dysolve, Storm was learning to spell multi-syllabic words: *responnsability (responsibility), *origanality (originality), *specificly (specifically), unmentionable. Yet, he still had not mastered the simple function words: *thay (they), *woun't (weren't), *jest (just), *thar (there).

This time, I was stern. "Storm, there's no excuse anymore not to learn the most common words. Others will judge you by your spelling of these simple words. Why? Because these words show up all over the place. So if you keep spelling them wrongly, your errors will be everywhere. And how long have I told you to learn them?"

"A year ago."

At school, his teachers echoed the same litany: "not working to ability, not working to ability." His teachers made him redo his Social Studies and English assignments. He just turned them in with no effort. They expected more from him now.

But his grades continued their rollercoaster ride (Figure 8)—until such time when he decides to choose a smoother journey.

Dyslexia Dissolved

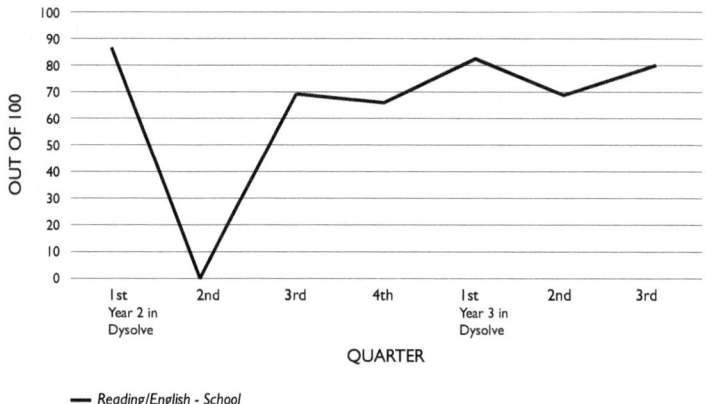

NOTE: No grade was assigned in the 2nd quarter of Year 2 because Storm missed too many assignments.

FIGURE 8
*Storm – School Reading/English Grades
in Year 2-3 in Dysolve*

NOTES

1. Dowswell, P. (2002). *True stories of heroes*. London: Usborne.
2. Research on the reading ability of children with autism dates back to the classic 1983 study of Frith and Snowling. Their results have been confirmed by subsequent studies. They conclude that this population shows difficulty with text comprehension even when subgroups are able to decode single words. See the research overview in Arciuli, J., & Brock, J. (2014). *Communication in autism*. Amsterdam: John Benjamins.
3. Self-injurious behaviors (SIB) are common in persons with autism but are not considered core symptoms of autism because SIB such as head banging also occur in other populations. Approximately 50% of the autistic population engage in some form of SIB, even if it is only at a specific period of their life span. SIB is thus more common in this group compared to all other populations. See Minshawi, N.F., Hurwitz, S., Fodstad, J.C., Biebl, S., Morriss, D.H., & McDougle, C.J. (2014). The association between self-injurious behaviors and autism spectrum disorders. *Psychology Research and Behavior Management, 7*, 125–136. Retrieved from https://doi.org/10.2147/PRBM.S44635
4. About 30% of patients with autism also have ADHD. When the primary diagnosis is autism, the most common ADHD symptom reported is hyperactivity. When the primary diagnosis is ADHD, the most common autistic symptom reported is problem with social interaction. ADHD and autism may share deficits in executive functions such as planning, decision-making and working memory. See for example Chantiluke, K., Christakou, A., Murphy, C.M., Giampietro, V., Daly, E.M.,…Rubia, K. (2014). Disorder-specific functional abnormalities during temporal discounting in youth with Attention Deficit Hyperactivity Disorder (ADHD), autism and comorbid ADHD and autism. *Psychiatry Research: Neuroimaging, 223*, 113-120.

5. Children with autism have been reported to use significantly more avoidance and venting strategies and fewer constructive strategies than their typical peers. Avoidance strategies include distraction. Venting can be vocal or physical and includes self-speech. Constructive strategies include goal-directed behaviors and support seeking from others. See for example Jahromi, L.B., Meek, S.E., & Ober-Reynolds, S. (2012). Emotion regulation in the context of frustration in children with high functioning autism and their typical peers. *Journal of Child Psychology and Psychiatry, 53*, 1250–1258. doi:10.1111/j.1469-7610.2012.02560.x
6. The children in Chapters 1, 3 and 5 are talented in art, 2 in sports, 5 and 6 in creative writing, and 5 in music as well.
7. The adverse effects of ADHD drugs on appetite and physical growth have been a concern in the field for some time. More adverse effects are discussed in Cortese, S., Holtmann, M., Banaschewski, T., Buitelaar, J., Coghill, D.,...Sergeant, J. (2015). Practitioner review: Current best practice in the management of adverse events during treatment with ADHD medications in children and adolescents. *Journal of Child Psychology and Psychiatry, 54*(3), 227–246. doi:10.1111/jcpp.12036
8. See the Teachers' Stories later in this chapter.
9. Language-processing deficits affect memory in even those without autism. See Chapters 1, 3 and 9.
10. Difficulties with emotion regulation are cause for concern in the population with autism, yet empirical studies are limited. See Note 5 above.
11. Dysolve specializes in addressing language processing alone. Storm needed psychological counseling as well.
12. The children in Chapters 2 and 5-8 displayed self-motivation. Patience in Chapter 1 eventually developed self-motivation to push past the obstacles.
13. In general, autism is associated with pain insensitivity. Thus, headache disorders have not been investigated among individuals with autism. One recent study, however, did report on their presence in this population. Victorio, M. (2014). EHMTI-0290. Headaches in patients with autism spectrum

disorder. *The Journal of Headache and Pain, 15*(Suppl 1):B37. doi:10.1186/1129-2377-15-S1-B37

14. Previously, severe speech and language impairment was a necessary criterion for a diagnosis of autism. Since then, emphasis has shifted to nonverbal communication. The population with autism shows a wide range of linguistic abilities, from exceptional verbal skills to little or no spoken language. Nevertheless, studies with representative samples do report language scores below average for this population. See Arciuli, J., & Brock, J. (2014). *Communication in autism.* Amsterdam: John Benjamins.

Instructor's Story

Chameleon
Evan

The Most Dangerous Animal

"What is the most dangerous animal to humans?" I asked Storm on his first visit to our Dysolve Center.

"Well, it wouldn't be the great white shark, because most people aren't in the ocean. So that would also rule out all marine creatures," Storm reasoned.

He continued, "I wouldn't consider tigers or lions either because they're only in some countries. So it's got to be some animal that's everywhere or almost everywhere…"

He concluded, "I know! It's the bee!"

Close. It's actually the mosquito, but Storm's reasoning impressed me, especially for a nine-year-old.

That was the smart, logical Storm. But there was another side to Storm. The other Storm sneaked up on you, making you spin around, worried about what he's up to behind your back. Or he'd hide under the desk at your feet while you're trying to work.[1]

"Hey, come out from under there! What are you doing?" I wanted him out of the shadows. Crawling out, he kept his head covered by a hoodie.[2]

As he walked by, he reached out his hand and touched my head.

"Don't do that!" I wanted him to understand that it's not appropriate behavior.[3] But he did it again the next time.

We leave a bowl of candy in the reception area. Some kids just grab the candy, others ask their parents if they could have any, and a handful eye it longingly because they know their parents don't allow them to have any. Storm didn't do any of these.[4] Instead, he'd sidle up when he thought nobody was looking, inched up his hand, poised for a quick extraction like the tongue of a chameleon. Another sleight of hand delivered the candy into his mouth, although none of us minded his eating the candy.

Meticulous Attention

For the first several months, Storm balked and moped through our exercises.[5] But as Storm himself saw improvements with his schoolwork, he finally grasped the value in cooperating with us on his custombuilt program.

He had had enough of the headaches and the voices and the images swirling uncontrollably in his head.[6] He could not read without screaming; he could not write because he couldn't remember how to spell.[7] He couldn't recite 6 times table when he got to 9 times.[8]

In the 13th month, he was ready to cross a big hurdle.

"Ready?" we asked.

He nodded.

He knew what to expect: that the headaches would come, but he stayed the course this time to push through. We lengthened our weekly sessions as the headaches declined; his face opened up.[9]

When our sessions ended, he hung around in the waiting room to chat with us. Nowadays, he kept his hoodie back.[10] He seemed to have grown a couple of inches, partly because he now stood straight.[11]

He brought in an art piece he had painted with meticulous attention.

"You did that yourself?" I marveled.

"Yep." He sounded proud.

"How long did it take you to paint it?"

"A couple of hours."

Storm working productively at his desk for several hours, now that's something.[12]

NOTES

1. Storm was not the only student at Dysolve to hide under the desk at times. Other students did the same when they faced cognitive overload and needed to shield themselves from further input, either verbal or visual, and sometimes both.
2. Individuals on the autism spectrum are often hypersensitive to sounds. Even noise in the environment may disturb them. Storm's habit of covering his head with a hoodie might have been a substitute for covering his ears with his hands, a typical behavior reported in the autism literature. See O'Connor, K. (2012). Auditory processing in autism spectrum disorder: A review. *Neuroscience & Biobehavioral Reviews, 36*(2), 836-854. Retrieved from https://doi.org/10.1016/j.neubiorev.2011.11.008
3. Autism spectrum disorders are characterized by problems with social interaction. Thus, socially inappropriate behaviors are common with this population.
4. In a small sample study, nearly half of the subjects with autism reported having no friends. Researchers attribute this to the lack of interpersonal skills and understanding of the reciprocal nature of social interaction. Storm's behavior reported here might have been due to his lack of facility in making requests (request strategies). Later, as his language-processing difficulties dissipated, he was able to make direct requests at the Dysolve Center. For research on conversational competence, see Chapter 9 of Arciuli, J., & Brock, J. (2014). *Communication in autism*. Amsterdam: John Benjamins.
5. See Note 5 in Dr. Coral's Story in this chapter.
6. Auditory and visual hallucinations are commonly associated with schizophrenia. The clinical connections between schizophrenia and autism have long been recognized in research, but the relation between the two disorders remains an open question. See Hommer, R.E., & Swedo, S.E. (2015). Schizophrenia and autism-related disorders. *Schizophrenia Bulletin, 41*(2), 313-314. doi:10.1093/schbul/sbu188
7. See Dr. Coral's Story in this chapter for further description.
8. The math-language connection is discussed in Chapter 1.

9. The cases in Chapters 1-6 reported having headaches. These headache events declined during the course of their Dysolve programs. Our instructors reported noticeable changes in the students' attitude and demeanor in conjunction with this decline in headache occurrence.
10. See Note 2 above.
11. In addition to Storm, the children in Chapters 3 and 5 also changed their physical posture when their academic performance improved.
12. Contrast the new Storm with the old one in his Mother's Story at the beginning of this chapter.

Teachers' Stories

Spiral of Self-Loathing

Authors' note: Stephanie and Richard Sackerman included Storm's video in their presentation Completing the Picture of Dyslexia: Twice-Exceptional Students *at the 2016 New Jersey Education Association Convention.*[1,2] *Over 100 teachers attended their presentation and praised Storm's contribution. (Excerpts of Storm's video are in Dr. Coral's Story in this chapter.)*

Richard Sackerman

As a Middle School teacher, I find that Storm's words really struck close to home. Day in and day out, we see students who, seemingly offhandedly, state that this teacher or that teacher "hates me." A quick followup with the student usually results in the student explaining whatever minor infraction occurred between him and the teacher. The student, really, just needed a way to vent out his frustration. For a student without a condition, this sort of issue could be solved with an airing of the grievance. For students with disabilities, it could be devastating—it could send them further down a spiral of self-loathing they fear they cannot escape.[3]

Stephanie Sackerman

Being an educator frames my impression of Storm when watching him relate his school experience. For me, three things stand out. First, Storm is incredibly honest. His candor when explaining simple day-to-day occurrences reminds me that a child with Storm's condition isn't just experiencing challenges at school. He has to deal with daily disruptions continually. Storm is also very introspective, particularly for someone his age. His ability to reflect on his experience with his teacher shows that he is very aware of his current reality.[4] Furthermore, the way he expresses himself with regard to his situation shows how caring he truly is. Storm is concerned for other children who, like him, have felt that way. It is terribly sad to imagine the impact that feeling that way had not only on Storm's ability to learn but also on his overall sense of self.

MY MESSAGE TO PARENTS

I really care about your child. I know he is your most treasured gift, and, trust me, it's my privilege to teach him. I do my very best every day to reach and teach all my students, but my job is not an easy one. It's complex and multilayered with many individuals I am trying to please: students, parents, administrators, school stakeholders, and myself. I put a lot of pressure on myself because my work is a huge responsibility. When I go home, I reflect on the day and think how I can improve on what I will adjust for tomorrow. And I worry about my kids. I wonder how they're doing tackling the homework that night; I think about where they are years after having taught them. I try my hardest, but I can only do what I can do with what I have and the information

I'm provided. I want to do a good job teaching all my students, and if I don't have the resources I need, I buy them with my own money, and if I can't find them, I write mentor texts myself.

I also feel frustration. Whether it's the tests used to classify a child or the timeline it takes to put a plan in place or even where the money in the budget goes, I have to remember that this is public education, and it's public policy. There are rules and a set way of doing things that have been prescribed by individuals who aren't in my school, my district, or sometimes even my state.

I wasn't trained specifically to teach a child with dyslexia. I'm someone just like you, trying just like you, to help your child the best way I can.

MY MESSAGE TO TEACHERS

Keep doing what you're doing. We're not in an easy spot, and it feels like we're on the frontlines all the time. Think back to why you started teaching. You didn't want to teach Science or Social Studies or Spanish—you wanted to teach children. Remember it's always about them. You know that children are precious and special but also vulnerable. It is our duty to make our classrooms a safe haven for all our children. Continue wielding your power to make a difference; you are.

NOTES

1. Stephanie Sackerman is a graduate of Columbia University's Teachers College with an MA in Curriculum and Teaching. Richard Sackerman holds a Master's in Secondary Education and a second Master's in Educational Leadership. Both are teachers in middle school in the state of New Jersey.
2. Sackerman, R.T., Jr., & Sackerman, S.A. (2016, November 10). *Completing the Picture of Dyslexia: Twice-Exceptional Students*. Paper presented at the New Jersey Education Association Convention, Atlantic City, NJ.
"Exceptional" refers to those who are outside the typical, at either end of the spectrum. Thus, one can be exceptional for having gifts or deficits. That is why those with both are called *twice-exceptional.*
3. Previous studies indicate that self-awareness of one's own mental state is impaired among individuals with autism. On the other hand, comparatively high levels of depression and anxiety are recorded in this population as well. It is not clear as yet how these findings may be reconciled. For the former topic, see Williams, D. (2010). Theory of own mind in autism: Evidence of a specific deficit in self-awareness? *Autism, 14*(5) 474–494. doi:10.1177/1362361310366314
For the latter topic, see Dickerson Mayes, S., Gorman, A.A., Hillwig-Garcia, J., & Syed, E. (2013). Suicide ideation and attempts in children with autism. *Research in Autism Spectrum Disorders, 7*(1), 109-119. Retrieved from https://doi.org/10.1016/j.rasd.2012.07.009
4. The behaviors reported here are not characteristic of autism. Impairment in introspection has been reported in autism research, but it is not clear as yet how such impairment relates to the development of self-concept. See for example Robinson, S., Howlin, P., & Russell, A. (2017). Personality traits, autobiographical memory and knowledge of self and others: A comparative study in young people with autism spectrum disorder. *Autism, 21*(3), 357-367. doi:10.1177/1362361316645429

Storm's Story

Pulled Apart

Authors' note: In revealing the child's thoughts here, we hope teachers may gain further insight on how their students with disabilities may view what happens in the classroom in a way that is different from what was intended.

Spoken to Loudly

The anger was caused by a teacher and the trouble with writing, pretty much all of 5th grade. My teacher, Mrs. Green, got mad at me for writing something down in a way that made sense to me. It was different than what she wrote. She came around and yelled at me for "not following directions."[1] It was for long division, and she threw me off by doing it her way.

The one teacher that gave me the most trouble was the one who failed as a communicator.[2]

She says, "I don't yell. I only speak loudly."

I know I got "spoken to loudly" a lot.[3]

I think my problems are related.[4] I have trouble spelling small words and remembering math facts.[5] I got frustrated and mad sometimes, and that didn't help.[6]

Some days were exactly the same because it was: Get there, not have Mrs. Green being disappointed, arguments, special classes, more minor arguments, recess, lunch, big argument, do stuff till buses leave. You could say it's a carbon copy.

[Here's what 5th grade was like:]

Day 1 – It was about two weeks into the school year and it was like I forgot something or [there was] a small conflict because I heard something this way but it was [supposed to be] another way.

Day 2 – One week later it was more arguing about stuff and general toxicity in the middle of the day and at the end somewhat.[7] The arguments got worse by the 30th day of school, and it was arguing every day. It was hard to learn with constant "You need to STOP" and "I've had it with you!"[8]

Day 3 – It was Day 2 over and over and over again every day and it was very hard to do anything in my core classes because of it. I had so many kids in my class who were "babied" if they felt bad. Everyone had to do something to make them the center of attention. But not for three of us. If we felt bad, it was pretty much "pfff—sucks to be you" or "suck it up."

    By that point I knew she was one of those teachers that had favorites and I know I wasn't one.
    She made me mad, sad and not like school for a loooooooooooooooooooooooong time. It was rinse and repeat.

Jibber-Jabber

Sixth grade was a big improvement to 5th because it was more learning and work instead of arguing 24/7. I liked my teachers and they liked me. It was a new school and my old teachers could not tell the new ones about me and how I acted.

ELA (English Language Arts) was hard because it was like I know it, I've been told how to do it, but I go to do it and I mess up. Most of the time I would do a writing piece and I'd get something wrong, not including spelling.

The homework was weird. I thought I could get away with not doing my homework. I still don't know why I thought I could, granted it was the me that throws bathroom jokes every five seconds.[9] I got away a few times when I had legitimate reasons like I left early, I was sick or no school, but that was it.

In the beginning it was like the 5th grade me but in a different school. The 6th grade me was the 5th grade me but with the bathroom humor and not doing homework every day.

When I was reading sometimes, I felt I was not in control, with my head hurting, spinning, and general mind boggling.[10] It's hard to explain. It feels like I'm in the center and I'm being pulled apart. I don't really know what I'm being pulled by, but I know it's there. It feels hard to keep calm and controlled and sane sometimes. Sometimes I "explode" at things and once it's out I'm fine. It's weird. The only time I'm not feeling that way is when I am sleeping.

My thoughts come to me like jibber-jabber, but it actually is a picture or a thought or even a video-like thought. It also is kind of hard to do things because I get ideas in segments. It works like this: I would look at a billboard and it relates to something and I think of something else like people doing backflips and then everyone winning.

MY MESSAGE TO MY 5TH GRADE TEACHER[11]

I feel overwhelmed a lot. Mrs. Green tells me all the time that I don't pay attention. Like today, we did something for a classmate who's going to a different school. I wrote it on the wrong paper. Mrs. Green yelled at me for not following the directions.

She's always telling me that I'm always too slow. I wish I could tell her, "Would you rather that I go fast and sloppy or slow and neat?" But I don't say that because she'll say that's giving her ATTITUDE. She's always saying that I don't respect her. Why should I respect her if she's not going to respect me?

I really want her to understand: *If we switched bodies, you'd see why I feel like this.*[12] Stop getting overworked every time I don't hear anything. Don't tell me something that doesn't help me. Don't tell me to pay attention when I am. Don't tell me that everything I tell you is an excuse.

Mrs. Green said, "Sorry class for taking away all this time to address Storm." Then everybody groans because it stops them from doing what they were supposed to. And this is getting really old! I don't always do my work because I don't get it.[13]

I try paying attention, but I get distracted easily. Even when I pay full attention to her, about 80% of the time, I don't get it. Six out of 10, I'll ask. The rest of the time, I guess. Then I get a lot of it wrong, and she yells at me again.

A long time ago, when Hannah got a headache, Mrs. Green told us that we had to be very quiet. But for me, she says, "Just wait and it'll die down in a little while."

But I think she really means, "So what?"[14]

At the beginning of the day, I feel good. But at the end of the day, I feel like I want to rip my head off and throw it into the ocean. Once all the work starts, the headache comes.[15] It's like the train—you can't feel it coming, and suddenly BAM! It's right there. It's like a truck hitting you—really sudden, really strong. And it doesn't go away till I get home.

NOTES

1. The teacher's perception of the situation may be different from the student's, especially one who has difficulty processing language. Regardless of intent, certain situations may cause such a student to shut down or feel anxious, leading to even more problems completing tasks.
2. Note the sophistication of Storm's syntactic structure: [The one teacher [that gave me the most trouble]] was [the one [who failed as a communicator]]. The preceding square brackets mark noun phrases and embedded relative clauses. Storm used a complex subject here, balanced by a complex object. The subject and object are syntactically parallel. Storm often produced such advanced syntactic forms in spontaneous speech.
3. Witticism is a trait of verbal precocity and high intelligence. See Hoh, P.-S. (Spring 2005). The linguistic advantage of the intellectually gifted child: An empirical study of spontaneous speech. *Roeper Review, 27*(3), 178-185.
4. Storm's self-awareness conflicts with findings in autism research. See Note 4 in the Teachers' Stories in this chapter.
5. See the math-language connection in Chapter 1.
6. See Note 5 in the Mother's Story and Note 5 in Dr. Coral's Story in this chapter.
7. Storm habitually used advanced nominals such as "toxicity" and uncommon words such as "discombobulate." He used these words correctly syntactically (sentence structure), semantically (meaning) and pragmatically (context).
8. The population with autism shows comparatively high levels of anxiety and sensitivity to criticism (see Note 3 in the Teachers' Stories and Note 4 in the Mother's Story in this chapter).
9. Besides his own account, the two sides to Storm were noted in Dr. Coral's Story and the Instructor's Story in this chapter.
10. See Dr. Coral's Story in this chapter.
11. Studies suggest that students exhibiting hostile and/or defiant behavior, in addition to low achievement, engender negative attitudes from teachers. See Cook, B.J. (2004). Inclusive

teachers' attitudes toward their students with disabilities: A replication and extension. *The Elementary School Journal, 104*(4), 307-320.
12. Storm pointed to the crux of the issue: others did not understand him because they could not experience his mental state directly. Conversely, trapped in his own brain, he could not compare his experiences with those of others to tell what was typical.
13. The students in Chapters 1, 3, 5, 6 and 9 also experienced difficulty following instructions before Dysolve.
14. Children, even those with disabilities, often notice cues that adults assume are beyond their ability to grasp. See Skye's Story in Chapter 3.
15. Recurrent headaches are common among our students with language-processing issues. See Chapters 1, 3, 5 and 6.

Key Takeaways

Do correct language-processing deficits in those with autism.

Set up conditions for self-accomplishment to motivate self-improvement.

Seek coordinated multimodal solutions for learners with coexisting conditions that may be related.

5

Will

Auditory Processing

Will

Dysolve Finding:
Deficits in language processing (including auditory processing) leading to dyslexia, ADHD symptoms[1, 2]

School Classification:
Speech and language impairment

School Services:
Speech/language therapy

Doctor's Diagnosis:
None provided

Auditory Processing

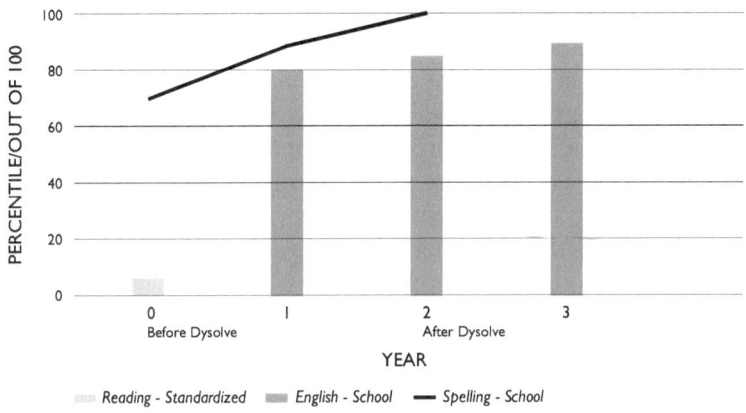

FIGURE 9

Will – School and Standardized Test Scores before and after Dysolve[3]

NOTES

1. The relationship between auditory processing deficits and reading disabilities is unclear at this stage of research in the field. The percentage of children with dyslexia who also have auditory processing deficits range wildly in the literature, hovering around a third of this population. Various hypotheses have been proposed for the role of auditory processing in reading development, but interventions based on these hypotheses have yielded mixed results. This has led some scholars to consider lately that we are dealing with a multidimensional disorder here. For an overview of this research, see Elliott, J.G., & Grigorenko, E.L. (2014). *The dyslexia debate*. New York: Cambridge University Press.
2. By *language-processing deficits*, we mean deficiencies in the processes involved in executing the language functions of speaking, listening, reading or writing.
3. Standardized scores were from the Iowa Tests of Basic Skills® (ITBS®) administered by the student's school. Standardized test scores were not available for older grades, when Will was in Dysolve.

Auditory Processing

Mother's Story

She Knew Things before I Told Her
Vivian

Second-Class Citizen

"Well, Mrs. Taylor, your son doesn't seem to be applying himself."

"He's doing what he can, you know. School's hard for him. It's always been hard for Will."

I braced myself for a repeat of last year's parent-teacher conference, and the one the year before, and the one before that. You'd think going through the same old script would toughen me for this dreaded meeting with my son's teachers, but it still hit me hard every time.

I felt myself going on the defensive again. "My other son is in the top 10 of his class. My daughter has a 4.0." I slipped in how well my other kids were doing, almost as if Will's struggles meant my husband and I came up short as parents. Oh yes, I did feel the difference, going from my other kids' classrooms to Will's.

Among Will's teachers, I felt like a second-class citizen.[1] Somehow, I felt I had to explain why he didn't—couldn't—apply himself. Why we didn't *make* him apply himself. Inevitably, this conversation always ended with my insisting, "Listen, we care about academics."

I'd suffered alongside my 12-year-old son, Will, who had struggled in school since the early grades.[2] That's hard because school is the main job of a kid. Will would come home from school with his head down most days.[3]

As if He didn't Show up

My husband said this once, and it upset me at first, but it was true: If Will didn't show up to take standardized tests, his scores would still have been the same. So here you have a kid, you're with him all the time, so you know he's bright. But as far as standardized tests were concerned, he barely registered. If he'd put *B*s all through in the answer options, or whatever, it wouldn't have mattered. It would have been the same score. It was as if he didn't show up to take the test.[4]

Our other children did well in these kinds of tests.[5] I knew there wasn't such a big difference between Will and his siblings. But you see his grades on these tests, and you go, "Oh my goodness, he needs help." We're all about helping our children, but we never seemed able to reach Will.[6]

His school was always saying, "Oh, he's not far enough behind to need services."[7]

But a second grader who couldn't read? When would he catch up? But his school would say, "Oh, that's your son—you just have to learn to cope with it."[8]

It just didn't seem right. What they were saying didn't add up.[9] I could tell there was a problem because I have my other older children to compare Will to.[10] I knew he couldn't be that different from them. After all, outside of class, Will was a bright, engaged boy.

One thing that gave me hope was that his comprehension was good, so I knew that he understood a lot.[11] His listening comprehension was stronger than his reading ability. When he listened to books on tape, he grasped it. There's definitely a big brain in that head, but he just wasn't able to show it on paper or show it on standardized tests.[12]

She Knew Things before I Even Told Her

By 7th grade, Will was two grades behind in reading.[13] When our pediatrician told us about Dysolve, we jumped right in. I thought, "What do we have to lose?" This didn't seem like it could hurt him.[14] A lot of time and money was already going into Will. We always had tutors for Will every year and in the summer.[15] I was a teacher myself; my husband and I value academics, and we're always willing to help Will.[16]

I was very nervous when Dr. Coral called us. What would she ask? What would she think of our Will? And about us, his parents?

Dr. Coral asked me a lot about how he *physically* felt. "Does he have a lot of headaches?" she asked.[17]

"Oh yes."

My Will always had headaches. Dr. Coral asked me about them. She knew things before I even told her.[18] I didn't realize how much Will's problem played a role in his health almost. He not only struggled academically, his brain kind of hurt at the end of the day, and I never thought of it that way.[19]

Dr. Coral said a lot of things that hit home. She asked a lot of questions, and then she said, "I can help."[20]

After the call, I felt relieved. Finally, someone understood our child and his need and was willing to take it on.[21]

The Belief System of Dysolve

I would say that the difference I noticed right away was the compassion that I felt when I got to the Dysolve Center—the understanding and appreciation of my child.[22]

Really, it almost brings tears to my eyes thinking, "Oh, he'll always struggle."[23]

But then someone said, "This is an intelligent boy. We can help him. We can change what's happening to him."

Just a few months into the program, I noticed a change in Will. His head used to be down when he got off the bus, defeated. His head was no longer down when he got off the bus.[24] He now believed he's smart and would learn how his brain needed to learn.[25] He now felt there's hope. All of us in the family felt very excited about our new journey with Will in Dysolve.[26]

I did see improvements in Will, though not right off the bat. I'm very this-is-the-way-you-do-things kind of person. My other children fit the traditional mold for school. They were the textbook students. You give them what they need; they give it back to you. Will was definitely a different type of learner. Dysolve was appreciating that but also helping him overcome his problem.[27]

Auditory Processing

The biggest thing about Dysolve for us is definitely the caring from the people who make up Dysolve, like Dr. Coral and her husband. It was incredible to me how much they believed in my child. I felt that they loved him; I still do. Will wanted to be there. Now, don't get me wrong, it's hard work, and Will is a person who doesn't always love doing the work, but I think he's a happier person because of this program. Because it was people who believed in him, saw in him what we couldn't even see at times academically.[28] They were very easy to work with and just wanted him to succeed.

We have lots of kids and are all over the board sometimes, but the Dysolve team would draw us back in.[29] They'd remind us, "Ok, you need to do this and that" in a nice way. It's like, "You want to do this for Will" and of course we do. You want to help your child in any way.

The program brings you in like a family. There was nothing hidden here. Everything they wanted you to know, you got to see. The more you know, the more you can help your child.[30]

I became involved as part of the Dysolve team and learned a lot about the Coral Method®.[31] It made it even more exciting for my child and for our entire family.

Dysolve affected even our family life, where I saw that Will's siblings kind of appreciated Will more. They understood more deeply how bright he is, how much he has to give. The belief system of Dysolve boosted everybody's confidence in Will's ability academically.[32]

He's Got It

By the eighth month in Dysolve, Will was thriving at school in 7th grade. He rarely complained of headaches anymore.[33] He had an 86% overall average that quarter. He kept his grades up while also getting into sports, band and theater.[34]

Our family could see that, finally, Will was beginning to take off and take charge of his future. He's very optimistic now and believes in himself.

Will is definitely a joiner of clubs. He's in a club where they're newscasters and they compete with other schools. They do research in a certain topic, like women in sports, and then do a newscast. This is his fourth year in it.

At the beginning, when he started in 4th grade, I was very nervous for him. To read everything, memorize it, and give it back to you, was almost like an impossible job for Will.[35] But he always wanted to do it; this was what interested him. He'd spend a lot of time preparing for it, and he'd do a good job. But his growth this year was phenomenal: though he had a much longer speech to memorize, it took him no time at all.

He had this new confidence. "Mom, I've got this."[36]

And I kept saying like, "Oh, no, no, Will, you've got to—"

And he'd say, "Mom, I've got this."

Not only that, I got the confirmation from his school teacher working in the newscasting program. She told me, "Thank you for working with Will. He did a great job."

But I hadn't been working with him that much this time. He's got it. He even got a nomination. He can do all the things now that he struggled with before. He's in plays and memorizing his lines. He does the readings in his Catholic school. He always volunteered, I'll give him that, even before he was a confident reader. But now, he doesn't need help. He can do it. That's so amazing and wonderful to see.

Setting Will Free

Twelve months into Dysolve, Will's world opened up. We'd been somewhat inconsistent at home with his training, but we'd put our best efforts forward given the business of our lives. Will left 7th grade with several awards.[37] The most important was Most Improved Student. As a mother present at the ceremony, I was so happy for him, and the look on his face was so great to see.

It's been a game-changer for Will. Dysolve retrained the brain and helped Will create the correct ways to read.[38] He is much more confident and now believes he can succeed. I can't wait for the future. It is wide open for Will.

What we wish for our son through the Dysolve Program is happiness and confidence. Not to be held back but to be able to pursue his dreams. He's often talked about being an architect or maybe an engineer. He's all over the board like young children are, but I think it's possible now and really, the sky is the limit.[39] He's still not the child that loves the academic part of life but at the same time, he can do it. He *knows* he can do it now. I always thought that he had this greatness about him, that he understood he worked differently. He persevered, and through hard work, he got stronger.[40] I'm very happy for him.

Dysolve is so different from any other program. They work with Will and *for* Will. It is so individualized that they can focus on his strengths while dealing with his "weak" spots.[41] Dysolve is setting Will free so he can make his own way, and we are all looking forward to what's in store.

MY MESSAGE TO PARENTS

I'm sure if you're like me in any way, you've tried a lot of things, spent a lot of money and had the same old answers and no results.[42] Have hope. This program works, but you have to work it. It's not no work involved on your child's part.[43]

It's like a new beginning, something new, something fresh that works and takes your individual child into account. It sees their potential, their part in this world, what they can do and what they have to offer.

Dysolve is individual and targeted, even though it is this big technology.[44] But it's also very much about your child. It's about *my* child. And if your child does it, it's about *your* child, and your child alone.

NOTES

1. There has been some research on teachers' attitudes on the inclusion of students with learning disabilities in the regular classroom. But research on teachers' attitudes toward the students themselves is scant. See Cook, B.G. (2004). Inclusive teachers' attitudes toward their students with disabilities: A replication and extension. *The Elementary School Journal, 104*(4), 307-320.
2. Prior research evidence points to high levels of stress for families of children with learning disabilities. Yet few studies investigate parental role in child outcomes. See Al-Yagon, M. (2015). Fathers and mothers of children with learning disabilities: Links between emotional and coping resources. *Learning Disability Quarterly, 38*(2), 112-128. doi:10.1177/0731948713520556
3. Besides Will, the posture of the children in Chapters 3 and 4 was also affected by their learning disability.
4. As shown in Figure 9 at the beginning of this chapter, Will's standardized reading scores registered at a low 5th percentile before Dysolve. A score below the 25th percentile is often used to classify a student as having dyslexia. See Snowling, M.J. (2000). *Dyslexia*. Oxford, UK: Blackwell.
5. Behavioral and genetic studies suggest that reading skills seem to be highly heritable. Still, more research is needed to understand how the environment and biology interact to produce different literacy outcomes in different families and in different members of the same family. See Snowling, M.J. (2008) Specific disorders and broader phenotypes: The case of dyslexia. *The Quarterly Journal of Experimental Psychology, 61*(1), 142-156. doi:10.1080/17470210701508830
6. Will faced language-processing deficits that required more than just extra tutoring or assistance. Until the underlying problems were corrected, the additional support was not effective. This was also true of the teacher and parental support given to all the other cases in this book.

7. The children in Chapters 1-6 of this book were told by their schools that they were not far enough behind in reading to qualify for special education services, even though almost all of them were two grades below when they joined Dysolve.
8. One dominant view in this field supports acceptance of the disability. In this view, schools can only help affected students cope with the problem. In contrast, Dysolve presupposes that in most cases, the problem is correctible. Thus our goal is to remove the condition for each child.
9. Apart from the mother in this chapter, the parents in Chapters 1-4 and 6 also voiced the same concern—that their children's learning problems were not fully recognized by their schools.
10. Vivian in this chapter could compare her son's development with those of her other older children to determine that a problem existed. Unfortunately for oldest or only children, parents may not realize this until much later. This happened to the cases in Chapters 1 and 2. Information on developmental milestones is available upon request at Dysolve.com and Dysolve Dyslexia on Facebook.
11. Besides Will, the cases in Chapters 1-3, 6 and 9 also demonstrated higher listening comprehension abilities compared to reading proficiency.
12. Almost all the parents in this book recognized their children's natural intelligence. Even so, many of them underestimated their children's true potential in academics until the students' problems were corrected in Dysolve. See for example the Father's Story in Chapter 1 and the Mother's Story in Chapter 4.
13. All the cases in this book except Max in Chapter 10 were below grade-level proficiency in reading before Dysolve. Most had fallen behind their classmates by at least two grade levels.
14. Vivian meant that Dysolve® is not an invasive method even though it is designed to change brain functions.
15. The parent in Chapter 3 also invested a lot of money into addressing her child's condition, but without success before Dysolve.
16. Some of the parents of our students are teachers and professors, including in English, languages, the communication arts,

and special education. Even advanced degrees in these fields are not sufficient to enable them to help their children with language-processing deficits.

17. Most of the children who come to us experience recurrent headaches, yet many do not tell adults about them. Some do not recognize them as headaches because they have become so much a part of their daily state. As Patience in Chapter 1 said, "I thought it was normal to have them." See Dr. Coral's blog *Their Heads Actually Hurt* in Dysolve Dyslexia on Facebook and child and parent blogs on the same topic.

18. At Dysolve, we make predictions on student behaviors and productions based on three decades of research and two decades of fieldwork.

19. The association between recurrent headaches and dyslexia (and ADHD) has not received much research interest. Recent studies do show a higher incidence of recurrent headaches among children with dyslexia, ADHD, and both conditions. Yet the explanations put forth remain controversial. For a review of studies, see Genizi, J., Gordon, S., Kerem, N.C., Srugo, I., Shahar, E., & Ravid, S. (2013). Primary headaches, attention deficit disorder and learning disabilities in children and adolescents. *Journal of Headache Pain, 14*(1), 54. doi: 10.1186/1129-2377-14-54

Our own fieldwork shows that headaches are common among students with dyslexia and co-occur with ADHD. Headaches or head pressure often occur when processing load increases. See also our blogs on this kind of headaches in Dysolve Dyslexia on Facebook.

20. See Note 18 above.

21. The success of a case depends on a multitude of factors that are internal and external to the child. Thus, we begin by assessing the ecosystem of support that includes the child's home and school environments. We address deficiencies in this ecosystem as needed to ensure that the child is adequately supported as he proceeds in his Dysolve program. It may be as simple as ensuring continuous, uninterrupted program participation or as involved as psychological counseling by an external provider.

22. See Note 18 above. Our knowledge base and accumulated expertise enabled us to determine accurately Will's true competence and strengths.
23. The parents in Chapters 1, 3 and 4 similarly voiced this concern that their children might struggle into adulthood.
24. Will's change in demeanor and attitude mirrored that of the children in Chapters 2-4, 6, 8 and 9.
25. At Dysolve, we explain to the child the problem that we are working together to resolve as a team. Our students favor this approach because it presupposes their intelligence in understanding the complex problem involved and their competence in helping us resolve it. Students often voice that they want to know the root cause of the problem. See Will's story at the end of this chapter. See also the Father's Story in Chapter 2.
26. Dyslexia does not only affect the child but the whole family as well. All the parents in this book described how the condition affected their family life and even extended family members.
27. Vivian explained that Will functioned differently as a learner when he first joined our program, but Dysolve focused on removing those learning differences instead of accommodating them, unlike other providers.
28. Vivian was not the only parent who had difficulty gauging her child's true academic potential. The parents in Chapters 1-4 did not as well.
29. The Dysolve Program is designed to accommodate interruptions to partipation, given the realities of family life. The recommended time for daily practice is also short for the same reason. In spite of these extenuating circumstances, Will's Dysolve program still enabled rapid improvement.
30. Dysolve educates parents so they may support their children. We believe that parents are their children's first and ultimate teachers.
31. Parents of our graduates often volunteer to advise other parents facing similar issues at the beginning of their journey. See the parent blogs in Dysolve Dyslexia on Facebook.
32. The child has to be supported by adults who show confidence in him, and he must have confidence in his own ability to

overcome the problem. These two factors were in Will's favor in his ecosystem of support. His self-perception about his ability to perform at the designated level is called *self-efficacy*. Research shows that students with high self-efficacy work harder, persist longer and achieve at higher levels. See Dale, H.S., & Pajares, F. (2009). Self-efficacy theory. In K.R. Wentzel & D.B. Miele (Eds.), *Handbook of motivation at school* (pp. 35-53). New York: Routledge.
33. The cases in Chapters 1-6 reported having headaches at school, which disappeared as they progressed in Dysolve. See also Note 19 above.
34. Due to the impact of dyslexia on social and family life, its resolution tends to free up resources for other social activities. Thus, a benefit of problem resolution is the improvement in the quality of life for the student and his family.
35. Until his language-processing deficits were resolved, memorizing lines was challenging for Will. This task is affected by processing speed, which is known to be suppressed among the majority with dyslexia. See Pennington, B.F., Cardoso-Martins, C., Green, P.A., & Lefly, D.L. (2001). Comparing the phonological and double deficit hypotheses for developmental dyslexia. *Reading and Writing: An Interdisciplinary Journal, 14,* 707–755.
36. Some of our students show great accuracy in gauging their own ability and readiness to progress to independent learning. See Dr. Coral's Story on Duke in Chapter 2.
37. In addition to Will, the students in Chapters 2 and 3 also received school awards for their progress, within the first year of Dysolve.
38. Once his underlying deficits were corrected, Will was able to read like his typical peers, as did the other students in this book. Compensatory strategies, used in other methods to help students with dyslexia cope with written language, were unnecessary.
39. The students' progress and new optimism paralleled their parents' newfound confidence in their children's future. See the cases in Chapters 1-9.
40. Some writers have attributed the resilience developed in dealing with dyslexia to the disproportionately high number

of successful entrepreneurs with this condition. However, a disproportionately high number of people with dyslexia also drop out of school and fail to realize their potential. For the former view, see for example Gladwell, M. (2013). *David and Goliath*. New York: Little, Brown and Company. For the latter, see Chapter 12 of this book.

41. As the Dysolve computer system custombuilds a program for each student, the program is more than just individualized. It is actually *individual-specific* and *individuated*. See Chapter 15 *Responsive Intelligence Technology*.
42. See Note 15 above.
43. The recommended training time on Dysolve games is 10-15 minutes for five days a week on average. Most of the cases in this book saw significant progress within the first year. Some stayed longer to acquire what they missed in their earlier grades.
44. See Note 41 above.

Father's Story

I can Fix this Problem
Vincent

Not Enough to be Self-Sufficient

When we were working with the school districts to get my son Will extra help, he was almost testing not far enough behind.[1] The school district wouldn't get him all the help he needed.[2] So we used tutors, sometimes after school, sometimes in the summer, and they would help, but did they help enough?[3] It was almost like, from year to year, Will was succeeding enough, but not enough to be self-sufficient.

It really struck us in 2nd grade, when Will's teacher said, "In all my years of teaching, I had never thought of holding a student back. But I gave it serious consideration for your son."[4]

That was an eye-opening moment. Will's teacher pointed out difficulties he was having with reading and writing in particular, and that his classmates were much farther ahead of him.

Eventually the teacher decided to advance Will to the 3rd grade nevertheless. We had Will's tutor continue to work with him over the summer and the school year for 3rd, 4th and 5th grade.

Will started enjoying books in 3rd, 4th, and 5th grades, but they were always the same kinds of books, *Diary of a Wimpy Kid, Nate the Great*—really simple books, small sentences. We read them over and over.[5] He kind of liked them. But when we tried to encourage him to read other books, any of the C.S. Lewis series—not interested.[6] Any of the Harry Potter series—not interested. He was having a hard time following the flow of the stories; he needed smaller sentences.[7]

How can One Reprogram a Brain?

At first, I was skeptical about Dysolve, thinking, "This isn't going to work. How can one reprogram the way a brain works?[8] Will needs to build his own tool set in order to deal with his problem."[9]

That tool set was what I myself developed in 5th, 6th grade. I had problems reading as well, and I developed those tool sets and worked with them. They helped me succeed through high school and college, until today.[10]

I look at confidence in different programs. As parents and consumers, we're looking around, trying to find somebody to buy a car from, or a doctor for surgery. When one of our children needed an operation, we came across a number of different doctors, and we were apprehensive. Then we came across one in New York City who said, "I can fix this problem."

I relate that to the Dysolve Program. Dr. Coral said, "I can fix this problem."[11] That gave me and my wife the confidence we were needing in a program to help our son.

A few months into Dysolve, I saw improvements in Will's reading, where he started reading bigger books and enjoying them.[12] You can catch Will now sitting in his room, reading a book instead of playing video games all the time, or watching TV shows all the time. I must also say that he still enjoys watching TV and playing video games, but that's not his number one source of entertainment anymore.

What makes me smile is seeing Will now in 8th grade. He comes home from school and says, "Dad, one of my favorite subjects is writing and reading."

"Oh, really?" That is so foreign to me. That's where Will's struggles used to be.

"I like sitting down and writing down my essays. My teacher likes my writing. She thinks I'm creative," says the boy who used to resist doing his homework.[13]

Will doing his schoolwork and being a self-motivator—this was one of his weaknesses before. My wife and I had to push him to do his homework.[14] I'm not going to lie, it's still a struggle pushing a 13-year-old to do his homework every night, but once he gets going, it's easier for him to be independent nowadays.

I'm a swim coach, and as a coach, you look into encouraging your swimmers and athletes. I find Dysolve and the people working there do just that: They're great coaches. They encourage and really want to see their students succeed.[15] While their students succeed, it brings them pleasure and joy. And that's what I see as a sign of a great coach.

MY MESSAGE TO PARENTS

There's work required for your student to succeed in Dysolve. The problem's not going to be fixed overnight.[16] It's not going to be fixed in one week, two weeks. Really, sticking it out, not seeing any improvement in three weeks, four weeks, as a parent, you start to think, "I thought it was going to be a quick fix. Are they going to help my child here?"

But Month 4, 5, I started seeing improvements with my son, from him doing the program easier, from him getting that enjoyment from reading independently.[17]

I find a lot of parents today spend a lot of money on sports programs. They're doing a lot of extra clinics, travel teams. They instill into their children the requirement to do their absolute best in these programs. Do these clinics. Go to these all-day affairs on the weekends. I would love to see parents do that for their children academically because I think the tools that you'll give them in a program like Dysolve will really help them way beyond high school, varsity sports, and Division 1 college sports.

It's going to help them with their future.

NOTES

1. See Note 4 in the Mother's Story in this chapter.
2. The cases in Chapters 1-6 were unable to obtain support services they requested. See Chapter 12 on the economics of dyslexia.
3. Reading progress in students with special needs may be negligible when we factor in the advances made by typical students year after year. The targeted goal should be grade-level proficiency, yet remediation methods popularly used in schools and by private providers often fail to reach it. Even reading experts at university clinics have failed to change the outcome significantly for struggling readers. See Fuchs, D., Compton, D.L., Fuchs, L.S., Bryant, V.J., Hamlett, C.L., & Lambert, W. (2012). First-grade cognitive abilities as long-term predictors of reading comprehension and disability status. *Journal of Learning Disabilities, 45*(3) 217–231.
4. Grade retention was also considered for the students in Chapters 1 and 4. Skye in Chapter 3 was retained, but it did not help her meet grade standards until her problem was resolved in Dysolve.
5. By reading over these simple books repeatedly, Will learned to memorize the words without having to decode them.
6. The students in all the other chapters also did not develop an interest in independent reading until their language-processing problems were resolved.
7. Because decoding words took up more mental resources than typical for Will, he could not deal with longer, more complex sentences.
8. See Chapters 14 and 15 on the new science.
9. With compensatory methods, which are popularly used in schools and by private providers, students are given a set of techniques to help them cope with their deficits for life. In contrast, with the corrective method of Dysolve, students read and write with the same techniques used by the typical population, after their problems are resolved.
10. Only about 15% of students with learning disabilities (LD) were able to go to college in 2014, compared to 66% of the

general population. The majority of students with LD have dyslexia. See Office of Special Education and Rehabilitative Services, Office of Special Education Programs. (2014). *36th Annual Report to Congress on the Implementation of the Individuals with Disabilities Education Act, 2014.* Washington, DC: US Department of Education.
11. When we can identify the specific language-processing deficits, we know the procedures needed to resolve them.
12. As Will's language-processing issues cleared, he was able to perform the numerous subprocesses of reading, such as word decoding and syntactic (sentence) analysis. Consequently, he was able to deal with texts that were more complex lexically (vocabulary), semantically (meaning) and syntactically. He was also able to sustain these operations for longer periods without encountering cognitive overload.
13. The students in Chapters 1 and 6 received awards from writing competitions after going through Dysolve.
14. All the parents in this book had to push their children to do homework, significantly more than typical. (The only exception was Grace in Chapter 7, who was unusually compliant and motivated.) These children worked independently on their homework and test preparation as their problems were corrected in Dysolve.
15. We encourage students to keep progressing because clearing each processing issue brings them closer to resolving their otherwise debilitating condition. As Dysolve charts out each student's expected trajectory of progress, we can see ahead what needs to be accomplished for problem resolution.
16. See Chapter 2 on progress in Dysolve that may stay latent for some time before emerging in the form of significant academic achievement.
17. Independent reading or reading for pleasure is one of the signs that dyslexia has been corrected. A child will only choose to perform the task voluntarily if it no longer exhausts mental energy to the point of physical discomfort, as often happens to our students who experience headaches from reading before Dysolve.

Dr. Coral's Story

Motivation

A Full Life

"Can you break down the word?[1] Take your time." I tried my most soothing voice to reassure Will, a 7th grader at our first training session.

Will hesitated, stumbled, and gave up without finishing the word. Surprise at the unexpected difficulty, annoyance at his own struggle, and sadness all flitted across his beautiful face.[2]

"Try again. Take your time."

Failed again. He couldn't even remember the whole word.[3] He stayed very still, but the emotions that swept across his face betrayed the mighty effort needed to keep himself in check. Part of his brain told him it should be easy, mindless; the other refused to obey. As in a dream, unable to will your foot to take a step. He leaned in.

"Slow it down. Try again."

Will's crystal-clear eyes reflected his confusion. The room was no longer stable but was starting to list.[4] He sank deeper into himself.[5] He shrank a few inches.[6]

"Oh, Will, you look so sad!" his mother, Vivian, exclaimed, watching his first session.

The effort melted his mighty will, his natural optimism. He could no longer hide his pain. I walked over and hugged him. "I know you're very bright. How do I know that? Because I've worked with a lot of bright kids like you, studied them and written about them.[7] You just have a processing problem to deal with, that's all. I'm not just saying that you're smart. I *know* you're smart."

He must have heard his parents and relatives reassure him how smart he was many times before. I thought it might help to have a stranger, an expert reiterate it for him this time.

Later Vivian told me that Will was quiet, pensive on their ride home that evening. In the enveloping darkness, he spoke up. "Mom, she cares."

It would take a granite heart not to care for Will. His beatific face opens to a kind and loving soul. Will was the kind of person who'd run to offer you a chair in a crowded room or walk up to you to chat if you're looking lost and alone.

He was frank about his problem. He'd tell his friends, "Oh, didn't you know? I have dyslexia!" An open and openhearted boy born with more than his fair share of optimism and exuberance.

Outside of this problem, Will led a full life. He ran for class president though he never won, acted in plays though he had trouble memorizing lines, volunteered to read in church though he stumbled, marched in the band, helped out at events big and small, and earned pocket money running a stand at a carnival. If I were to pick one student who'd still be fine in life without the help of Dysolve, it would be Will.[8]

Auditory Processing

His large and loving family, with deep and valued ties to many in his hometown, would have ensured that. Grandparents, uncles, aunts, cousins—a large extended family, a family not in want. A cherished childhood rich with many, many happy memories.

Will's parents, Vivian and Vincent, doted on every one of their many children. Children give away much about their home life. Will and his siblings showed their parents' careful tending. Impeccable manners, immaculate dressing. Vivian was the kind of mother who'd be the first—and often the only one—to volunteer at her children's schools. She and her husband have this gift of making you feel that you're their good friends for life. This rare, precious quality is in their Will.

True, Will was down at times from having to struggle through yet another day at school, but he always bounced back.[9] And quickly. Life was a creation, a discovery, an adventure—sculpting winning sand castles, renovating the house with his Dad, and sharing their love of cars at off-road events. There was too much to life to let his dyslexia dampen it for long. And Will already had his dream carved out—to build things, to be an architect.

Catching the Tailwind

Will was one of the first batch of students to try out our online games when Dysolve transitioned to full automation. Unlike games for entertainment, Dysolve games have a singular, practical goal: correct a specific deficit. That means daily practice, not just when you feel like it. It also means stretching your capability to the limit, not walking away when you're frustrated; and sometimes tolerating discomfort like head pressure, not quitting because you've had had enough.[10]

Everybody needs a reward. For Will, the reward is going to the college of his dreams, to become an architect. From my own son's experience, I knew how much the interest of an older boy meant to a younger one. At that time, our son was studying architecture at Cornell, a top-ranked school in this field. We introduced our architect-to-be to the architect student-to-be. The undergrad gave Will a Cornell T-shirt in the school's vibrant red. Vivian sent us a photo of Will wearing his Cornell shirt. His Mom had to wash it every day because he was wearing it every day.[11]

Will joined Dysolve in September of 7th grade. A few months later, his training was interrupted often by the holiday season and other family obligations. We pressed his family to make Dysolve their priority.[12] As processing problems are challenging to correct, any improvement has to be reinforced immediately so as not to lose that hard-won gain. Our fieldwork shows that changes can happen very quickly with the brain, so long as the learner keeps pushing to break through.[13]

Will's academic work started to improve five months into Dysolve, although in reality it was only three months of intensive work after discounting the interruptions to training.[14] Eight months after he joined Dysolve, Will's academic life took a 180-degree turn. He graduated 7th grade with the Most Improved Student Award from his school.[15]

Almost to a year since he joined Dysolve, we asked Will to talk to one of our younger students, Prince.[16] Fourth-grader Prince was going through a particularly rough patch and needed a morale boost from somebody closer to his own age.

The younger boy looked up tentatively when Will walked into the room. They shook hands and sat down.

"I know what it's like because it was like that for me too at the beginning," Will assured Prince.

"At first, the games were like catching the tailwind of an airplane. I couldn't do anything about it. It just blew me away. Then, slowly, I passed one game, then another, and another. And it became very easy."[17] Will spoke in metaphors, the language of Prince.

The younger boy leaned in. His face opened up. I left the room to let them chat. When I went back in, the two boys were talking animatedly about their shared love—cars.

"Can I see Will again?" Prince begged me.

We made that Prince's reward when he scored in his games.

Upright

Will needed barely a year of Dysolve to correct his dyslexia. His teachers noticed his remarkable turnaround. His tutor of many years noticed it. Old friends of the family commented on the new Will.[18]

A year out of the program, Will returned to our Dysolve Center to volunteer as a MathCounts coach for students in middle school.[19] He was now a freshman in high school. By now he was taller than I. A young man, standing upright.[20] A veneer of guardedness now shielded his old child-like openness, as it should.

We nodded to each other, greeting from afar.

THE PROBLEM AND OUR SOLUTION

Our initial evaluation showed that Will experienced processing deficits that affected both language reception and production. He faced problems with auditory processing and verbal production. During Dysolve exercises initially, he frequently could not retain the exact forms of words he heard.[21] "Just saying some words launched me into a tailspin." An articulate person describing his inexplicable difficulty.[22]

Our Dysolve team knew right from the start that Will would succeed, just by watching him play his games.[23] Although he was often fidgety during our manual exercises, he was able to control his restlessness during gameplay.[24] This restlessness led his parents to research ADHD when he was younger.[25]

We asked Will before he started on his first game, "Do you want to switch to another chair?" We always advise students not to sit on swivel chairs, because they have to keep still and focus all their energy on the game, especially if it's a speed game.[26]

"Oh, I didn't realize it swivels. I'm ok." Will stayed put, crouching to sprint at the starting gate.

Auditory Processing

He clicked the Start button. Game over in just 10 seconds. He didn't get past. Start button again. Game over. Back to Start. Game over. Repeat cycle. Again. And again.

Will did not pause or look around each time he failed. He got right back in the game. Re-hit Start. Over and over again. His swivel chair as still as he was. Torso angled forward. Eyes laser-focused on the screen. Only his fingers moved, tapping the keys.

Will was the only Dysolve student who was not distracted by another person tapping on the keyboard next to him. We could work at the adjoining desk, and Will would just keep going at his games without so much as a glance up. His intensity was palpable. He was going to beat this thing, and he willed it to happen before high school.

Will would go through 40 fails in one stretch and still get back into the game without so much as a pause. He kept fighting his way through, past his ego, past his headaches, past the old habits of mind that clung on stubbornly. Will. How could such a fighter not succeed in life?[27]

Will's Dysolve measures showed a gradual climb, with improvements sometimes plateauing for weeks before climbing again.[28] Figure 10 shows this signature pattern for auditory processing in a span of 12 weeks. With Word List 1, Will's performance plateaued from Weeks 5-11, meaning he kept failing his games consecutively for six weeks. With Word List 3, he plateaued twice, from Weeks 2-6 and Weeks 8-12, meaning that he failed two-thirds of the time. We expect frequent failures because Dysolve has to expand a learner's capability beyond his present limit. After all, it is not easy to reorganize the brain. *During those times when improvement is latent rather than overt, it is critical that the student does not give up.*[29] When Will's underlying deficits cleared, his school grades shot up suddenly in 7th grade during his first year in Dysolve.[30]

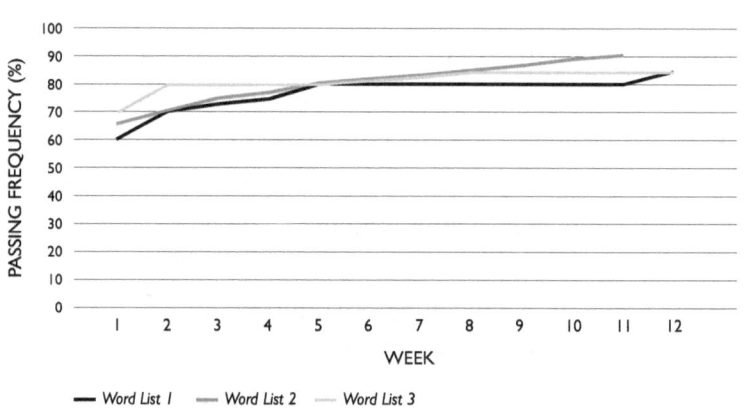

FIGURE 10
Will – Gradual Improvement in Auditory Processing in Year 1 of Dysolve

After this intense struggle, Will was better prepared than his classmates for the big jump in expectations in 8th grade for everyone. He received 100% in spelling for the first time and the highest score in the first paper of his English class. He discovered his love of writing.[31] His English scores now registered consistently in the 80s—a big change from registering below the 10th percentile in standardized reading tests in earlier years.

QUESTION

Luckily for Will, his parents brought him to Dysolve two years before high school. He still had time to catch up before preparations for college admission. So is it better to correct the problem when the student is younger or older? Based on our experience, both have their pros and cons.

Young children sometimes surprise us by the speed at which their brains readjust to new demands.[32] Sometimes, they clear a hurdle in just one session. However, children in pre-K or kindergarten may not be motivated to change because they do not fully appreciate the long-term consequences of dyslexia. Also, parents have to be committed to supervising them, at the very least to make sure they do play their games daily. On the other hand, early correction may avoid the detrimental effects of a learning disability on self-image and attitude towards academics.[33] As early as kindergarten, some of our students already label themselves as "stupid." For our younger graduates, their early disability, once resolved, is a faint memory soon to be forgotten.[34] Besides, they do not have much to catch up on if they fall behind in the early grades.

By 5th grade, students typically acquire 10,000 new words or more a year.[35] Therefore, the longer that language problems stay uncorrected, the harder it is to catch up. On top of spelling acquisition, older students face increasing demands from more subject matter to study and lengthier homework. At the same time, however, they can tap into their more developed cognitive abilities to learn new skills and self-correct. That is, they are more metacognitively aware—knowing how they themselves function as learners and thinkers.[36]

We saw this in action when observing Will in front of the computer screen. Every time he failed a game, he reanalyzed what he did wrongly and how he could do it better the next time. When he misspelled words, he changed his hypotheses to internalize the right spelling rules.

Older students also have larger long-term goals. Will had his sights on being an architect. He knew what he needed to accomplish to get there. He would put up with the uncomfortable exercises, the frustration of consecutive fails, the challenge of climbing a summit where the trails are so slippery he couldn't hang on to prevent from sliding right back down again and again.

Why? Because he understood what was waiting for him when he got to the peak.[37]

NOTES

1. Dyslexia research has long associated the condition to the lack of phonological awareness—the ability to detect and manipulate the sounds (phonemes) and sound patterns of one's language. However, finer-grained explanations for this deficit remain speculative to date. The segmentation hypothesis proposes that deficient underlying phonological representations primarily caused this deficit. Phonological representations are the learner's mental representations of the sound structures of words. For a brief overview of the theoretical background, see for example Boada, R., & Pennington, B.F. (2006). Deficient implicit phonological representations in children with dyslexia. *Journal of Experimental Child Psychology, 95*(3), 153-193. Retrieved from https://doi.org/10.1016/j.jecp.2006.04.003
2. Students with dyslexia often fail to recognize deficits in their linguistic ability. The condition is strongly associated with the lack of phonological awareness. See Note 1 above.
3. Individuals with language-processing deficits are often seen as "forgetful." See Chapter 1.
4. See Will's Story at the end of this chapter.
5. Through our observational studies and case study methodology, we see up close the concrete instances that cumulatively lead to defeatism.
6. See the Mother's Story in this chapter on Will's posture before Dysolve. See also the change in posture reported in Chapters 3 and 4.
7. As with so many of our students, Will is twice-exceptional. "Exceptional" refers to those who are outside the typical, at either end of the spectrum. Thus, one can be exceptional for having gifts or deficits. That is why those with both are called *twice-exceptional*. Even though many of them register IQ scores in the average or slightly above the average range, their actual intelligence levels are usually higher because their achievement is suppressed by language-processing deficits prior to their joining Dysolve.

8. Will is an exception to the general trend due to his robust ecosystem of support and personal strengths. See Chapter 12 for the grim outlook for the population with learning disabilities in the US.
9. Most of our students, as with the cases in this book, do not feel well physically at school. Head pressure often builds up in the course of the school day due to cognitive overload. We recommend downtime right after school to allow the headaches to dissipate. See descriptions of this problem in Chapters 1, 3-6.
10. Our own fieldwork shows that headaches are common among students with dyslexia and co-occur with ADHD. However, the exact physiology of these events is not clear at this point. The association between headaches and dyslexia (and ADHD) has not received much research interest. Recent studies do show a higher incidence of recurrent headaches among children with dyslexia, ADHD, and both conditions. Yet the explanations put forth remain controversial. One hypothesis uses overlapping brain mechanisms to account for the associations. A second hypothesis suggests that learning disabilities and ADHD create stresses that induce headaches. A third speculates that frequent headaches hinder learning and cause ADHD behaviors. A fourth proposes a common disorder underlying headaches and ADHD. Which is the cause? Which is the effect? Depending on the hypothesis, headaches can be either. For a review of studies, see Genizi, J., Gordon, S., Kerem, N.C., Srugo, I., Shahar, E., & Ravid, S. (2013). Primary headaches, attention deficit disorder and learning disabilities in children and adolescents. *Journal of Headache Pain, 14*(1), 54. doi:10.1186/1129-2377-14-54
11. In Chapter 2, the gift of a university computer bag had a similar motivational effect on Duke.
12. See Chapter 11 on prioritizing this condition as a crisis.
13. See Uno's case in Chapter 8.
14. Tremendous improvements within three months were also recorded for the cases in Chapters 8 and 9 going through the automated program.
15. The cases in Chapters 1 and 3 also received Most Improved Awards from their schools.

16. See the description of the meeting between Will and Prince in the next chapter.
17. Our students report that linguistic-cognitive tasks that were initially difficult quickly became easy with practice, indicating the speed of brain reorganization.
18. Changes in demeanor were also reported for all the other cases in the book.
19. For further description of this volunteer program, see the Founder's Story in Chapter 7.
20. See Note 6 above.
21. See early works on auditory processing and learning disabilities in these references: Heath, S.M., Hogben, J.H., & Clark, C.D. (1999). Auditory temporal processing in disabled readers with and without oral language delay. *Journal of Child Psychology and Psychiatry, 40*, 637-647. doi:10.1017/S0021963099003947. Sternberg, R.J., & Grigorenko, E.L. (1999). *Our labeled children: What every parent and teacher needs to know about learning disabilities.* Cambridge, MA: Perseus. Snowling, M.J. (2000). *Dyslexia.* Oxford, UK: Blackwell.
22. Students with language-processing deficits often exhibit seemingly paradoxical behaviors on the surface. The surface contradictions can be resolved by understanding their root causes. For example, Duke in Chapter 2 was highly intelligent but could not read. Storm in Chapter 4 was verbally articulate but could not spell. Prince in Chapter 6 used sophisticated words but could not follow instructions. Max in Chapter 10 could read but could not write.
23. Some Dysolve interactive games require, and hence encourage, focused concentration for extended periods. Two of the most commonly reported characteristics of ADHD are "easy distractibility" and "short attention spans." Research also notes that these traits are highly variable even within the same individual and are task- and context-dependent. See Wender, P.H. (2001). *ADHD: Attention-deficit hyperactivity disorder in children, adolescents, and adults.* New York: Oxford University Press.
24. The cognitive overload often manifested itself as physical symptoms characteristic of ADHD. See Chapter 6 on ADHD.

25. Will was not diagnosed with ADHD. However, he and Patience in Chapter 1 did exhibit typical symptoms similar to the other cases who were diagnosed with the condition by their pediatricians. On the other hand, Duke in Chapter 2, who was diagnosed with ADHD, did not exhibit all the characteristic symptoms frequently, such as restlessness.
26. Processing speed has often been mentioned as a core component of the deficits underlying dyslexia. However, its role and relation to other components are still unclear in the research literature. See Elliott, J.G., & Grigorenko, E.L. (2014). *The dyslexia debate.* New York: Cambridge University Press.
27. By junior high school, even typical students start to exhibit two distinct patterns of responses to challenging academic situations. One group shows a pattern of helplessness and blames failure on lack of ability, which members view as a fixed entity. In contrast, the other group shows a pattern of optimism because ability is seen as changeable. These self-theories play a critical role on motivation at school. Their impact is magnified when students have learning disabilities. For the general topic of motivation, see Wentzel, K.R., & Miele, D.B. (2009). *Handbook of motivation at school.* New York: Routledge.
28. Dysolve® measures improvements at the micro level. See Chapter 14 *Computational Microlinguistics.*
29. Self-motivation becomes the remaining factor for success when other critical variables, such as program efficacy and a positive learning environment, have been secured.
30. School grades of Dysolve students typically tend to follow a knee-of-the curve upward trajectory rather than a gradual climb when underlying deficits are corrected. This can be seen in the other chapters of this book.
31. The students in Chapters 1 and 6 later won writing awards. See also Skye's and Storm's own writing in Chapters 3 and 4 respectively.
32. Third grader Uno in Chapter 8 and second grader User2 in Chapter 9 experienced huge improvements within a short span of 3-4 months.

33. Although the cases in this book demonstrate that Dysolve can resolve language-processing problems for older students, we promote early screening in preschool before the onset of detrimental psychosocial and other effects.
34. See Uno's case in Chapter 8.
35. Shaywitz, S. (2003). *Overcoming dyslexia*. New York: Vintage Books.
36. Understanding and talking about one's own learning and thinking processes builds metacognition.
37. Will's maturity, as the oldest student in this book, may explain his goal-oriented performance.

Will's Story

Nothing's Going to Hold You Back

Carrying a Car

Before Dysolve, it was hard to pass tests. Spelling, I got like 40s. I would spend so long studying for spelling tests, but it wouldn't really show that I studied at all.[1] It took me two hours a night for each day of the week for me to get a 70, which isn't even that good.

Homework was super hard. It would take me three hours to get a bit done.[2] It seemed impossible. In school, everybody seemed so much better than me in almost everything, besides math.[3] Everybody was progressing, and I wasn't. It just wasn't working for me. I knew there was something wrong, something that had to be fixed.[4]

During classes, I would get major headaches.[5] I'd have to go to the nurse's office. I felt terrible physically. Dyslexia really holds your body back, because every time you tried to do something, it'd give you a headache, say, it'd make you feel depressed or sad because you couldn't do it.[6]

When I entered Dysolve, it was pretty hard. It took me a while to get used to the program. It was emotionally challenging, it was physically challenging, and it was personally challenging. During training, I would get a headache.[7] I wouldn't want to do it anymore, but I knew I had to keep on going or I wouldn't make it anywhere.[8]

At first, the program felt like me carrying a car or something like that, super-heavyweight. You really couldn't move anywhere. *Progressing through, I felt the load just got lighter and lighter until it became easier and very easy.*[9]

What really pushed me through, to keep on going was to do like everybody else, to get good grades in tests. I wanted to bc like my classmates and all my good friends.[10]

After going through Dysolve for a year, I went to my tutor over the summer, who complimented me on my great ability with writing now, which I never really had. My teachers were happy for me. They saw great improvement. They're impressed by my writing, my spelling grades, ELA grades, all of them, really. My friends realized I had more time to hang out with them because I didn't have to spend so much time on schoolwork anymore.[11]

MY MESSAGE TO DYSOLVE STUDENTS

You just have to keep on going.[12] Don't give up. If you keep on going, you'll make it somewhere. With Dysolve, you're going to get so much farther. Speed was a huge improvement for me. It's your homework time—it takes so much less time for me now.[13] Really, anything you do, it'd be so much faster than you did before. You'll have skills that other people don't have.[14] Use those skills to help yourself and others around you.

One of my hopes gained through this program was to be an architect, to design structures. The program helped me realize I can do anything. Nothing's going to hold me back.[15] And nothing's going to hold *you* back.

MY MESSAGE TO TEACHERS

Students can tell that teachers have favorites.[16] In my class, the teacher favored every girl and two of the smartest boys. When these students did something bad, the teacher ignored it. The punishment is greater for the rest of us. We get yelled at just for talking in class.

Teachers don't get the reasons for grades being low. They think that you are not trying or are being careless. Teachers should know that some of us are trying our hardest but can't get the answer.[17] Or we make mistakes we don't notice.[18]

Teachers should give more detailed instructions for assignments.[19] We can get overwhelmed when there are not enough props for essay writing. Outline what to do and also what *not* to do.[20]

NOTES

1. Research shows that spelling error patterns differ between those with and without dyslexia. Dysolve students shift from former patterns to the latter as their language-processing problems are corrected. Thus, spelling error patterns serve as early signs of problem resolution. See Dr. Coral's Story in Chapters 1-4. See also Bernstein, S.E. (2009). Phonology, decoding, and lexical compensation in vowel spelling errors made by children with dyslexia. *Reading and Writing, 22*(3), 307-331.
2. See Note 14 in the Father's Story in this chapter.
3. The students in Chapters 2, 3 and 6 were also strong in math. Studies on the population with dyslexia have not been able to establish a spatial advantage. Spatial talent is helpful in some areas of math. High-ability students in math generally fall into three groups: those who have strong visual-spatial skills, those who favor verbal-analytical skills, and those who use a mixture of both. See the classic study by Krutetskii, V.A. (1976). *The psychology of mathematical abilities in schoolchildren.* Chicago: University of Chicago Press. Dyslexia research has instead focused more on weaknesses in math. See Gilger, J.W., Allen, K., & Castillo, A. (2016). Reading disability and enhanced dynamic spatial reasoning: A review of the literature. *Brain and Cognition, 105,* 55–65.
4. Instead of this view that the deficit needed correction, some in the field consider this problem a "learning difference." See Chapter 17 *Our Answers to Your Questions*.
5. See Notes 17 and 19 about headaches in the Mother's Story in this chapter.
6. Language-processing issues can affect a person physically due to recurrent headaches caused by cognitive overload and posture changes reflecting feelings of defeatism.
7. See Chapter 6 on headaches and ADHD symptoms.
8. See Note 37 on motivation in Dr. Coral's Story in this chapter.
9. The brain reorganizes and adjusts functionally in response to new input and activities. This is called *neuroplasticity*.

10. Being like their friends was also the motivating factor for the boys in Chapters 2, 6 and 8.
11. One of the primary reasons for a corrective program such as Dysolve is to improve quality of life by removing the condition.
12. Duke in Chapter 2 and Prince in Chapter 6 also encouraged other students not to give up.
13. Some Dysolve games are designed to improve certain aspects of language processing, which collectively affect text comprehension and information retrieval, i.e., tasks involved in homework assignments.
14. Some Dysolve games help develop advanced linguistic-cognitive skills.
15. This new optimism was echoed by the students in Chapters 1-3 and 6.
16. See Storm's Story in Chapter 4.
17. See the Principal's Story about the lack of teacher preparation in learning disabilities.
18. Monitoring one's linguistic production to detect errors requires additional mental resources that a student with processing deficits may not have.
19. See Patience's message in Chapter 1 about the need for teachers to break down instructions even further for students with processing difficulties.
20. Will gives sound advice on the need to provide clear constraints for assignments. Students need to know what *not* to do in addition to what to do. See Storm's story in Chapter 4 on the problems he encountered in trying to determine the former without his teacher's explicit instructions.

Key Takeaways

Self-motivation, a strong support system and predictive analytics help ensure students' success.

Even extremely low reading achievement may be improved quickly.

Language-processing deficits should be corrected immediately regardless of age.

Dyslexia Dissolved

6

Prince

ADHD

Prince

Dysolve Finding:
Language-processing deficits leading to dyslexia and ADHD symptoms[1, 2]

School Classification:
ADHD

School Services:
Academic Intervention Services for Reading

Doctor's Diagnosis:
ADHD

ADHD

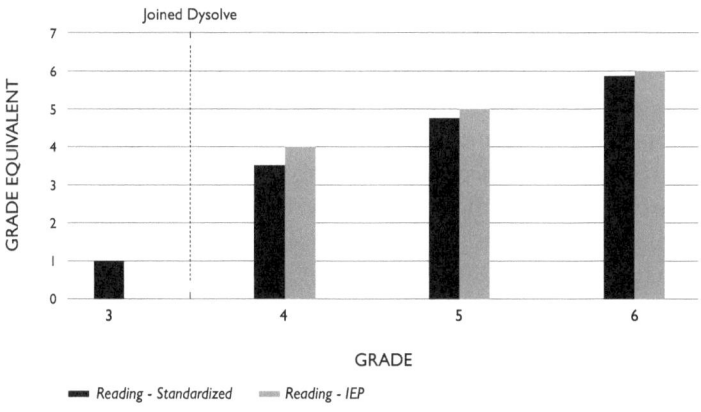

FIGURE 11
*Prince – School Standardized Reading Scores
by Grade Equivalent
before and after Joining Dysolve*[3]

NOTES

1. By *language-processing deficits*, we mean deficiencies in the processes involved in executing the language functions of speaking, listening, reading or writing.
2. *ADHD* refers to Attention Deficit/Hyperactivity Disorder. It is also referred to as *ADD* as well as other labels that have been updated over the years. The core components of this condition are inattention, hyperactivity and impulsivity.

    ADHD is described in detail in this chapter. There are many unanswered questions associated with this condition in the research literature. See for example Hinshaw, S.P., & Scheffler, R.M. (2014). *ADHD explosion: Myths, medication, money, and today's push for performance.* New York: Oxford University Press.
3. Prince's standardized reading scores are based on STAR Reading Assessment and Fountas & Pinnell Benchmark Assessment Systems administered by his school. *IEP* refers to Individualized Education Program (or Plan). The IEP scores in Figure 11 are from Prince's IEP Progress Reports documenting his achievement of targeted goals.

Dr. Coral's Story

Language-Related ADHD

Can You See Me Now?

On my screen was a T-shirt with a big green frog covering the whole chest. No human head though. Prince had leaned so far back in his chair that that was all I could see.

"Prince, hey, Prince. Can you sit up, please?" That must have been my 11th request. It was our weekly conference online.

Thump! He swung forward so swiftly that I missed his face again. Now one eyeball filled the whole screen. Prince's.

"Can you see me now? Can you see me now?" he teased.

"Sit back. I need to see your whole face." I tried again.

No luck. Ka-thump! I caught glimpses of jackets hanging on the door, part of a table leg, a couple of earth-toned decorations, then his ceiling. Prince had knocked his device off the table.

"Come on, I need to see you." I waited patiently for the 10-year-old.

He appeared head to hip, standing in silhouette.

"I still can't see you," I cajoled.

"How about now?" His eye sockets cast deep shadows skyward, lit up with a desk lamp from the chin up, horror-movie style.

Finally, he showed up on my screen right side up, sitting down, fully lit. "Are you ready to begin?" he said mockingly, glancing sideways with mischievous eyes and a disarming dimple.

If babies weren't so cute, the human race might not have survived. I named him *Prince* because he could be so charming.

Prince wasn't always fooling around when we conferenced. Most of the time, he couldn't help it. His language-processing problems were so severe that his ADHD symptoms often popped up like whack-a-mole.[1] Prince would flop around like a wet rag doll. Torso slumped on the table, or arched back on the chair, leaning to the right, to the left, and sometimes sliding off completely onto the floor.[2]

He'd climb out from under the table. "Wait—I have to ask my Mom something." And he'd be gone again.[3]

We could only work with Prince in small doses, before his ADHD erupted. He had one of the worst cases of ADHD we'd ever seen.[4]

When Prince joined Dysolve in 4th grade, I told his Mom that it would take more than a year to resolve his problems. I seldom am so sure that a student would need that long. On most Dysolve indices, Prince's scores fell in the Very High Risk range whereas most of our students with dyslexia scored mainly in the Medium - High Risk ranges only. So deep and broad-ranging were Prince's processing deficits I was confident we couldn't clear them any sooner.

Prince was only reading at the 1st grade level in 3rd grade. There was also the ADHD to contend with. Only Adeline, his Mom, would commit to their resolution, no matter how long it took.

Alpha Mom

Adeline was a stealth alpha mom. Alpha moms go all out to take care of their children's needs, no matter how high the obstacles. Adeline did this quietly in her low-key way, but with the same effective results.

Her college degree and professional training gave her the tools to educate herself on her son's condition. She bought books to learn as much as possible about dyslexia and ADHD, and even found out about the weaknesses in an education system that does not include extensive teacher training in special needs.[5]

"If they only take one course in the exceptional child and only cover dyslexia in one week, which is about three hours at most, how is that enough preparation?" she wondered.

Research, learn, practice. And commit. Adeline even offered to advocate for us to get help to other students at Prince's school.

Because of the severity of Prince's problems, Adeline agreed that he needed face-to-face consultation on top of online games. We could have done it with online conferencing, but when Prince said that he preferred onsite visits, Adeline drove him to our Dysolve Center every Sunday evening, 45 minutes one way. Night came before they left. Adeline would pack in her van two kids plus her elderly mother who could not be left alone at home. They waited in the parking lot for an hour. That's what family does for one another.

After a full day's work, Adeline returned home to start her *other* job as a single mom.[6] Her professional efficiency she passed on to Prince. He started our first training session with a fancy leather organizer. Prince took out his notebook and used to-do lists. Adeline had nurtured the value of being organized. If only every parent would do this favor for their children—and for their teachers.

Despite his dyslexia and ADHD, Adeline did not let Prince slack in his homework and test preps. They practiced every single night for a vocabulary test the following week, distributed parts of a book report throughout the languid days of summer, and completed a science fair project through the winter weeks.[7] Prince's teachers peppered his report cards with "We can always count on him to do his best!" and "Prince is a hard worker."

In return, Adeline did not skimp on rewards for Prince. While the rest of us struggled through a particularly bruising winter, Adeline packed her kids into the car and drove three hours to the Winter Olympics Site at Lake Placid for a day's outing. Another trip to Hershey Park would follow when Prince graduated from Dysolve.

It was a two-way street. "I want to design cars. The first one is for my Mom. It's a van because she needs to drive five people and a dog." Prince dedicated his future to his Mom first.

"Look, Mom, see what I got!" He had to share everything with Adeline, tousling her hair while she smiled.

They were always connected—his arm draped around her shoulders, his body leaning against hers.

"Don't forget my reward!" He rubbed his nose against hers playfully. She smiled back. That was *her* reward.[8]

Good Student, Good School

Prince was very exact in his description of what was happening to him. He had an affinity for metaphors.[9]

"I'm outside the building going round and round trying to find the door in."

Most of the time, he could see no door open to get in. Locked out of his own mind.

Over a year into Dysolve, his head still hurt and he was still fidgety. More often than not, he got frustrated with himself. When he couldn't articulate a word, he started slapping his own mouth. I caught his hand. The only way to stop him was to resolve his problem.

During calmer moments of reflection, he cheered himself on.[10] "I think there're about five stories. I'm on the third floor now!"

Prince wanted to do well. He could *see* himself as a good student. He wanted to please. He would put in the effort, no matter how much. Only when the effort still turned in a disappointing score would he get discouraged momentarily. He was very sensitive about doing poorly. He referred to a low score he received in a quiz as "the-thing-we-will-not-talk-about."

Adeline had carefully chosen a close-knit, caring school community to put down roots. Prince's teachers were skilled and gentle with their students. His school allowed him to walk about the room, use a stress ball and chew gum if he needed to accommodate his ADHD. By 4th grade, his school curriculum expected students to use basic literary terms and recognize genres. His teachers did their best to help Prince meet their standards. Whenever Adeline queried, his teachers replied promptly in great detail.

It was a setting that cradled his problems, yet there was so much more that Prince needed.[11]

Meds

Prince had taken medications for his ADHD in 2nd grade, but before he started Dysolve in 4th grade, Adeline had stopped them. Could he function without these chemicals?[12] She wanted to know.

Despite his restlessness, we were able to keep Prince going at Dysolve, as did his Mom at home. He kept up his school grades. But then 19 months into Dysolve, his teachers started to complain of attention issues that were getting out of hand. At Dysolve too, Debbie, one of our instructors who worked with Prince, reported similar problems.

Adeline started questioning her earlier decision. Should he go back to taking medication? Would a counselor on adolescent behavior help? Around this time, Prince grew several sizes, an 11-year-old the height of a 14-year-old.

Things were coming to a head.

New Prince

"Did you see the new Prince?!" Debbie asked me, barely controlling her excitement.

Twenty months into Dysolve, it finally clicked for Prince. His transformation happened in one momentous week in October, just as fall foliage changed overnight.[13] As instantly as toddlers enter the terrible twos.

"Yes! I saw it too!" I texted Debbie back, after our session.

Prince came into the room, took out his binder, and laid out his notes. He directed me, "Come on, let's do this. Quiz me. I want to read. Let me read it to you. Let's do the questions."[14] He used up the full hour and didn't want to stop. He sat upright throughout, all business.

After our session, we walked out together to meet his mother in the waiting room. I told him, "You have everything. Brains, looks, charm, talent, a loving family." Adeline beamed.

"Come to my birthday!" He invited me without checking with his Mom first.

"Oh, I don't know. I'm not sure I want to hang out with 12 boisterous boys," I hesitated.

"Oh, but you come to my house on my actual birthday! My friends are coming the day before." That was the most earnest invitation that we had ever received from a 12-year-old.

That was *our* reward.

THE PROBLEM

Prince started Dysolve in 4th grade with a host of language-processing deficits. His reading was two grades behind. He had frequent headaches and could not remember instructions and information.[15] His Teacher Rating Scale on the Behavior Assessment System for Children - 2nd Edition carried an at-risk score of 92 percentile for hyperactivity and 88 percentile for attention problems.[16] He could not distinguish between *b* and *d*.[17]

"Restless" showed up repeatedly in our observation notes during our initial evaluation.[18] His error rate in a reading test was 46.2%.[19] Prince reported that he felt head pressure at school especially at test time or when studying at home.[20]

Five months into Dysolve, Prince was still confusing *b* with *d* in his spelling. He made a lot of spelling errors in general, but his verbal ability was strong. Thus, his sentences were usually wellformed even though they contained a lot of spelling errors. Figure 12 shows this discrepancy—high error rates for spelling but few for syntax (sentence structure).[21] Like some of our students with dyslexia, Prince seemed so articulate in speech yet could not spell and write.[22]

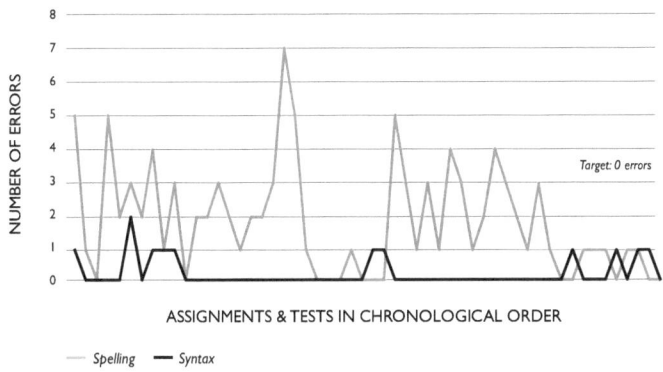

FIGURE 12
*Number of Spelling and Syntactic Errors
Per Written Sentence/Answer in the First 6 Months of
Dysolve*

Six months into Dysolve, Prince was discouraged by a failing score in a science test.[23] "My Mom and I took hours and hours, and we did mock tests on it."

I looked at his science test. It was on types of rocks—*sedimentary, metamorphic, igneous.* What do these words mean to an 11-year-old? To Prince, they're just more words to add to the pile of confusing words with no meaning to him.[24] How was one word different from another? And their definitions? Just more words.[25]

I went to Prince's classroom to observe him at school. I noted that the longest duration that he worked on his class assignment was five minutes, at the beginning. From there on, he did not work for longer than a minute at a stretch.[26]

His posture declined noticeably in the course of the first period. Here are my observation notes:

8:15 – Start of class.

8:25 – Put away his worksheet into his desk (not completed). Pressing down the lid of his desk. Rolling a pencil down his desktop. Reorganizing the inside of his desk.[27]

8:30 – Legs propped up, body slumped on desk. Not working.

8:35 - Slumped, now sitting on edge of seat. Not working.

8:40 – Circle time - playing with something on the floor, not attending to other students answering teacher's questions.[28]

8:43 - Stretching and folding his legs, rocking back and forth slightly.[29]

8:45 - Back at his seat—rocking in chair, looking around, worked on worksheet for less than one minute. Stretched his legs out to the desk in front of him.

Prince's 4th grade class was managed competently by two experienced co-teachers. However, unless a teacher watched him continuously, she would not have noticed the intermittent way he attended to his assignment.[30] When one of them came around to him, he attended to it, but when she walked away to focus on another student, he stopped working.

I asked Prince later as to why he did not do his work in class.

"What are we supposed to do? I don't know what the question is asking." He was frank about it in the privacy of our conference room.

OUR SOLUTION

To help chart the progress of Prince and students like him who have ADHD, we quantified their ADHD symptoms. For example, *Hyperactivity Magnitude Score (HMS)* refers to the severity of language-related ADHD symptoms, as computed by Dysolve's proprietary algorithms.[31] (See the Instructor's Story in this chapter.)

At Dysolve and at school, Prince frequently displayed symptoms of cognitive overload, when the brain is overwhelmed by the input it has to process. The language demands were beyond his present ability to meet. The goal is to reduce a student's HMS through the Dysolve Program. As his HMS declined, Prince's concentration span lengthened and his language retention improved.

By the eighth month in Dysolve, Prince was able to store scientific terms (lexical storage) and definitions accurately. Spelling was not always accurate but the words at least kept to the right number of syllables generally— *hominids, embryology, vestigial, *ethalean (ethylene), *clorafill (cholorophyll)*.[32]

At 14 months, when we retested Prince with a new set of multisyllabic technical terms, he correctly retrieved all words except for *combinatorial*. A month later, his spelling was accurate on a list of more common words except for mistakes that could have been made by any one of his classmates—*genearation* (*generation*), *discustion* (*discussion*).[33]

To help him function more effectively in the classroom, we taught Prince request strategies. We gave him schemas such as "I'm not sure about _____. Can you please explain it to me?"[34] That is, we made the effort of requesting information from the teacher easier by giving him the scaffold. That gave him the confidence to ask in the first place.

Before he asked, we taught him to self-check first: What did he know? What did he not know? What was his class supposed to do? Why were they doing it? These strategies were designed to build his metacognition—his awareness of his own thinking processes and problems.[35] Metacognition is needed to help him understand his capabilities and weaknesses as a learner and to overcome the latter.

BREAKTHROUGH

By 16 months, the small victories along the way were no longer sufficient to keep Prince motivated to plow ahead. He sorely needed a morale boost. We presented him with an Achievement Certificate listing the 20 new abilities he'd acquired since joining Dysolve.

Our instructors were worried about Prince. His Mom was worried. It had been a long uphill climb, and though he had made progress, he was not anywhere near the peak yet.[36] He crossed some hurdles along the way, but boy, it was a big hill.

I suggested getting an older student to talk to Prince. An older boy. We did not have to look far. Eighth-grader Will, who was in Dysolve at that time, would be perfect.[37] Both boys were gentle, kind people. Both would benefit from the arrangement. Prince would get encouraged. Will would get a confidence boost from serving as a role model. It was part of a chain we had set up in our local community several years ago, kids helping kids.[38] Then the younger kids would grow up and become mentors themselves.

The meeting with Will perked Prince up—momentarily. By the 19th month, he was feeling the full weight of the remaining challenges and finding it hard to press on. His teachers, our instructors, his Mom all saw that his problem was dragging him down.

Then, it clicked.[39]

Overnight, Prince changed into the ideal student he had aspired to be. Twenty months into Dysolve, his teachers reported he was doing well at school. The attention issues faded into the background. He jumped up several levels in reading in the middle of 5th grade.[40] He no longer needed his mother's help; he was reading and prepping for tests on his own.[41] He received 100 in two vocabulary tests in a row and won a poetry-writing contest.[42,43] He made the Honor roll.[44]

"I just need five more points to make High Honor roll," he told me in 6th grade.

That was reward enough for him.

QUESTION

What is ADHD? As with dyslexia, ADHD is poorly understood in research, with many questions still unanswered. In fact, many critical questions about this common condition are not even asked as yet, as indicated by the endnotes in this chapter and others in Part 1 of this book.

Restlessness is a classic symptom reported in the ADHD literature. However, the term does not quite capture the physical "agitation" we have observed, as seen in Prince in this chapter and other Dysolve students. Dysolve students are enrolled in our program because they have difficulty processing linguistic input. This difficulty often causes cognitive overload when the brain feels overwhelmed, which manifests itself as headaches and other physical symptoms. Our students describe their overwhelmed brains as being "on fire." To relieve these physical symptoms, some students feel the urge to fidget, move or walk about.

When cognitive overload occurs, the affected student can elect to continue with the task and tolerate this physical discomfort, abandon it and "distract" himself with another activity as a manifestation of harm avoidance, or shut down to block further input. Harm avoidance has been studied in adults with ADHD but not much with children. The term "inattention" often associated with ADHD does not convey accurately its nature and cause. A more accurate description may be *disattention*—a conscious attempt by the affected individual to reduce cognitive overload by stopping further processing of input. Unfortunately, such behaviors are often misunderstood as inattention, distractibility or defiance in the classroom.

Presently, schools and providers determine the presence and severity of ADHD with checklists, questionnaires or rating scales filled in by parents, teachers and sometimes the children themselves. Authorities in the field recommend also interviews to determine the patient's developmental history and possibly classroom observations as well. Thus, ADHD is presently diagnosed with subjective, qualitative reports mostly given by nonspecialists. The risks of over- and under-diagnosis are wellknown in the field.[45]

In place of these traditional subjective ratings, Dysolve uses objective, quantified measures based on over 20 years of fieldwork on observable symptoms and other empirical data.[46] This allows us to determine the exact nature, sources and severity of language-related ADHD for each person affected and to chart its decline quantitatively in Dysolve.[47]

NOTES

1. Max in Chapter 10 also displayed severe ADHD symptoms.
2. Only Prince and Max in Chapter 10 displayed this symptom. Some of our cases outside of this book hid under the table in the evaluation room when they felt overwhelmed cognitively.
3. Prince was displaying avoidance behavior at this point, to sidestep exercises that he found difficult. Avoidance behavior is also common among second language learners in the typical population. Avoidance behavior is scarcely studied in children with ADHD.
4. The children in Chapters 1, 2, 4, 5 and 9 also displayed ADHD symptoms such as restlessness but did not get out of their seats during our sessions, unlike Prince in this chapter and Max in Chapter 10. The girls in Chapters 3 and 7 were not restless at Dysolve. Uno's behavior in Chapter 8 is unknown because we did not interact with him as he progressed through the fully automated program.
5. See the Principal's Story in Chapter 7 and the economic cost of dyslexia in Chapter 12.
6. Three of the 10 mothers in this book headed single-parent households.
7. The parents in all chapters of this book helped their children with homework more than typical before they joined Dysolve.
8. Language acquisition studies show that social rewards in the form of more engaged responses from their children can induce parents to create more opportunities for conversational interactions, thus accelerating their linguistic development. Conversely, withdrawn children, whatever the cause, may create the opposite effect. The effect is magnified for expressive or precocious children as well as for those with language delay or deficits. See Hoh, P.-S. (Spring 2005). The linguistic advantage of the intellectually gifted child: An empirical study of spontaneous speech. *Roeper Review, 27*(3), 178-185.
9. Metaphors are challenging to create because they require speakers to maintain and manipulate simultaneous representations of the object or event and the thing it is being compared

to. Language studies show that young children have great difficulty understanding metaphors. Yet the children in this book tend to create them spontaneously as a habit. See Chapters 3-5. See also Hoh, P.-S. (Spring 2005). The linguistic advantage of the intellectually gifted child: An empirical study of spontaneous speech. *Roeper Review, 27*(3), 178-185.
10. Research on children with ADHD has tended to focus on emotion dysfunction while studies on emotion regulation in ADHD have yielded inconsistent findings. In contrast, Prince in this chapter had a cheerful disposition outside of his struggles with academic work. His ADHD symptoms, as described here, emerged mainly during academic tasks. For a recent research overview, see Van Cauwenberge, V., Sonuga-Barke, E.J.S., Hoppenbrouwers, K., Van Leeuwen, H.K., & Wiersema, J.R. (2017). Regulation of emotion in ADHD: Can children with ADHD override the natural tendency to approach positive and avoid negative pictures? *Journal of Neural Transmission, 124*(3), 397-406.
11. School staff are not trained to deal with students like Prince who face cognitive overload during performance of routine classroom tasks.
12. See the controversy surrounding ADHD medication in Schwarz, A. (2016). *ADHD nation*. New York: Scribner.
13. Prince's transformation was unusually abrupt, unlike the other cases in this book. See Dr. Coral's Story about latent changes in Chapter 2.
14. Prince was able to work at length without displaying ADHD symptoms when language-processing deficits were cleared.
15. Our own fieldwork shows that headaches are common among students with dyslexia and co-occur with ADHD. Headaches or head pressure often occur when cognitive load increases. The association between recurrent headaches and dyslexia (and ADHD) has not received much research interest. Recent studies do show a higher incidence of recurrent headaches among children with dyslexia, ADHD, and both conditions. Yet the explanations put forth remain controversial. One hypothesis uses overlapping brain mechanisms to account for the associations. A second hypothesis suggests that learning

disabilities and ADHD create stresses that induce headaches. A third speculates that frequent headaches hinder learning and cause ADHD behaviors. A fourth proposes a common disorder underlying headaches and ADHD. Which is the cause? Which is the effect? Depending on the hypothesis, headaches can be either. For a review of studies, see Genizi, J., Gordon, S., Kerem, N.C., Srugo, I., Shahar, E., & Ravid, S. (2013). Primary headaches, attention deficit disorder and learning disabilities in children and adolescents. *Journal of Headache Pain, 14*(1), 54. doi:10.1186/1129-2377-14-54

16. See the discussion on subjective and objective measures for ADHD in the Question section of this story. See also Hinshaw, S.P., & Scheffler, R.M. (2014). *ADHD explosion: Myths, medication, money, and today's push for performance.* New York: Oxford University Press.

17. Our students often confuse *b* with d, as do other individuals with dyslexia. This may have misled some people to think that dyslexia is a visual-processing problem. The confusion happens often with *b* and *d*, which are close in sound. It tends not to happen with *p* and *q*, which are not phonetically similar.

18. See also Chapter 10.

19. Prince's reading error rate of 46.2% meant that he misread one word in almost every other line of a four-stanza poem with an average of seven words per line.

20. See Note 15 above.

21. The error rates were based on the number of orthographic (spelling) and syntactic (sentence grammar) errors per sentence or answer in Prince's written assignments from school in the first six months of Dysolve, as provided to us. The written answers ranged from single phrases to a maximum of three sentences. Single-word answers were not considered. All sentential and grammatical errors were counted.

22. The students in Chapters 2, 4-5 and 10 were also highly articulate in speech.

23. Unless the underlying deficit is corrected, the affected student has to expend an inordinate amount of time studying material that others can acquire quickly.

24. Problems with lexical (word) retrieval occurred often to the cases in this book.

25. This partly explains why students with dyslexia and ADHD cannot remember language-based information.
26. Prince's behavior is explained in the Question section of this story.
27. See the Question section about disattention.
28. Owing to difficulty processing verbal instructions, Prince was often unsure as to what he was supposed to do. At other times, he could not understand written instructions to complete class assignments.
29. This behavior was also observed with the case in Chapter 10.
30. Even the support of a co-teacher was insufficient to address Prince's learning problem. Since continuous one-on-one assistance for every student in need is not economically viable, a solution such as Dysolve® is needed. See Chapters 12 and 15.
31. This information is proprietary. To find out your child's ADHD indices, contact Dysolve.com.
32. Error patterns differ between spellers with dyslexia and those without. Studies found that spellers with dyslexia tend to commit more errors related to their difficulty with segmentation (breaking words into single sounds) and phoneme identification (recognizing sounds in words). For example, they reduce consonant clusters (*str→st*), and substitute consonants. They omit vowels and substitute vowels that are not even phonetically similar. They often leave out word endings (*-s, -ed*). In contrast, writers without dyslexia produce words that sound like the target words (phonetically accurate) even when they are not spelled correctly (orthographically inaccurate). Thus, they may substitute same-sounding words (homophones: *buy→by*), use the incorrect letters for unstressed vowels (*attitude → att*a*tude*), and overgeneralize the silent *–e* rule (*plan→plane*). Spelling instruction is needed for students with dyslexia, but research shows that it is more effective before 4th grade. See Bernstein, S.E. (2009). Phonology, decoding, and lexical compensation in vowel spelling errors made by children with dyslexia, *Reading and Writing, 22*(3), 307-331.
33. Prince's pattern of progress in spelling was similar to those in Chapters 1-3.

34. A schema is a pre-established script that lays out expectations for participants in the interaction. For further description of request strategies and schemas, see for example Bargiela-Chiappini, F., & Haugh, M. (Eds.).(2009). *Face, communication and social interaction.* London: Equinox.
35. Metacognition comprises knowledge about one's thinking (monitoring) and self-regulatory mechanisms such as planning, testing, revising and evaluating strategies and checking outcomes. Metacognition is thus important in learning outcomes. For a more detailed definition, see Dinsmore, D.L., Alexander, P.A., & Loughlin, S.M. (2008). Focusing the conceptual lens on metacognition, self-regulation, and self-regulated learning. *Educational Psychology Review, 20*(4), 391-409. doi:10.1007/s10648-008-9083-6
36. Prince took over six months longer to correct major underlying deficits compared to the other children in this book, who mostly resolved theirs within the first year. Prince's training period was predicted by Dr. Coral at the beginning of his program. See the beginning of this story.
37. See Dr. Coral's Story in Chapter 5.
38. See the Founder's Story in Chapter 7.
39. See Chapter 2 on latent changes.
40. Other cases in this book also experienced big jumps in reading levels.
41. See also Chapters 1-5 and 7 for advancements to independent learning.
42. The students in Chapters 1-5 and 9 also generally attained spelling or vocabulary test scores in the 90s-100 after joining Dysolve.
43. Patience in Chapter 1 also won a writing contest.
44. The students in Chapters 1-3 and 5 also received academic recognition.
45. See Hinshaw, S.P., & Scheffler, R.M. (2014). *ADHD explosion: Myths, medication, money, and today's push for performance.* New York: Oxford University Press.
46. See the Instructor's Story in this chapter.
47. See our answer to Questions from Doctors in Chapter 17.

Mother's Story

A Place that Focused on Language
Adeline

Faith

Homework time—our least favorite time of the day. Coming home from work and trying to tackle a reading assignment with my son Prince was the last thing either of us wanted to do. He was exhausted from trying hard all day in school. He hated reading. I can't tell you how many times I had to uncrinkle a paper or tape it up so he could hand it in. Some nights we would both want to crinkle up that paper. Prince loves to learn. He was always seeking new information but please not from a book and don't make me write about it. He would get frustrated and erase his work so hard it would rip up his paper.

In 3rd grade he had a co-teacher in his classroom who recognized he needed more help than the extra reading time. She tested him and said he qualified for the Wilson Program.[1] Thankful for the Internet, I researched the program and read that it was supposed to be for students with dyslexia. The teacher could not say, "Yes he has dyslexia," but she did confirm that the program was used for this population. So we finally had a direction. Prince made small gains in 3rd and 4th grade but not enough to get him to grade level in reading despite the Wilson Program.[2] He was still struggling with reading in 4th grade.

I knew there was more inside Prince that needed to come out. Because he was still struggling with reading even after the school's interventions, I took him to Dysolve. Moreover, his school seemed more concerned over his attention issue. But I wanted to find a place that focused on his language.[3] His pediatrician recommended Dysolve.[4]

Prince had been evaluated earlier for special education in 1st and 3rd grade, but his school said he did not qualify for services because he was in the Average range.[5] I did not know what specific techniques were used in Prince's school—but I wasn't confident in the interventions for his reading. I was frustrated with the school for waiting for him "not to respond to intervention" before they would give him the support he needed.[6]

But here at Dysolve, I can help him myself.[7] It's hard to find time to do everything and this program on top of it, but if I was positive in it, he'd be too. The Dysolve Program was a big commitment but I had hopes of seeing big rewards.[8]

What kept me going? My faith in Prince. He's a very intelligent boy but struggles with expressing it. I had to find him a path to get through.[9] I did not want to see him discouraged. I want his education to be a positive experience.[10] I want to see progress in his reading. I saw improvement quickly in just a couple of months in Dysolve, like changes in his reading. We weren't working on reading directly at the beginning of his Dysolve program, but still he could see his mistakes and stop and correct them and read a little longer.

He's starting to be a little more confident and not give up so quickly.[11] He's more excited about learning now, always looking to do better.[12]

It helps to know he's not alone. Bringing in an older boy for him to talk to at Dysolve was a good idea.[13] Prince always knew he was different because he could compare himself to his brother. In 4th grade Prince started noticing he was called out of class for extra help, and the other kids noticed too.[14]

I kept going back to the school. Prince was lucky—his school has a great elementary teaching staff, but the teachers, when they're in college, didn't learn enough about dyslexia and ADHD.[15] I continued to communicate my concerns with Prince's progress through emails and conferences, but it wasn't until I went to Dysolve and they evaluated him there did we begin to get the help we needed.[16]

Once I had the finding of Prince's language-processing deficits from Dysolve, the school agreed to re-evaluate him. School evaluations are not helpful for kids with dyslexia because they do not test for it. Still, we had to go through the motions. Finally in the summer before 5th grade, the Committee on Special Education agreed Prince would qualify for services because he failed to "RTI" (respond to intervention).[17] Imagine if they had listened to me in 1st grade or if the state provided schools with a test for dyslexia. So in 5th grade, Prince qualified for special services. But by 5th grade, maybe you've lost the kid![18]

Navigate with His Mind

When Prince was in 1st grade, I asked his doctor and others about his attention issue and about meds. He improved a bit on meds, but he was still struggling at school.[19] I took him off meds on the weekends and in the summer in 2nd, 3rd, 4th grades.[20]

He went to Dysolve in 4th grade. I asked Dr. Coral, "Do you think there's something going on here?"[21]

I decided to stop Prince's ADHD medication that summer and have him make progress without it.[22] His school was always focused primarily on the attention issue. I felt unspoken pressure to put him back on medication when they said they noticed how much harder he was struggling to focus.[23] At the school meeting with the special ed team, I told them, "He won't be taking it." I want him to navigate with his mind.

Now in 6th grade, Prince is more independent, reading on his own.[24] He picks up a book to enjoy himself. He wants to read above his grade level.

At this time in my life, I have to take care of my Mom and my boys. I've learned some things. One, there's always time even when there's no time. Two, there's no use getting upset about a situation you can't change. Three, giving up is not an option.[25] If I walk away, then there's nobody for my kid. I don't want to see him struggle, suffer. When I can give up extra time and lose some sleep to help him, I do it.

MY MESSAGE TO EDUCATORS

Schools and preschools need to teach to the kids. Don't put them in a box. There's a large group of kids out there who don't learn that way. This should start early in preschool education. Looking back, there were early signs that Prince had dyslexia. Elementary educators need better training in recognizing these signs.[26] The schools are constantly testing the children's reading level instead. Why don't they build in a screening tool to look for these early indicators?[27] That is really the key to helping these kids.

MY MESSAGE TO PARENTS

Parents know their children best. You need to be persistent in fighting for what your children deserve.[28] *Always listen to that voice inside—it's usually right.*[29] Seek support from other parents. It helps to know you are not alone and you can learn from the experiences of others.[30]

NOTES

1. The Wilson Reading System is based on Orton-Gillingham. Orton-Gillingham is an instructional approach for reading remediation developed in the 1930s. This compensatory approach is meant to help struggling readers cope with dyslexia. Orton-Gillingham is *not* designed to remove dyslexia as a chronic condition. It is commonly used in schools and by private providers in some parts of the US. Despite such methods, school statistics on students with learning disabilities are disappointing, with poor prospects for readers still struggling in middle school. See the research review in Elliott, J.G., & Grigorenko, E.L. (2014). *The dyslexia debate.* New York: Cambridge University Press.
2. The cases in Chapters 2, 3 and 9 also did not progress to grade-level reading proficiency on Orton-Gillingham-based methods before they joined Dysolve. The students in the other chapters similarly did not advance, but their schools' methods were not disclosed to us.
3. Adeline had done her research: she knew that these conditions coexisted with language difficulties.
4. Five of the 10 cases in this book came to Dysolve through physician recommendations.
5. The students in Chapters 1-5 also did not qualify for needed services even though their standardized reading scores were generally below the 25th percentile—the threshold used in research to determine the presence of dyslexia. See research standards in Snowling, M.J. (2000). *Dyslexia.* Oxford, UK: Blackwell.
6. The issue is whether to adopt a reactive or preventive approach.
7. Dysolve designs a program sustained by the child's ecosystem of support that includes his parent(s) as a vital contributor to its success. Sometimes, parents are asked to monitor and provide feedback or coach as needed.
8. Adeline recognized Prince's true capability, which was adversely suppressed intermittently by his ADHD symptoms.

9. Adeline approached her child's problem logically and methodically, like Frances in Chapter 3.
10. Adeline's sentiment is echoed in the Professor's Story in Chapter 8.
11. As his Dysolve program removed language-processing deficits, Prince was able to lengthen reading time and other language-based tasks.
12. Self-perception about one's ability to perform at the designated level is called *self-efficacy*. Research shows that students with high self-efficacy work harder, persist longer and achieve at higher levels. See Dale, H.S., & Pajarcs, F. (2009). Self-efficacy theory. In K.R. Wentzel & D.B. Miele (Eds.), *Handbook of motivation at school* (pp. 35-53). New York: Routledge.
13. See the description of this meeting in Dr. Coral's Story in Chapter 5.
14. See the perception of a student needing special services in Skye's Story in Chapter 3.
15. See the Principal's Story about lack of teacher preparation on special education.
16. The parents in Chapter 1, 3 and 4 also approached their schools with Dysolve evaluation results to get support services.
17. The parents in Chapters 1-4 also struggled to obtain special services till their children were in 5th grade.
18. See Chapter 12 on the economics of dyslexia.
19. Storm in Chapter 4 struggled academically before Dysolve despite taking ADHD medication.
20. Drug holidays—days off from medication—are often prescribed for ADHD medication due to its adverse effect on children's growth. See Ibrahim, K., & Donyai, P. (2015). Drug holidays from ADHD medication: International experience over the past four decades. *Journal of Attention Disorders, 19*(7), 551-568. doi:10.1177/1087054714548035
21. Adeline asked whether language difficulties could cause Prince's ADHD symptoms.
22. The scope of our work is confined to the educational side, beyond which is the medical and clinical.

23. Some parents have reported being pressured by school staff to medicate their children. See Schwarz, A. (2016). *ADHD nation*. New York: Scribner.
24. Almost all the other cases in this book also proceeded to independent reading, as one of the indicators that their processing problems had been resolved.
25. The parents in Chapters 1-5 echoed a similar message not to give up.
26. Informational materials on the signs of dyslexia are available upon request at Dysolve.com and Dysolve Dyslexia on Facebook.
27. Dysolve also advocates for early screening of young children, so as to spare them the hardships experienced by the cases in this book. This early screening can occur at Dysolve before pre-K.
28. This sentiment is echoed by the other parents in this book.
29. The research summaries provided in the endnotes in this book contain a recurring theme: Even experts in the field do not have conclusive findings on most issues, if the topics have been studied at all. In the absence of definitive knowledge, Adeline is right: Parents need to trust their own instincts and act decisively to do what is right for their own children.
30. Adeline offered to advocate for other children at her son's school. Parents can indeed benefit from the experiences of others who had gone before them. To this end, Dysolve Dyslexia on Facebook contains blogs written by parents for other parents.

Instructor's Story

Be Alarmed
Evan

Funny Kid

"Wait! I want to show you my new game. It's a… SHOOTING game!" Prince said in mock horror. He always liked to share whatever was happening in his life. After coming to our Dysolve Center for half a year, he was getting comfortable with me. Maybe a bit too comfortable.

"BE ALARMED!" He exclaimed with his usual flair. I laughed. He's a funny kid.[1]

But I wasn't laughing when I conferenced with him. His Mom, Adeline, had to drag him to the front of the screen so we could start our session. He plopped into his chair, moping, facing sideways.

"Ok, can we start?" I tried to stay upbeat.

"Ughmmmm—" He tried to prop his head up with his hand, but soon both head and hand were on the desk.

"Hey, Prince, come on, sit up."

"Whhhhaaaat?" He looked up slightly. But he fell off the screen. I swear he was purposely positioning his device so it would keep sliding off.[2]

I kept losing him onscreen. Twelve minutes later, he sat up. "Are we done yet? I'm going to get my Mom!" Before I could answer, he was gone.

Quantifying ADHD[3]

Sometimes, Prince would begin our sessions with good humor and dramatic flair. But more often than not, his head would toss and then his whole torso. Soon he could hardly keep himself in his seat. And even before he fell off his seat, we knew his mind was barely there.[4]

These were all symptoms of cognitive overload, when Prince was overwhelmed by the input.[5] We had quantified these ADHD symptoms at Dysolve. We knew Prince's ADHD symptoms and indices.

In Prince's sixth month at Dysolve, we recorded this:

Week 1	Exercise RF390-2-4C administered 8.3 HMS
Week 2	Exercise RF405-2-4C administered 7.3 HMS
Week 3	Exercise AR221-9-1A administered 7.4 HMS[6]

HMS refers to Hyperactivity Magnitude Score, as computed by Dysolve's proprietary algorithms. One of the goals of the Dysolve Program is to reduce the student's HMS. As with our other students, we expected to see a sharp fall in Prince's ADHD indices rather than a gradual decline.[7]

But we did not expect a vertical drop—the week Prince conquered his ADHD symptoms and emerged as a different learner.

Happy Ending

"Here's my impersonation of Evan."

At one of our last meetings, Prince took my seat behind my desk and huddled over my computer, perching my glasses over his nose and looking up.

"My, Prince, how much you've grown!" He put on his deepest 12-year-old voice. We were all laughing.

A happy ending.

NOTES

1. Humor is a sign of high intelligence. See Hoh, P.-S. (2008). Cognitive characteristics of the gifted. In J.A. Plucker & C.M. Callahan (Eds.), *Critical issues and practices in gifted education* (pp. 57-83). Waco, TX: Prufrock Press.
2. Prince might be exhibiting avoidance behavior due to the expected physical agitation and discomfort such as headaches arising from linguistic-cognitive tasks.
3. See Note 16 and the Question section in Dr. Coral's Story in this chapter.
4. Max in Chapter 10 displayed similar symptoms such as sliding off his chair.
5. Cognitive overload led Prince to lose control. Impaired self-regulation is a reported trait of ADHD.
6. See Dr. Coral's Story in this chapter and Note 31 at the end of that story.
7. Disappearance of ADHD symptoms was more gradual in the other cases in this book.

Prince's Story

You Push through the Headaches

Stressful to Read

It was stressful to read. So when you read, your head starts to hurt.[1] I felt the pain every time I read. Everywhere. Everyday.[2]

Science was hard. The teacher was really looking to do things that some people couldn't. It's like asking, What is life?[3] I don't know what life is. Of course I just said it in my head. I didn't challenge the teacher.

When I think about my Dysolve program, I think there're about five floors. I think I'm on the third floor. At first, I was locked out. When I reached the stairs, sometimes it's hard to walk up, but I pushed and I pushed. I'm stretched to the limit. I hope I finish it.

I had to read a bunch of things at the Dysolve Center and at home. You try to push through the headaches, and it worked.[4] Halfway through the program, the headaches were gone. Every day now, I don't have headaches.[5] So YAYY!

Now everything is a lot easier to do. EVERYTHING.

Now, I can read better. I made it to page 20 in 10 minutes! Science is a little hard but not that hard anymore. Math is my best subject, but Science is my second best.[6]

When I found out at school that I was on the High Honor roll, I was so happy I wanted to call my Mom.

MY MESSAGE TO DYSOLVE KIDS

You were probably nervous when you first came to Dysolve, just like me. But you showed up anyway, and you found they're really nice people.

But you will encounter some hardships. When you finish a Dysolve game, you will go on to a more challenging one. You got to try to finish the games even if you feel you're going to pass out.[7]

Before when you're reading, it's like you're at the doctor's because your fingernail fell off. You're screaming because of the pain in your head and your fingernail. Now [with Dysolve] it doesn't hurt anymore when you're reading.

Keep pushing. At first, it's like pushing 20 airplanes all at once.[8] Before for me, it was really hard, really challenging. Afterwards, it was a lot easier. Now I make people laugh when I'm being silly. I can relax now.[9]

NOTES

1. The children in Chapters 1, 4 and 5 described in their stories how their heads used to hurt.
2. Recurrent headaches are barely studied in ADHD research. See Note 15 in Dr. Coral's Story in this chapter.
3. Prince meant that Science was impossible for him to deal with, due to his severe language-processing difficulties. However, he eventually mastered the subject with our help. See Note 6 below.
4. Every one of the students in this book learned to push through to improve processing ability.
5. The children in Chapters 1-6 except 2 reported that their recurrent headaches had disappeared when their academic performance improved while in Dysolve. Duke in Chapter 2 had a high tolerance for pain and did not report having frequent headaches (see Dr. Coral's Story). Grace in Chapter 7 was exceptionally quiet. The children in Chapters 8 and 9 were much younger.
6. This was a huge improvement, considering that Prince faced cognitive overload in the science class previously and could not follow his teacher's instructions.
7. Prince's affinity for hyperbole is another indicator of his high intelligence.
8. Will in Chapter 5 described the beginning of his Dysolve program as equivalent to carrying a car. Prince had an affinity for hyperbolic statements to entertain.
9. We note this change in personality in almost every successful case at Dysolve.

Key Takeaways

Ask whether ADHD symptoms can be caused by language-processing deficits.

See whether ADHD symptoms dissipate when language-processing issues are resolved.

Use objective, quantified measures to determine ADHD severity and to chart progress, in place of present subjective ADHD evaluations.

7

Grace

Dyslexic or Poor Readers

Grace

Dysolve Finding:
Non-standard English; language-processing deficits leading to dyslexia[1, 2]

School Classification:
Not provided

School Services:
Academic Intervention Services for English

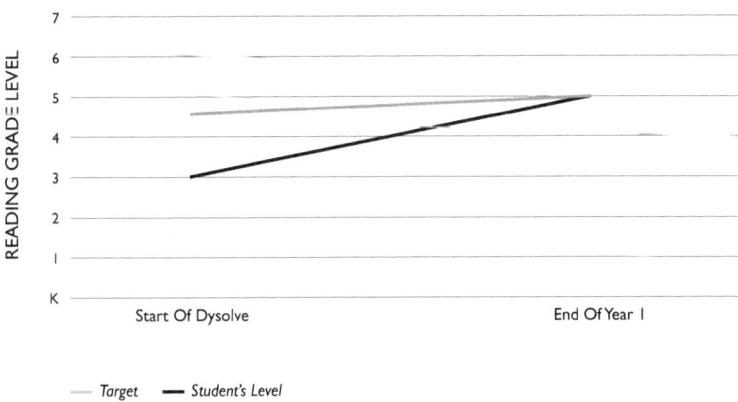

FIGURE 13
Grace – Advanced by 2 Grade Levels in Reading in a Year in Dysolve[3]

NOTES

1. The English language is made up of many varieties or dialects. Linguists define Standard English as the "neutral" dialect that does not draw a negative response. See further explanation in Dr. Coral's Story in this chapter.
2. By *language-processing deficits*, we mean deficiencies in the processes involved in executing the language functions of speaking, listening, reading or writing.
3. Data based on Benchmark Reading Level were provided by Grace's school.

Dr. Coral's Story

Dialect vs. Deficit

Total Silence

The application form had 25 staples edging it, when a single staple would have kept it folded through the US Postal Service till it reached our office.

We had distributed our forms at a local elementary school to offer our dyslexia intervention services to struggling students for free.[1] The form with 25 staples was one of the responses. We invited that family to meet with us.

Mrs. Chantelle Smith clutched her big bag tightly in front of her as I invited her to sit down. She came with her grownup daughter, Bianca, who spoke for her.

As our interview went on, Mrs. Smith's total silence became more and more awkward for all parties in the room.

"Is the sun bothering you?" I noticed that Mrs. Smith was squinting in the morning sun streaming across my office. She shook her head. I couldn't get her to utter a single word.

Bianca and I arranged for her little sister, Grace, to work with us once a week. Grace was in 5th grade but was reading at the 3rd grade level.[2]

At the end of our meeting, Mrs. Smith still didn't speak and didn't get up. She nudged her daughter Bianca.

"Er," Bianca started, "how much is this going to cost?"

Nothing, I told her. Grace was going to be our scholarship recipient for a full year.

Relieved, the women got up to leave. "Bye, thank you," Bianca said. Her mother's farewell was barely audible.

For many of our sessions in the first year, Grace also did not speak outside of our oral exercises. She mainly nodded or shook her head.[3]

Natural Intelligence

She was a graceful girl with beauty, poise, intelligence, talent, a doting family, and a calm dignity that would stand her well in adulthood. But Grace could not read.

I opened to a page on *The American Story*.[4]

Grace read it slowly and calmly, with some stumbles here and there.

"Good," I said when she was done. "Now tell me what it means."

Silence.

"How about this paragraph? What does it say?" I narrowed down what Grace had to cover.

Silence.

"How about just this sentence?"

A teardrop swelled up under her right eye, catching the sun's afternoon ray and tumbling down her ebony cheek to the confounding page below.

"She's sad," her sister Bianca whispered to me.

None of what Grace just read made any sense to her. It was as if she was just a vessel for the words to pour forth, leaving no trace of their meaning behind. Grace could "read" many of the words because her stepdad had made her memorize and overlearn them.[5] But she could not put them together in a sentence to extract their meaning.

Even in moments of frustration, humiliation and deep hurt from all the incidents much like this one, Grace maintained a dignified exterior that bespoke a natural intelligence that had barely been tapped into.

We tapped into that intelligence to help her. We explained her problem to her.[6] Each time we introduced a new technique, we explained how it would work.[7] She listened intently with her big, clear eyes and complied. She wanted to do better.[8] But she did not speak for the first four months except for the exercises and "Hi" and "Bye."

Roofless

Grace's brain adjusted quickly to the new demands.[9] Sometimes, it did within a week, but often within a session. We wanted to keep going, week after week, until her processing problems were all resolved.

But Thanksgiving came; then Christmas and New Year. Grace's family stopped bringing her; every adult in the household was busy.[10]

We called her home and left messages. Grace would have wanted us to. At every session, she did her practices faithfully and diligently, completely attentive. She kept going and going until the hour was up. Her will was tangible.[11] For the child's sake, we hounded the adults.

Grace finally returned in February.

"I'm so sorry. First it was Fanksgiving, then Christmas." Her sister didn't use the interdental *–th*.[12]

In fact, her whole family spoke that way: *ruthless* was the same as *roofless*. We worked on clearing these problems as quickly as we could, before her family stopped bringing Grace altogether.

Stepfather's Story

"I said, 'You did WHAT?!!!' Boy, I was mad! And she said, 'I threw it out. I thought it was junk from school.'"

Grace's stepdad was recounting how she lost a whole year's worth of Dysolve notes because her Mom had discarded them during spring cleaning.[13]

Grace's stepfather was the one who fretted most when nobody else could drive Grace over to our center while he was working. He made flashcards for Grace and accepted our vocabulary workbooks gratefully.[14] He worried whether she could follow in her older siblings' footsteps and go to college.

Losing a year's worth of work was not the only setback for Grace. There were other setbacks, such as missed appointments because of camp or an emergency. Or sporadic practices because of a broken computer. Or weak execution from caretakers who did not follow our instructions exactly. All these we had already factored into the development of the Dysolve Program. We knew that Dysolve would have to operate within the hustle and bustle of family life populated with individuals with diverse competencies, and competing needs and obligations.[15] We did not build Dysolve to operate in an ideal world.

In spite of these obstacles, Dysolve should still achieve its goal. And so it did for Grace. By the end of 5th grade, her school decided she would not need services the following year.

Dyslexia Never Happened

A year since she started Dysolve, Grace gazed straight at me for a full 10 seconds.

"I understand now."

That was the most she had ever said voluntarily. She kept looking straight into my eyes, as if there was more she wanted me to understand.

There was no need for words. I patted her hand. I could see how much she had changed in the past 12 months from our data and her performance graphs.

"I know. You're going to be fine." I knew her family wouldn't bring her much longer, now that she was catching up at school.

A year later, I bumped into her stepdad at the store.

He sounded proud and relieved. "Grace is doing very well at school. She don't remember what she did with you. She's too busy playing sports and hanging out with her friends nowadays."[16]

I was happy for Grace. The best outcome occurs when the deficit is corrected early, leaving no deleterious effects.[17]

No memory, no scar. As if dyslexia never happened.

THE PROBLEM

A dialect is a language variety, a version of a language. This dialect may differ from other dialects of the same language by sound (phonologically), words (lexically), sentence structure (syntactically) and such. Particular dialects may be associated with particular communities divided by ethnicity, socioeconomic class, etc. African American English, popularly called *Ebonics*, is a dialect of American English used by some African Americans. From a linguist's point of view, one dialect is not superior or inferior to another. Dialects have their own grammars and grammatical rules. They are all rule-governed and fulfill communicative functions for their speakers. Society unfairly assigns prestige and stigmatized values to certain dialects based on economic, social and political factors, not linguistic reasons.[18] Linguistically speaking, the standard dialect is not superior to other dialects. Linguists therefore define Standard American English as the socially "neutral" (unmarked) dialect that does not draw a negative response.

When minority students speak non-standard English, others sometimes are too quick to blame language problems on their dialect. The same happens to children from households where English is a second language (ESL).[19] In truth, even for seasoned specialists, it takes time and careful analysis to tease apart dialectal differences from processing issues. Superficial observations are not sufficient for us to answer the question, Is it a dialect or a deficit?

The patterns of language output are different from these two sources. For example, a family speaking non-standard English may not use the sound /ð/ (*the*) at all. They may use /d/ in its place, so that *this* sounds like *dis*. A speaker of this dialect who does not have a processing disorder can be taught to recognize /ð/ missing in her phonetic repertoire when she's learning Standard English.

She can start to recognize that, "Ok, I don't have this sound /ð/. This is how I'm supposed to say /ð/. I have to replace it in some words that I'd been saying /d/." This does not mean that the learner's own dialect is deficient—she just has to acquire Standard English to advance in certain areas, such as academics.

In contrast, when a student actually has a processing deficit, her patterns of errors are different from dialectal or ESL features. The case study in this chapter, Grace, at first produced spelling forms that are not typical of dialectal or ESL sources, such as *sogh* and *rua*. Spelling forms of students with dyslexia may become so mangled that we cannot even tell the number of syllables in the word, such as *buobf*.[20] The journey to awareness and application usually takes a lot longer for processing deficits.

OUR SOLUTION

Grace had both issues: dialectal differences and processing deficits. We started her program at Dysolve by distinguishing the dialect from the deficit.

Grace's family spoke non-standard English. They substituted the labiodental fricatives /f, v/ for the interdental fricatives /Θ, ð/.[21] So in their dialect, *thin* sounded the same as *fin*. They reduced consonant clusters (sequence of consonants), simplifying articulation.[22] So *bold* sounded like *bode*.

We taught Grace the consonants and vowels of Standard English absent in her speech. Concurrently, we tackled her processing deficits. Before Dysolve, reading for Grace meant matching the words on the page with the ones she had overlearned through flashcards her stepdad made, which she dutifully memorized every day. She did not actually decode the words she was "reading." Thus, her misreadings often involved similar-looking words: *quiet* for *quite*, *thought* for *through*, *thought* for *though*, *George* for *gorge*.

After clearing her underlying processing deficits, we taught her how to build her decoding skills. Two months into Dysolve, Grace was able to monitor the number of syllables in unfamiliar words, even while she used the wrong letters in some syllables, such as **vintrillaqust* (*ventriloquist*), **acquatinse* (*acquaintance*), **abondent* (*abundant*), **anonamous* (*anonymous*), **triumfint* (*triumphant*).[23] By the end of her program in 5th grade, Grace was spelling correctly words she encountered for the first time at our sessions: *navigators, peplum, scrambler, clandestine*.

QUESTION

What type of reader was Grace? In some quarters of the fields of education and reading remediation, she would have been classified as a "poor reader" rather than a student with dyslexia. Social bias can influence some to ascribe Grace's language problems to nurture and those of other students to nature. That is, Grace's deficits may be considered non-dyslexic and environmental in origin while those of another student from a different ethnicity and socioeconomic class may be ruled as dyslexic and neurological.[24]

A label is not a solution. At Dysolve, we focus instead on identifying the specific language-processing deficits involved in each case in order to correct them. *At this individual-specific, micro level, classifications do not matter and have no value.*[25]

Why did Grace keep silent in our presence? Perhaps she was apprehensive of authority. More likely, she was in her shell because of her problem; she kept her problem because she was in her shell.[26] Language needs practice. We encouraged Grace to speak, if only to herself in the privacy of her bedroom at first. We encouraged her to write daily in her journal.

By the end of 5th grade, Grace caught up with her peers. Her school decided she would not need support services when she moved up to 6th grade. We decided she would not need our services either.

Happily, we parted ways.

NOTES

1. See the Founder's Story in this chapter.
2. The cases in Chapters 2, 3, 5 and 6 were also two grades behind in reading when they joined Dysolve. Support services, when available, did not help them catch up.
3. Skye in Chapter 3 also spoke little at the beginning of her Dysolve program.
4. Armstrong, J. (2006). *The American story: 100 true tales from American history*. New York: Alfred A. Knopf.
5. The effects of training, such as memorizing written words by rote, can help a student with dyslexia recognize words. But she may not get word and textual meaning because of her underlying problems.
6. The Coral Method® empowers the student to use her natural intelligence to learn how her own mind works, to control and manage it by developing metacognitive and metalinguistic awareness. Metacognitive awareness is knowledge of one's own thinking processes and limitations. Metalinguistic awareness is knowledge of one's own language processes and abilities.
7. See the Principal's Story in this chapter about empowering students.
8. The students in Chapters 2 and 5 were also strongly motivated to do better.
9. See Chapter 2 about latent changes.
10. The students in Chapters 5 and 8 also faced interruptions to their training. Yet their Dysolve programs were still effective.
11. See Note 8 above.
12. Substituting the interdental fricative /θ/ with the labiodental fricative /f/ is common in many dialects of English and among second language learners as well as children. Linguistically, one sound (phoneme) is not superior or inferior to another.
13. Grace joined Dysolve in its early years before we moved to automation.
14. The cases in this book were supported daily by biological parents, a stepfather, an adoptive mother, siblings and grandparents.

15. See Note 10 above.
16. One of our goals is to enable the student to enjoy the life of a child or adolescent by giving her the gift of time, when academics no longer take up a disproportionate amount of family time. See Will's Story in Chapter 5.
17. Unfortunately, by the time students come to us, the psychological effects have often set in, hurting self-esteem, motivation, social relations and sometimes familial ties. See Chapter 11.
18. This is studied in the field of Sociolinguistics. To learn more, read the works of William Labov and Walt Wolfram or search under the key words "language variation," "language and society," or "language in society."
19. Hasty judgments may deny the students concerned the opportunity to seek the assistance they need for their processing deficits. This happened to some of the students who eventually came to Dysolve. Confirming the sources of students' linguistic features requires painstaking analysis of their patterns of errors, related behaviors, contextual information and so forth.
20. This spelling example is from User2 in Chapter 9.
21. See Note 12 above.
22. Omitting a consonant from a string of consonants (consonant cluster reduction) is a common phonological process among native speakers (*library* [laibrəri] → *libary* [laibəri]), dialects, second language learners and children (*sandwich* [sændwɪtʃ] → *sammich* [sæmɪtʃ]).
23. See the discussion on spelling patterns in Dr. Coral's Story in Chapters 1-3 and 6. Error patterns differ between spellers with dyslexia and those without. Studies found that spellers with dyslexia tend to commit more errors related to their difficulty with segmentation (breaking words into single sounds) and phoneme identification (recognizing sounds in words). For example, they reduce consonant clusters (*str* → *st*), and substitute consonants. They omit vowels and substitute vowels that are not even phonetically similar. They often leave out word endings (*-s, -ed*). In contrast, writers without dyslexia produce words that sound like the target words (phonetically accurate) even when they are not spelled correctly (ortho-

graphically inaccurate). Thus, they may substitute same-sounding words (homophones: *buy→by*), use the incorrect letters for unstressed vowels (*attitude → att__a__tude*), and overgeneralize the silent *–e* rule (*plan→plane*). Spelling instruction is needed for students with dyslexia, but research shows that it is more effective before 4th grade. See Bernstein, S.E. (2009). Phonology, decoding, and lexical compensation in vowel spelling errors made by children with dyslexia, *Reading and Writing, 22*(3), 307-331.
24. See the criticism against this differentiation between dyslexic and nondyslexic poor readers in Elliott, J.G., & Grigorenko, E.L. (2014). *The dyslexia debate*. New York: Cambridge University Press, pp. 10-11.
25. See the critique against this field's focus on classification in the Engineer's Story in Chapter 9.
26. Skye in Chapter 3, from a different ethnic and socioeconomic group, also spoke little at the beginning of Dysolve.

Principal's Story

Create New Pathways
Laura DiStefano[1]

Demographics and Grouping

I have been in the field of Special Education for over 10 years, first as a teacher, then an administrator, and now a principal. Just when I thought I had it figured out as to which parents would be the most supportive of their children with special needs, I come across situations that blow up my whole perspective. It all comes down to the value placed on education in the home.

It is impossible to predict the value placed on education merely from demographics. One would presume that parents and guardians from wealthier districts would be better equipped at assisting their children at home. However, those parents and guardians may work longer hours in more demanding careers in order to live in those well-to-do areas. Conversely, one might presume that parents and guardians from a lower socioeconomic area may not be educated enough to assist their children; yet the value placed on education itself may be extensive.

Our assumptions have real consequences, particularly when assigning students to academic groups. One approach is to place all students with a certain reading lexile (level) together.² This type of homogenous grouping allows students to read lower-level primary source to achieve the same learning objective as the other groups. Heterogeneous grouping, on the other hand, is an approach that allows a mix of high-ability and low-ability students to work together toward the same learning objective. This type of student grouping helps the low-ability students raise their level to meet the high bar of the other students. As a principal and a former teacher, I prefer the second approach.

It can be very convenient for a teacher to assume that students with a reading disability cannot handle a challenging assignment. The instruction then becomes less rigorous and students are not pushed to achieve their true potential. This type of teaching does a disservice to all students. If we, as educators, raise the bar incrementally, the student will rise to meet it and *want* to rise to meet it.³ Students are savvier than we give them credit for when it comes to underlying messages. Students will begin to believe that they are not capable of learning if they are consistently placed in the "lower-ability" group.

Unfunded IDEA[4]

In New York State, special education is one of the many unfunded mandates. IDEA (Individuals with Disabilities Education Act) is a marvelous law that changed the landscape of public education; however, it needs to be funded appropriately by both the state and federal governments. IDEA stipulates that every student be provided the opportunity for a free and appropriate education. However, "appropriate" does not necessarily mean the very best. IDEA requires public schools to meet the needs of all students, regardless of disability.

Parents and educators are in agreement that every student deserves every opportunity possible to achieve academic success. However, school districts must also be fiscally responsible to the taxpayers in terms of costs and benefits of resources.[5] Public school districts in New York State are funded by a combination of state aid and taxes. Many middle- to upper-class districts do not receive a majority of their funding from state aid, which means that district administrators must weigh the students' needs with that of the tax base.

Many school districts purchase district-wide licenses for academic and/or remedial programs, which can be quite expensive. In addition to the licensing costs, training the educators to use these programs creates another extensive expense.[6] Most licensing agreements require that any teacher using the program be trained by the program's company prior to student use.

The cost of special education can be quite extravagant. Educational training, educational software, and educational consultants are only a few of the areas that make up the lucrative business of education. Emphasis on high-stakes testing, beginning with the passage of No Child Left Behind, opened a market for test preparation programs and publications, especially for those in need of remediation.

Given the realities in Special Education, educators must always balance equity versus equality. Providing special education services in the public school system is about leveling the playing field so all students have equal access to educational opportunities. Parents and guardians may advocate for their children to receive services that their children may not actually need.[7] While this is completely understandable, this is not the purpose of Special Education. Educators must take caution when planning special education services with parents and guardians. Leveling the playing field is not the same as providing students with disabilities more than they need to be successful. Providing too many services to a child that may not require them can put the student at a disadvantage in areas such as study skills, critical thinking, and problem-solving.

What Happens when They Get a Job?

Our primary goal as educators is to help our students reach the academic level to graduate from high school. Again, decision-making here involves providing students with what they may need in order to level the playing field, with graduation as the ultimate goal. Special education services provide students with explicit instruction by specialized teachers; however, these services are not the only way to allow all students equal access to education.

Accommodations and program modifications can be written into a student's Individualized Education Program (IEP). For example, a student who is in 9th grade with a history of receiving multiple years of multisensory reading instruction may not need more of the same.[8] He may still struggle with reading, but now the reading disability is affecting other content areas that are necessary requirements for graduation. If a student cannot read a test in Global

Studies, then that test cannot be an accurate assessment of Global Studies knowledge. A reading deficit should not affect other content areas in terms of grading. An accommodation in the form of the test being read out loud to the student would level the playing field to assess content knowledge. At this point, the IEP is not giving specialized instruction; yet the student is still being given equal access to education.

From an educator's point of view, I am not satisfied with the level of special education that public schools provide nationally. Students with disabilities are graduating from high school in greater numbers, which is to be commended.[9] However, as educators, we must reflect on whether the students are learning the skills to be successful in life after high school. Colleges and universities across the country have come a long way in accommodating students with disabilities. At many institutions of higher learning, students with reading disabilities have access to various accommodations, such as text-to-speech software. These types of accommodations allow students who struggle with reading to have the same opportunities for post-secondary education. While I applaud this equal access, I often wonder what happens when that student is hired for a job.

Although all workplaces are mandated to have protections for employees with disabilities, learning disabilities are invisible. Many people still do not fully understand learning disabilities, particularly dyslexia, where one's faculties are average to above average. Outwardly, a person with dyslexia presents as any average citizen would in most circumstances. This can lead to a person with dyslexia being disciplined for incompetence, when a mistake was caused by his disability.

Brain Plasticity[10]

I do not believe that we, as a society, empower our children and teenagers enough. I understand that parents and guardians are concerned about how a label might affect their children, and children can certainly be sensitive to labels. Students, especially preteens and teens, need to know if they have a disability, and then must be empowered to understand the disability's effect.[11] Once students understand their disability, they can begin to gather the tools to overcome it. Explaining the research and science behind brain plasticity allows students to develop metacognition in a concrete way.[12] Students constantly question what they learn and why they have to learn it. Learning how their brain works and understanding the new pathways that can be created enables students with learning difficulties to have hope in a solution.

There is still much to learn about brain plasticity and the world of education. Many educators are delving more into creating opportunities for students to develop metacognitive skills. The research on retraining one's brain must be an integral component of every teacher preparatory program. Educators at every level must have a firm grasp on this knowledge in order to inform students and parents.

My team and I have taught our high school students the basics of brain plasticity. Our students were engaged and had many questions about their own brains. Once students realize that they have the power to change their own brains, they become much more invested in their own learning. Many students with dyslexia have above-average cognitive capabilities and can certainly understand how brain plasticity can be used to combat their disability.[13]

It is imperative that educators teach students to reframe how they view personal learning obstacles. Instead of a student making the assumption that she will never be a good reader, she must be taught that she has the potential but may need to just take a different route.[14] This needs to take place before any program can be effective for adolescents. Students should ask themselves the following questions: What's in front of me? What are the obstacles? Now that I know, what plans can I make to get through these obstacles?"

Unfortunately, unlike my school which has a small student population, many schools across New York State and the country have very large student-to-teacher ratios. When a teacher has 150 students, it is difficult to develop a trusting student-teacher relationship. Teachers may not know their students well enough to have a conversation about personal learning obstacles. In such an environment, teachers hesitate to initiate that conversation because of the potential for a negative response.

Educate the Educators, Individualize the Method

Academic institutions must do a better job at educating faculty and staff about the different disabilities. General education teachers are not provided enough professional development to truly grasp the meaning of specific disabilities, including dyslexia. In my experience, I have known general education teachers who assume a learning disability means the student is lower functioning in all academic areas. This is a myth that must be foiled. One-sized interventions, especially in general education settings, do not work as effectively as individualized methods.[15]

Canned programs in education can only bring a student so far before that student requires the teacher to intervene. Using a prescribed approach may work for the typical student; however, teachers must plan for the outlier. The multisensory approach for students with dyslexia has been preferred in the schools in which I have been an educator.[16] Many students have expressed feelings of negativity toward it once they hit adolescence. Once students get into junior high, specifically 8th grade and older, many have expressed to me feeling childish drawing out letters in the air, doing prescribed movements, and saying nonsense words.[17] *They feel more self-conscious about the remediation than if they were given no specialized instruction at all to address their reading difficulties.*[18]

In my experience, many behavioral issues from adolescent students could be attributed to attempts to mask a learning disability. Middle and high school students often act out in negative ways in order to draw the attention away from an academic deficit.[19] Poor behavior is much more socially accepted in the teenage world than not being able to read well. Teachers must be cognizant of this phenomenon and react to the underlying issue as opposed to the behavior.

Teacher preparation programs at colleges and universities across the nation have been improving when it comes to exposing all teacher candidates to the educational effects of disabilities. While newer teachers are being trained, teachers who have been in the field for many years may require more knowledge on this subject.[20]

Unfortunately, teachers in public schools are inundated with various professional development programs that are sorely needed. But there is never enough time in the day, year, or summer. The demands placed upon public educators seem endless at times, particularly in the areas of standards and assessments.[21] Professional development in the area of learning disabilities is offered but not mandated by many school districts. Moreover, sometimes teachers have to pay for certain professional development activities out of pocket, which also limits opportunities for teacher learning.

Artificial Intelligence

As we move further into the 21st century, I see the teacher's role in the learning process as changing to that of a facilitator and guide, rather than passing on information at the board. This generation of students has come of age with the Internet and all of its information literally in their pockets. Educators need to embrace this fact instead of fighting against it. With the rise of artificial intelligence, educators have an incredible opportunity to target specific areas of the brain and to create those new pathways. I believe artificial intelligence is a tool to be used, to be valued, and to be funded in public education. However, at no time can artificial intelligence be viewed as a replacement for the art of human teaching.[22]

In an ideal world, I would like to see schools use computer-based, ongoing (formative) assessments to target the skills that still need to be learned, as opposed to the content that still needs to be taught.[23] Prescribed programs, in my opinion, focus too heavily on the teaching and not as much on the learning. Teachers are held captive by the instructions of a program and rarely veer off of the directed path due to the fear of compromising the program's integrity. While these methods may work for some students, I would like to see an instructional program, especially for reading disabilities, that works for *all* students. Furthermore, it must be student-centered, not program-centered.[24]

Artificial intelligence allows the teacher and the student to receive realtime results, which guides that next step in instruction. Too often, these students get frustrated with the age-appropriateness of the instruction and/or the lack of academic expectations. Student apathy and disengagement stems from this frustration. *Using artificial intelligence to target interventions and increase the speed of positive results will help stem the tide of student apathy.*

MY MESSAGE TO TEACHERS

All of your students have their own strengths and weaknesses. Celebrating students' strengths is a necessity, but so is helping students recognize their weaknesses in order to help them grow academically and socially. These difficult conversations are the building blocks that make your students grow into young adults who can persevere in the sight of adversity.

Only with these tough conversations is the student with a disability truly going to know what she's up against to overcome it. It is equally difficult for the parent to hear that his child has a disability. But in the long run, that parent is going to be appreciative and will say to you: "You put yourself in an uncomfortable position so that you can help me help my child grow."[25]

Assisting a student in understanding the obstacles that stand in her way, and collaborating on a plan to conquer those obstacles is your most integral role as an educator. Embrace it and do not fear it.

NOTES

1. Laura DiStefano is the Principal of an alternative high school in New York that serves both general education and special education students. She has worked in teaching and administrative positions in Special Education for more than 10 years. She has a Master of Education degree in Students with Disabilities and a Master of Science in Leadership for Educational Change.
2. Lexile measures or levels are popularly used by schools to indicate students' reading ability or text difficulty.
3. This has been the philosophy at Dysolve as well. Dysolve students are challenged to meet high expectations even though they have language-processing deficits. They often surprise their parents and teachers by performing way above what was originally thought to be their potential. See Chapters 1-4.
4. *IDEA* stands for the Individuals with Disabilities Education Act. IDEA is a federal law that requires schools to provide a free appropriate public education (FAPE) to children with disabilities. IDEA requires schools to evaluate students for disabilities and provide appropriate services at no cost to parents. IDEA also protects the parent's right to have a say in the educational decisions affecting their children.
5. See Chapter 12 on the economics of dyslexia.
6. This teacher training cost is removed with an automated program such as Dysolve®.
7. In many cases in this book, the parents at first merely wanted to make sure their children did not drop out of high school.
8. Multisensory instruction is predicated on the assumption that children, especially struggling readers, learn best when more than one sense is used. Multisensory instruction is often incorporated into reading programs based on Orton-Gillingham, which pioneered it. But note that a comprehensive review of the research to date concludes that "Despite the enthusiasm for multisensory approaches held by many specialist dyslexia teachers...the theoretical grounds and scientific rationale for their use are questionable" - Elliott, J.G., & Grigorenko, E.L.

(2014). *The dyslexia debate*. New York: Cambridge University Press, p. 150.
9. About 69% of students served under the IDEA (Individuals with Disabilities Education Act) graduated with a regular high school diploma in 2014-2015—meaning that close to a third did not. Figures are from the US Department of Education, Office of Special Education Programs, Individuals with Disabilities Education Act (IDEA) Section 618. Cited in National Center for Education Statistics. Retrieved from https://nces.ed.gov/programs/coe/indicator_cgg.asp
10. *Brain plasticity* refers to the ability of the brain to change or reorganize itself. It is also called *neuroplasticity*.
11. The Coral Method® used in Dysolve entails explaining the problem to the student and enlisting her help in resolving it. See Dr. Coral's Story in this chapter and Chapters 1 and 3.
12. Metacognition involves knowing one's own processes and abilities as a learner, thinker and problem-solver.
13. Many of our Dysolve students have high intelligence and are twice-exceptional.
14. When their underlying processing problems are corrected, students can follow the learning path of typically developing learners. See Chapter 17 as to why we do not use the term *learning difference*.
15. Programs in reading remediation and intervention often advertise that they are "individualized," "personalized" or "adaptive." This merely means that students are placed into particular levels, with the same cookie-cutter kits used for all students at a certain level. It does not mean that each student gets a unique instructional unit based on her unique needs. This is why Dysolve uses the term *individuated* instead—because each student in Dysolve does get a customized program built just for her.
16. See Note 8 above.
17. By junior high, existing remediation methods typically fail to help struggling readers. See Elliott, J.G., & Grigorenko, E.L. (2014). *The dyslexia debate*. New York: Cambridge University Press.

18. Dysolve® was designed to overcome inhibiting factors such as learner's self-consciousness. Users can play Dysolve games alone in the privacy of their homes.
19. See the Professor's Story in Chapter 7 *Uno*.
20. There is no federal mandate for dyslexia training in teacher preparation programs. Some states have mandated training, which varies from state to state.
21. Common Core Learning Standards and others.
22. Dysolve® as an artificial intelligence program is designed to resolve deeply rooted processing problems. This task is beyond the capability of human educators. Dysolve® does not instruct students on their school curriculum, the province of human teachers.
23. As ongoing assessment is critical, Dysolve® integrates continuous evaluation with corrective training.
24. We use the term *individuated* at Dysolve.
25. This gratitude is expressed by Patience's father in Chapter 1.

Founder's Story

Not-For-Profit
Evan Y. Haruta

We couldn't Say "No" to a Child

Raising a child into a well-adjusted, productive citizen takes a lot of care. Raising a child with a condition takes a lot of caretakers. Grace's parents did not have a college education and the resources to cover the cost of intervention. They were not alone in finding it hard to pay for the services needed to correct their child's condition.

Grace was one of the early students we helped in Dysolve through our community service. In the process of our volunteer work, we saw up close the hardships families in need faced. Solving dyslexia was not enough.

One-on-one consultations with specialists are expensive because, well, specialists are expensive. Moreover, Dr. Coral was the only expert with the broad knowledge to resolve the most challenging cases. The Coral Method® as an in-person service kept the number of students we could help small. The Coral Method® as an in-person service kept the number of *paying* students even smaller. We did not want our solution to benefit only the well-to-do.

To bring down the cost of our services, Dysolve had to be automated. It took Dr. Coral and her team 80-hour workweeks over more than six years to build the intelligent program behind the new Dysolve. We purposely priced the basic program at a rate below the average household expense for entertainment. Even at that low price with a fully automated program, some families were still having difficulty covering Dysolve.

We couldn't say "no" to a child in need. So we reverted to old-fashioned barter in some cases. A father did landscaping services for us in return for Dysolve for his children. A mother helped out with our office work. Some former students and their parents returned to work for us in paid assignments, recouping some of the money they had spent on Dysolve.

Ideal World

In 2017, we founded a not-for-profit, IDLWorld, to offer assistance to more families in need in a systematic way as we scaled up. This was not just for direct intervention services for students. Our team of veteran teachers offered workshops to families and faculty to help build the ecosystem essential for students to fend off defeatism and thrive.

As our students graduate from the Dysolve Program, we interest them in our gifted program that is based on the national MathCounts program. The MathCounts program enables students in middle school to train and compete at regional and national levels. Local programs are usually coached by professionals in STEM such as engineers and math teachers. But our volunteer MathCounts program uses high school students as coaches. Our former student-coaches went on to top undergraduate programs in the country such as Cornell, Carnegie Mellon, and the US Naval Academy.

The appointee to the US Naval Academy is the first generation in his family to go to college. Years ago, while he was in 5th grade, we saw his potential and mentored him for seven years. He was admitted to a selective institution with an acceptance rate below 10%. We did the same for his sister, who graduated from Cornell University.

We want to offer the same opportunity to excel to all our students, including those who come to us at the lowest point in their academic career. As Dysolve grows and gets stretched thin in many directions, IDLWorld steps in to carry on our original mission, to tend to talent, to mend what is broken, to make sure every child gets the wings to soar.

IDLWorld has a lot to educate the world—how to solve a 100-year-old problem, how to assist students in school, how to nurture children at home, how to create a more understanding and supportive society.

In an ideal world, every child learns.

In an ideal world, every person excels.

In an ideal world, every family finds fulfillment.

NOTE

Grace could not remember her experience in Dysolve to tell her own story because it was a long time ago.

Key Takeaways

Ask whether reading problems are due to dyslexia instead of dialect or socioeconomic disadvantage.

Distinguish between dialectal vs. deficit sources when addressing reading problems.

Focus on identifying the student's specific problem instead of boxing her into a category.

Dyslexia Dissolved

8

Uno

First Subject of AI System

Uno[1]

Dysolve Finding:
Language-processing deficits leading to dyslexia[2]

School Classification:
None

School Services:
After-school homework help, support of reading specialist

Other Diagnosis:
None

First Subject of AI System

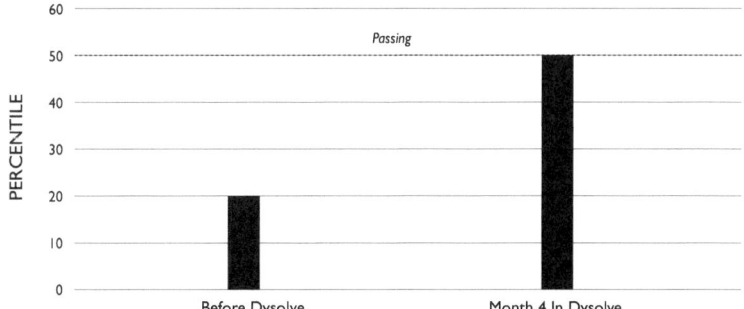

FIGURE 14
*Uno – Passed State Reading Tests
after 4 Months in Dysolve[3]*

NOTES

1. We called this case *Uno* because he was the first student to use the fully automated Dysolve system.
2. By *language-processing deficits*, we mean deficiencies in the processes involved in executing the language functions of speaking, listening, reading or writing.
3. State reading tests were administered by Uno's school in New York.

First Subject of AI System

Dr. Coral's Story

Artificial Intelligence[1]

The Problems

We solved dyslexia. Case after successful case proved it for us. Our corrective program was short-term, but the results were permanent.[2] We knew what dyslexia was and how to remove it.[3] But that was not good enough. We had to figure out how to deliver our solution, the Coral Method®.

"Every child is a snowflake." We echo that a lot at Dysolve. In the two decades I have worked with children with language-processing deficits, I have never seen two students with identical problems.

So there is no one answer to the question, How do you solve dyslexia? For the question, How do you solve *a person's* dyslexia?—there are perhaps as many answers as there are people affected.

These conditions call for solutions specific to each individual. At Dysolve, we build individual-specific programs to identify individual-specific problems to correct individual-specific deficits. That is a lot of work. At the beginning with the Coral Method® done manually, each child required weekly face-to-face consultations with our specialists and daily practices at home with parents' help.

Even though the consultations usually took no more than an hour each time and the daily practices only 15 minutes on average, it was still a labor-intensive solution. That drove up cost. Many families could not afford this solution in terms of time and money.

Even if they could, we could not. We could only see so many students in a day. Most disorders in the medical field are treated by a large contingent of physicians and specialists across the country. Not dyslexia. Our small team at Dysolve was the only one able to correct the condition successfully.[4]

This expertise funnel was a huge problem. Moreover, I was the only expert at Dysolve who could custombuild evaluation and corrective programs in realtime and make adjustments in realtime. The job required over 30 years of accumulated expertise.[5] We could never train somebody else fully enough to meet these demands.

That was just the problem at our end for the manual method. Students' success depended on parents' commitment as well. The adults had to follow our instructions to assist their children at home. Some adults were more capable and consistent than others. The logistics of driving their children to our center or keeping their weekly online conferences was too much for some households. Teachers could not step in to help since they were not trained in the Coral Method® and the Dysolve Program was not designed to meet short-term curricular goals. Dysolve focused on underlying deficits so students *could* meet curricular goals.

First Subject of AI System

Our Solution

What if we cloned Dr. Coral? What if every student got to interface with Dr. Coral on demand?

Our answer: artificial intelligence (AI). We had to build an expert system, a program that acted autonomously like a human expert.[6] This synthetic expert not only had to analyze the learner's data but make decisions on evaluation and training. It had to custombuild all the evaluation and training units for every user and deliver them on demand. The intelligent system would keep the essence of the manual Coral Method's success: the individual-specific nature of its programs. We called this expert system *Dysolve®*, for *dissolve dyslexia*.

Around that time in 2013, cloud computing was beginning to gain traction.[7] We housed Dysolve® on our cloud server to meet each user's unique needs on demand, 24/7. We gamified the student's experience. The student would log in to his user account and play the games that Dysolve® delivered. Behind the scenes, the games would send all kinds of data about that student through his game responses back to Dysolve® for analysis as well as decision-making.[8]

Did Dysolve® overcome all the obstacles?
Make every student's program individual-specific—check.
Make evaluation inexpensive—check.
Make training program affordable—check.
Keep caretakers' support minimal—check.
Make service convenient—check.
Make program fun—check.
Keep training activities short—check.

Keep training period short—check.
Make correction permanent—check.

Still, would Dysolve® work as well as our old method?

Breakthrough

With the old Coral Method®, we got to know each child and family intimately. We shared their joy and felt their pain. We laughed with them and sometimes wept for them. The children's successes made us as proud as their parents. The new Dysolve® would take this deeply fulfilling part of our work away.

Still, after more than six years of intensive development, after too many missed holidays and family time for our programmers and designers, we were ready to release Dysolve®. It was time to let Dysolve® show us what it could do.

We launched Dysolve® on Valentine's Day, 2017. A year before, the US Patent and Trademark Office had awarded us the software patent for it.

The first student registered for the new, automated Dysolve system.[9] We called him *Uno*. He was just a name in our system.[10] His only contact with us was a brief online conference at the beginning. We let Dysolve® take care of Uno.

From Uno's data, we could see that he registered mostly in the Medium - High Risk scores on Dysolve indices in his initial screening. His game play was consistent most weeks except June - August when he was traveling. Even

First Subject of AI System

with the interruption, his game performance did not regress. Figure 15 shows a sample of his game data. The chart records the number of times he failed to pass the games. Each line represents a different speed, 50-60 and 60-70 WPM (Words Per Minute). The highest peak for each line comes early in the graph, meaning that Uno struggled more at the beginning of each new speed presented. From the sharp drops in these peaks down to zero fails, we can see that his brain adjusted quickly to these new, higher speeds each time.[11]

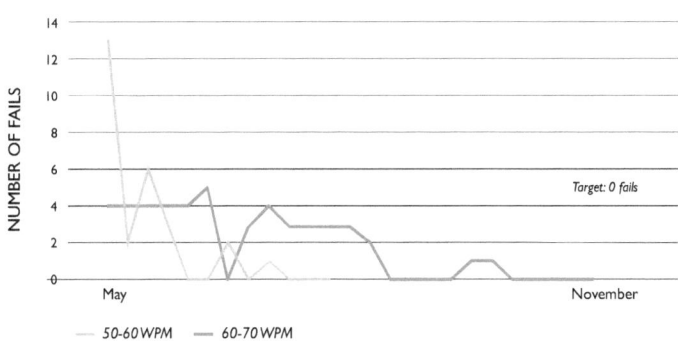

FIGURE 15
Uno – Declining Number of Fails in Dysolve Games within a 6-Month Period

Then in the fourth month of Uno's program, his Dad met with us. He whipped out his phone and showed us Uno's state reading test scores from school. It took us a second to register what the graph meant. It looked like a checkmark, a short, slight dip at the beginning and a sharp, straight rise at a 60-degree angle to the fourth month of Dysolve. Within a trimester, Uno had shot up from failing state reading tests in the bottom quintile to passing in the middle quintile (Figure 14). His school projected that he would be fine, tracking in the middle from there on.

So the computer expert was better than the human expert. It could generate and track billions of datapoints for each student to cut out redundancies and inefficiencies in the training, to attack each deficit with laser focus. It navigated through the labyrinth of the learner's brain with precision and decisiveness. *The territory Dysolve® could track and the mileage it could traverse was beyond a human.*

Later, parents of our graduates would say, still awed to the very end, "It was magic."

Dysolve® could save all the Unos in the world.

Dr. Coral could never.

NOTES

1. Artificial intelligence systems simulate intelligent human behavior. See Chapter 15 for further discussion.
2. For the cases in this book, major deficits were removed by the end of the first year, as reflected in academic achievement. Effects were stable during the study period, which extended past six years for the longest recorded case.
3. See Chapters 13-15.
4. See the cases in this book. Successful correction of the condition entails that the student involved can perform at or above grade-level competence in English/Reading while moving towards independent work. Additionally, comorbid conditions such as recurrent headaches should dissipate or disappear altogether.
5. Expertise is often demonstrated through improvising skills nurtured through substantial practical experience. The experience acquired through a myriad of instances in turn enables the expert to apply intuitive or pre-conceptual forms of know-how that are situation-specific. In some quarters of organization theory, the expert is viewed as one who can operate competently in the space where formal language and theoretical frameworks have not yet translated the "buzzing, booming confusion" of concrete experiences into neat conceptual categories. We would instead emphasize that the expert in dyslexia intervention needs to operate concretely and holistically within a specific case instead of reducing it to an empty category. See the Engineer's Story in Chapter 9.
6. Artificial intelligence (AI) systems abound in today's digital and physical worlds. Some control simple physical tasks while others perform "thinking" operations such as culling data for analysis. The latter type tends to serve as assistants to human decision-makers by gathering relevant information for them. Dysolve® is different. Our AI system acts as the researcher, analyst, decision-maker and administrator. Dysolve® decides what to do for each student and administers it autonomously. It is thus a type of AI system called *computer expert system*. See Chapter 15 for further discussion.

7. In our case, cloud computing allows us to deliver an affordable service on demand by developing and managing our data center and AI system centrally and remotely via the Internet. Users can tap into these resources without downloads, installations or new hardware. Millions of users can access our system at the same time.
8. See Chapter 15 *Responsive Intelligence Technology*.
9. This is done by signing up at Dysolve.com.
10. Human intervention was not necessary because our AI system could act autonomously throughout Uno's program.
11. See Chapters 14 and 15 for further discussion.

First Subject of AI System

Professor's Story

Buster vs. Puffy the Vampire Fish
Father

Class Clown

My son was the class clown. Like the silent-film comic Buster Keaton, you could always count on him to fall off his chair or make a face. Homework time at the kitchen table became the preferred time for an impromptu comedic act while at school his chaplinesque skills would be particularly sharp when asked a question.[1] Reading a passage aloud resulted in even more antics.[2] I had come to call him *Buster* for this reason.

Second grade was perhaps the most challenging as Buster's teacher, a traditionalist instructor, grew impatient whenever he fell off his chair at school, said something silly or distracted another child sitting near him. During the parent-teacher conferences, discussions often focused on his disruptive behavior rather than academics.[3]

Buster was a slow reader and far behind his classmates, some of whom were reading the *Harry Potter* series while he struggled with books labeled well below grade level. He worked with a specialist in the classroom in a reading group with several students whose second language was English although Buster is a native speaker.[4] He was making some progress at school but it was not as much or as fast as his teachers wanted him to advance.[5] As a matter of fact, he was not progressing as fast as *he* wished to progress. Buster was aware that he could not read as well as his friends and he would often comment at home about his weak reading abilities.

Buster would say, "I am not a good reader. I am not as good as Henry or Calvin. They pick the thick chapter books from the book bin. The teacher makes me pick the baby books."[6]

On library days, although he couldn't read them, Buster also chose those fat books. He stored them in his backpack and carried them home where they sat for the week unread. Clearly book choices were important in 3rd grade in front of your friends.

Horror-Movie Nemesis

Buster's mother and I attributed his behavior to immaturity. After all, every night he would still cover himself in his favorite stuffed animals. We couldn't get him to read a book at night in bed like his older brother. Instead, Buster preferred to examine each animal, care for it, and place it in deep conversations with another animal friend. His imaginary animal kingdom would unfold for hours under the sheets of his bed.[7] The glow of the nightlight serving as the spotlight of his private stage.

It wasn't until we received his low state testing scores in reading early in 3rd grade that I suspected Buster needed more help than he was getting in his reading group.

A different approach needed to be taken before another year of slapstick masked his insecurities. I didn't want another year of low self-esteem to take hold and permanently leave a bitter taste of school that, once acquired, is difficult to alter.[8]

I spoke with Dr. Coral at Dysolve and I decided to have Buster give the program a try. The website stated it would only take about 15 minutes a day using the online system, and Buster loved vidcogames, so I thought he might enjoy the activities enough to not notice he was getting further reading help.[9] After the initial screening and a video conference with a learning specialist at Dysolve, it was determined that a language-processing issue existed and that Buster would benefit from the program.[10]

At first Buster enjoyed the focused time with Daddy without his siblings around and the use of a special program that was only for him and him alone. But soon he struggled with the game activities.[11] *Puffy the Fish* proved to be the most menacing. After a few weeks of regular sessions, Buster would moan when Puffy's puckered face appeared as the next game.

"But I beat him yesterday, Dad. Why is Puffy back again?" Buster protested.[12]

"You must beat him with faster speeds every time," I would explain.[13]

It would take more bribes and words of support to get Buster to complete his game each day.[14] Buster would sometimes come up with excuses why a certain day was not a good day to fight Puffy. Like a horror-movie nemesis, Puffy would seemingly recover from his demise just the day before. The specialists at Dysolve had explained to me how much concentration some of the games took. I knew Buster resisted playing sometimes because his time with Puffy was a struggle and no one enjoys struggling with difficult tasks, not an eight-year-old boy for certain.

Over and over, Puffy would fill up with air and burst before him into smaller fish and bubbles. Buster would place his head on the table, defeated.[15]

Tomb of Tomes

One evening after school, about eight weeks into the program, Puffy didn't pop. Buster looked at me and smiled.

"I beat him, Dad," he declared triumphantly.

"You see, you can do anything with practice. Keep beating that vampire fish even if he comes back," I replied with a wink.

Buster went from mixed results with Puffy encounters to more consistent victories within a matter of weeks. He had learned to, at some point, process language more effectively than he had ever done before.[16]

Books about animals began to replace the plush toys in his bed. Then Buster went in his older brother's room and raided his *Diary of a Wimpy Kid* collection. Then he sacked all the books we had about the *Berenstain Bears* family and then plundered all of the *Mr. Men* series by Roger Hargreaves. Each morning I would find Buster with a curtain of books around him, as if building his fortress against the oncoming forces. His night owl scenarios that he once played out were replaced by the fictional tales of children's authors. Buster had become a reader.

At the second parent-teacher conference in the third trimester of 3rd grade, Buster's teacher could barely contain herself.

"Your son has made a miraculous jump! He is now at grade level for reading according to his test scores," she declared proudly.

"That's amazing. Thank you for all of your hard work with him," I said. I prefaced what I was about to say: "I'm sure many of the interventions you've done have helped."[17]

Then as diplomatically as I could: "But I would like to tell you about something we started just four months ago at home. It's called *Dysolve*."

His teacher listened to me tell of our online work with Dysolve® and she jotted down the Dysolve.com URL with interest.

Buster is closing in on his final months of 3rd grade. He is currently reading *Wonder* by R. J. Palacio after seeing the movie four times. Like many kids, he was drawn to the story of a boy on the margins of acceptance that struggles to feel like everyone else. I watch him read the novel with interest. "Does he like it because he identifies with the plight of the protagonist?" I wonder myself. "Or does he enjoy the fact that he is holding a fat chapter book like the ones he has seen his friends hold so many times at school?" I suspect both questions may lead to the correct answer.

I am grateful for Buster's restored confidence and consequently his renewed sense of purpose at school. He is no longer the clown at school but rather the kid who loves animals and blurting out the answers. (He is still working on taking turns.) At home he has always been one to fall asleep in a world of stories and his new confidence has unlocked a tomb of tomes that once upon a time remained too far away for him to reach. It seems that Puffy the Vampire Fish has been vanquished, never to return again.

MY MESSAGE TO SCHOOL ADMINISTRATORS

Buster was never diagnosed with a learning disability.[18] He was not a kid that demonstrated any major differences that caused concern for teachers and administrators.[19] He was reading below grade level and needed extra help. He worked each day with the reading specialist at the school. Buster's below-average performance on reading scores qualified him for after-school homework help with a teacher. Until he used Dysolve, he showed slow progress but not enough to reach grade level.[20]

In spite of sparsely using the program for six weeks during summer vacation travel, Buster was reading at grade-level expectations less than half a year after starting the Dysolve Program.[21] The program seemed to target some of the issues he had in processing language. Once these obstacles were corrected, Buster's school performance improved. He became a more focused and serious student.[22] He enjoyed learning more than ever before. What is more, Buster gained self-confidence. Not only was he a reader, he was a motivated learner on the path for scholastic success.

Given the relatively low cost of Dysolve as well as the short amount of time one needs to dedicate each day to the method, school administrators should consider using such a program to complement traditional reading instruction. *Dysolve's targeted activities can benefit learners on the margins and pull them into grade-level performance in a focused and efficient way.*[23] Given that schools often invest in other online learning programs, I would urge administrators to use school budgets wisely for a program like Dysolve.

NOTES

1. The link between problem behaviors and reading difficulties is well established in research. However, there are competing theoretical models to explain the association. First, a common factor such as poor attention may underlie both conditions. Second, behavior problems lead to reading difficulties because off-task or disruptive behaviors may take attention away from reading tasks. Third, reading difficulties cause problem behaviors such as acting out and avoidance. Fourth, problem behaviors and reading difficulties cause each other. The father's account here suggests that the third model explains the causal relationship. This is supported by the Principal's Story in Chapter 7. For a brief overview of the current inconclusive state of research on this topic, see for example Morgan, P.L., Farkas, G., Tufis, P.A., & Sperling, R.A. (2008). Are reading and behavior problems risk factors for each other? *Journal of Learning Disabilities, 41*(5), 417-436.
2. See the Principal's Story in Chapter 7 on why students act out.
3. The issue is not behavior vs. academics but rather behavior *due to* academics. See Note 1 above. See also this topic in Chapter 6 on ADHD, where the school focused on behavior while the mother rightly sought the root cause of the behavior in the execution of academic tasks.
4. ESL problems are different from language-processing problems. These students should not have been grouped together for the same kind of support. See Dr. Coral's Story in Chapter 7 *Dialect vs. Deficit.*
5. Many students receiving remediation see "some" progress but not enough to reach grade-level competence. See Chapters 2-6 and 9.
6. Even young children do notice differences in the way they are being treated, as do their peers. The effect on self-esteem can be deep and long-lasting. See Skye's story in Chapter 3.
7. Skye in Chapter 3 also engaged in solitary imaginary play.

8. As a college professor and researcher, this father was well aware of the affective (emotional) factors in learning and their impact on future performance.
9. This is the reason for the gamification of Dysolve®, which distinguishes it even more from homework.
10. Typically, the system sends the student to initial screening right after registration at Dysolve.com. During the screening period, a Dysolve specialist conferences with the student and caretakers to ensure that the student's ecosystem of support is adequate. At the end of initial screening, the system generates an evaluation report that summarizes risk factors and switches automatically to corrective training. See Chapter 15 for further description.
11. We expect students to struggle with Dysolve games as they are designed to correct deficits.
12. Puffy the game, as with other Dysolve games, is just the skin or shell. As such, game activities may look the same superficially, but their content and other variables may differ from activity to activity. See Chapter 15 for further description.
13. Some Dysolve games work on processing speed, a known component of the deficit underlying dyslexia. See the research overview in Johnson, E.S., Humphrey, M., Mellard, D.F., Woods, K., & Swanson, H.L. (2010). Cognitive processing deficits and students with specific learning disabilities: A selective meta-analysis of the literature. *Learning Disability Quarterly, 33*, 3-18.
14. We encourage families to develop a reward system to motivate students in the program. Dysolve games automatically generate treasure points in their user accounts.
15. Duke in Chapter 2 and Will in Chapter 5 were exceptionally motivated to win despite repeated fails.
16. See Chapter 14 for further discussion on the new science.
17. Reading remediation programs at school generally use compensatory methods. Thus improvements are usually limited because the underlying deficits remain. See Chapters 2, 3 and 6.
18. Over half of students with dyslexia are not classified at school to receive special services. See Chapter 12.

19. Buster's school should have been concerned about his reading difficulties, since they were unexpected in light of his supportive environment, his parents' educational background, his natural intelligence, motivation and absence of contributing factors. See Shaywitz, S. (2003). *Overcoming dyslexia*. New York: Alfred A. Knopf.
20. The other cases in this book also did not reach grade-level proficiency in reading with other intervention methods before Dysolve®. See Note 17 above.
21. Interruptions in training also occurred to the students in Chapters 5 and 7. Nevertheless, their Dysolve programs were still effective.
22. Buster's transformation mirrored those of the other children in this book.
23. Buster likely represents a majority of struggling learners who fall just below grade-level standards but do not present any other issue. His case suggests that this group of students can benefit quickly from an automated corrective program such as Dysolve®.

First Subject of AI System

Key Takeaways

An automated, individual-specific solution is needed for each person's dyslexia.

An AI program can clear processing deficits quickly and permanently.

Some failing readers can advance to passing in just a few months of Dysolve®.

Dyslexia Dissolved

9

User2

Second Subject of AI System

User2

Dysolve Finding:
Language-processing deficits leading to dyslexia, speech impairment, ADHD symptoms[1]

School Classification:
Speech/language impairment

School Services:
Speech/language therapy; Academic Intervention Services for Reading and Speech Improvement

Doctor's Diagnosis:
ADHD[2]

Second Subject of AI System

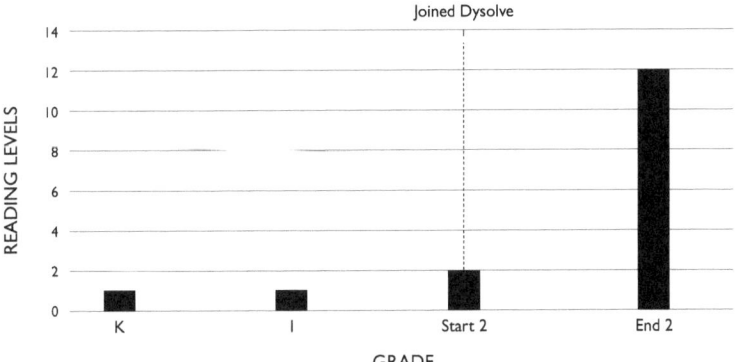

FIGURE 16
User2 – School Standardized Reading Scores before and after Joining Dysolve[3]

NOTES

1. By *language-processing deficits*, we mean deficiencies in the processes involved in executing the language functions of speaking, listening, reading or writing.
2. *ADHD* refers to Attention Deficit/Hyperactivity Disorder. It is also referred to as *ADD* as well as other labels that have been updated over the years. The core components of this condition are inattention, hyperactivity and impulsivity. There are many unanswered questions concerning this condition in the research literature. See for example Hinshaw, S.P., & Scheffler, R.M. (2014). *ADHD explosion: Myths, medication, money, and today's push for performance.* New York: Oxford University Press.
3. Scores were from standardized Fountas and Pinnell Assessment administered by student's school, as converted into number levels. User2 also scored 100 consistently in school spelling tests after three months in Dysolve. She used to score in the 60s with a lot of help from her mother.

Second Subject of AI System

Engineer's Story

Problem Resolution
Evan Y. Haruta

Doing any Less is Not an Option

I am trained to diagnose problems when computer systems break down. These are complex operating systems, with many processes running in parallel at any given time. We can't afford to let these systems break down because they schedule your air flights, monitor your bank accounts, and manage your health data.

When a system fails, I have to figure out what is going wrong and *why* it's going wrong. To an extent, I consider what the programmers operating these systems are telling me. Sometimes, they tell me some of the symptoms. But at other times, they point to things that are not actually part of the problem. In any case, the symptoms don't tell me what the root cause is. I have to work my way back to the source of the problem. I can often perceive what less experienced engineers may fail to see. Some people call it intuition.[1] But what is intuition, really? In my case, it's close to three decades of accumulated knowledge and experience with tens of thousands of cases.

When I was first introduced to the field of dyslexia intervention by my wife, Dr. Coral, I was struck by how different it was from my field although both areas deal with problem identification. They needn't be. With computer programs, problem identification is for the purpose of problem resolution. With dyslexia, it's not always clear what the diagnosis is for.[2]

Dr. Coral, trained as a linguist, a scientist in a technical field, operates by the same principles that I apply to programming.[3] Though the contents of our analyses differ, we both deal with volumes of data to find patterns in order to locate sources of problems.[4] Often, the data are chaotic, seemingly random on the surface, highly variable from situation to situation, dynamically changing, morphing this way and that as influenced by a multitude of shifting factors. In spite of this complexity, it is our job to identify the specific problem and resolve it. Doing any less is not an option.

This is not the case with the field of dyslexia intervention presently. It seems to me parents are paying for problem classification only. When they pay several thousand dollars for a neuropsychological evaluation or standardized testing, they get a diagnosis of "dyslexia," or "mixed receptive-expressive language disorder," or "executive function disorder" or some such fancy term.[5] Then they have to find another provider to do something with that diagnosis. This is different from other clinical disorders. In those cases, the physician usually diagnoses the disorder and treats it or refers you to another specialist who can treat it. *What good is a diagnosis if you don't know what to do with it?*[6] Then you're only paying for a label.

If I take, say, 2,000 cases of the programming problems I've encountered through the years, I can also group them and give them distinct labels. I can associate each label with a set of symptoms and call it a "classification." If I only dispense a classification to a new case and consider my job done, I'd be fired.

Additionally, a cookie-cutter approach cannot be used to diagnose operating system problems that come across my desk. This standardized approach would almost never work. Due to the incredible complexity of these operating systems, a lot of time has to be spent first on understanding the problem. If you use lots of little diagnostic tools to get little pieces of information, you still have to assemble all of them together to see what it all means. More likely, these standard tools leave big gaps in the information you need to solve the problem. The same is true with diagnosing a person's dyslexia. The brain is too complex to be understood through cookie-cutter, standardized kits that leave big gaps in information. That's why a computer system like Dysolve® that produces case-specific, comprehensive, up-to-date assessments in micro detail is needed.

No Such Thing as Broken Carness

If your car breaks down and you take it to a mechanic, you're not going to be satisfied if he says, "I have a diagnosis for you: Your car is broken."

There is no such thing as broken carness.

You want the mechanic to tell you which part is causing the car to break down. And so it should be with dyslexia. You want to know why your child can't read. Dyslexia is not the thing you need to diagnose. This end state, where your child can't read, is not the source of the problem. You can *see* this end state, dyslexia, for yourself. When you rule out all other possible factors why your child can't learn to read, you know something is wrong. You know your child is bright, she *wants* to learn, you're helping her with homework every day, you're doing all you can to support her learning as are her teachers, and yet she's struggling with reading.[7] That's dyslexia.

But what is *causing* the dyslexia? That's the question. In my field of computer science, given a problem to identify as a software engineer, I have to get to the line of code or the bit or byte that is in error. That's what Dr. Coral also does in dyslexia intervention. She has to get to the root cause of dyslexia for that specific case—the lines of code in my lingo.[8] (Now with the AI system Dysolve®, dyslexia *is* defined by lines of code.) Then Dr. Coral can correct the problem. She doesn't label the problem because then there would be millions of labels at the micro level she operates in.[9] Besides, she'd be wasting precious resources on problem classification instead of focusing on the crucial task of problem *resolution*.

Second Student

Dysolve is focused on problem identification for the purpose of problem resolution. The first student, Uno, in the automated Dysolve Program improved in his reading from failing to passing in state tests in under four months. Could Dysolve® replicate these remarkable results? In other words, was Uno a fluke?

The second student, User2, was a second grader. Her mother contacted Dysolve in the spring to find out about our program but decided to wait for school services. By late fall, User2 had regressed noticeably despite receiving new intervention services at school, causing her parents much alarm. They brought her back to Dysolve.

"Can you tell if she's worse off than before? Can you? Can you?" her mother, Marianne, prodded anxiously.

Yes, Dr. Coral could tell. User2 couldn't even speak clearly.[10] The quality of her voice had deteriorated; listeners had to strain to understand her now.[11]

User2 enrolled in the automated Dysolve Program immediately. Within nine months, she advanced by 500% in reading levels (see Figure 16).

Total Expense Long-Term

Like Marianne, some parents waver when searching for the solution to their children's dyslexia. Some parents look at the expense short-term instead of the problem long-term. They think, "I have to pay $200 a month for this program, but I only pay $30 an hour for a tutor." If the problem goes away with the program, that's just a finite cost.[12] Since a tutor can't remove the condition, you're paying this extra expense for longer. Your total cost with the tutoring method includes all the other expenses from the damaging psychosocial consequences, and perhaps even psychosomatic effects later, when your child has to deal with dyslexia chronically throughout her life.[13] Add in lost income from lesser educational and career options, and the coping or compensatory method becomes way too expensive for anyone to bear.[14]

When companies consider which software services to buy, they calculate the total expense long-term. They don't just compare price but the quality of the outcome. They would rather not pay a little bit to solve this small part of the problem and a little bit to solve another part. They know it gets expensive managing all the programs they cobbled together that don't end up working anyway.

MY MESSAGE TO PARENTS

I often see a parent asking on social media, Did anyone try this or that? Then someone comments, Yes, I used it. It's a great program!

That's not enough information to make a critical decision that affects your child's future. In fact, be very critical about what you get. Ask very specific questions:
- Did the program *solve* the problem for their kid?
- Even if they said that the program "fixed" their kid, it's still a subjective answer. Does that mean they don't need extra help anymore? Do their kids still have to work harder than others? Are their kids now at grade level, below grade level, or at the top of the class?[15]
- Follow up with more questions: Are all symptoms gone or do some symptoms remain? Do they still need coping techniques?[16]

- Can you get cases? Can you get numerical data? Which students passed or failed in which grades? What are their state test scores?[17]
- Ask the evaluator or educator: Can you explain how the problem is related to the behavior? Can you predict how taking care of this issue will affect this other issue?[18]
- If you're using the diagnosis to get support services, ask: What support services does your school offer? What is the school's track record? Do the students who use these services attain grade-level reading? How many? What happened to the others?[19]
- What were participants' GPA prior to the program and after?

When a programmer updates me on a problem that we worked on, she is very specific in her answer. She doesn't say, "Oh things are better now."

She says, "Symptoms XYZ are gone."

Why should you settle for less?

NOTES

1. Expertise is often demonstrated through improvising skills nurtured through substantial practical experience. The experience acquired through a myriad of instances in turn enables the expert to apply intuitive or pre-conceptual forms of know-how that are situation-specific. In some quarters of organization theory, the expert is viewed as one who can operate competently in the space where formal language and theoretical frameworks have not yet translated the "buzzing, booming confusion" of concrete experiences into neat conceptual categories. In the account here, the author points out the need for the expert in dyslexia intervention to operate concretely and holistically within a specific case instead of reducing it to an empty category. To learn more about expert practice, see practice literature and the works of process philosophers. For example, Styhre, A. (2011). Practice and intuitive thinking. *International Journal of Organizational Analysis, 19*(2), 109-126. doi:10.1108/19348831111135065
2. Presently, students generally need to produce a formal diagnosis of dyslexia to get special education services at school. But neuropsychological evaluations that typically provide such diagnoses do not include intervention plans. Conversely, schools provide and administer such plans but do not diagnose. See the father's critique of this state of affairs in Chapter 2. See also recent attempts to ameliorate the situation by recommending a shift from "assessment for diagnosis" to "assessment for intervention" in the *Diagnostic and Statistical Manual of Mental Disorders - Fifth Edition* (DSM-5) published by the American Psychiatric Association.
3. Linguistics as a cognitive science uses linguistic data to understand the workings of the brain. As a science, it uses empirical evidence to test and disprove hypotheses. It requires theories to have not only descriptive and explanatory adequacy but also predictive power. That is, in Linguistics, theories must not only describe and explain satisfactorily human behaviors but must also predict accurately future phenomena or output that has not been observed as yet.

4. Outside of Dysolve, the present field of dyslexia intervention does not generally engage in identifying the complex of specific language-processing deficits underlying language-based conditions for each individual affected.
5. See Implications for Dyslexia Intervention section in Chapter 15 for a discussion of how traditional evaluations have been superseded by dynamic, comprehensive, continuous assessment in micro detail due to advances in technology.
6. Researchers have critiqued for some time the practice of not linking diagnosis to remediation. See Elliott, J.G., & Grigorenko, E.L. (2014). *The dyslexia debate*. New York: Cambridge University Press. See also Note 2 above.
7. Experienced teachers have told us that they recognize when dyslexia is involved prior to any formal diagnosis. The parents in this book similarly sensed that there was a problem that needed addressing.
8. See discussions on the root cause of dyslexia in Chapters 3 and 13.
9. See Chapter 14 *Computational Microlinguistics*.
10. Children with speech disorders, which are different from mere speech delay, often also have difficulty with recognizing the sounds and sound patterns of language (phonological awareness). Followup studies show that they continue to face literacy problems at 12 years old, especially if they have other language impairment. See Holm, A., Farrier, F., & Dodd, B. (2008). Phonological awareness, reading accuracy and spelling ability of children with inconsistent phonological disorder. *International Journal of Language and Communication Disorders, 43*, 300–322. See also Hulme, C., Nash, H.M., Gooch, D., Lervåg, A., & Snowling, M.J. (2015). The foundations of literacy development in children at familial risk of dyslexia. *Psychological Science, 26*, 1877–1886.
11. Listeners also faced difficulty understanding the spoken language of Skye in Chapter 3.
12. The cases in this book showed that their language-processing deficits were corrected for the most part within a year. Some stayed more than a year to catch up on linguistic skills and knowledge missed in earlier grades. The subscription cost of Dysolve in the Basic Plan at the time of this writing is

$200/month or $2,400/year. See Chapter 12 for a comparison with costs incurred for leaving the problem uncorrected.
13. See Chapter 12 on the cost of dyslexia.
14. See Chapter 12 for sample calculations of long-term costs for leaving the problem uncorrected.
15. Many of our students are above average in intelligence. When their language-processing deficits are corrected, they tend to excel academically, as seen in the cases in this book.
16. Dysolve graduates tend to perform as well as or better than their typical peers. The goal of Dysolve is to enable our students to process language in the way that the rest of the population does.
17. Ask for specific test scores or grades of individuals, not vague testimonials. If a testimonial said that the student "improved/progressed/got better," what does that actually entail? Ask for individual-specific data, not generalized averages from studies. If the group's average rose above failing, how many students actually did? If the study investigated an aspect of academic achievement, what about overall grades in that subject?
18. The research literature and our own fieldwork show that many conditions involved here are comorbid (co-occur). Can providers explain their causal relationships? Do they have a multimodal program in place to address these interrelated problems? See Chapter 4.
19. See Chapter 12 on school statistics.

Mother's Story

She Skyrocketed
Marianne

No Short-Term Memory

"I can't do it! I don't know how to!" My daughter, Bella, used to scream at me during homework.[1] She refused to even pick up the pencil to attempt it. I used to spend 2-3 hours of homework every night trying to help her.[2]

Now I say, "Just do it."

And she says, "Ok!"

My seven-year-old Bella is creative, imaginative, and expressive.[3] But she couldn't deal with anything on paper. I made flashcards for her to learn simple words like *and* and *the*.[4] We'd go over them many, many times, but Bella couldn't make them stick.[5] Testing showed that her long-term memory is great. However, Bella has no short-term memory. Bella has ADHD.[6] Her teachers say she's "consistently inconsistent" at school.

I was concerned and frustrated that Bella was inconsistent with her academic skills despite receiving Academic Intervention Services (AIS) for Reading and Speech Improvement since kindergarten. She received remedial instruction in nursery school for reading and writing, but she still struggled in kindergarten. Bella's kindergarten teacher referred her to the Response to Intervention (RTI) team.[7] An RTI Intervention Plan was already in place for Bella by the end of kindergarten.[8]

The problems continued in 1st grade.[9] Bella still had trouble writing letters and numbers. She only recognized slightly over half of the sight words for her grade. Her school determined that she was struggling with English Language Arts (ELA) standards. Her reading score in a standardized test was Below Average.[10]

A teacher told me about Dysolve. I thought it was a great program, but I wanted to get Bella's school to support her first. I got Bella speech therapy at a local hospital over the summer before 2nd grade. She then received speech therapy at school the following fall. But Bella started doing strange things, like saying *t-oy* and *wa-ter* with pauses in between, like a robot. At home, she shut down at times and had difficulty communicating with her little sister. Bella even had trouble saying her sister's name.

100s

I took Bella back to Dysolve. Her growth was fast in Dysolve. After four months of Dysolve, Bella's speech cleared up and her stuttering dissipated. Her teacher saw more growth and said Bella's focused more. Before, even with my help, she got 60s and 70s in her spelling tests. Now she consistently gets 100s on spelling tests. Now she thinks she's great at spelling and wants to spell. There's a new confidence about her.

Her teacher gives her time to process, to put words on paper. Bella's speed has definitely gone up. She's trying independently to write and spell phonetically. Now she's willing to try and more apt to do it herself. Before, her teacher would scribe for her in class. I didn't want Bella to get used to the teacher scribing for her. I put a stop to it, as I wanted her to be challenged.

After two months of Dysolve in 2nd grade, Bella wrote in her journal: "*i f I wa bi w tkfps.*" (*If I were a grown up, I would take care of pets.*)

Four months later, her writing is getting easier to make out, "*Hwie bekus it si buobf.*" (*Hawaii, because it is beautiful.*)

Her teacher wrote, "Her spelling has improved and now consists of more than just letters. Now it has a meaningful letter-sound connection."

Bella went up three reading levels within four months of Dysolve. Bella didn't read before. She only looked at the pictures in the book previously. Now she's more apt to read. She attends to and recognizes sight words.

With the AIS at school, the improvement was slow. But since Bella started Dysolve, she skyrocketed. Now in her sixth month, Bella is expected to achieve four out of the five reading and writing goals of her Individualized Education Program (IEP) from school. She is progressing gradually in the 5th goal and may still achieve it by year's end. (See Figure 17.)

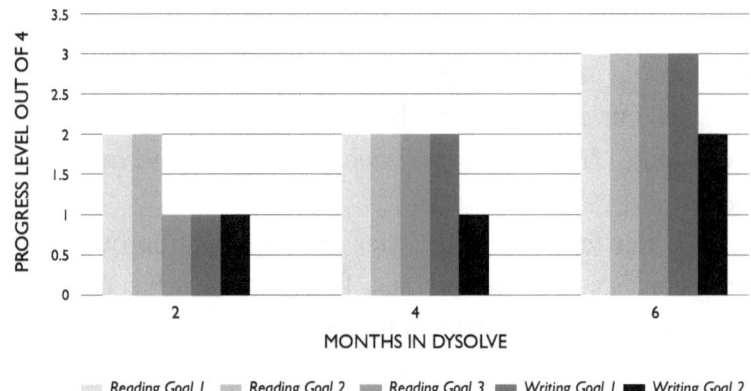

FIGURE 17
*Bella – Expected to Achieve IEP Goals
after 6 Months in Dysolve[11]*

NOTES

1. ADHD has been associated with impaired academic achievement in the research literature. Many studies tie low academic achievement to the lack of effort or motivation in this population. However, questions remain as to whether the cause is actually inability, as in the case in this chapter. The studies often involve boys and older youth. Pre-adolescent girls, like Bella in this chapter, are an understudied group in ADHD research.
2. The parents in Chapters 1-6 also spent an inordinate amount of time on homework before Dysolve.
3. Even though Bella was expressive in spoken language, she had speech articulation issues. Bella was also expressive in art.
4. Small function words such as *the* and *and* are not acoustically prominent and are thus easily missed in spoken language.
5. See similar problems with forgetfulness in Chapters 1 and 4.
6. While several groups of researchers have identified working-memory deficits in ADHD, others have not. Results have been mixed and tend to focus on boys rather than girls. See for example Rhodes, S.M., Park, J., Seth, S., & Coghill, D.R. (2012). A comprehensive investigation of memory impairment in attention deficit hyperactivity disorder and oppositional defiant disorder. *Journal of Child Psychology and Psychiatry and Allied Disciplines, 53*(2), 128-137. doi:10.1111/j.1469-7610.2011.02436.x
7. Response to intervention (RTI) is a process used by schools to help struggling students by first identifying their needs through assessment measures and addressing them with appropriate interventions. If a student does not respond to the initial interventions, more focused methods are used.
8. Unlike the other cases in this book, Bella did get support services early from her school district.
9. That is, the school's support services did not help Bella attain grade-level competence, just like the other cases in this book.
10. Total Reading score from the Wechsler Individual Achievement Test – 3rd Edition (WIAT-III).

11. An IEP is an Individualized Education Program (or Plan) for students with special needs to receive support services in public schools. *IEP* also refers to the legal document that charts the student's needs, evaluative and support services, and targeted goals. IEPs are covered by the Individuals with Disabilities Education Act (IDEA).

    IEP goals were converted to numeric values in Figure 17. Achieved = 4; Progressing Satisfactorily = 3; Progressing Gradually = 2; Progressing Inconsistently = 1; Not Achieved = 0.

Second Subject of AI System

Key Takeaways

Use evaluations that are integrated with remediation so that deficits are resolved.

Act immediately to minimize the cost of addressing the problem and its secondary effects.

Calculate the total long-term cost of each method and avoid a patchwork of approaches that don't yield the same collective result.

Dyslexia Dissolved

10

Max

Writing Disability

Max

Dysolve Finding:
Language-processing deficits leading to writing difficulties, ADHD symptoms[1, 2]

School Classification:
Other Health Impairment (OHI)

School Services:
Occupational therapy, psychological counseling, co-teaching classes[3]

Doctor's Diagnosis:
ADD[4]

NOTES

1. By *language-processing deficits*, we mean deficiencies in the processes involved in executing the language functions of speaking, listening, reading or writing.
2. When Max did produce written language, it was generally wellformed in all respects, including in terms of mechanics (spelling and punctuation), diction (word choice), syntax (sentence grammar), semantics (meaning) and pragmatics (contextual appropriateness). His handwriting was neat and legible and thus did not contain common signs of a writing disorder/disability called *dysgraphia*. Max's problem occurred at the composing stage of the writing process.
3. Co-teaching classes contain at least two teachers. Often, one teacher covers the material for the whole class while the second is a special education teacher who attends to students with special needs.
4. *ADD* stands for Attention Deficit Disorder. It refers to the same condition popularly called *ADHD* (Attention Deficit Hyperactivity Disorder). We use *ADHD* in this book. In some quarters, the label *AD/HD* is used instead. The label may yet undergo another revision. See the Engineer's Story about problem classification in Chapter 7. Chapter 6 describes a case with ADHD.

Dr. Coral's Story

Early Childhood Deprivation[1]

Paradox

"I've been waiting all week to see you!"

"Me too! I wanted to see you again!"

Nine-year-old Max intrigued me. The first time we met, we conversed about the great white shark, the origin of birds, and vocal cord transplants, all within the first five minutes. He read profusely and had amassed a vast storehouse of knowledge. Conversations with him were **spitfire flights through** space and time to all corners of the universe. He was full of humor and chuckled over the ironies of the adult world.[2]

So what was he doing at Dysolve?

Max was a paradox.[3] He could read but could not write. His contradictory behavior baffled his teachers, who blamed it on defiance. They thought, here's a rebel. Why else would a kid put up with reprimands rather than write down a few sentences, or even just one? Why put up with punishment for 60 minutes rather than just get the insipid chore over in five?

Homework time stretched on for three hours each night in 4th grade, with Max staring at a blank page in front of him. His adoptive mother reasoned, bribed, threatened, pleaded and begged to no avail.[4]

Yet Max seemed to read well. Early in our program, I asked Max to read a chapter from a science textbook. No problem. He read it fluently and summarized its content. He shared what he had learned from his voracious reading at home about the animal kingdom.

Then it appeared.

At one of our sessions, Max became increasingly fidgety. With his head tilted back, torso arched, he started rocking in his chair, stronger and stronger.[5] BRRRRR—BRRR—BRRR. He made a sound similar to the one made by my guinea pig when it was afraid. But Max's was involuntary.

With all that frenzied exhalation, Max sank down and down deflated until he slid completely off his chair onto the floor.[6] When he climbed back up, I noticed that his fingers were bleeding. He had bitten his nails down to the flesh in the anxiety of daily living.[7]

His school day was a series of penalties.[8] Recess time was taken away so he would finish his work. His beloved music class was taken away so he would learn not to delay. He ran away from school a couple of times.

Clearly, this child needed someone who understood him, someone who had been in his shoes and could empathize. From our pool of Dysolve graduates, we found a mentor for Max.

The mentor showed up in a gray and fuschia outfit and cotton candy hair.

She greeted Max, "Hi, I'm Skye."

To be continued in the second book in this series...

NOTES

1. The most compelling evidence to date for the environmental factor in ADHD comes from studies of children in institutional settings who were later placed with adoptive or foster families. Elevated levels of inattention and hyperactivity/impulsivity have been reported in this population, with the severity of effects dependent on the duration and severity of early deprivation. See for example Kennedy, M., Kreppner, J., Knights, N., Kumsta, R., Maughan, B.,...Sonuga-Barke, E.J.S. (2016). Early severe institutional deprivation is associated with a persistent variant of adult attention-deficit/hyperactivity disorder: clinical presentation, developmental continuities and life circumstances in the English and Romanian Adoptees study. *Journal of Child Psychology and Psychiatry, 57*(10), 1113–1125. doi:10.1111/jcpp.12576
2. Max exhibited many of the traits of intellectually gifted children: curiosity, vast knowledge, preference for adult interaction, philosophical thinking, insight, humor. See Hoh, P.-S. (2008). Cognitive characteristics of the gifted. In J. Plucker & C. Callahan (Eds.), *Critical issues and practices in gifted education: What the research says* (57-83). Austin, TX: Prufrock Press.
3. Most of our students with language-processing deficits show paradoxical behaviors on the surface: perceptive but inarticulate; articulate but unable to read; intelligent but failing in school, etc. These paradoxes can be resolved by understanding the root causes of the conditions involved.
4. Many of our students reported spending too much time on homework before their language-processing deficits were corrected. See Chapters 1-6.
5. Max's behaviors are similar to those of Prince's in Chapter 6 on ADHD.
6. Prince in Chapter 6 also repeatedly slid from his chair to the floor during Dysolve exercises, as an extreme symptom of hyperactivity.
7. Approximately 25% of children with ADHD have a comorbid (co-occurring) anxiety disorder, characterized by excessive

worry, difficulty shifting attention and inflexibility. The cause of anxiety in ADHD is unknown at this point in research. One hypothesis suggests that anxiety is due to faulty information processing and hypersensitivity to information and sensory stimuli in the environment. Research also indicates that sensory issues, anxiety and ADHD are associated with similar neurological structures, which co-occur in some people. See for example Reynolds, S., & Lane, S.J. (2009). Sensory over-responsivity and anxiety in children with ADHD. *The American Journal of Occupational Therapy, 63*(4), 433-440.
8. Max's school records documented his sensory processing difficulties, yet these did not seem to be taken into consideration in dealing with his behavior in the classroom.

11

Lessons Learned

The Ones who Walked away

Did we pick and choose only successful cases for this book? No—these were randomly selected from the ones who stayed.[1] So long as we could pinpoint the specific language-processing deficits, we could work methodically through to correct them.[2] The students just had to stay long enough in Dysolve to let that happen.

Many chose not to. A hyperactive seven-year-old whose stepdad brought him to Dysolve but who left when their restaurant business moved away. A ten-year-old whose mother flitted from one program to the next every few months. A nine-year-old who cursed every time he tripped over a word—he left for Maine in the summer in a red convertible and never came back. A sixth grader whose physical ailments could not budge his busy parents to action. High school students who only had a narrow band of deficits to correct but who instead rushed impatiently to end their education. Twenty-year-olds who schemed to hide their literacy problems from their employers. Grown men who worried about their future as day workers.

During brief moments of reflection, we wonder what happened to the ones who walked away. Did they turn out fine? Or did they join the pool of sad statistics from Special Education?[3] Which ones among them had the resilience to fight against all odds?[4] Which ones failed?

The Ones who Failed in Society

Authors' note: As seen in our cases, self-resilience and positive environments serve as moderating factors against risk behaviors in certain individuals. Be that as it may, we recount below the general trends besetting this population for schools and policy makers to note the vulnerabilities faced by this group as a whole.

While about 20% of the general population have dyslexia caused by language difficulties, over 50% of youth offenders in the criminal justice system have language difficulties.[5] Standardized assessment identified 52%-65% of youth offender subjects in some studies as language impaired. In one such study, 92-96% of youth offender subjects failed to meet their mean age targets in reading and language tests.[6] Similarly poor results were obtained in other studies on literacy tests. These language results of youth offenders are similar to those of the cases in this book prior to their joining Dysolve.

As with our cases, youth offenders disclosed in these studies that they struggled to understand their teachers' verbal instructions and to read school assignments. This resulted in work avoidance, a scenario that also played out every night in our students' pre-Dysolve days. Coupled with the feeling that they were put down by others due to their language difficulties, youth offenders in studies reported negative attitudes towards education, consequently harming their academic achievement.

These youth offenders often expressed themselves aggressively, particularly towards authority figures such as teachers and parents. Research repeatedly confirms that many young people with conduct disorders have difficulties with language usage (pragmatics). Collectively, their language difficulties, poor behavior and low self-esteem drive them away from the mainstream to groups whose identities are defined by risk behaviors and delinquency. Notably, one study reported that these youth subjects preferred not to confide in others about their personal problems.[7] Thus, parents and teachers may be unaware of the internal turmoil experienced by such youths and may be caught off guard by any ensuing drastic action taken by the latter.

Inability to express their feelings of frustration thus creates and perpetuates a vicious cycle of helplessness, confrontation, disengagement, avoidance, inadequacy and aggression that eventually leads many of them to end up in the criminal justice system.

The grim statistics in the next chapter tell their story.

Key Findings

The cases in this book reveal these recurrent themes:
- Chances are, it's dyslexia.

- Dyslexia can be corrected.
- You should be in crisis mode.
- Trust yourself.
- Don't settle for less.

Chances are, It's Dyslexia

Dyslexia comes in many forms and affects people from diverse backgrounds. A person diagnosed with other disorders, such as autism or ADHD, may also have language-processing deficits that need addressing as well. In fact, dyslexia co-occurs with many of these conditions.[8]

The language-processing deficits underlying dyslexia affect not only reading ability but a broad range of areas from the cognitive to the psychosocial and physical.[9] Until we identify the root cause of each disorder, surface effects may seem unrelated, puzzling, paradoxical, intractable and even hopeless.

Given the ubiquity of the various symptoms reported in this book, it should come as no surprise that dyslexia affects 20% of the population in the US.[10] Whenever you have the question, What's wrong with my child?, start by eliminating deficits in language processing as the possible source. This evaluation can now be done easily and inexpensively at Dysolve.com—before you search for more expensive and less likely solutions.

So we ask teachers, parents, caretakers, school administrators and the public: *Give the child the benefit of the doubt.* Reserve judgment and action until you have talked to him and explored deeply with him the possible source of his behavior. This is our Coral Method® way.

Dyslexia can be Corrected

Authorities in the field claim that dyslexia is a chronic, lifelong condition. Authorities in the field cannot agree on what dyslexia is.[11] The children in Part 1 of this book attained grade-level reading proficiency and above even though they struggled with reading for years and qualified as dyslexic according to the standards established by the field.[12]

The answer lies in finding the root cause of each child's dyslexia. As each child is a snowflake, we have to design an individual-specific evaluation to define the individual-specific problem to create an individual-specific solution to correct it. This requires a lot of expertise in multiple disciplines and data analytics best relegated to a computer expert system using artificial intelligence.[13] *There is only one such computer expert system for dyslexia in the world—Dysolve®.*

As a child's language-processing deficits dissolve, so do many of his co-occurring conditions such as recurrent headaches and ADHD. The result sometimes is a different learner, a different person.

You should be in Crisis Mode

In a crisis, we act quickly to turn things around quickly. The cases in this book show that this is possible with dyslexia.

Consistent practice through a year helps resolve major language-processing deficits in most cases. The families in this book made sacrifices for the short-term for a dyslexia-free life for the long-term.

Dyslexia does not occur in a vacuum. It does not simply go away because your child or student is not reading at the moment. The deleterious effects on her psyche, social relations, wellbeing, etc. can be profound and long-lasting. Every time a failing reader hears about another student's success at school or at home, she feels the sting of her own struggles. Every time a learner with dyslexia sees others rewarded for their academic accomplishments, he feels beaten down further for his lack of results for the great effort he had put in.

We were able to save the third graders and younger children from these negative feelings about themselves and their education. By 4th-5th grade, this negativity has usually taken hold. For most children, school is challenging enough without this extra burden. At some point, the struggling student may turn inward and reject further attempts to improve her situation.[14] The failing learner may lash out to protect his ego.[15] This may come sooner than you expect. We see children change from state to state within a matter of months if not weeks. *We cannot help someone who no longer wants to be helped.*

Even without these secondary effects, reading difficulties alone have amplifying consequences. In Linguistics, we talk about the snowballing effect in language acquisition. A snowball starts small but as it rolls downhill, it grows bigger and bigger—not incrementally but enormously—and soon its great weight causes it to plunge headlong faster and faster. Every child going through the typical course of language acquisition benefits from this snowballing effect. First, in small, mincing steps, the child learns to say first words. Within a matter of months, the words become phrases, and the phrases grow astoundingly into a multitude of sentences to fit every occasion. Pleased with this growth, parents and caregivers feed the learning child book after book to accelerate this amazing development. A strong reader may read a staggering 1.8 million words yearly while a poor reader may cover a mere 8,000.[16] A struggling reader is thus arrested in her language development while her peers hurtle miles ahead. Trying to catch up, even by 2nd grade, becomes a challenge. This is why if you see "some progress" in your struggling reader, *it may be negligible when you compare it to her classmates' even more astonishing progress.*

Research shows that language and learning problems often exist in a tangled web of related issues including ADHD, anxiety, depression, defeatism, self-injurious behaviors, suicide ideation and on and on.[17] Language-processing deficits should not be allowed to fester. Something very involved has to take place to remove an ingrained problem, one that has been there probably since early infancy.

Schools say, give it time. Parents think, let's wait another year. The families in this book understood that they were fighting for nothing less than their children's lives. We have not heard from the parents of older children who waited. What is their story?

Trust Yourself

Trust yourself because you know your child best. If you sense your child has a problem, pursue it. Don't let others talk you out of it or tell you to wait and see how it unfolds. You may not like what you see next. Trust yourself because authorities in this field do not often have the answers you need. Many topics related to this condition are understudied or have inconclusive or conflicting results. Just look at the endnotes in the preceding chapters on what the research says and the state of the science in Chapter 13.

Nearly two-thirds of the general student population actually fail standardized reading tests year after year (see Chapter 12).[18] When even reading experts cannot change this trend given the present state of knowledge, schools are often left without firm guidance (see Chapter 13). Struggling readers may fall into a group that researchers call "non-responders."[19] The fact that such a label even exists tells you something—that there is an entrenched group of children that formal instruction cannot reach.

Do not let labels and terminology camouflage the answers you need. In fact, forget labels.[20] Your child is not a category. You need the specialist to explain in plain language what his problem is exactly and how to remove it. *Someone who says that this cannot be done has not put in the hard work.* Dysolve has done the hard work for you. Take advantage of it.

Don't Settle for Less

It is possible to be classified with a math disability and earn 80-90s in math two years later.[21] It is possible to advance from *below* the 20th percentile in standardized reading to *above* the 80th in two years.[22] It is possible to shoot from the bottom quintile to the middle in four months.[23] It is possible to advance from not knowing how to spell "*the*" to scoring 100s in spelling tests after three months of Dysolve games.[24] It is possible to get a failing student with autism, ADHD, oppositional defiant disorder and dyslexia to score in the 90s in school grades.[25]

Set high expectations because low ones become self-fulfilling prophecies. Don't settle for less just because your child has a disability/disorder/learning difference. But when a program promises big benefits, they will not come quickly or easily. Instill the discipline to work consistently in the program until latent changes surface.[26]

Don't settle for some "research" evidence of a sliver of an improvement in some aspect of reading in a sample group's average.[27] Show us the successful students who can now function like the rest. Don't settle for programs and providers that cannot show you case after case of actual students who joined the ranks of independent learners that succeed and excel without further assistance. Don't settle for programs that require 45 minutes of daily practice *indefinitely* because their effects are temporary. In fact, don't settle for programs that make family life too difficult or your child's education too costly.

Don't settle for less—because you know your child is bright. Don't settle for less because you have big dreams for her, and so does she.

NOTES

1. Later books in this series document other cases who completed their Dysolve programs.
2. To date, we have been able to identify the sources of language-based conditions in 100% of Dysolve students. Of these, 0.13% have additional issues in domains we do not cover such as vision.
3. See school statistics in Chapter 12.
4. Resilience comprises character strengths that enable one to cope, adapt and thrive in the face of adversity. Rather than view resilience as a static, intrinsic trait of one's personality, it may be more productively treated as a learned aptitude developed through experiences of adversity.
5. Statistics and research findings referenced in this section can be found in Hopkins, T., Clegg, J., & Stackhouse, J. (2016). Young offenders' perspectives on their literacy and communication skills. *International Journal of Language & Communication Disorders, 51*(1), 95–109.
6. The assessment used was the Clinical Evaluation of Language Fundamentals – 4th Ed. (CELF-4).
7. See Sanger, D., Moore-Brown, B.J., Montgomery, J., Rezac, C., & Keller, H. (2003). Female incarcerated adolescents with language problems talk about their own communication behaviours and learning. *Journal of Communication Disorders, 36*, 465–486. See also Sanger, D., Scheffler, M., Drake, B., Hilgert, K., Cresswell, J.W., & Hansen, D.J. (2000). Maltreated female delinquents speak about their communication behaviours. *Communication Disorders Quarterly, 21*, 176–187.
8. See Chapters 3-6 and 10.
9. These include recurrent headaches discussed in Chapters 1 and 3-6. A Dysolve Source Chart showing the impact of language-processing deficits is available upon request at Dysolve.com and Dysolve Dyslexia on Facebook.
10. The 20% figure is cited by the US Department of Health and Human Services, National Institutes of Health, and National Institute of Child Health and Human Development.

11. See Elliott, J.G., & Grigorenko, E.L. (2014). *The dyslexia debate*. New York: Cambridge University Press.
12. The 25th percentile threshold in reading assessment is often used to determine that a student has dyslexia. See Snowling, M.J. (2000). *Dyslexia*. Oxford, UK: Blackwell.
13. See Chapter 15 *Responsive Intelligence Technology*.
14. See Skye's Story in Chapter 3.
15. See Duke's Story in Chapter 2.
16. Shaywitz, S. (2003). *Overcoming dyslexia*. New York: Alfred A. Knopf.
17. These issues are illustrated to varying degrees by the cases in Part 1 of this book.
18. The 2017 NAEP (National Assessment of Educational Progress) report shows that the percentage of students performing at or above proficiency in reading did not improve from 4th to 8th grade. The number stayed constant at 35% through the grades for public schools nationwide. This means that the 65% who performed below proficiency in 4th grade likely remained so through the years. The reading score for 12th grade only improved by 1%. Retrieved from https://www.nationsreportcard.gov/
19. University experts admit that even their best programs cannot improve poor reading performance. See Fuchs, D., Compton, D.L., Fuchs, L.S., Bryant, V.J., Hamlett, C.L., & Lambert, W. (2012). First-grade cognitive abilities as long-term predictors of reading comprehension and disability status. *Journal of Learning Disabilities, 45*(3) 217–231.
20. See the Engineer's Story in Chapter 9 for a critique of classification and Implications for Dyslexia Intervention section in Chapter 15 for a discussion of how traditional evaluations have been superseded by dynamic, comprehensive, continuous assessment in micro detail due to advances in technology.
21. See Patience's case in Chapter 1.
22. See Skye's case in Chapter 3.
23. See Uno's case in Chapter 8.
24. See User2's case in Chapter 9.
25. See Storm's case in Chapter 4.

26. See Chapter 2 on latent changes.
27. See Questions from Schools in Chapter 17.

PART 2

Present and Future

Dyslexia Dissolved

12

The True Cost of Dyslexia

Evan Y. Haruta

We All Pay for Dyslexia

Nationwide, we spend more than twice as much for each special education student as for the general education pupil.[1] In New York State, about a third of the education budget goes to 9% of students, who are in special education.[2] Most of them have learning disabilities (LD), which are mainly dyslexia and its co-occurring disorders. This 9% is less than half of those with dyslexia, which is 20%.[3,4] This means that if we bring the other half of the students with dyslexia into special education, special education may gobble up two-thirds of the education budget, leaving only one-third (33%) for the remaining 80% of students (Figure 18).

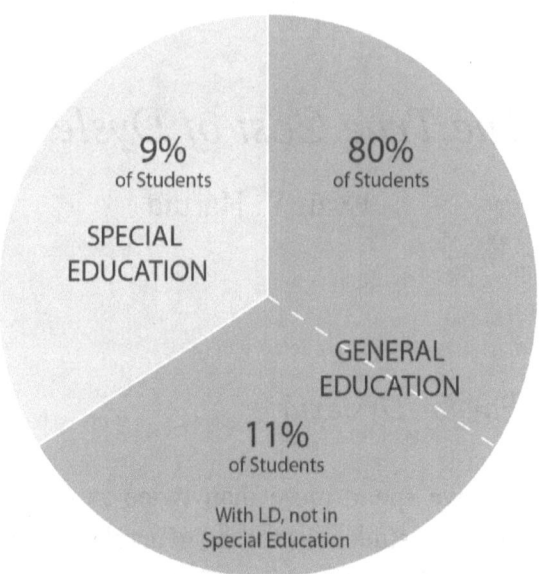

FIGURE 18
NY State Education Budget Allocations and Student Populations

Clearly, with present methods, the special education budget cannot feasibly accommodate all students with LD, which is why schools are forced to limit the number of students in this pricey pool. Thus even 5th graders who read at the 3rd grade level do not always qualify for school services. The present economics of dyslexia make it impossible for schools to honor the spirit of the Individuals with

Disabilities Education Act (IDEA), which promises a free appropriate education for all students with disabilities.

School districts typically cobble together a variable mix of federal, state and local funds to pay for special education. Special education spending in the US is over $70 billion a year nationally.[5] But even $70 billion a year is not enough for special education in the US, given present methods. The federal government underfunds special education, as do other sources. Although the IDEA includes a federal commitment to fund 40% of special education, the US government actually only coughs up around 16-17%.[6] This leaves more than a $10 billion shortfall for states and local school districts to deal with year after year.[7]

On top of this, special education is fast expanding. From 2006-2012, New York State's special education expenses increased by more than 26%.[8] Schools face increasing pressures from parents' growing awareness of dyslexia and more frequent diagnoses of this condition. As a result, other parts of school budgets are being squeezed out, such as sports programs, field trips, music and art.

Consequently, although dyslexia only occurs in about 20% of the population, we all pay for the present state of special education. And it is not sustainable.

Why is Special Ed so Expensive?

Special education expenses include teacher salaries and benefits, professional development for teachers, licensing fees to use commercial programs, registration fees to get teachers certified to use these programs, purchases of educational materials to use these programs, assistive technologies and hardware, purchases of evaluative materials from commercial publishers, etc., etc.

A small school in New York spends $10,000 on training for each one of its teachers in a popular commercial program based on Orton-Gillingham (OG).[9] One OG training course alone may cost each teacher over $2,000 while the training program requires 100 hours of teacher training for one module.[10] The site license for another popular OG offshoot, Barton Reading and Spelling System, costs $9,500. The Barton program involves 10 levels, with each one taking the student and teacher 3-5 months to complete. Another popular OG offshoot, Wilson Reading System, costs each classroom over $1,000 in materials including the teacher's kit and manual. Additionally, the small student-to-teacher ratio in special education also drives up expenses.

What does It Buy Us?

What do these exorbitant expenses from our taxpayer money buy us? Nationwide, these are the returns from our investments:
- Nearly two-thirds of students fail standardized reading tests in 4th, 8th and 12th grades.[11]
- Nearly three-quarters of students with reading disabilities (RD) stay classified throughout school.[12]
- Students with LD, most of whom have RD, drop out of high school at a rate almost three times that of others.[13]

- Nearly 85% of students with LD do not go to college (v. 34%).[14]
- Nearly 50% of prison inmates cannot read or write.[15]

If the general student population is unable to satisfy educational requirements, what hope is there for those whom reading experts call "low responders" and "non-responders"? University researchers acknowledge that even their best programs cannot improve poor reading performance.[16]

Cost Comparisons

Schools and private providers primarily use compensatory methods to help students cope with dyslexia, which means costs are incurred on an ongoing basis for the long-term. A corrective method such as Dysolve is needed to stop the cash outflow by moving students out of special education quickly and permanently. That is, present methods incur unending expenses while Dysolve incurs one-time costs. Add to this the cost advantage of automation, and the economic difference magnifies.

For illustration, we use a midsize school district in upstate New York. In the state of New York, general education cost in 2013 was just over $11,000 per student but special education was close to $30,000 per student.[17] This sample school district serves 700 special education students with reading disabilities. The cumulative cost keeps rising steeply with present compensatory methods, as about 75% of this group of 700 students continue to need special education services year after year, as shown in Figure 19.[18] On the other hand, the cumulative cost of using Dysolve is comparatively infinitesimal because of the low expense of a fully automated program.[19] After the first two years of Dysolve, students typically return to the less expensive general education pool.[20] Costs can be even lower as data analytics help to increase computer system efficiency, shortening remediation time. At the time of this writing, some Dysolve students in special education reached grade-level reading in just 2-3 months.

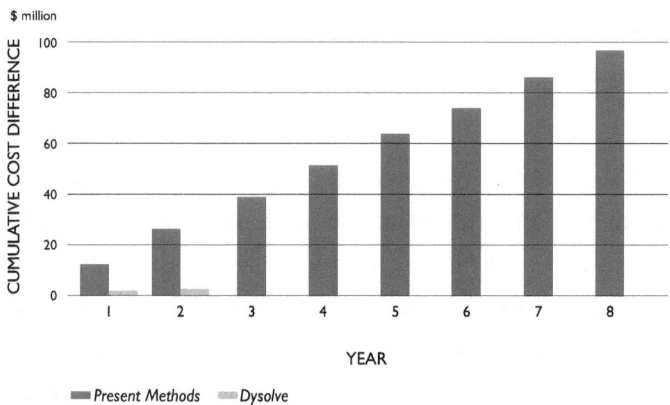

FIGURE 19

Cumulative Cost Difference of Special Ed Program vs. Dysolve for 700 Students at a NY School District[21]

The True Cost of Dyslexia

As shown in Figure 19, the cumulative cost difference between using Dysolve and the present methods in special education is close to $100 million for this cohort of 700 students. The *total* cost of using present methods at this midsize school district in New York is more than $155 million over the span of elementary and middle school for this cohort of 700 students in special education.[22] We can see why the district cannot take in the other 700 students with dyslexia who also need services, like some of the cases in this book.[23]

In contrast, the corrective method of Dysolve keeps the total cost under $20 million for the 700 students using the automated program.[24] Why is there such a big difference in cost? The answer: correction and automation. Owing to its corrective solution, Dysolve costs are not incurred indefinitely. Artificial intelligence and computing technology remove the costs of teacher training, licensing fees, program materials, test packets, testing specialists, administrative costs, etc., etc.

We discuss these implications further in Chapter 16 *Responsible Education.*

Individual Toll

The cost of Dysolve is presently $2,400 per student for one year.[25] This covers both continuous evaluation and training. Compare this with current alternatives:

Neuropsychological evaluation	$5,000[26]
Reading camps	$15,000[27]
Special dyslexia school	$160,000+[28]

Private school	$63,000+[29]
Homeschool – parent's lost income	$270,000+ [30]
Tutor	$10,000+[31]

Furthermore, since most students with learning disabilities do not go to college, they may miss out on the higher lifetime earnings that higher education offers. High school graduates typically earn about 66% less than Bachelor's degree holders during a 40-year working life.[32] The annual difference in earnings can grow to nearly $800,000 over that lifespan.[33]

These calculations do not even include the cost of medications for comorbid conditions and the wide-ranging effects of dealing with an invisible disability—not to mention the daily toll on the quality of life. We have tried to capture glimpses of these from the families who so generously opened their doors and hearts in Part 1 of this book.

How much do shattered dreams and abandoned hopes cost? How much does the missed potential of inventors, architects, engineers, artists, programmers and thinkers cost society?

Authors' note: The father in Chapter 1, who was in law enforcement, saw how other struggling learners engaged in risk behaviors even though his own child was shielded by a positive home environment. We present below the general trends for this vulnerable population.

Societal Cost

In the field of criminal justice, literacy deficits are widely accepted to be a major cause of crime. The typical juvenile inmate in the US is at the 9th grade level by age (15.5 years old) but reads at the 4th-grade level.[34] The average prison inmate has not attended school beyond the 10th grade and cannot achieve above a 7th grade level academically. This poor academic performance is attributed to the fact that at least 50% of them have a specific learning disability.

Data from the National Institute for Literacy showed that 43% of people with the lowest literacy skills live in poverty and 70% of this group have no full- or part-time employment.[35]

Therefore, *the average inmate in correctional facilities in the US is functionally nonliterate, never held a steady job, was a juvenile delinquent previously, and likely has a learning disability.*

NOTES

1. National Education Association. (2017). *Background of Special Education and the Individuals with Disabilities Education Act (IDEA)*. Retrieved from http://www.nea.org/home/19029.htm
2. Cunningham, D.H. (2015). *The education dollar: A look at spending and funding trends*. Albany, NY: NY State Association of School Business Officials. Retrieved from https://www.nysasbo.org/uploads/files/1442244064_Spending%202015%20%285%29.pdf
3. Office of Special Education and Rehabilitative Services, Office of Special Education Programs. (2016). *38th Annual Report to Congress on the Implementation of the Individuals with Disabilities Education Act, 2016*. Washington, DC: US Department of Education—9% of general population ages 6-21 served.
4. The 20% figure is used by the US Department of Health and Human Services, National Institutes of Health, National Institute of Child Health and Human Development.
5. About 16-17% of the special education budget is from the federal government. Federal funding for special education in 2011-17 ranges around $12 billion. See *Fiscal Year 2016, 2017 Budget Summary* at the US Department of Education site. See also Ellerson, N. (2017). *School budgets 101*. Alexandria, VA: American Association of School Administrators. Retrieved from https://www.aasa.org/uploadedFiles/Policy_and_Advocacy/files/SchoolBudgetBriefFINAL.pdf
6. See Note 3 above for the source.
7. See Note 1 above for the source.
8. See Note 2 above for the source.
9. This figure was provided by a Principal in a 3rd-5th grade school in New York, personal communication.
10. These figures are from the providers' websites:
    http://oginstruction.com/certified-level/,
    https://bartonreading.com/price/#license
    https://store.wilsonlanguage.com/just-words

11. The 2017 NAEP (National Assessment of Educational Progress) report shows that the percentage of students performing at or above proficiency in reading did not improve from 4th to 8th grade. The number stayed constant at 35% through the grades for public schools nationwide. This means that the 65% who performed below proficiency in 4th grade likely remained so through the years. The reading score for 12th grade only improved by 1%. Retrieved from https://www.nationsreportcard.gov/
12. Gunning, T. (2003). The role of readability in today's classroom. *Topics in Language Disorders, 23*(3), 175-185. In 2013-2014, only 9.2% of special education students aged 14-21 in the US transferred to general education. See Note 3 above for the source.
13. Office of Special Education and Rehabilitative Services, Office of Special Education Programs. (2014). *36th Annual Report to Congress on the Implementation of the Individuals with Disabilities Education Act, 2014.* Washington, DC: US Department of Education.
14. See Note 13 above for the source.
15. Vacca, J. (2004). Educated prisoners are less likely to return to prison. *Journal of Correctional Education, 55*(4), 297–305. See also National Center for Education Statistics. (1994). *Literacy behind prison walls.* Washington, DC: US Department of Education, Office of Educational Research and Improvement. Retrieved from https://nces.ed.gov/pubs94/94102.pdf
16. See Fuchs, D., Compton, D.L., Fuchs, L.S., Bryant, V.J., Hamlett, C.L., & Lambert, W. (2012). First-grade cognitive abilities as long-term predictors of reading comprehension and disability status. *Journal of Learning Disabilities, 45*(3) 217–231.
17. See Note 2 above.
18. Close to 75% of special education students remain classified throughout school. See Note 12 above.
19. At the time of this writing, the basic Dysolve fee is $200 a month per student, which includes full access to the online program 24/7 and 15 minutes a month of live assistance.

20. Dysolve generally resolves major language-processing problems in 1-2 years on average. Students sometimes stay longer to catch up on reading and writing acquisition missed in earlier years.
21. As about 25% of LD students eventually leave special education, we deduct 16 students from the 700 LD group from each of the 8 years of schooling before high school (= 176 students over 12 years of schooling). Dysolve annual cost is $2,400 for each of the 700 students for the Basic Plan. Students in Dysolve will also incur general education costs of $11,000 per pupil. We deduct $11,000 from both the Dysolve and present special education costs to derive the cost difference. Dysolve costs end in the second year as students typically leave the program to return to general education at that time. The Basic Plan is fully automated with minimal live assistance and is presently used by the majority of students in Dysolve.
22. The $155 million total cost of using present methods is obtained in this way: $30,000 per special education pupil x 700 students less 25% of students leaving special ed in gradual increments as given in Note 21 above over the span of 8 years.
23. Fewer than half the students with dyslexia receive special education services. See Note 3 above for the source.
24. Some students may require human assistance in Dysolve, but the additional cost is still minute compared with present special education expenses.
25. This is the subscription rate for using the online games with minimal human consultation. This Basic Plan is used by most Dysolve students at the time of this writing.
26. This was the fee that Frances in Chapter 3 paid. Neuropsychological evaluations generally cost $2,000 - $6,000+.
27. This was the fee that Frances in Chapter 3 paid for two summers.
28. The figure is derived from $40,000 of annual tuition over four years. Search for these schools under "language-based learning difference" or "language-based learning disabilities."
29. Some families place their children with special needs in smaller, private schools such as parochial schools in hopes of a more nurturing environment. The figure is based on $7,000

in annual tuition for 3rd-12th grades. Reading difficulties become obvious in 3rd grade.
30. Some families try to address their children's needs through homeschooling. The figure is based on a low annual income of $30,000, which a parent may forgo to homeschool his/her child for 3rd-12th grades.
31. This figure is based on tutoring services at $40/hour once a week for nine months from 3rd-10th grade when dyslexia is not corrected.
32. College Board. (2018). Lifetime earnings by education level. *Trends in higher education.* Retrieved from https://trends.collegeboard.org/education-pays/figures-tables/lifetime-earnings-education-level#Key%20Points
33. In 2015, median earnings for high school and college graduates were $30,500 and $50,000 respectively. US Department of Education, National Center for Education Statistics. (2017). Annual earnings of young adults. *The Condition of Education 2017* (NCES 2017-144). Retrieved from https://nces.ed.gov/fastfacts/display.asp?id=77
34. Statistics and facts in this section are from Vacca, J.S. (2008). Crime can be prevented if schools teach juvenile offenders to read. *Children and Youth Services Review, 30*(9), 1055-1062. Retrieved from https://doi.org/10.1016/j.childyouth.2008.01.013
35. See Note 34 above for the source.

Key Takeaways

Present methods leave half of students with dyslexia without services at school due to cost.

Those with learning disabilities make up at least half the prison population in the US.

Corrective, inexpensive solutions such as Dysolve are needed to stop the current drain on special education resources and the trend towards delinquency and crime.

13

State of the Science

The State We Inherited

The children and their families in Part 1 who suffered for years because of their dyslexia are but a tiny, tiny fraction of the 10 million students with reading disabilities who struggle in the US school system each year, and the tens of millions before them.[1] As seen in the statistics in Chapter 12, the prognosis is dismal for those who have not improved by late elementary and middle school. Reading researchers acknowledge that even the best and most intensive intervention programs available have not been able to help the group labeled "low responders" and "nonresponders."[2] How did this problem end up in this state?

Many of the present conceptions and issues surrounding dyslexia can be traced back to the history of its study and treatment. We give a brief tour of that history below to explain the state we inherited and our points of departure.[3]

Dyslexia emerged as a problem with a name in the late 1800s in Europe. The earliest reports by physicians described cases of adults who acquired text-blindness or word-blindness following a stroke, brain injury or disease. In the 1880s, German ophthalmologist Rudolph Berlin used the term *dyslexia* (meaning 'impaired word') to describe adult cases of reading problems due to cerebral disease. Interestingly, Berlin's adult patients complained of headaches when reading, much like the children in Part 1 of this book.[4]

From these adult cases of physical causes, interest grew in studying children who faced reading difficulties without brain trauma or disease. In medical reports of "congenital word-blindness" in children, the assumption was that the dysfunction was present since birth. These early case studies were reported primarily by specialists in vision such as ophthalmologists and eye surgeons because patients sought to locate the source of the problem in their sight.

Then as now, the physicians noted that affected children were bright but could not learn to read. These early reports stated that the children's intelligence was intact, as was their oral (expressive) language and other abilities such as math (although research now shows that speech impairment and math disability can co-occur with dyslexia). The condition was thus seen as a local or specific rather than generalized cerebral dysfunction. The children's condition came to be known as *developmental dyslexia*, as opposed to loss of reading ability in adulthood.

In 1902, a Glasgow ophthalmologist and surgeon, James Hinshelwood, provided a detailed account of congenital word-blindness that he attributed to defective visual memory of words and letters. Hinshelwood's work is important to note here because of the various threads of investigations and interventions that he initiated. First, since the child involved had difficulty learning to read by sight alone, Hinshelwood suggested using a multisensory teaching method and personal instruction, a precursor to today's special education.[5] Second, he believed that the deficit was confined to the visual memory center of the brain. Vision therapy continues to be used by some quarters today even though dyslexia is now widely accepted to be a language, not visual, disorder. Most significantly, Hinshelwood stated that diagnosis should be possible because the disorder's traits are distinct and easily understood. That sentiment remains among some of today's dyslexia specialists.[6]

The instructional aspect of dyslexia was expanded by American psychiatrist and neuropathologist Samuel Orton in the 1930s. Since regular instruction failed to get children with dyslexia to acquire written language, Orton suggested repetitive drills on sound-letter associations to secure them and to remove image reversals.[7] Orton's associate and psychologist Anna Gillingham applied his principles to remedial instruction that sequentially introduces the structure of the English language, from phonemes (sounds) to morphemes (parts of words) and spelling rules.

This Orton-Gillingham (OG) approach spawned many of the present remedial reading programs in schools and private services in the US, including the Wilson Reading System and Barton Reading and Spelling System. Generally, these OG methods involve overlearning written language through visual, auditory, kinesthetic and tactile means. They came to be called "multisensory instruction" and remain popular today. But note that a comprehensive review of the research to date concludes that "Despite the enthusiasm for multisensory approaches held by many specialist dyslexia teachers...the theoretical grounds and scientific rationale for their use are questionable."[8]

The Orton Dyslexia Society was established in 1949. The Orton Society became the present US-based International Dyslexia Association (IDA), which still advocates for the OG "explicit, systematic, multisensory" and "structured literacy" approach to reading instruction.[9] Academic journals in this field such as *Annals of Dyslexia, Reading and Writing*, and *Perspectives on Language and Literacy* are published by the IDA. Special schools for dyslexia and advocacy groups continue to promote the OG approach up to the present.[10]

The OG phonics approach involves identifying single sounds and then combining them into words, as well as the reverse procedure of segmenting words into single sounds.[11] At the same time, a competing whole-word approach pioneered by psychologist Grace Fernald emerged. Nevertheless, regardless of philosophical bent, pioneer after pioneer insisted on examining each child carefully to *understand his specific strengths and deficits so as to plan a comprehensive, dynamic educational program for that child.*

As more specialists and researchers entered this emerging field, the picture of dyslexia became increasingly robust—and complicated. The earlier hypothesis on visual deficits was supplanted by discovery of auditory and other deficits. Various linguistic, cognitive and perceptual processes and their various permutations in different subpopulations were discovered to be relevant. Comorbid (coexisting) conditions such as ADHD clouded the picture even further.[12]

Orton hypothesized that reversal errors (e.g., *b/d*) in dyslexia were caused by mirror images in the right brain hemisphere of the images in the left hemisphere dominant for language.[13] Orton's hypothesis is of course not supported by the evidence today. Yet the myth about letter reversals is still widespread among the public up till now.

The anatomical basis of dyslexia suggested by early researchers was investigated more intensively since the 1960s until today. With the advent of noninvasive neuroimaging technology such as fMRI (functional magnetic resonance imaging), researchers searched for physical markers of dyslexia in the brain.[14] Neuroanatomical differences appear to exist between dyslexic and non-dyslexic brains in group data. However, given this early state of neuroscience, the possibility of diagnosing dyslexia in individuals through brain scans is unlikely in the near future.[15]

A hundred years following the earliest accounts of dyslexia in Europe, the US government established several Centers for the Study of Learning and Attention to support research on learning disabilities. One of these centers at Yale University conducted a longitudinal study in 1983-84 that aimed to answer some of the critical questions surrounding dyslexia. One of the conclusions from the Yale study was that reading difficulties occur on a continuum. As one of the study's authors said:

> By not recognizing shades of gray represented by struggling children who haven't yet failed enough to meet a particular criterion, schools may be underidentifying many children who will go on to experience significant reading problems.[16]

By now, a mountain of studies shows that phonemic and phonological awareness is an important factor for the occurrence of dyslexia. Phonemic awareness is sensitivity to the sounds in words. Phonological awareness is sensitivity to the sound patterns of spoken language. But other types of linguistic ability, such as orthographic (spelling) and morphological (word structure) awareness were also found to be significant in other studies. Understandably, research and intervention focused on smaller and thus more manageable units while larger units of language received less attention. Nevertheless, the field started to recognize that multiple deficits affecting the processing of different components of language were involved in dyslexia.[17]

How does one diagnose an amorphous condition with multiple deficits? The traditional answer is to sample relevant traits in batteries of tests. One dominant approach involves quantifying identified discrepancies since the reading difficulty is considered to be "unexpected" given the individual's cognitive abilities.[18] Neuropsychological assessments thus examine students' language/reading achievement in the context of their cognitive profiles. But which cognitive variables should be sampled? IQ scores were included at one point but has since been abandoned.[19] Lack of empirical evidence led researchers to conclude that such assessments "failed to provide sufficient value-added benefit to justify their use" in informing appropriate intervention.[20] The most recent edition of the *Diagnostic and Statistical Manual of Mental Disorders* (DSM-5), commonly used as guidance, recommends a shift from "assessment for diagnosis" to "assessment for intervention." Nevertheless, traditional neuropsychological assessments remain popular in pockets of the country, as is the IQ criterion.

The other major approach is to assess reading skills directly within a Response to Intervention (RTI) framework. RTI is aimed at identifying at-risk students early and mitigating reading problems with increasingly intensive interventions as needed. Still, even with this direct approach, researchers note that "high-quality research studies have proven largely incapable of indicating how to help those who have not benefitted sufficiently from earlier high-quality interventions."[21]

Thus, the field acknowledges that existing expertise falls short in helping a significant group of failing readers. As seen in the cases in Part 1 of this book, although the details differ, the trajectory of reading and learning failure follows a similar gloomy path—unless a transformative intervention averts it.

Some reading researchers consequently call for qualitative changes to reading intervention since quantitative changes such as 100 hours of instruction have failed to produce desired reading outcomes.[22] Others call for "data-based individuation" that responds to each person's profile and needs, much as the early pioneers recommended.[23] But until the launch of Dysolve®, no such program could be individuated to this degree as researchers acknowledge that teachers simply do not have the high-level expertise required to respond capably to each student's deficits.[24]

As noted in Chapter 12, more than half of students with dyslexia do not get special services at school. Many of them are not even diagnosed. But for the fraction of affected students who are diagnosed, remediation mainly involves compensatory methods such as OG to help them cope with dyslexia.[25] They spend more time learning and overlearning the rules of language that others acquire easily. The intensive instruction is thought to be necessary because dyslexia is widely accepted at present to be chronic and lifelong.

The assumption that dyslexia is a lifelong condition was challenged by psychologist Paula Tallal, who developed the FastForword program.[26] Program users played interactive games to correct certain aspects of their auditory processing, but later studies found other areas of dysfunction that were equally important but not addressed in Tallal's invention.[27] The excitement over a "cure" abated in the late 1990s when the promise remained largely unfulfilled.

In 2014, Julian Elliott from the University of Durham and Elena Grigorenko from Yale University published *The Dyslexia Debate*, a comprehensive review of the dyslexia research to date.[28] Topic after topic, they concluded that the results of studies were conflicting, inconclusive or inadequate for claims widely propagated in the field.[29] At the end of their exhaustive study, the researchers proposed abandoning the term *dyslexia* as it is "inadequate for both classification and diagnosis."[30]

While the field of dyslexia research continues to grapple with fundamental questions about this disorder, the field of dyslexia intervention grew into the present patchwork of competing approaches, uneven support services, government agencies and private providers, dyslexia or reading specialists of various compensatory methods at varying levels of certification, assistive technologies, and alternative therapies that the OG-oriented IDA deems "controversial."[31] The 10 cases in this book illustrate the hodgepodge of services and programs used in and out of school before these students found the solution in Dysolve.

The Solution

The present state of uncertainty in the field notwithstanding, some of its most prominent scholars have already identified above what is needed to solve the most resistant cases of reading difficulty. In bringing together all the requirements that have been expressed over the years, we arrive at the specifications for the model program:

> *A comprehensive, data-driven, dynamic, responsive, individuated program for each student based on a comprehensive, data-driven, dynamic, responsive, individuated, continuous evaluation of her abilities and deficits.*

The problem is, teachers are not equipped to deliver such a program. It would require a vast amount of high-level expertise that teacher preparation programs do not, and cannot, cover.

We used all the specifications of the model program to build Dysolve®. This was why Dysolve® was able to transform the failing readers in Part 1 of this book to thriving learners. The next chapter describes how this transformation can be done on a massive scale.

Our solution emerged outside of the field of dyslexia research and practice. Dysolve® was made possible through sharp departures from accepted assumptions. Below we discuss some of the major points of departure.

Dyslexia-Free Life [32]

The foundational assumption that one is born with dyslexia for life was established early when cases were labeled as "*congenital* word-blindness."[33] This assumption was strengthened by observations that the young children involved came from good home environments that could not possibly have caused the reading problem. The assumption was solidified when dyslexia research adopted innateness theory from Linguistics and interpreted it as meaning that "language is innate."[34] Actually, innateness theory is complicated and subject to differing interpretations even within Linguistics.[35] It is easy to assume innate faculties to be fixed—unchanging and unchangeable. This assumption was compounded by neuroanatomical evidence that dyslexic brains are indeed different.[36]

Neuroplasticity—the ability of the brain to change and reorganize itself—is a relatively new concept.[37] Before neuroplasticity was popular, as it is now, we worked early in Dysolve on harnessing this pliable nature of the brain.

Even when linguistic and neuroanatomical features are found in young children, we cannot assume that these did not develop in early infancy. Much of one's language develops upon exposure to the native language, so that an American baby born in the US speaks English while an American baby born in Kenya speaks Kikuyu. Linguists in fact do not agree on what innateness means.[38] And even if certain tendencies were present at birth, that does not mean we cannot change them with practice. This is the new promise of neuroplasticity.

Define the Deficit, Not Dyslexia

We sympathize with researchers Elliott and Grigorenko who proposed dispensing with the term *dyslexia* owing to the confusion it generates.[39] Consider the following definitions of dyslexia from wellknown sources. We have underlined and labeled the parts for discussion:

Definition 1
Dyslexia is <u>a specific</u>[a] learning disability that is <u>neurobiological in origin</u>[b]. It is characterized by difficulties with <u>accurate and/or fluent word recognition and by poor spelling and decoding</u>[c] abilities. These difficulties typically result from <u>a deficit</u>[d] in the <u>phonological component</u>[e] of language that is often unexpected in relation to other cognitive abilities and the provision of <u>effective classroom instruction</u>[f]. Secondary consequences may include problems in <u>reading comprehension</u>[g] and <u>reduced reading experience that can impede growth of vocabulary</u>[h] and background knowledge. - International Dyslexia Association[40]

a. The categorical term "specific learning disability" can easily mislead the layperson to think of dyslexia as a single, unitary, clearly defined condition, which it is not.

b. This phrasing may mislead the layperson to assume that one is born with a dyslexic brain. The innateness question is far from settled.

c. This definition mixes reception (word recognition and decoding) with production (spelling). Production should be under writing, not reading. In any case, why are these three traits selected but not others? Reading is complicated and comprises many subprocesses. Why not lexical retrieval?[41] Why not anaphoric grounding of information nodes in the mentally represented text?[42]

d. Typically, affected individuals show more than one language deficit.[43]

e. Other components of language such as the morphological (word structure) and semantic (meaning) are also affected but receive less attention in research.

f. Does it mean that struggling readers from poor learning environments are excluded?[44]

g. Why are problems in reading comprehension considered secondary consequences and not traits that characterize dyslexia?

h. Reduced reading experience is said to impede vocabulary growth here, but the relationship is actually bidirectional. Limited vocabulary makes reading harder. Moreover, oral vocabulary may not be affected.

State of the Science

Definition 2
Dyslexic children and adults struggle to read fluently, spell words[i] correctly and learn a second language[j], among other challenges. - Yale Center for Dyslexia and Creativity[45]

i. As with the IDA definition above, the Yale definition mixes reading with writing.
j. Dyslexia here seems to be a broad condition that goes beyond reading difficulty. Second language learning requires a different set of skills. Reading difficulties need not impede oral language acquisition.

Definition 3
Dyslexia is a brain-based condition. It causes[k] difficulty with reading, spelling, writing and sometimes speaking[l]... Some people with dyslexia don't have[m] trouble sounding out or "decoding" words...Characteristics of dyslexia often include...Difficulty reading aloud with the proper tone and grouping words and phrases[n] together...Trouble writing or copying[o] letters, numbers and symbols[p] in the correct order...
- Understood[46]

k. Dyslexia is seen as the cause rather than the condition itself.
l. Dyslexia has expanded here beyond a reading disability to become a generalized language dysfunction.
m. This suggests different profiles for dyslexia.
n. Reading aloud with proper prosody involves phonological (sound) processing. But grouping words and

phrases together involves syntactic (sentence) processing.
o. Writing comprises a set of subprocesses that are different from copying. At the very least, copying may not require retrieval of forms from memory.
p. This definition seems to extend dyslexia beyond natural language.

Definition 4
Dyslexia is a learning disorder that affects your ability to read, spell, write, and speak.[q] Kids who have it are often smart and hardworking, but they have trouble connecting the letters they see to the sounds those letters make.[r] - WebMD[47]

q. Dyslexia has expanded here beyond a reading disability to become a generalized language dysfunction.
r. Actually, children who can make sound-letter associations may still face difficulty with the other subprocesses of reading.

To summarize, the confusion with the term *dyslexia* comes from
- implying that it is a single, specific condition or a broad dysfunction covering all language functions and beyond
- viewing it as both the cause and the condition itself
- sampling some traits without full consideration of prevalence, salience, their interrelationships and causal connections

- sampling some language components without full consideration of prevalence, salience, their interrelationships and causal connections
- sampling some reading subprocesses without full consideration of prevalence, salience, their interrelationships and causal connections

Let us set this straight: We will use *dyslexia* as an umbrella term to cover a spectrum of reading difficulties caused by underlying language-processing deficits. The brain has to process language when we speak, read, write and understand speech. This involves many processes, and any one of them can be deficient for various reasons. Each person's dyslexia is the collection of surface symptoms or effects of these underlying deficits. The reading difficulty, or dyslexia, is apparent: the child cannot learn to read despite much effort. What is not obvious is the complex of underlying deficits. It is this complex of underlying deficits we have to identify for each individual. At Dysolve, we call it the *root cause of dyslexia*.

Each complex of deficits may affect more than just reading, in which case dyslexia co-occurs with difficulties in other language functions such as writing. But the writing difficulty on the surface is called *dysgraphia*.[48] The underlying deficits may also affect speech, which is why dyslexia coexists with speech disorders, as seen in Chapters 1 and 9.

Language-processing deficits therefore create difficulties on the surface that may collectively be grouped under the general category of *language-based conditions*. That is, language-based conditions include dyslexia, dysgraphia, speech disorders, etc. The roots of these conditions can be traced to underlying language-processing deficits. When you can find each specific deficit, you no longer need indirect measures to gauge surface symptoms or discrepancies.[49] *The condition is defined directly by the deficits themselves.*

Only by locating each root cause can we correct the condition. When underlying deficits are corrected, dyslexia resolves itself on the surface since the latter is mainly a symptom of the former.

However, it is not easy to identify each underlying problem because each person with dyslexia has a different complex of language-processing deficits. Usually, each person has multiple, interrelated deficits that influence one another, as seen in our cases in Part 1. Each person thus presents a different and unique profile of deficits and related conditions. As mentioned above, the idea of multiple deficits that occupy a whole spectrum of difficulties on a continuum is already accepted in dyslexia research.[50]

In a nutshell, dyslexia is not a condition, disability or disorder. It is many conditions, disabilities or disorders. This much should have been apparent from the diversity of cases in Part 1 of this book. The dyslexia cases in the second book in this series are very different from the ones you read here and the cases in the third book, and so on.

Thus, when these unique cases are grouped together in dyslexia studies, results tend to vary from study to study. This partly explains why studies tend to yield conflicting and inconclusive findings.[51]

So how do you solve dyslexia? You don't. You solve the deficits that underlie each person's dyslexia. Therefore, there is not one solution for dyslexia. *There are many, many solutions for many, many dyslexias.* That is why nobody solved it before us.

New Science

To locate and remove specific language-processing deficits requires deep knowledge of language and language processing. Technical knowledge of language resides in Linguistics, the scientific study of language. But knowledge of language processing for the purpose of dyslexia diagnosis and intervention was not in any existing discipline when we first started two decades ago. We had to develop the new field of Computational Microlinguistics at Dysolve.[52]

Owing to the origin of dyslexia study, dyslexia was investigated by specialists outside of these essential fields, in medicine and psychology instead, and the responsibility of diagnosis remains in these traditional fields up to the present.

Chapter 14 explains this new science and Chapter 15 describes the new technology that supports it.

Correct, Not Compensate

Without the necessary knowledge and tools to locate the underlying deficits, present remediation methods thus focus on compensating for the surface symptoms, dyslexia. Furthermore, the field settled on compensation rather than correction because of the early assumptions of congenital word-blindness and innate language. Teachers, educational psychologists, reading specialists and tutors try their best to alleviate students' struggles with compensatory methods such as Orton-Gillingham, structured literacy or multisensory instruction. But without removing the underlying deficits, the rules of language remain difficult to internalize because, as a Dysolve student said, they "don't make sense" to someone with problems processing language. While special education students struggle to learn and overlearn these rules year after year, special education budgets continue to expand alarmingly beyond their projected size.[53]

The logical solution is to remove the obstacle to learning, to get struggling students to learn to process language as others do. That obstacle is the root cause of dyslexia, the complex of underlying deficits for each student. Once their processing deficits are corrected, struggling students perform like their peers, as happened in the cases in Part 1.

Functional, Not Physical Brain

Interest in the biological basis of dyslexia started early. Brain sciences will no doubt yield all kinds of interesting discoveries about us in this new frontier in this millennium. But we are not there yet on many fronts. Scientists do not yet know how to read individual brain scans for language. The scientific reality is far from the hype in the popular media often accompanying brain images lit up in fluorescent colors. As neuroscientists at Boston Children's Hospital acknowledge:

> It is important to note that to date it is not possible to reliably identify brain alterations characteristic for dyslexia in a single subject and it is unclear whether this will be possible in the near future (or ever)...Furthermore, while neural measures enhance the overall prediction accuracy of behavioral measures, their additional contribution is moderate and may not warrant the high costs and logistical problems associated with using MRI with young children (yet).[54]

Even if we could identify dyslexia from brain scans, they do not show us how to transpose a wrongly activated area to the correct one.

Scientists can work patiently for decades to solve these challenges. But growing children cannot. Every year that we delay, we risk losing millions of them to academic failure, defeatism and delinquency. This is why we focus on the functional brain instead of the physical brain at Dysolve.[55]

So long as we are accurate in our new science of Computational Microlinguistics, struggling students can learn to function like their peers, or better, right now. And so long as we are good at this predictive science, we can locate deficits in the functional brain and replace present compensatory methods with our corrective solution. Someday, we may well see how our functional brain maps onto the physical brain.[56]

But we don't have to wait for the future to help the student today.

NOTES

1. The figure is from the US National Institutes of Health. In 2015–2016, 6.7 million students received special education services in the US. When we combine the percentage of these students who were classified with specific learning disability, speech or language impairment and other conditions known to involve language-processing deficits, the percentage is close to the 80% used widely as the fraction of students with dyslexia out of this population. As slightly less than half of the students with learning disabilities actually get services at school, we estimate that the total with dyslexia amount to over 10 million. The 2015-16 data are from the US Department of Education, Office of Special Education Programs, *Individuals with Disabilities Education Act (IDEA) database.*
   Retrieved from
   https://www2.ed.gov/programs/osepidea/618-data/state-level-data-files/index.html#bcc.
   In addition, the US child population for ages 6-17 in 2018 is 49.5 million. Using the established 20% figure for dyslexia, the at-risk population is 9.9 million. Source:
   https://www.childstats.gov/americaschildren/tables.asp
2. See Fuchs, D., Compton, D.L., Fuchs, L.S., Bryant, V.J., Hamlett, C.L., & Lambert, W. (2012). First-grade cognitive abilities as long-term predictors of reading comprehension and disability status. *Journal of Learning Disabilities, 45*(3) 217–231. See also Vellutino, F.R., Scanlon, D.M., Zhang, H., & Schatschneider, C. (2008). Using response to kindergarten and first grade intervention to identify children at-risk for long-term reading difficulties. *Reading and Writing, 21*, 437-480.
3. The historical facts are from Mather, N., & Wendling, B.J. (2012). *Essentials of dyslexia assessment and intervention.* Hoboken, NJ: John Wiley & Sons. And Shaywitz, S. (2003). *Overcoming dyslexia.* New York: Alfred A. Knopf.
4. See Chapters 1 and 3-6 on recurrent headaches.
5. See the Orton-Gillingham approach below in this chapter.

6. See Shaywitz, S. (2003). *Overcoming dyslexia*. New York: Alfred A. Knopf.
7. Dyslexia is now known to be a language, not visual, disorder. It is also not characterized by letter or image reversals although these do occur with some people with dyslexia for various reasons.
8. Elliott, J.G., & Grigorenko, E.L. (2014). *The dyslexia debate*. New York: Cambridge University Press, p. 150.
9. Stated on IDA's website https://dyslexiaida.org/history-of-the-ida/.
10. Search under "language-based learning difference" or "language-based learning disabilities" to see the schools for dyslexia.
11. OG practitioners call this combining of sounds into words "blends." But this is not technically correct. Technically speaking, blends are new words formed by deleting internal structures of syllables and merging the remaining structures. An example of a blend is Skye's formation of the word *yield* from *yell* and *field* in the next chapter.
12. See what the research says on ADHD in the Notes in Chapter 6.
13. Some letter reversals, such as *b/d*, are probably caused by the similarity in sounds instead.
14. These fMRI studies require child subjects to stay still for some duration and cannot involve tasks needing much motion such as speaking. There are also statistical issues associated with these studies including in the interpretation of brain scan results. For a review of the research on the neuroanatomical profile of dyslexia, see Eckert, M. (2004). Neuroanatomical markers for dyslexia: A review of dyslexia structural imaging studies. *Neuroscientist, 10*(3), 1–10.
15. See the quote about using MRI on young children at the end of this chapter.
16. Shaywitz, S. (2003). *Overcoming dyslexia*. New York: Alfred A. Knopf, p. 28.
17. See the research review in Elliott, J.G., & Grigorenko, E.L. (2014). *The dyslexia debate*. New York: Cambridge University Press.

18. Actually, the affected students' underachievement is expected when we know the underlying deficits involved.
19. See Rose, J. (2009). *Identifying and teaching children and young people with dyslexia and literacy difficulties. (The Rose Report)*. Nottingham, UK: DCSF Publications.
20. Fletcher, J.M., Stuebing, K.K., Barth, A.E., Denton, C.A., Cirino, P.T., Francis, D.J.,...Vaughn, S. (2011). Cognitive correlates of inadequate response to reading intervention. *School Psychology Review, 40*, 3-22, p. 20.
21. Quoted in Elliott, J.G., & Grigorenko, E.L. (2014). *The dyslexia debate*. New York: Cambridge University Press, p. 141. The study is Wanzek, J., & Roberts, G. (2012). Reading interventions with varying instructional emphases for fourth graders with reading difficulties. *Learning Disability Quarterly, 35*(2), 90-101.
22. Vaughn, S., Cirino, P.T., Wanzek, J., Wexler, J., Fletcher, J.M., Denton, C.D.,...Francis, D.J. (2010). Response to intervention for middle school students with reading difficulties: Effects of a primary and secondary intervention. *School Psychology Review, 39*(1), 3-21.
23. See Fuchs, D., McMaster, K.L., Fuchs, L.S., & Al Otaiba, S. (2013). Data-based individualization as a means of providing intensive instruction to students with serious learning disorders. In H.L. Swanson, K.R. Harris, & S. Graham (Eds.). *Handbook of learning disabilities* (pp. 526-544). New York: Guilford Press. See also Fuchs, L.S., Fuchs, D., & Compton, D.L. (2010). Commentary: Rethinking response to intervention at middle and high school. *School Psychology Review, 39*, 22-28.
24. See the researchers mentioned in Note 22 above.
25. Other remedial methods include Lindamood-Bell, which focuses on "sensory-cognitive functions" to help each person reach his/her potential. Go to https://lindamoodbell.com/webelieve
26. Tallal, P. (2012). Improving neural response to sound improves reading. *PNAS, 109*, 16406-16407. See also patent publications by W.M. Jenkins, M.M. Merzenich, S.L. Miller, B.E. Peterson, & P. Tallal.

27. See Goswami, U., Mead, N., Foster, T., Huss, M., Barnes, L., & Leong, V. (2013). Impaired perception of syllable stress in children with dyslexia: A longitudinal study. *Journal of Memory and Language, 69*(1), 1-17. Retrieved from https://doi.org/10.1016/j.jml.2013.03.001
28. Elliott, J.G., & Grigorenko, E.L. (2014). *The dyslexia debate.* New York: Cambridge University Press.
29. The fields of ADHD and autism research face the same problem of uncertainty as well, leaving the causal relationships of these conditions that are comorbid with dyslexia unclear. See the Notes in Chapters 4 and 6.
30. Elliott, J.G., & Grigorenko, E.L. (2014). *The dyslexia debate.* New York: Cambridge University Press, p. 178. They suggested a more specific construct that can be measured such as "reading disability" (word-reading difficulty). We address this question in Chapter 17.
31. Pennington, B.F. (2011). Controversial therapies for dyslexia. *Perspectives on Language and Literacy, 37*(1), 7-8.
32. Dyslexia as a lifelong condition is echoed by such organizations as the Yale Center for Dyslexia and Creativity, the Mayo Clinic and the not-for-profit Understood.
33. See Berlin's work at the beginning of this chapter.
34. Quote from Shaywitz, S. (2003). *Overcoming dyslexia.* New York: Alfred A. Knopf, p. 45.
35. See for example Elman, J.L., Bates, E.A., Johnson, M.H., Karmiloff-Smith, A., Parisi, D., & Plunkett, K. (1999). *Rethinking innateness.* Cambridge, MA: MIT Press.
36. More recent work is oriented towards a more dynamic view of the brain. See for example Krafnick, A.J., Flowers, D.L., Napoliello, E.M., & Eden, G.F. (2011). Gray matter volume changes following reading intervention in dyslexic children. *NeuroImage, 57*(3), 733-741. doi:10.1016/j.neuroimage.2010.10.062
37. See early works in for example Brauth, S.E., Hall, W.S., & Dooling, R.J. (Eds.). (1991). *Plasticity of development.* Cambridge, MA: MIT Press.
38. The nature/nurture debate in Linguistics is reframed in MacWhinney, B. (Ed.). (1999). *The emergence of language.* Mahwah, NJ: Lawrence Erlbaum.

39. Elliott, J.G., & Grigorenko, E.L. (2014). *The dyslexia debate*. New York: Cambridge University Press.
40. https://dyslexiaida.org/definition-of-dyslexia/
41. *Lexical retrieval* means the retrieval of words. This itself is a complicated process involving extraction of not just word forms but also their meanings, phonetic representations, etc. See the description of the retrieval of the word *yield* in the next chapter.
42. Anaphoric grounding involves connecting incoming new information chunks to existing mental representation of the text. See Givón, T. (1995). *Functionalism and grammar*. Amsterdam: John Benjamins.
43. The field acknowledges that multiple deficits are involved, and this is seen in the cases in Part 1.
44. The distinction between dyslexic vs. poor readers is controversial in the field. See Elliott, J.G., & Grigorenko, E.L. (2014). *The dyslexia debate*. New York: Cambridge University Press.
45. http://dyslexia.yale.edu/dyslexia/what-is-dyslexia/
46. Understood is a not-for-profit aimed at educating parents on learning and attention issues. Go to https://www.understood.org/en/learning-attention-issues/child-learning-disabilities/dyslexia/understanding-dyslexia
47. WebMD is a popular Internet source for health information. (https://www.webmd.com/children/understanding-dyslexia-basics)
48. The term *dysgraphia* is also confusing. Sometimes it refers to all writing difficulties. In some quarters, it is only confined to the mechanics of handwriting and does not cover composing.
49. See neuropsychological assessments discussed above in this chapter.
50. See Note 16 above.
51. See the research review in Elliott, J.G., & Grigorenko, E.L. (2014). *The dyslexia debate*. New York: Cambridge University Press.
52. This new science is described in the next chapter.
53. See Chapter 12.

54. Ozernov-Palchik, O., & Gaab, N. (2016). Tackling the early identification of dyslexia with the help of neuroimaging. *Perspectives on Language and Literacy*, *42*(1), 11-17, p. 15.
55. See Chapters 14 and 15.
56. This is also the goal of Linguistics: that we will eventually find the biological underpinnings of present theoretical models of language.

Key Takeaways

Researchers are still grappling with fundamental questions about dyslexia.

Lacking essential knowledge, even intensive "evidence-based, best-practice" intervention methods remain ineffective for a significant number.

Researchers call for individuated programs, but the level of expertise required is beyond that of teachers, providers and specialists outside of Dysolve.

14

Computational Microlinguistics[1]
Coral P.S. Hoh

The Challenge

In the previous chapter, we laid out the problem of dyslexia:
- It is not a single condition but a whole spectrum of difficulties.
- Each person affected has a different complex of underlying language-processing deficits.
- Each person affected usually has multiple deficits.
- The deficits are interrelated in different ways.

To solve dyslexia, therefore, we had to first recognize the complexity of the problem. We give a brief overview of the problem below.

Structure-Complex

Yield. You read the word *yield* on this page right away. But wait—the word is not really on the page. These are just marks on the page. Somehow these marks triggered something in your brain to make you see the word *yield*.

Activated in your brain is a whole network of associations tied to the components of language: the orthographic (spelling: Y-I-E-L-D), phonetic (sounds: [jild]), semantic (meaning: 'to give way'), morphological (affixes: *-s, -ed, -ing*), syntactic (sentence structure: *We do not yield*/SUBJ-AUX-NEG-VERB), etc. There are also affective (emotional) associations tied to the history of your own encounters with this word, such as the context in which you first learned *yield*, your experiences with drivers who do or do not yield, and so forth.

But these activated associations are just the tip of the iceberg. Let's go deeper. Let's take the phonetic or sound component. The word *yield* is made up of the phonemes (sounds) /j, i, l, d/. Each phoneme is in turn made up of smaller atoms of sounds called *phonetic features*. Figure 20 shows the Phonetic Feature Matrix for English consonants. Each phoneme is differentiated from all other phonemes by its unique combination of binary features at this atomic level.[2] Thus, each phoneme or sound is actually a composite of smaller units.

Features	p	b	m	t	d	n	k	g	ŋ	f	v	θ	ð
Consonantal	+	+	+	+	+	+	+	+	+	+	+	+	+
Sonorant	−	−	+	−	−	+	−	−	+	−	−	−	−
Syllabic	−	−	−/+	−	−	−/+	−	−	−/+	−	−	−	−
Nasal	−	−	+	−	−	+	−	−	+	−	−	−	−
Voiced	−	+	+	−	+	+	−	+	+	−	+	−	+
Continuant	−	−	−	−	−	−	−	−	−	+	+	+	+
Labial	+	+	+	−	−	−	−	−	−	+	+	−	−
Alveolar	−	−	−	+	+	+	−	−	−	−	−	−	−
Palatal	−	−	−	−	−	−	−	−	−	−	−	−	−
Anterior	+	+	+	+	+	+	−	−	−	+	+	+	+
Velar	−	−	−	−	−	−	+	+	+	−	−	−	−
Coronal	−	−	−	+	+	+	−	−	−	−	−	+	+
Sibilant	−	−	−	−	−	−	−	−	−	−	−	−	−

FIGURE 20
*Part of the Phonetic Feature Matrix
of English Consonants*

We can do the same with the semantic or meaning component. The word *yield* can similarly be differentiated from all other words in the English lexicon by atoms of meaning called *semantic features*. Figure 21 shows a sample of words that are synonyms of *yield*. Thus a word is like a molecule made up of smaller atoms of meaning or semantic features. These atoms, such as ±PERMANENCE, recur in other words, in different combinations with other semantic features.

Features	
Yield	+GIVE IN, +PRESSURE, +AUTHORITY +WILL, +SIDES, -PERMANENCE
Capitulate	+GIVE IN, +PRESSURE, -AUTHORITY -WILL, +SIDES, +PERMANENCE
Submit	+GIVE IN, +PRESSURE, -AUTHORITY -WILL, -SIDES, +PERMANENCE
Relent	+GIVE IN, +PRESSURE, +AUTHORITY +WILL, +SIDES, -PERMANENCE
Succumb	+GIVE IN, +PRESSURE, +AUTHORITY -WILL, +SIDES, +PERMANENCE
Defer	+GIVE IN, -PRESSURE, -AUTHORITY +WILL, +SIDES, -PERMANENCE

FIGURE 21
Sample - Componential Analysis of the Lexical Field of Yield

In short, components of language can be broken down further into smaller and smaller discrete units at the atomic level. Some, like the phonetic and semantic components, can be defined by binary values not unlike the binary code of programming. Although natural language may seem amorphous, highly variable and ever-changing to the layperson, it can nevertheless be studied as a system of stable structures of discrete units.[3]

Imagine language as a gigantic Rubik's Cube. Each component is made up of subcomponents; each subcomponent is made up of smaller sub-subcomponents, and on and on down to the little atoms of language. But that is not all. We still have to understand how each component and subcomponent and sub-subcomponent interfaces with other parts of this complex structure.

Say we take the semantic-syntactic interface, specifically how meaning features of words constrain how words are combined into sentences. Figure 22 shows a semantic-syntactic representation of a sentence.[4] The sentence example used is *"Orwell is sure that his political activity improves his work."*

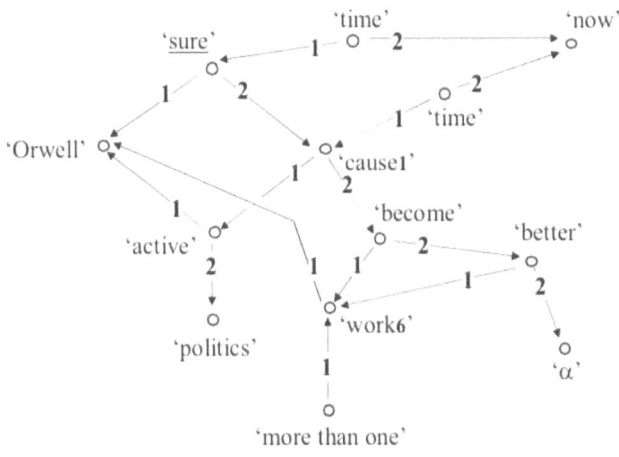

FIGURE 22
Representation of the Semantic-Syntactic Structure of a Sentence

Understanding a sentence therefore involves activation of this kind of network in addition to many other representations at many levels throughout the various components and subcomponents of language.

The foregoing gives a cursory preview of the complexity of linguistic structures. It is but a brief glimpse of the structure-complex we call *language*.[5]

Problem-Complex

Knowledge from Linguistics gives us the description of this structure-complex. But to solve the problem of dyslexia, we need to know what the brain *does* with language, and more specifically how the dyslexic brain responds to language. This was the answer that was not available from existing disciplines when we first started in Dysolve. It was the knowledge we had to build up ourselves for over two decades.

To illustrate the problem, let's consider how Skye in Chapter 3 learned the word *yield*:
1. Bring up a visual image of a person yelling.
2. Retrieve the word *yell*.
3. Bring up a visual image of a field of grass.
4. Retrieve the word *field*.

Computational Microlinguistics

5. Analyze the internal structure of *yell*:[6]

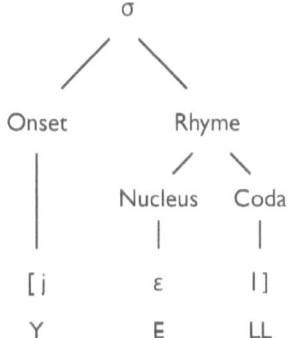

6. Analyze the internal structure of *field*:

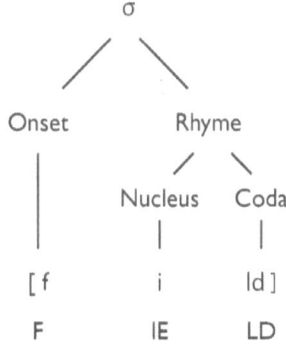

7. Delete the rhyme of *yell*:

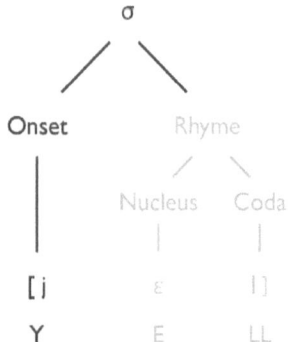

8. Delete the onset of *field*:

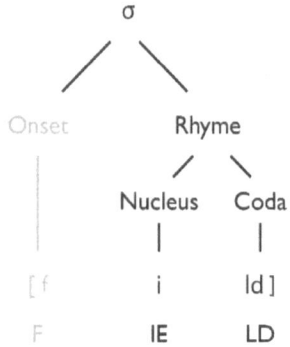

9. Blend the remaining parts of the two structures:

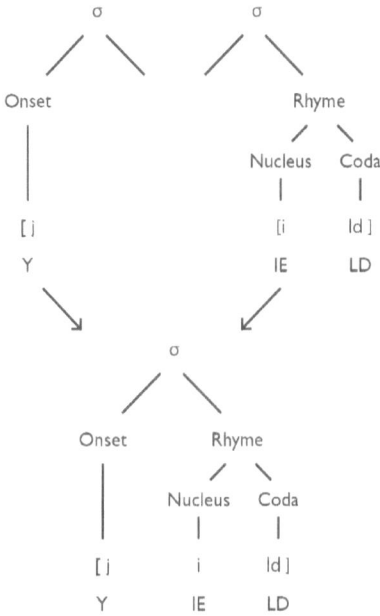

10. Obtain the word *yield*.

Steps 1-10 allowed Skye to learn and store the word *yield*. To retrieve the word later to use in an appropriate context, Skye had to go through the same operations 1-10 again. All these she had to do laboriously and consciously, unlike us.

The result? Cognitive overload—when the brain gets too overwhelmed to perform further processing. Skye used to experience recurrent headaches due to this processing overload.[7]

Despite its astounding complexity, we process natural language rapidly, and for the most part automatically and subconsciously. However, individuals with dyslexia do not typically process language this way. The *yield* example above shows that lexical storage for Skye in some cases required a clunky set of associations that involved visual images, other lexical (word) items, parts of other syllables, etc. Of course, Skye did not store every word in this way. She used a haphazard, chaotic assortment of means to enable lexical storage. This we had to clean up for Skye.

Computational Problem

To resolve Skye's problem, we had to be able to see her language-processing deficits with clarity. This was a challenge, given the complexity of language processing. How big a challenge?

Let's illustrate with a few examples below. Consider first the semantic component of language. In this semantic component, we see each word represented by a set of binary features as shown previously in Figure 21. Figure 21 is just a tiny sample—we would need to add many, many other words with their own sets of binary semantic features. How many words are there in the mental lexicon represented in our heads?[8] How many billions of atoms of meaning are associated with these words? The number becomes very large very quickly.

Next consider a tiny phonetic subcomponent. In this phonetic subcomponent, we consider the possible bisyllabic words in English containing the sound /p/.[9] Syllables assume certain forms because sounds can only co-occur with certain other sounds in a language. For example, /kp/ do not begin a word in English.[10] These restrictions are called *phonotactic constraints*.[11] Knowing a language includes knowing these phonotactic constraints. A competent native speaker knows how to coin new words that sound like English words because they abide by these phonotactic constraints. By the same token, the native speaker knows when her spelling does not seem right because it violates these constraints. Figure 23 shows a sample of the number of possible forms of bisyllabic words with /p/ in English.

V + /p/ + V	= 18x1x18 = 324
V + /p/ + V + C	= 18x1x18x24 = 7,776
V + /p/ + V + CC	= 18x1x18x34 = 11,016
V + /p/ + V + CCC	= 18x1x18x17 = 5,508
C + V + /p/ + V	= 23x18x1x18 = 7,452
C + V + /p/ + V + C	= 23x18x1x18x24 = 178,848
C + V + /p/ + V + CC	= 23x18x1x18x34 = 253,368
C + V + /p/ + V + CCC	= 23x18x1x18x17 = 126,684
CC + V + /p/ + V	= 22x18x1x18 = 7,128
CC + V + /p/ + V + C	= 22x18x1x18x24 = 171,072
CC + V + /p/ + V + CC	= 22x18x1x18x34 = 242,352
CC + V + /p/ + V + CCC	= 22x18x1x18x17 = 121,176
CCC + V + /p/ + V	= 4x18x1x18 = 1,296
CCC + V + /p/ + V + C	= 4x18x1x18x24 = 31,104
CCC + V + /p/ + V + CC	= 4x18x1x18x34 = 44,064
CCC + V + /p/ + V + CCC	= 4x18x1x18x17 = 22,032
V + C + /p/ + V	= 18x24x1x18 = 7,776
C + V + C + /p/ + V	= 23x18x4x1x18 = 31,104
CC + V + C + /p/ + V	= 22x18x4x1x18 = 28,512
CCC + V + C + /p/ + V	= 4x18x4x1x18 = 5,184
V + C + /p/ + V + C	= 18x4x1x18x24 = 31,104
V + C + /p/ + V + CC	= 18x4x1x18x34 = 44,064
V + C + /p/ + V + CCC	= 18x4x1x18x17 = 22,032
V + C + /p/ + C + V	= 18x3x1x1x18 = 972
C + V + C + /p/ + C + V	= 23x18x3x1x1x18 = 22,356
CC+ V + C + /p/ + C + V	= 22x18x3x1x1x18 = 21,384
CCC+ V + C + /p/ + C + V	= 4x18x3x1x1x18 = 3,888
V + C + /p/ + C + V + C	= 18x3x1x1x18x24 = 23,328
V + C + /p/ + C + V + CC	= 18x3x1x1x18x34 = 33,048
V + C + /p/ + C + V + CCC	= 18x3x1x1x18x17 = 16,524
C + V + C + /p/ + C + V + C	= 23x18x3x1x1x18x24 = 536,544
CC + V + C + /p/ + C + V + C	= 22x18x3x1x1x18x24 = 513,216
CCC + V + C + /p/ + C + V + C	= 4x18x3x1x1x18x24 = <u>93,312</u>
	TOTAL 2,675,548

FIGURE 23
Sample - Number of Possible Bisyllabic Words with /p/ in English

The number of possible words easily exceeds 2.6 million quickly.[12] But that is just for one sound in English and for only bisyllabic words.

And that does not even get us close to the problem of dyslexia. On top of understanding the problem of language, we have to understand the problem of language processing. This means knowing and predicting how different individuals, both typical and dyslexic, receive and produce language in the course of daily functioning in varying contexts in various modalities in a multitude of permutations.

Do you see where we are going with this? This is largely a computational problem. The problem of language processing, specifically dyslexia, cannot be solved easily by a human being. Yes, we did resolve dyslexia for individuals in our pre-automation days. But as our number of students grew, it quickly became very difficult to record, track, cross-reference and interpret billions of datapoints. But this is what computers do best.

Computational Microlinguistics

We had to learn how individual brains work beyond what was available in the emerging fields of the neurosciences. Specifically, we had to understand and predict how different brains respond to Dysolve-generated tasks.

We called our new field *Computational Microlinguistics*. Its goal is to solve the computational problem defined above. Computational Microlinguistics is distinct from the established field of Computational Linguistics, which investigates the computational and mathematical properties of language and develops natural language processing systems. Natural language processing (NLP) uses the tools from computer science and artificial intelligence to develop computer systems that can produce and receive language, like humans. *Natural language processing* is distinct from the term *language processing* used in this book. The former refers to computers; the latter to humans. Whereas the old field is aimed at having machines match humans' language capability, our new field is aimed at having machines *correct* humans' language difficulties.

How can a computer program correct a person's linguistic difficulties? Dysolve® does so through a type of artificial intelligence we call *Responsive Intelligence Technology*^{TM}. Dysolve® is the first computer system to have this responsive intelligence technology. The term captures the autonomous capabilities of Dysolve® to prompt and respond to input to correct users' language-processing deficits.

Through Dysolve's responsive actions, the system effects changes to the language user's abilities. To ensure desired effects, we built the architecture of Dysolve® on the knowledge we accumulated from our successful fieldwork with the Coral Method®. This knowledge is also the foundation of our new science, Computational Microlinguistics. We continue to expand Computational Microlinguistics as the intelligent system yields new discoveries from accumulating detailed user data.

Traditionally, the term *Micro Linguistics* is used to refer to the theoretical description of the components of language. We use the term *Microlinguistics* in the new science to mean, in addition, the incremental, micro changes we effect on language users' abilities. Computational Microlinguistics helps us find micropatterns and assign meaning to microfeatures in users' program data. Computational Microlinguistics was essential to the understanding and resolution of the dyslexia cases in Part 1 of this book. This new science will equally be necessary for resolving the diversity of language-based conditions in the future.

NOTES

1. See the end of this chapter for the description of Computational Microlinguistics.
2. If you go down the column of binary features for /p/ and its neighbor /b/ in the Phonetic Feature Matrix, you see that these consonants are only differentiated by the feature $\pm$Voiced, meaning that these phonemes differ in the onset of vibration of the vocal cords.
3. See the works of the founding figure of modern Linguistics, Ferdinand de Saussure. Saussure's *Cours de linguistique générale* or *Course in general linguistics*. Bally, C., & Sechehaye, A. (Eds.). (1915). *Course in General Linguistics - Ferdinand de Saussure*. (Baskin, W., Transl.). New York: McGraw-Hill.
4. The model is from Mel'čuk, I., & Beck, D. (2016). *Language: From meaning to text*. Moscow: Academic Studies Press.
5. The term *natural language* is used traditionally in Linguistics to refer to human language. Natural language is distinguished from artificial language used in computer science.
6. The syllable comprises the onset and rhyme. The onset comprises all beginning consonants preceding the first vowel. The rhyme can be further divided into the nucleus and coda. The nucleus comprises the vowel(s). The coda comprises any consonant(s) following the nucleus. See the reference in Note 11 below.
7. Skye's recurrent headaches are described in Chapter 3.
8. *Mental lexicon* refers to the representations of words in our heads. This would include the network of associations to the various components of language as described at the beginning of this chapter. How many words do we know? The question is not easy to answer because it depends on how we define "word." See Brysbaert, M., Stevens, M., Mandera, P., & Keuleers, E. (2016). How many words do we know? Practical estimates of vocabulary size dependent on word definition, the degree of language input and the participant's age. *Frontiers in Psychology, 7*, 1116. doi:10.3389/fpsyg.2016.01116

9. Bisyllabic or two-syllable words with /p/ include *happy* (C+V+/p/+V). Phonetically, *happy* has only one /p/ in the middle although it is spelled with two *P*s.
10. Unless it is a foreign borrowing.
11. Phonotactic constraint is a wellknown concept in Linguistics and is discussed in introductory texts. See for example Radford, A., Atkinson, M., Britain, D., Clahsen, H., & Spencer, A. (2009). *Linguistics: An introduction*. Cambridge: Cambridge University Press.
12. Of course not all combinations here are realized in the English lexicon. But linguistic competence includes knowing which combinatorial forms are *possible* in English.

Key Takeaways

The problem-complex of dyslexia requires a computational solution.

This computational solution requires a new science that describes, explains and predicts how individuals with dyslexia process language.

This new science, Computational Microlinguistics, enables us to change language users' abilities.

15

Responsive Intelligence Technology[1]

Coral P.S. Hoh

System and Human Requirements

In Chapter 12, we explain why the present state of special education is unsustainable. In Chapter 13, we summarize how the field of dyslexia research and practice ended up in this state. In Chapter 14, we describe the complexity of the solution needed to end this state.

Now in this chapter we describe the solution. In the preceding chapter, we clarify why it has to be a computational solution. Given the nature of dyslexia as described in Chapter 14 and current realities, the computer system to be developed has to meet the following requirements.

System requirements:
- Deliver through the cloud
- Access through portable devices
- Be compatible with different devices

- Allow 24/7 access
- Have nanosecond response time capability[2]
- Centralize update management[3]

Human requirements:
- User-friendly interface
- Minimal adult assistance[4]
- Training in privacy[5]
- Short training sessions[6]
- Short training program[7]
- Permanent effects[8]
- Affordable program[9]

It took our team over six years to build a computer program that satisfies all these requirements. But it took over 30 years to accumulate the knowledge needed to conceptualize it in the first place. We were awarded the US patent for this computing technology in 2016.

Computer Expert System[10]

For each student, Dysolve consists of the automated program and the ecosystem of human support.[11] The components of the automated program are in a continuous feedback loop as explained below.

Student

Let's call our student Abby. Abby has grown up with a "plug and play" mentality: she expects the software to work flawlessly upon first use, without any adjustments on her part. To meet such expectations, Dysolve does not require downloads or installations.[12] Abby simply signs up at Dysolve.com and starts playing the games generated for her. She can log into her user account via her Internet-connected device at any time to play new games.[13]

Games

Unlike other online educational games, Dysolve games are generated by a computer expert system. The difference is this: all other manufacturers' games are premade and reused for groups of students, regardless of whether the programs are labelled "individualized," "individual-based," "personalized," "customized" or "adaptive." In contrast, each Dysolve game is custombuilt as a result of the expert system's continuous assessment of Abby's deficits and its decision-making on the next best step in their resolution.

Dysolve® thus acts intelligently, expertly and flexibly to deliver what Abby needs next instead of what the inventory contains. In fact, Dysolve® does not have any inventory of games at all since each game is built anew and used just once for the intended user. This flexibility and precision is facilitated by Dysolve's collection of extensive micro data on Abby's capabilities from her game responses. That is, Dysolve's responsive games serve as the interface for the bidirectional extraction of huge amounts of data, from the user to the system and vice versa, as the system works on changing the user's abilities.

Student's Program

To summarize, *Abby's Dysolve program did not exist before she started playing her games.*[14] As the games extract data to enable the system to identify Abby's deficits, Dysolve® develops a program for her that targets them for correction. Abby's program grows and changes as she continues in Dysolve.

This dynamic quality of each student's program is a hallmark of our artificial intelligence (AI) technology. It allows the student's program to adjust to her current abilities so as to expand or enhance them. Continuous capture of her current abilities enables this adjustment to occur dynamically. At the same time, the system uses its considerable resources to predict and advance her in this carefully orchestrated trajectory.

In education in general, the ability to pinpoint a student's exact competence at any point is precious. The ability to manage and control her development, priceless.

AI System

Abby's Dysolve program is controlled by the expert system on our server. The expert system acts as the artificial "brain" that evaluates, identifies, corrects, monitors, cross-references, verifies and adjusts to Abby's language-processing issues one-on-one. This AI system can design, administer and modify every student's program one-on-one in realtime for millions of users on demand. That is to say, this expert system far exceeds what any human expert can accomplish.

Responsive Intelligence Technology^{TM}

An AI system simulates human intelligence by performing tasks that require thinking and perception. Even simple routine tasks such as responding with the same answers to the same queries from customers may involve AI. The sophisticated expert work done by Dysolve® requires a type of AI that we call *Responsive Intelligence Technology*^{TM}.

A responsive intelligence system has full autonomy and exceptional expertise, as explained below.

Full Autonomy

Some AI systems in other industries serve as assistants by culling data for human decision-makers. These synthetic assistants act when prompted by their human managers. In contrast, Dysolve® is the autonomous decision-maker for all tasks required to carry a student from program registration to program completion.[15] It can lead a student through the program without human intervention at all because it is fully "aware" of her abilities and deficits and highly sensitive to any changes or improvements. As such, it can be highly responsive to each user.

Of course, traditional online programs for reading remediation can also deliver users from enrollment to graduation. But traditional programs do so unintelligently by using the same path and cookie-cutter units for everyone. "Individualized," "individual-based," "personalized," or "adaptive" programs may use several path options to move groups of students through, but their instructional units, no matter how large, are premade and preset. Dysolve® has no preset paths or units—it custombuilds a program for the student in realtime as it interacts with her.

Whereas other programs may require a user to prompt them to act, Dysolve® is the one that directs the student. This is necessary for dyslexia intervention because the expert system is the only one that knows what best to do next.

Exceptional Expertise

To be able to act completely autonomously without human intervention in the middle, responsive intelligence systems have to be built on exceptional expertise in their fields of operation. In the field of dyslexia intervention where human specialists lack this level of expertise to solve the problem, a responsive intelligence system is obligatory.

Recall that in Chapter 13, reading researchers point out that schools lack the high-level expertise needed to help struggling readers who are resistant to remediation.[16] In dyslexia research and practice, bits of information for partial solutions are scattered among different human specialists. To solve the problem fully, our team placed all essential knowledge and information, especially that from our own fieldwork, within one agent—an autonomous decision-maker and administrator in software, Dysolve®. Therefore, this AI system's decision-making is based on the accumulated expertise of more than one expert; its database far exceeds the cumulative experience of any one team. *A responsive intelligence system is the expert of all experts.*

Individuated Programs[17]

Owing to their defining characteristics, responsive intelligence systems can custombuild one-of-a-kind corrective programs for users in realtime. These systems modify their programs dynamically as they receive new user input. In other words, the system is flexibly responsive to the user at all times. Because the term *individualized* is widely used for programs that are not actually individual-specific, we refer to a student's Dysolve program as *individuated* since each one is uniquely distinct from other users' Dysolve programs.

Recall in the preceding chapter that reading researchers asked that certain criteria be met in dyslexia intervention, which we grouped together as specifications for the model program:

> *A comprehensive, data-driven, dynamic, responsive, individuated program for each student based on a comprehensive, data-driven, dynamic, responsive, individuated, continuous evaluation of her abilities and deficits.*[18]

The model program that meets all these specifications is Dysolve®. We built Dysolve® to implement individuated assessment and training. Individuated assessment entails that the intelligent system knows how to identify the unique complex of deficits of a learner. Of the many areas of digital customization, dyslexia intervention may well be one of the most suitable and beneficial. We do not need to waste taxpayers' money having students complete lengthy programs designed for somebody else or for everybody else. An intervention program should directly address that student's unique complex of deficits, nothing more.

Advantages of Responsive Intelligence

Besides individuation, the capabilities of responsive intelligence systems create these advantages:
- Perfect memory
- Extensive data analysis
- Objectivity
- Superhuman perception

We illustrate these advantages with a scenario below.

Imagine the interaction between the student Abby and human expert Dr. Coral during a typical live consultation. Dr. Coral perceives certain surface cues Abby exhibits. Dr. Coral suspects that these cues are really symptoms of a deeper problem. Dr. Coral designs tests for Abby to probe deeper and deeper to the underlying deficit. At times, Dr. Coral repeats a test to confirm a result. At other times, Dr. Coral presents a different test to confirm the same result. But constantly Dr. Coral returns to her collected data to cross-reference findings and use these to determine the next course of action. As Abby improves, Dr. Coral also does regular sweeps of Abby's overall performance to make sure she is progressing as predicted. All the while, Dr. Coral adjusts her assessment plan as she incorporates new information. Dr. Coral does the same in designing training tasks for Abby.

These are now done by the responsive intelligence system, Dysolve®. Like Dr. Coral, Dysolve® can also backtrack to recheck previous results as needed. The difference, though, is that Dysolve's database ensures perfect memory of all interactions. It is as if Dysolve® never forgets. It "remembers" what Abby did two nights ago at 8:01 PM. It records what errors Abby made with segmentation of four-syllable words on February 22, April 1, and June 27 at 10:36 PM. Dr. Coral was sleeping at that time and could not possibly observe Abby for every gameplay. But Dysolve® stands ready 24/7 to monitor Abby's every key stroke.[19]

It can cross-reference billions of datapoints for Abby, and for millions of other students. It studies user data—deficits, strengths, gameplay habits, progress, areas resistant to change—for enlightening patterns. Dysolve® uses these learning analytics data to enhance its efficiency in helping every student. As an intelligent system, Dysolve® also mines accumulated data to perform predictive analytics so as to anticipate Abby's future performance, prime her for greater improvement and accelerate her progress.

From the student's perspective, the computer system seems impassively non-judgmental. Abby may feel embarrassed when she fails to perform in front of Dr. Coral or anybody else. This inhibition is often lowered in the anonymity of the online world.[20] Thus Abby may feel more comfortable interacting with games onscreen—even though Dysolve® captures every little detail of her performance.[21]

In fact, Dysolve® perceives features too fine for human perception. When an adult fieldtester tried one of our games, Dysolve® kept sending her back to a certain activity. Why? Even though her language problem was not obvious to us, she used to have a lisp as a child because her front teeth were knocked out prematurely in an accident. Dysolve® detected traces of that earlier language deficit.

Dysolve® also detects and reacts in speeds faster than we can execute. Activities previously administered by human specialists are now in code, specifically APIs (application programming interfaces). Think of APIs as digital worker bees. These digital worker bees zip back and forth between Abby's device and the computer system in fractions of a second. Dysolve's custombuilt APIs do what our team used to do manually, such as pulling each bit of information from Abby's gameplay and sending it back to the server. On the server backend, the API wakes up a program that can execute thousands of decisions and then sends the output back to Abby's device within milliseconds.

Implications for Dyslexia Intervention

Technology can be defined as an invention that expands human capacity. That is to say, it enables us to perform beyond our natural ability. This transformative change reframes how we think and act on existing issues.

Ever since we launched Dysolve®, we have been asked, Is it better than XYZ? Of course it is. But that is not the right question because Dysolve® is a prototype with no counterpart for comparison. As patented technology, it can only be the only system of its kind.

Dysolve® opens up a new way of doing things. For one, it removes the guesswork in present diagnostic and evaluative tools. Presently, the test developer first administers a new test item to a sizable group already known to have the condition in order to obtain normative data.[22] If the desired number of group members score satisfactorily against a preset threshold, the new test item is accepted. If not, another test item is developed and tested. In other words, test development in this traditional approach involves calibrating and recalibrating the diagnostic instrument through trial and error to get results that match the known data.[23]

This guesswork is removed because Dysolve® makes it possible to obtain microfeatures of a person's exact deficits.[24] It does not cost much more to do it for millions as opposed to one. It does not cost much more to run evaluations every second through continuous capture as opposed to just once. In contrast, traditional evaluations are typically done only once at the beginning for diagnosis of dyslexia. Only samples of problems can be assessed because it takes a specialist a lot of time to administer traditional testing such as neuropsychological evaluations. The traditional evaluations thus cost thousands of dollars per student.[25] Even then, the traditional approach can only yield a static, one-time partial snapshot of the problem at a general level as opposed to a dynamic, comprehensive representation of the student's abilities in micro detail.

An intelligent training program additionally removes the limitations of present compensatory methods.[26] The teacher no longer needs to waste time teaching over and over again through various multisensory means, say, syllabification rules on how to break a word into its syllables.[27] As the AI system can determine the student's functional abilities directly, the expert system "knows" when the student is primed to syllabify certain words correctly.

This new way of doing things comes from a new way of thinking about the issue. This requires, in turn, new language, as language can trap us. First, dyslexia is not *a* problem. It is multiple problems, multilayered and multimodal in multiple permutations, interconnected by causal chains and cause-effect feedback loops. It is a problem-complex.[28]

This new way of thinking helps the field of dyslexia intervention catch up with the powerful capabilities that computing technology and artificial intelligence already offer: individuated assessments, learning analytics, predictive analytics, and responsive intelligence.

So is Dysolve® better than the old approaches? The new and old approaches are incommensurable. Reframe the question, please.

Dyslexia Dissolved

How do we know that Dysolve's individuated programs are effective? That the identified deficits are cleared? That dyslexia has been corrected?

The cases in Part 1 show these:
- A 5th grader with speech impairment, dyscalculia and dyslexia, who previously registered in the 32nd percentile in English and 14th percentile in Math, consistently scored 86-94 in these subjects after two years in Dysolve. She won an essay-writing contest and received Most Improved Awards from school.[29]
- A 5th grader with ADHD and behavioral issues whose state reading scores barely registered in the

2nd percentile, scored 83 in English after three years in Dysolve. He received a school award for conduct and became a mentor to younger students.[30]

- A 5th grader who did not speak for the first half of the year in school in the lower grades and who previously registered in the 16th percentile in Reading despite Orton-Gillingham reading intervention, advanced to the 82nd percentile and consistently earned 96-99+ GPA after two years in Dysolve. She received a Most Improved Award from school and became a MathCounts coach.[31]
- A 5th grader with autism, ADHD and oppositional defiant disorder who previously registered in the 25th percentile in Reading, earned 88 in Reading after three years in Dysolve. He contributed to a presentation at a New Jersey Education Association annual convention.[32]
- A 7th grader whose standardized reading scores barely registered in the 5th percentile earned 89 in English after a year in Dysolve. He received a Most Improved Award and was nominated for his newscasting role.[33]
- A 4th grader with severe ADHD who was two grades behind in reading reached grade-level proficiency in the third year and Honor roll in the first year of Dysolve. He received a Most Improved Award and won a poetry-writing contest.[34]
- A 5th grader who was two grades behind in reading reached grade-level proficiency after a year in Dysolve. She was placed out of Academic Intervention Services and became a star athlete.[35]

For all these students, the hours of homework with the support of parents, grandparents and older siblings ended with Dysolve. They started to function like their peers. They said they could no longer retrieve their old habits of speaking, reading, spelling and writing. The new patterns of behavior are simply who they are now. They live their talents and shine in their own way, just like other children.

When Dysolve became a fully automated intelligent program, its first student advanced from failing state reading tests in the bottom quintile to passing in the middle within four months. The second student who previously read at a kindergarten level in 2nd grade advanced by 500% in reading levels in nine months. The third student who previously failed reading tests reached grade-level proficiency in five months. The fourth student advanced by one grade level in two months…

NOTES

1. Responsive Intelligence Technology™ is a type of artificial intelligence technology that involves iterative interaction between a computer system and another party. The term is defined under the section by this name in this chapter.
2. This rapid response time allows the system to run numerous algorithms without a typical speaker noticing any perceptible delay in language output, given the speed of language processing. See the Responsive Intelligence Technology section in this chapter.
3. Users do not have to spend time and resources getting software updates as these are done on the server.
4. Dysolve games are designed to require minimal, if any, external assistance from teachers or caretakers.
5. Students can play Dysolve games alone in privacy without any assistance. This may be important for older students who wish to avoid the social repercussions of having a disability. See the Principal's Story in Chapter 7.
6. Dysolve gameplay is usually recommended for about 15 minutes a day.
7. Students typically cleared major deficits in 1-2 years in the manual method. In the new automated method, students are advancing to grade-level proficiency in shorter timeframes on average.
8. Dysolve graduates continue to function like their typical peers more than six years after joining the program. This is the maximum length of our longitudinal studies to date.
9. The Basic Plan with full automation and minimal human intervention costs $200/month or $2,400 a year at the time of this writing, which is less than the average annual household expense for entertainment of $2,913 in 2016. Bureau of Labor Statistics. (2017). Consumer expenditures – 2016. *Economic News Release* (USDL-17-1175). US Department of Labor. Retrieved from https://www.bls.gov/news.release/cesan.nr0.htm

10. An expert system is an AI system that performs the role of a human expert in such tasks as data analysis, testing and decision-making.
11. The Dysolve ecosystem of human support includes the Dysolve team, parents and caretakers at home, teachers and support staff at school, doctors, counselors, tutors, other specialists the child is seeing, etc.
12. Dysolve users do not need downloads or apps. Downloads and apps are "fixed" computer programs that need to be upgraded every time a bug or fix is created.
13. Most Internet-connected devices work except iPad and some mobile phones that do not support HTML5 games that Dysolve® uses.
14. Dysolve games may use the same skin or shell (the "look" of the game), but their content, purpose and presentation vary.
15. An example of a student who went through Dysolve® without human intervention is Uno in Chapter 8.
16. See Fuchs, D., Compton, D.L., Fuchs, L.S., Bryant, V.J., Hamlett, C.L., & Lambert, W. (2012). First-grade cognitive abilities as long-term predictors of reading comprehension and disability status. *Journal of Learning Disabilities, 45*(3) 217–231. See also Vellutino, F.R., Scanlon, D.M., Zhang, H., & Schatschneider, C. (2008). Using response to kindergarten and first grade intervention to identify children at-risk for long-term reading difficulties. *Reading and Writing, 21*, 437-480.
17. The term *individuated* is defined in the section titled "Individuated Programs." See also Fuchs, D., McMaster, K. L., Fuchs, L.S., & Al Otaiba, S. (2013). Data-based individuallization as a means of providing intensive instruction to students with serious learning disorders. In H.L. Swanson, K.R. Harris, & S. Graham (Eds.). *Handbook of learning disabilities* (pp. 526-544). New York: Guilford Press.
18. See Fuchs, L.S., Fuchs, D., & Compton, D.L. (2010). Commentary: Rethinking response to intervention at middle and high school. *School Psychology Review, 39*, 22-28.
19. Dysolve® only has access to users' game responses. It does not record extraneous information, unlike automated personal assistants.

20. See for example Suler, J. (2004). The online disinhibition effect. *CyberPsychology & Behavior, 7*(3), 321-6. doi:10.1089/1094931041291295
21. See Note 19 above.
22. Normative data characterize the typical traits of a defined population. Normative data merely serve to characterize rather than explain phenomena or behaviors.
23. Up to the time of our US patent award in 2016, other patent applications in this and related fields for new assessment instruments followed this traditional approach. Even recent applications to the patent office after that date still rely on known data from dyslexic and nondyslexic populations to select test items to include. See for example Rello-Sanchez, M.L., & Ballesteros, M. (2017). *US Patent Application No. US 2017/0308654 A1*. Alexandria, VA: United States Patent and Trademark Office.
24. See Chapter 14 *Computational Microlinguistics*.
25. The neuropsychological evaluation administered to Skye in Chapter 3 cost $5,000.
26. Compensatory methods include Orton-Gillingham-based, multisensory, structured literacy methods. See Why is Special Ed So Expensive? section in Chapter 12 and Correct, Not Compensate section in Chapter 13.
27. See the discussion on the foundation of Orton-Gillingham methods in Chapter 13.
28. See Problem-Complex section in Chapter 14.
29. See Chapter 1 on Patience.
30. See Chapter 2 on Duke.
31. See Chapter 3 on Skye.
32. See Chapter 4 on Storm.
33. See Chapter 5 on Will.
34. See Chapter 6 on Prince.
35. See Chapter 7 on Grace.

Key Takeaways

The computer expert system Dysolve® uses AI to surpass human capability and expertise.

Dysolve's responsive intelligence enables comprehensive continuous capture of abilities in micro detail, superseding standardized, normative evaluations.

Responsive intelligence generated individuated programs that resolved reading difficulties for the cases using Dysolve® in Part 1.

16

Responsible Education

Evan Y. Haruta

Anger

Many school teachers and administrators are shocked by the anger towards school expressed by many families of children with dyslexia. This anger permeates parent support groups in social media. Just take a peek at some of these groups on any given day.[1] Our teacher reviewers were upset by the parents' stories in this book. Parents may not speak candidly to the adults who oversee their young children for a big part of each day.[2]

As educators and parents ourselves, we sympathize with both parties caught in a difficult, previously unsolvable situation.[3] Families expect their children to learn at school. Teachers *want* their students to learn at school. But the field of study did not produce a solution for schools to use with children with reading disabilities.[4] Meanwhile, existing bandaid solutions cost too much to give to every child affected.[5] Families resent this rationing. And when they do get it, they are disappointed that it's just a bandaid.[6] In private meetings, Directors of Special Education tell us that parents of middle schoolers especially are furious.[7] By then, these parents realize that intervention methods have not worked, while high school and college admissions loom ahead. Desperate, some parents threaten to sue and some in fact proceed with litigation.[8] But what can schools do when even the best available compensatory methods cannot reliably lift the student to grade-level proficiency?

But now that the solution is here, we expect the situation to change for students with dyslexia in every school in the US. There is no reason for teachers to tell parents to just wait for their children to get better.[9] There is no reason for school administrators to move failing students through the system till they leave.[10] There is no reason for Special Education to take up so much of our public funding while locking out half the students in need.[11] It is no longer acceptable to yield meager results on taxpayers' hard-earned investment.[12] There is no excuse to claim instructional practices are "research-based" or "evidenced-based" when the actual research evidence is lacking or inconclusive.[13] There is no reason to let the majority—or even a minority—of students fail to meet reading standards.[14]

The Dysolve team built the solution that removes these previous obstacles.[15] It is time for schools to serve as positive learning environments for *all* students, where staff and families can work together as partners.[16] All they have to do now is keep their children playing games on the computer. What can be easier than that?

Owning the Problem

In Chapters 12 and 13, our overview of the state of the field clarifies how schools came to inherit a difficult situation with no way out. Yet at the same time, we have to recognize that the school system as structured also contains inherent weaknesses.

Let me explain with an analogy. When a doctor sees a patient with a medical condition, she owns that problem. She works on understanding that condition, its source and treatment options. Until such time when she recognizes that the condition's treatment is beyond her capability, she keeps that patient as her responsibility. She does not pass the child to somebody else at the end of the year. But schools do—the child with a reading disorder is passed from teacher to teacher. Every few years, that child leaves his current school. The new teacher or school does not have a full history of what happened to that child in previous years.[17] The new family entering the school system also does not know what happened to the children before theirs.[18]

This is one of the reasons why we wrote this book. We have laid it all out there—the problem at the individual level, the problem in the field, the problem in the school system, and the economic problem to society.[19] The knowledge gap has to be filled for all parties involved.

Now that you know, what would you do next?

Saving A Life

Among the many competing priorities in life, this comes first for us—saving a child. It may not be obvious because the child involved is not bleeding or crying out in pain. But it is no less a crisis when the problem determines the path each child will take in life. We work intensively in crisis mode for each child because we know how dark a path the alternative can be.[20] It is not just a job. The parents in Part 1 of this book, and the kind teachers who have stepped up along the way, understand this. They spoke up to serve as role models for others who live and work with affected children we will never reach. Our parents and teachers told their stories candidly to inspire others to save other children—because now it can be done.

Unlike first-time parents, school administrators and teachers know when this juncture between promise and defeatism comes up for each child. After that point, that child's path in life is set for the most part. In our work, we have met many older parents who tell us that their children could have benefited from a program like Dysolve, but it is too late now because these youths have already given up.

MY MESSAGE TO SCHOOL ADMINISTRATORS

In a lifetime, a breakthrough like Dysolve only happens once, if at all. You can be skeptical, critical or unconvinced.[21] But you owe it to your students, families, teachers and taxpayers to check it out. You probably have students who have not improved through any available reading intervention for years. Why not let them try this new technology at a fraction of the cost you allocate annually?[22] The yield, as you can see from Part 1, can be huge.

Unlike other programs, you do not incur with Dysolve installation costs, software or hardware expenses, teacher training fees, materials and test kit purchases.[23] If families subscribe to the service outside of school, you do not even incur any costs, including licensing fees. Since Dysolve is automated, students can simply play its games outside of school. Any needed human supervision is handled exclusively by Dysolve's own specialists without additional costs.[24] Unlike your compensatory methods which have to be delivered by your teachers, Dysolve does not require school staff to run any part of its program. This frees school teachers to carry out what they are trained to do—cover the school curriculum. Dysolve works at a deeper level to correct specific underlying deficits while teachers help students develop global skills on the surface.

At the same time, Dysolve supports the work of our students' schools, for we all share a common goal of ensuring that children fulfill academic standards. To monitor your students' progress and share data, Dysolve can place them together on your own group platform.[25] This allows your school to benefit from the system's analytics capability to improve students' performance in tests.

Review our students' improvement in the beginning of each chapter in Part 1 and the summary at the end of Chapter 15. Can your students who scored below the 10th and even 20th percentile in standardized reading tests advance to independent work and Honor roll within 1-2 years? Can your students advance by 3-5 reading levels in 2-5 months? If the answer is "no" to any of these, then check out Dysolve.com.

While nearly 20% of students can officially be classified as dyslexic, around two-thirds of students do not pass standardized testing.[26] As a reading expert pointed out, the 20% is an arbitrary figure on a continuum of language difficulties.[27] Therefore, many more students can be helped by a program such as Dysolve that corrects language-processing deficits. Especially for the bulk of students who perform just under the passing threshold, corrective training for a short period may efficiently and permanently lift them up to reading standards.[28] Although Dysolve serves every age including adulthood, early screening in preschool would save taxpayers the heavy expenses of remediation in later grades. Dysolve can identify children at risk before they begin to learn to read.

As dyslexia is a perplexing condition on the surface, Dysolve offers professional development on this topic to school faculty and staff. We train educators on how to recognize symptoms in their classrooms and deal with different student profiles. Just as important, we advise on the most effective pedagogical approaches for different types of deficits so as to economize resources and maximize efforts.

We have created the solution to reading disabilities. We now own the responsibility of supporting your application of this solution to the children in your care.

There is no reason to let another child go through what the students in Part 1 of this book endured.

NOTES

1. To find some of these parent groups, search under "dyslexia" on Facebook.
2. The parents in Chapters 1 and 4 voiced this reservation.
3. See Chapter 13 *State of the Science*.
4. By "solution," we mean a method that effectively removes the underlying deficits causing the condition. Methods that merely help students cope but do not remove underlying deficits—compensatory methods—are not solutions for dyslexia.
5. See Chapter 12 on the cost of existing methods.
6. See the Principal's Story in Chapter 7.
7. Reading researchers do know that struggling readers in middle school will likely not improve. See Elliott, J.G., & Grigorenko, E.L. (2014). *The dyslexia debate*. New York: Cambridge University Press.
8. See a landmark 30-year review of such legal cases in Rose, T., & Zirkel, P. (2007). Orton-Gillingham methodology for students with reading disabilities: 30 years of case law. *The Journal of Special Education, 41*(3), 171-185.
9. The families in Chapters 1, 3, 4 and 6 were told by their schools to wait.
10. Nearly three-quarters of students with reading disabilities stay classified throughout school. See Gunning, T. (2003). The role of readability in today's classroom. *Topics in Language Disorders, 23*(3), 175-185. In 2013-2014, only 9.2% of special education students aged 14-21 in the US transferred out to general education. Office of Special Education and Rehabilitative Services, Office of Special Education Programs. (2016). *38th Annual Report to Congress on the Implementation of the Individuals with Disabilities Education Act, 2016.* Washington, DC: US Department of Education.
11. See Chapter 12 *The True Cost of Dyslexia*.
12. See Chapter 12 on reading statistics.
13. The lack of scientific evidence is reiterated repeatedly in the research review in Elliott, J.G., & Grigorenko, E.L. (2014). *The dyslexia debate*. New York: Cambridge University Press.

14. The 2017 NAEP (National Assessment of Educational Progress) report shows that the percentage of students performing at or above proficiency in reading did not improve from 4th to 8th grade. The number stayed constant at 35% through the grades for public schools nationwide. This means that the 65% who performed below proficiency in 4th grade likely remained so through the years. The reading score for 12th grade only improved by 1%. Retrieved from https://www.nationsreportcard.gov/
15. See Chapter 15 for elaboration on the traditional obstacles that Dysolve® overcame.
16. The adversarial relationship between schools and families is apparent in Chapters 1, 3 and 4.
17. School records including IEPs provide snapshots of students' abilities instead of continuous narrative. The cost of accumulating comprehensive data would have been prohibitive with traditional methods. However, computer technology makes this possible. Dysolve® in fact performs continuous assessment on every student and mines the data to enhance efficacy.
18. Most parents do not realize that less than a quarter of students with reading disabilities improve sufficiently to get declassified. See Note 10 above.
19. See Part 1 of this book, Chapter 13 and Chapter 12 respectively.
20. This dark path includes the deleterious effects mentioned in research on reading and learning disabilities and their comorbid conditions: anxiety, negativity, sleep disturbance, task avoidance, defeatism, meltdowns, maladaptive and self-injurious behaviors, and suicide ideation. See also the statistics on youth offenders in Chapter 12.
21. See Chapter 17 *Our Answers To Your Questions*.
22. At the time of this writing, the basic cost of Dysolve is $200/month per student to use the online program on demand with minimal human assistance. See cost comparisons between Dysolve and present methods in Chapter 12.
23. See Chapter 12 for the costs of compensatory methods and programs. In contrast, Dysolve is a corrective program.

24. The monthly subscription also covers human assistance as defined by the plan purchased.
25. Upon request, Dysolve sets up group platforms for institutions and single providers so that their patients or students can be placed together and their progress monitored.
26. See Note 14 above.
27. See Shaywitz, S. (2003). *Overcoming dyslexia.* New York: Alfred A. Knopf.
28. Uno in Chapter 8 represents one such successful case. See the Professor's Story in that chapter.

Key Takeaways

The solution of Dysolve® enables schools to serve all students with dyslexia.

Dysolve® frees teachers to focus on the curriculum and schools to invest in other areas.

Dysolve's creators own the responsibility of educating schools on the solution to dyslexia while schools own the responsibility of getting every child to read.

17

Our Answers to Your Questions

Context

In 2014, Julian Elliott from the University of Durham and Elena Grigorenko from Yale University published *The Dyslexia Debate*, a comprehensive review of the dyslexia research to date. We quote at length their conclusions on assessment and intervention to bring the state of the field in sharp relief because of the existing research-to-practice gap:

> It has been repeatedly demonstrated that systematic instruction...can significantly reduce the proportion of children who are later considered to be reading disabled. However, initial gains in the first years of schooling are not always sustained...To date, there is no clear consensus as to the most appropriate measures, methods, or timing...To date, work in genetics, neuroscience, and cognitive science is not sufficiently advanced to be able to generate additional guidance for educational practice with such children. At the current time, other than recommending "more of

the same," researchers are uncertain about how to assist those with the most complex and intractable reading difficulties. There is little evidence to support the use of any special approaches for dyslexia, as key elements of dyslexia teaching programs are typically the same as those routinely employed in the reading disability literature. Complementary approaches such as motor training, auditory and visual interventions, the use of fatty acids, and biofeedback have yet to demonstrate significant evidence of effectiveness...the crucial task is to identify the individual's particular reading strengths and weaknesses and address these directly.[1]

The key conclusions from these leading researchers form the context for our answers below:
- A significant group of struggling readers do not show permanent gains from present remediation methods.
- There is little evidence to support the use of any of these specialist approaches for dyslexia.
- Nobody in the field knows how to help them.
- *The solution is to identify the individual's specific deficits and address them directly.*

Our Answers to Your Questions

Questions from the Public

Do you really have the cure for dyslexia?
Dyslexia is not a disease to be cured. Reading difficulties (dyslexia) are caused by language-processing deficits. Dysolve can clear these deficits to remove reading difficulties. As the processing deficits and reading difficulties vary from person to person, Dysolve can customize solutions to correct them. So yes, Dysolve has the solution for dyslexia. And yes, Dysolve has corrected dyslexia in individuals. See the cases in Part 1 of this book.

I thought dyslexia was lifelong. Why do you say it can be corrected?
Most providers and programs still treat dyslexia as a chronic condition. Popular methods merely teach students how to cope with or compensate for dyslexia. This is because these traditional methods are not able to identify the specific deficits underlying the condition for each person. In contrast, Dysolve corrects the problem by getting to the source. Students who graduated from Dysolve more than three years ago have stayed on the Honor roll without putting in more effort than typical.

What do you think dyslexia is, exactly?
We use *dyslexia* as an umbrella term to cover a spectrum of reading difficulties caused by language-processing deficits.[2] We process language when we speak, read, write and understand speech. The reading difficulty, or dyslexia, is apparent: the child cannot learn to read despite much effort. What is not obvious is the complex of deficits underlying the con-

dition. It is this complex of underlying deficits we have to identify in order to correct dyslexia. We call it the *root cause of dyslexia* at Dysolve.

Dyslexia is the collection of surface symptoms in the reading domain of these underlying deficits. These deficits may affect more than just reading, in which case dyslexia co-occurs with other language difficulties such as speech and writing.[3]

Language-processing deficits therefore create difficulties on the surface that may collectively be grouped under the general category of *language-based conditions*.[4] Language-based conditions include dyslexia, dysgraphia, speech disorders, etc.

Do people with dyslexia see letters backwards?
Some researchers discount this as a myth because dyslexia is not a visual disorder.[5] However, our Dysolve students do often confuse *b* and *d* due to their phonetic (sound) similarity.[6] Thus, students *seem* to see letters backwards because they cannot associate the right shape with the right sound. They tend not to confuse *p* and *q*. In dyslexia research, much is still unknown about the visual processing of written text during reading. Instead of simply rejecting the myth outright, we continue to investigate the relationship between visual and language processing at Dysolve.

What is the relationship between learning disabilities, reading disabilities and dyslexia?
The term *learning disabilities* is also referred to as *specific learning disabilities*. The Individuals with Disabilities Education Act (IDEA) defines *specific learning disability* as a

disorder which results in the imperfect ability to listen, think, speak, read, write, spell, or calculate.[7] Most students classified with learning disabilities fall into the subcategory of reading disabilities.[8]

Excluded from this legal classification are those with learning problems caused by physical or intellectual disabilities, emotional disturbance, or environmental/economic disadvantage. That is, reading difficulties may be due to other factors and need not be caused by a reading disability or dyslexia.

In practice, however, it is not always easy to separate out conditions arising from different sources, especially when many of them coexist. Nor is it always possible, even in research, to determine causal relations. This is why Dysolve focuses on correcting specific deficits, regardless of their origin.

Do you consider dyslexia a disability, disorder or learning difference?
Different terms are used in different fields. As the word "disability" connotes a permanent condition, we would encourage schools to replace it since dyslexia is correctable. A "disorder" is a disruption to regular functions in the body and is diagnosed in the medical field. As reading difficulties are resolved outside of medicine, we will refrain from calling dyslexia a "disorder." "Learning differences" between typical and dyslexic brains disappear when the latter can be retrained to function like the former.

We use the term *language-processing deficits* to refer to the problems underlying dyslexia and its co-occurring conditions. All these conditions come under the general category of *language-based conditions*. A condition is a nontypical state interfering with age-appropriate activities and general wellbeing. Dyslexia is a collection of language-based conditions involving reading.

Why do you call dyslexia a "deficit" while others consider it an advantage?[9]

Many of our students with dyslexia also have special talents, especially in visuo-spatial abilities. The children in Part 1 want to be designers, engineers, architects, programmers and inventors. We recognize that dyslexic brains have both strengths *and* language-processing deficits.

Our approach is to remove these deficits while nurturing their talents so that they have a *double* advantage. It is not coincidental that graduate after graduate of Dysolve catapults from the bottom quintile in school performance to the top—their intrinsic strengths allow them to excel when their deficits are removed.

Dysolve focuses on their deficits because these often create debilitating effects that hinder their talent development, such as recurrent headaches and feelings of defeatism. While we celebrate the successes of individuals with dyslexia, we are mindful of the majority of children with reading disabilities who never got the opportunity to show their true potential. Consider the grim statistics in Chapter 12.

What is your vision?

Harmonious collaboration among educators, families, doctors, specialists, providers, advocates and the public to create a dyslexia-free world in our lifetime.

Our Answers to Your Questions

How can I help?
Spread the message that dyslexia does not just affect the 1 in 5 people who has it but all 5 people who pay taxes for Special Education and who may benefit from the future discoveries of the creative thinkers who had dyslexia. Spread the word that dyslexia can now be corrected. Educate others about this condition from the new findings at Dysolve.com and Dysolve Dyslexia on Facebook.

Questions from Schools

Why have I not heard of this breakthrough before?
Before 2017, we could only help a small number of students since it was very time-consuming to custombuild evaluation and training for each person manually. When Dysolve was automated, we conducted beta testing with a small sample at first. As our solution impacts the lives of children and their families in a deeply emotional way, we have to act responsibly at every step. With the publication of this book, we are now ready to engage with schools and other sectors.

Even the most prominent experts at the most prestigious institutions did not solve this problem. How can you claim that you did?
It is not a question of the amount of knowledge but the right kind of knowledge. Chapters 13-15 explain why existing fields of study could not solve the problem of dyslexia. The solution had to come from the right expertise in the right area. The delivery of this solution also needed technology

that just emerged in recent years. It took our team more than 30 years of research, 20 years of fieldwork involving thousands of hours of close interaction with students and their families, and six years of programming to build this solution. No other group made this investment.

Can you fix all students with dyslexia?
Dysolve can correct the language-processing deficits causing dyslexia provided that students practice diligently according to the training frequency, session duration and program period prescribed. How much a student improves with Dysolve depends on how well her brain responds to corrective training. See the cases in Part 1 of this book.[10]

Most of our students don't have problems as severe as the ones featured in your book. Is Dysolve still appropriate for them?
Absolutely. See Uno's case in Chapter 8. Students who are performing just below grade-level proficiency may advance quickly through the automated program, as Uno did within four months. Dysolve can therefore help move such students out of special education quickly. In this book, we feature mainly the most severe cases with many coexisting conditions to emphasize the efficacy of Dysolve in resolving even the most intractable of problems.

How many students can you work with at the same time?
Dysolve® is an automated program. It can accommodate all students at once.

How can you tell that your students with dyslexia have high intelligence?

We specialize in twice-exceptionality (talent + disability), and most Dysolve students are twice-exceptional.[11] Dr. Coral wrote on giftedness traits for the National Association for Gifted Children.[12] These traits include metacognitive awareness, the ability to monitor one's own thinking. Although children with dyslexia display language difficulties, they often show high metacognitive awareness. Even when they cannot execute language tasks, they usually do not have difficulty understanding what is required of them. Some of them are highly articulate and witty. Gifted children enjoy humor because of the mental challenge involved in creating it.

Where does Dysolve stand in relation to other programs and providers?

Dysolve uses leading-edge patented technology that is not available to others and thus delivers benefits not found elsewhere. Its technological advantages allow it to correct dyslexia, whereas most existing programs are compensatory in that they keep dyslexia as a chronic condition (e.g., Orton-Gillingham, multisensory, structured literacy).

On the basis of existing programs, dyslexia was defined as a lifelong condition. In contrast, Dysolve can correct—and has corrected—dyslexia for individuals because it can customize corrective solutions for each person while keeping costs low through automation. It can uniquely run continuous assessments 24/7 and make realtime program modifications while interacting with each student because it has all necessary knowledge and protocol at its immediate disposal. Its high efficiency usually allows students to practice in short bursts and yet still improve a lot faster than in other programs. See Chapter 15.

What is your track record?
We have identified the specific language-processing deficits in 100% of our cases. Dysolve has effectively corrected reading difficulties to enable performance at average or higher without more effort than typical in 100% of our graduates. In 0.13% of cases, students also have issues in other domains that Dysolve does not address, namely visual and cognitive impairment.

What do we have to do if we use Dysolve at our school?
Dysolve covers all support services and materials needed to run the program at your school. Your school may allocate space for students to play their Dysolve games with minimal supervision or assign students to do so at home. Dysolve's training does not interfere with the school curriculum.

Will Dysolve replace teachers?
Dysolve focuses on underlying deficits that the school curriculum does not, and cannot, address. Thus Dysolve's work does not overlap with teachers' responsibilities. Because more than half of students with dyslexia do not receive special services presently, Dysolve actually enables special education teachers to make better use of their resources to help all students in need.[13]

Although it can work autonomously, Dysolve does use human specialists to take care of the human side of learning. Students do need encouragement and sympathetic supervision that only human teachers can provide.

Since Dysolve's correction of underlying deficits takes time, school teachers have to support struggling readers with the school curriculum so that they do not fall too far behind academically in the interim. After processing deficits have been removed, teachers are still needed to help Dysolve graduates catch up with their peers in terms of spelling and vocabulary acquisition, subject content, etc. By working in tandem with Dysolve, teachers often find more fulfillment in their own work because now their instructional efforts yield greater results.

What will happen to the other methods schools have been using?
Compensatory methods that instruct students on the structural patterns of language can still be used at the end of their Dysolve programs—when underlying deficits have been corrected and the rules of language make sense. Dysolve removes the need for repetition and overlearning because it makes such instruction effective. Since the instruction was not offered to all students with dyslexia previously, Dysolve enables schools to apply these methods to a larger group. For schools that do not provide such instruction, Dysolve can offer this support.

What will happen to traditional evaluations?
Dysolve does not use evaluations administered externally because we need comprehensive, detailed and continuous assessment to correct dyslexia and other language-based conditions. Dysolve's own assessment is in a form that only

it can generate and interpret.[14] *Dysolve's customized evaluation feeds directly into Dysolve's corrective training.*[15] No other evaluation is necessary.

The new efficiencies created by computing technology replace costly traditional evaluations that were administered one-on-one by specialists and that are beyond the budgets of many families and schools while falling short of what is needed to identify underlying deficits to remove the condition.

Is your method research- or evidence-based?
Although these terms are popular and often assigned to existing methods and programs, scientific rigor has not always been applied uniformly in the field of reading and dyslexia research.

A landmark 30-year review in the *Journal of Special Education* found problems in published Orton-Gillingham studies, including the lack of rigor and objectivity in their methodologies as well as in their data reporting and analyses.[16] Such studies also did not allow for direct or systematic replication because their procedures were often not operationally defined.

In addition, many of the studies did not report on the fidelity of implementation, as required of efficacy research by the Institute of Education Sciences, US Department of Education. *Fidelity of implementation* refers to the strength and qualities of implementation so as to determine whether the intervention's impact could have been influenced by the way it was implemented.[17] For instance, the National Reading Panel (2000) excluded many published studies from its review of the effectiveness of phonemic awareness training due to insufficient methodological rigor and other reasons.[18]

The crucial question is, Can a method resolve reading disabilities permanently? For the answer, we need to look at older readers. But studies on older readers are sparse, as is "high-quality research evidence" for the multisensory component of specialist approaches to dyslexia teaching.[19] Researchers found "no compelling evidence" that multisensory instruction can benefit this population.[20] Most critically, adolescent readers getting the best of existing methods continue to struggle with reading.[21]

Research-based
Our solution to dyslexia was the product of over 30 years of research in many specialized fields and over 20 years of fieldwork with populations across a broad spectrum of language-based conditions. Our prior work resulted in the creation of a new discipline, Computational Microlinguistics, which made this solution possible. This solution clarified what was missing in the field of dyslexia research and practice previously that prevented problem resolution earlier. See Chapters 13 and 14.

Evidence-based
Dysolve is evidence-based in a way that was not technically possible previously: its quantitative measures and analytics data show us concretely which specific deficits have been corrected and to what degree for each student. For instance, student Abby can perform Activity 7-82011B with 92.6% accuracy at a speed of 0.43 sec/word during the week of July 15-21 while Activity 7-82011C advanced her to 95.4% ac-

curacy at a speed of 0.33 sec/word during the week of July 22-28. Dysolve's analytics enable the collection and mining of empirical data not previously available or even imaginable. See Chapter 15.

All the same, we expect our method to be reviewed and rigorously examined by external, independent researchers using traditional methods of study in the coming years.

Do you work with schools?
Yes. Schools or school districts can serve as test beds, pilot programs or research partners. Students in your schools can be placed under your group platform at Dysolve to enable data sharing and close monitoring to improve their test performance at school. We provide professional development in the form of workshops and educational materials. We collaborate with school faculty and administration to present and publish at national and international fora.

How can my school get involved?
Work with us to identify students who can benefit from corrective training. At the same time, by bringing special education costs down, we can help you accommodate more students who could not be supported before. Contact us at Dysolve.com or 844-DYSOLVE. Direct teachers and parents to Dysolve.com and Dysolve Dyslexia on Facebook to learn about dyslexia and its coexisting conditions. Also consider partnering with us to serve as a model for other schools.

But these students' scores showed high risk levels in Dysolve's more comprehensive, detailed testing. You can talk to us through Dysolve.com before you commit to our program.

How much improvement can I expect to see?
See the cases in Part 1 of this book. The improvement for these students was much more than their families ever expected. Dysolve knows what needs to be done for a student to advance.

How fast he progresses and whether he reaches the destination depends on several factors. Some are within his control, such as always performing at his current best. Some are within his family's control, such as scheduling events around his Dysolve training so that he can practice regularly without constant interruption. Part of it also depends on how his brain responds to training. Our past records show that young brains adjust quickly to training.

Some students with dyslexia have excelled without going through your program. Why should mine?
Some students with dyslexia can excel academically, but the achievement usually comes at a high cost, in terms of the time and effort spent on schoolwork compared to typical peers.

Dysolve aims to correct the condition so that students can function like their classmates, without putting in many more hours for their studies. The extra time and effort reduces social time and removes certain majors and career options. These students who excel in spite of dyslexia are in

Our Answers to Your Questions

Questions from Families

My son has a lot of other issues including ADHD. Why should I attend to something that is not so urgent at the moment?
His more pressing issues may be related to dyslexia. For example, ADHD and dyslexia coexist, and both co-occur with language difficulties.[22] These difficulties can cause cognitive overload, which in turn can manifest itself in different ways, including hyperactivity, headaches, moodiness, meltdowns, etc. The cases in Chapters 4 and 6 show how these issues subsided when language difficulties were resolved.

I don't know what my child's problem is. We've taken her to a lot of specialists, but their test results seem to point to different things. How can you help?
As language-processing deficits are very common, you may want to start by eliminating them as the source of your child's problem. The cases in Part 1 show the diversity of surface symptoms.

If your child's problem is indeed due to language-processing deficits, Dysolve will help identify them for correction. The evaluation has to get to the specific deficits involved to help you make sense of your child's behaviors and issues. This is Dysolve's goal.

Tests that do not get down to this level of micro detail may fail to relate symptoms that seem perplexing on the surface. With many students, standardized tests by other providers did not detect any issue although these learners displayed problematic behaviors such as extreme anxiety.

a small minority: only about 15% of students with learning or reading disabilities go to college.[23]

Many students with dyslexia are twice-exceptional (talent + disability). Perhaps these students you reference would have performed even better had their dyslexia been corrected. Some students can maintain passing grades when they first join Dysolve even though they have dyslexia because their high intelligence allows them to compensate for their reading difficulty. For these students, Dysolve aims to get them to perform higher, at their true potential, and to clear coexisting conditions such as recurrent headaches and language-related ADHD.

Don't you think my child will outgrow the problem?
No. No reading researcher would claim that for dyslexia. Dyslexia is different from a developmental lag in reading (delayed reading). With dyslexia, a delay in intervention may make it even harder to catch up to grade-level reading. Your child's reading problem can grow in severity and he may acquire other issues such as negativity towards academics and harmful behaviors. As shown by the cases in Part 1 of this book, usually by 2nd-3rd grade, uncorrected reading problems have already created negative behaviors that are not easy to remove. You should act immediately.

What is the best age to use Dysolve?
The person who uses Dysolve has a language-processing problem. Since we have to process language every single day, even when we are not in school, it is a serious problem. It should be taken care of immediately. If your child is in school, she may start to feel the repercussions of her lang-

uage difficulties, which may harm her self-esteem and relations with peers. When psychological and social effects of dyslexia emerge, they create additional obstacles to progress.

If you mean the best age to see the most or quickest improvement, it depends on many factors. Dr. Coral answered this question in Chapter 5.

Our family lives on my husband's income because I have to homeschool our kids. Can you lower your fees further?
It took a lot of investment to build the artificial intelligence system behind Dysolve® and to deliver it through a user-friendly platform. Yet we set Dysolve fees reasonably to keep it affordable for as many families as possible.

Some children are homeschooled because of dyslexia and/or ADHD. Dysolve is designed to correct the problem so that fees are not incurred indefinitely. The long-term cost of letting the problem remain can be as much as $800,000—the income difference between high school and college graduates over their working life.[24]

Families with children who need an educational service such as Dysolve have a right to demand that it be provided to them for free through schools.

My daughter is already in high school. Why wasn't this solution offered to her earlier?
It took time to build Dysolve®, and it only launched in 2017. Every student has a different form of the problem. To identify and correct each student's problem, we had to custombuild evaluation and training for everyone. As such, we could only work one-on-one with a selected number of

students each year—until now. We did offer prototypes to several school districts, but their administrators did not act, even though they witnessed their students who enrolled privately in Dysolve achieve the remarkable results seen in Part 1 of this book.

Dysolve is designed for all ages. It is never too late to correct a condition that would otherwise be lifelong.

Can my child who has dyslexia ever excel?
See Skye's story in Chapter 3. Because Skye had been using other parts of her brain to compensate for her deficit earlier, she recounted how she developed enhanced abilities from that previous experience. When her dyslexia was corrected and she could function as effectively as her classmates, she excelled in certain areas because of the special abilities developed earlier to compensate for her deficit.

Students who have dyslexia and special talents constitute a significant group with the label of *twice-exceptional children* in giftedness research.

How can I get involved?
If your child has reading difficulties or any of the conditions described in Part 1, contact us at Dysolve.com to get further insight, even if you have no plans to enroll. If you know of a friend, relative or neighbor with the condition, tell this person to learn about the new findings. Spread the word that dyslexia is a common condition and can be corrected. Join our volunteer team at idlworld.org.

Questions from Doctors

Can you fix ADHD too?
As language-processing deficits are corrected in Dysolve, ADHD symptoms tend to dissipate as well. ADHD symptoms in these cases, especially hyperactivity, are caused by cognitive overload. Our work only involves ADHD symptoms that occur in individuals with language difficulties.[25] The scope of our work does not allow us to determine whether ADHD occurs outside of language processing. See Chapter 6.

How can you be sure about ADHD?
As seen in over 1,200 hours of close observation, the cases in this book exhibited characteristic patterns of ADHD symptoms that could be identified definitively, quantified, monitored and modified. Out of this sample of 10 cases, seven of them exhibited hyperactivity. See Chapters 1, 2, 4-6, 9-10. Similar patterns of behavior were recorded in many other cases in our two decades of fieldwork.

As you know, ADHD is presently diagnosed by other providers through subjective ratings. We have replaced these subjective ratings with objective, quantified measures for the severity of ADHD, based on empirical data. This removes the risk of subjectivity inherent in reports by nonspecialists and self-reports in traditional diagnoses. Dysolve's quantified ADHD measures are derived from proprietary algorithms based on our fieldwork.

Can you help those with autism?

Language-processing deficits are common in those with autism spectrum disorder. Dysolve corrects these deficits. While individuals with autism may have other issues that Dysolve does not address, improving language functioning in this population certainly contributes to their overall competence. See Chapter 4.

How do you diagnose dyslexia?

We can easily determine that a child has a reading difficulty, or dyslexia, by ruling out other factors such as motivation, home/school environment, etc. Rather, the question is, What is *causing* the dyslexia? The root cause of dyslexia for an individual is usually a complex of language-processing deficits. Identification of these deficits can be represented as a computational problem. The solution to this computational problem requires knowledge of Computational Microlinguistics and responsive intelligence technology, as explained in Chapters 14 and 15.

How do you know that the problem is language processing and not something else?

We solve each problem logically: we trace surface symptoms to their underlying sources and then retrace underlying deficits to surface problems. Following problem identification, we provide an explanatory framework with predictive power that accounts for all present and future behaviors.

The development of this framework is governed by the principles and parameters of our science, Computational Microlinguistics. As scientists, we test our hypotheses and predictions against empirical data. Our method was developed through decades of research and fieldwork. Language-processing deficits are very common, which is why nearly 85% of students with learning disabilities have reading difficulties.[26]

Can you explain the symptoms associated with dyslexia?
Dyslexia involves reading difficulties. To appreciate the complexity of the reading process, imagine building from scratch a robot that can read. What would you need to program into this robot? You would need to include procedures for the robot to decode words, to associate letters in words to sounds, to retrieve stored words, to select word forms with the right meanings, etc., etc.

Reading involves many processes and subprocesses. To read well, we have to orchestrate all these processes smoothly. Any number of these can be disrupted by underlying deficits in language processing.

As a result, the affected individual may read haltingly, misread words, substitute words, skip lines, slow down considerably as he reads, forget what he read or face difficulty learning to read. The same underlying deficits may also disrupt other language functions, which is why dyslexia often coexists with speech and auditory processing disorders. See Chapter 13 on the definition of dyslexia.

Should I continue to recommend neuropsychological evaluations?
Dysolve does not use these evaluations. See our answer on traditional evaluations in *Questions from Schools*.

Our Answers to Your Questions

Is there any harm associated with using Dysolve®?
No. It is not invasive. Students merely play online games. These are not recreational games and are not addictive.

What can I do for my patients?
Consider these:
- Request free informational materials from Dysolve.com to distribute to patients you suspect have language-processing deficits and comorbid conditions.
- Encourage affected patients to screen for language-processing deficits by enrolling in your Dysolve group platform.
- Contact us to set up your group platform so you can monitor your patients in this group and coordinate services with us.
- Spread the word to colleagues in your field that there is now a solution for dyslexia, learning disabilities and their coexisting conditions such as ADHD.
- Request educational materials that we have used in presentations at medical centers and annual conventions to learn more about the solution to dyslexia, ADHD and learning disabilities.

Questions from Researchers

Since dyslexia is a confusing term, do you agree that we should discard it?
We agree that the term has been used in confusing ways. This is why Dysolve identifies and targets specific *deficits*,

not the general condition of dyslexia itself. However, for practical reasons, the word *dyslexia* should continue to be used because a problem needs a name to focus public attention and mobilize campaigns. "Language-processing deficits" or "decoding problems" just does not have that kind of power.

Where are your double-blind, peer-reviewed studies?
The automated Dysolve Program just launched in 2017 and is still in beta testing. We invite schools to enroll students in Dysolve and university researchers to conduct large-scale, longitudinal control studies and publish their results in peer-reviewed journals. To validate our results, these studies should be conducted by independent researchers with no affiliation to us, other providers, or organizations originating from or oriented towards a particular method, approach, or ideology.

Their study design should follow the recommended criteria of the Institute of Education Sciences (2013) and the National Reading Panel (2000) for efficacy research, as well as recommended guidelines for fidelity of implementation, procedural reliability, and interrater reliability.[27] There is a need for methodological rigor that has not always been uniformly implemented in reading research, as explained in our answer to the question above on evidence-based method.

Our own researchers will continue to publish case studies that illuminate the details of individual profiles of dyslexia.

Our Answers to Your Questions

Based on your own work, what do you think causes dyslexia?
Dyslexia is caused by language-processing deficits. The real question is, What caused the language-processing deficits? Given the diversity of cases we have seen, a variety of factors are likely involved. While our research in this area is ongoing, the focus of Dysolve is on correcting these deficits, regardless of their origin.

Can you distinguish between reading difficulties caused by a neurological disorder vs. deprived learning environments?
In practice, this is difficult and counterproductive because of the intricate interplay of genetic and environmental factors. Other researchers do not make this distinction as well.[28] Dysolve focuses on removing the reading difficulties regardless of their source. This is illustrated in Chapter 7.

How can I get involved?
Engage with us to start this new conversation on dyslexia. Conduct control studies on the efficacy of Dysolve®. Where our program shines above all others, encourage schools to use it. Where we fall short, inform us so we can work harder to improve on the implementation of our solution. You chose this field because you care about the children you study. We learned about this field because we wanted to help the children we encountered. Let us work together to do better.

NOTES

1. Elliott, J.G., & Grigorenko, E.L. (2014). *The dyslexia debate*. New York: Cambridge University Press, p. 164-165.
2. See the confusion in the various definitions of dyslexia in Chapter 13.
3. Reading and speech difficulties co-occur in the cases in Chapters 1, 3 and 9; reading and writing difficulties in Chapters 4 and 10. See further elaboration on coexisting conditions in Chapter 13 on the definition of dyslexia.
4. We will avoid the term *disorder* because it refers to disruption of regular functions of the body by a disease diagnosed in the medical field.
5. This myth is discounted in Shaywitz, S. (2003). *Overcoming dyslexia*. New York: Alfred A. Knopf, p. 100.
6. The children in Chapters 2, 4 and 6 confused *b* with *d*.
7. 20 US Code 1401 (30).
8. Nearly 85% of students with learning disabilities have reading disabilities. Source: The Center for the Study of Learning, Georgetown University Medical Center. (nd). *Frequently asked questions about dyslexia*. Retrieved from http://csl.georgetown.edu/dyslexia/faqs.shtml
9. See for example Eide, B.L., & Eide, F.F. (2011). *The dyslexic advantage: Unlocking the hidden potential of the dyslexic brain*. New York, NY: Penguin.
10. See also Dysolve results at the end of Chapter 15.
11. See Chapter 2 on twice-exceptionality.
12. See Hoh, P.-S. (2008). Cognitive characteristics of the gifted. In J. Plucker & C. Callahan (Eds.), *Critical issues and practices in gifted education: What the research says* (pp. 57-83). Austin, TX: Prufrock.
13. *38th Annual Report to Congress on the Implementation of the IDEA,* 2016—9% of general population ages 6-21 served by Special Education. But 20% of students have dyslexia. This 20% figure is used by the US Department of Health & Human Services, National Institutes of Health, National Institute of Child Health & Human Development.
14. See Chapter 14 *Computational Microlinguistics*.

15. This was the intent of research pioneers and reading researchers—link evaluation with remediation. The most recent edition of the *Diagnostic and Statistical Manual of Mental Disorders* (DSM-5) recommends a shift to "assessment for intervention."
16. Rose, T., & Zirkel, P. (2007). Orton-Gillingham methodology for students with reading disabilities: 30 years of case law. *The Journal of Special Education, 41*(3), 171-185.
17. Institute of Education Sciences. (2013). *Common guidelines for education research and development: A report from the Institute of Education Sciences, US Department of Education and the National Science Foundation.* Retrieved from http://www.nsf.gov/pubs/2013/nsf13126/nsf13126.pdf
18. National Reading Panel. (2000). *Teaching children to read: An evidence-based assessment of the scientific literature on reading and its implications for reading instruction.* Bethesda, MD: National Institute of Child Health and Human Development.
19. See the research review in Elliott, J.G., & Grigorenko, E.L. (2014). *The dyslexia debate.* New York: Cambridge University Press.
20. Vaughn, S., & Linan-Thompson, S. (2003). What is special about special education for students with learning disabilities? *Journal of Special Education, 37*, 140-147.
21. See Fuchs, D., Compton, D.L., Fuchs, L.S., Bryant, V.J., Hamlett, C.L., & Lambert, W. (2012). First-grade cognitive abilities as long-term predictors of reading comprehension and disability status. *Journal of Learning Disabilities, 45*(3) 217–231. See also Vellutino, F.R., Scanlon, D.M., Zhang, H., & Schatschneider, C. (2008). Using response to kindergarten and first grade intervention to identify children at-risk for long-term reading difficulties. *Reading and Writing, 21*, 437-480.
22. See for example Costa, H.C. et al. (2013). Emergent literacy skills, behavior problems and familial antecedents of reading difficulties: A follow-up study of reading achievement from kindergarten to fifth grade. *Research in Developmental Disabilities, 34*(3), 1018-1035. See also Shanahan, M. A. et al. (2006). Processing speed deficits in attention deficit/hyper-

activity disorder and reading disability. *Journal of Abnormal Child Psychology, 34*, 585-602. See also Germanó, E., Gagliano, A., & Curatolo, P. (2010). Comorbidity of ADHD and dyslexia. *Developmental Neuropsychology, 35*(5) 475-493.

23. Office of Special Education and Rehabilitative Services, Office of Special Education Programs. (2014). *36th Annual Report to Congress on the Implementation of the Individuals with Disabilities Education Act, 2014*. Washington, DC: US Department of Education.

24. College Board. (2018). Lifetime earnings by education level. *Trends in higher education*. Retrieved from https://trends.collegeboard.org/education-pays/figures-tables/lifetime-earnings-education-level#Key%20Points.
In 2015, median earnings for high school and college graduates were $30,500 and $50,000 respectively. National Center for Education Statistics. (2017). Annual earnings of young adults. *The Condition of Education 2017* (NCES 2017-144). US Department of Education. Retrieved from https://nces.ed.gov/fastfacts/display.asp?id=77

25. Dyslexia and ADHD are known to coexist. See Germanó, E., Gagliano, A., & Curatolo, P. (2010). Comorbidity of ADHD and dyslexia. *Developmental Neuropsychology, 35*(5) 475-493.

26. See Note 8 above.

27. See Notes 17 and 18 above.

28. See for example Vellutino, F.R., Fletcher, J.M., Snowling, M.J., & Scanlon, D.M. (2004). Specific reading disability (dyslexia): What have we learned in the past four decades? *Journal of Child Psychology & Psychiatry, 45*, 2-40.

18

An Ideal World

Full Circle

"If you guys want to earn a 97.5 average, pay attention and do as Patience does!" said the English teacher to her class.

It is 2018. Patience, who once had a speech impairment, dyscalculia and dyslexia, now leads as the role model at school. Skye, who was functionally mute in elementary school, is, in the words of her teacher, a "rock star" in high school. Skye teaches younger students how to succeed in Dysolve and in life. On the weekends, she coaches MathCounts, together with Will. Will's mother, Vivian, volunteers to talk to schools, libraries, churches, in fact anyone she sees needs help with language processing. Frances, Skye's mother, freed from taking care of her own daughter, devotes her spare time to training other children and advising their parents. Duke uses his past experiences with bullies to connect with young children and mentor them. Duke's parents, Conny and Ken, tell those affected by language issues—from preschoolers to adults—to seek the help they need. Prince is preparing to follow in Will's footsteps, to lift up other students with his candid humor. Storm is lamenting the end of the school year because school is no longer rinse and repeat but "so much fun!" By the way, Storm now volunteers to do extra assignments at school. Storm's mother, Helen, happily helps us out in any way she can. Parents Adeline, Charles and Faye are persuading friends, neighbors, colleagues to get their children into the program that would clear up their chronic struggles. Uno's Dad, the professor, is doing what he does best—educating faculty, doctors and not-for-profits about the problem of dyslexia and its solution. Parent Marianne talks to school teachers about how her daughter, User2, skyrocketed in her first year in Dysolve. Patience's teacher, Ms. White, is telling her colleagues, "It works!" Max's pediatrician invited Dr. Coral to give a presentation to physicians at a medical center.

As one of our programmers said, "I honestly believe that making such impact in someone's life ends up affecting hundreds of others positively, because that person will not keep it to herself. She will look out for others and help them." Our talented programmers patiently worked with us through many long nights for over six years. They are still with us today.

None of the families we approached for this book turned us down to tell their story. They all wanted to pay it forward.

An Ideal World

Transformation

Each child in Part 1 became a different person when we resolved the problem. Each parent was relieved, liberated from the burden of not knowing. In each family, the evening hours of dreaded cries and recriminations transitioned to happy talk of future possibilities. Imagine multiplying this transformation 10 million times—to all the households with children affected by dyslexia in this country.[1]

Imagine these exceptional children growing up to fulfill their talents and realize their dreams. What is in store for them and for society? Imagine when other students—those in the middle getting by with average grades—are challenged to reach higher because few are performing below them anymore to offer that cushion of comfort. What would it be like for their teachers to get this opportunity instead of the strain of differentiating their instruction into a dozen distinct forms? What would teachers bring to their classrooms when their energy is no longer sapped by negative attitudes, lack of motivation, delinquency, acting up, meltdowns, bullying, fits of anger, fist fights…?[2]

Now imagine the opposite: The endless struggle within the school system felt by the children, their families, their teachers, and the administrators who carry the moral and financial weight of that responsibility. The fights rending families and school environments apart. The students who fall through the cracks down the spiral of defeatism, self-injurious behaviors and delinquency.[3] The limited future of the future of our society—school dropouts sliding into the working poor, nonliterate workers unable to lift themselves out of poverty, those filling the ranks of the criminal justice system.[4, 5, 6] This is the present.

It no longer needs to be our future, as it has been for 100 years. Technology has overturned the state of affairs. Now, it is the old, ineffective approach that is too costly to sustain.[7] The new approach costs a fraction *and* solves the problem.[8] The solution returns a balance to education spending, where the bulk of funds should be devoted to nurturing the bulk of students.

The economic, social, psychological and health impact of dyslexia and the coexisting conditions of ADHD and other language-based conditions also need rebalancing. These societal costs and individual toll diminish if not disappear when preschoolers are screened for language-processing deficits before they start to read.

Artificial intelligence can now wipe these tangible and intangible costs away, as if dyslexia never happened.

Dissemination

From our local community in the heart of the Empire State, we see our solution spread—through the old infrastructure of dyslexia support that concerned parents, educators and advocates had already built for this issue—to the rest of the country. Then country by country, our international colleagues help us construct in their homeland the answer to their fellow citizens' cries for help in their native tongues.

The early adopters, the parents in this book, are driven by their commitment to their children to do everything possible to give them a fighting chance in life. Their pediatricians are committed to their professional oath to find a way to ameliorate their patients' suffering. One by one, the struggling learners seeking medical help enter this new world of high achievers. Soon the school bureaucracy responds to the growing stridency of change from the half of the special needs population they serve. One by one, schools fall in compliance with new dyslexia legislation rolling through the nation.

Dysolve Dyslexia

Dysolve® is more than a solution to a problem. It changes how we think of the issue and reframes the question itself. It is a new way of doing things in a seamless, digital world. You simply plug and play. There is no thick manual to go through; no instructions to remember. The computer will simply prompt you. You don't have to plan what to do next or remember what you did—it's all in the system. The adult in the child's life doesn't need formal training to help him. Nor does his teacher. In fact, the student doesn't really need supervision to play his games. If you ever run into a problem, the friendly voice at the other end of the phone guides you through. If the system senses you need help, a friendly face appears in your online conference to support you. Much of the encumbrance of the old way of doing things has simply dissolved. You wonder, Why didn't we do this before?

It is 2018. 2018 technology is nothing like 2008 technology. To all the dedicated teachers who fretted at the end of the day what more they could have done for their struggling students, to all the administrators who worried about how best to budget for the next school year, to all the doctors who searched everywhere for a permanent solution for their patients, to all the parents and caretakers who sacrificed family time and resources to support their children with special needs, to all the activists who devoted decades to this cause even as their own children who were affected had all grown up, to all the children who face their reading problems bravely at school every day, to all the adults who continue to wonder why they cannot read—we present Dysolve.

NOTES

1. The figure is from the US National Institutes of Health. In 2015–2016, 6.7 million students received special education services in the US. When we combine the percentage of these students who were classified with specific learning disability, speech or language impairment and other conditions known to involve language-processing deficits, the percentage is close to the 80% used widely as the fraction of students with dyslexia out of this population. As slightly less than half of the students with learning disabilities actually get services at school, we estimate that the total with dyslexia amount to over 10 million. The 2015-16 data are from the US Department of Education, Office of Special Education Programs, *Individuals with Disabilities Education Act (IDEA) database*.
Retrieved from
https://www2.ed.gov/programs/osepidea/618-data/state-level-data-files/index.html#bcc.
In addition, the US child population for ages 6-17 in 2018 is 49.5 million. Using the established 20% figure for dyslexia, the at-risk population is 9.9 million. Source:
https://www.childstats.gov/americaschildren/tables.asp
2. See Chapters 2-4.
3. See Chapters 4 and 12.
4. Students with learning disabilities drop out of high school at a rate almost three times that of typical peers. See Office of Special Education and Rehabilitative Services, Office of Special Education Programs. (2014). *36th Annual Report to Congress on the Implementation of the Individuals with Disabilities Education Act, 2014.* Washington, DC: US Department of Education.
5. High school graduates typically earn about 66% less than Bachelor's degree holders during a 40-year working life. The annual difference in earnings can grow to nearly $800,000 over that lifespan. See College Board. (2018). Lifetime earnings by education level. *Trends in higher education*.
Retrieved from

https://trends.collegeboard.org/education-pays/figures-tables/lifetime-earnings-education-level#Key%20Points. In 2015, median earnings for high school and college graduates were $30,500 and $50,000 respectively. US Department of Education, National Center for Education Statistics. (2017). Annual earnings of young adults. *The Condition of Education 2017* (NCES 2017-144). Cited in National Center for Education Statistics. Retrieved from https://nces.ed.gov/fastfacts/display.asp?id=77

6. About 33% of prison inmates have the lowest literacy skills v. 20% of the general population. See National Center for Education Statistics. (1994). *Literacy behind prison walls.* Washington, DC: US Department of Education, Office of Educational Research and Improvement. Retrieved from https://nces.ed.gov/pubs94/94102.pdf
7. See Chapter 12 *The True Cost of Dyslexia.*
8. The cumulative 8-year cost difference between using Dysolve and the present methods in special education is close to $100 million for 700 students in a midsize school district in New York. See cost comparisons between Dysolve and present methods in Chapter 12.

References

Acquarone, S. (2018). *Signs of autism in infants: Recognition and early intervention.* New York: Routledge.

Al-Yagon, M. (2015). Fathers and mothers of children with learning disabilities: Links between emotional and coping resources. *Learning Disability Quarterly, 38*(2), 112-128. doi:10.1177/0731948713520556

American Psychiatric Association. *Diagnostic and Statistical Manual of Mental Disorders*, 5th Edition. Arlington, VA: American Psychiatric Association.

Arciuli, J., & Brock, J. (2014). *Communication in autism.* Amsterdam: John Benjamins.

Ashkenazi, S., Black, J.M., Abrams, D.A., Hoeft, F., & Menon, V. (2013). Neurobiological underpinnings of math and reading learning disabilities. *Journal of Learning Disabilities, 46*(6) 549–569. doi:10.1177/0022219413483174

Baker, S., Gersten, R., & Lee, D. S. (2002). A synthesis of empirical research on teaching mathematics to low-achieving students. *Elementary School Journal, 103*, 51–73.

Bally, C., & Sechehaye, A. (Eds.). (1915). *Course in General Linguistics - Ferdinand de Saussure.* (Baskin, W., Transl.). New York: McGraw-Hill.

Bargiela-Chiappini, F., & Haugh, M. (Eds.).(2009). *Face, communication and social interaction.* London: Equinox.

Bereiter, C., & Scardamalia, M. (1983). Does learning to write have to be so difficult? In A. Freedman, I. Pringle, & J. Yalden (Eds.), *Learning to write: First language/second language* (pp. 20-33). London: Longman.

Berninger, V.W., & Richards, T.L. (2002). *Brain literacy for educators and psychologists.* Amsterdam: Academic.

Bernstein, S.E. (2009). Phonology, decoding, and lexical compensation in vowel spelling errors made by children with dyslexia, *Reading and Writing, 22*(3), 307-331.

Boada, R., & Pennington, B.F. (2006). Deficient implicit phonological representations in children with dyslexia. *Journal of Experimental Child Psychology, 95*(3), 153-193.

Retrieved from https://doi.org/10.1016/j.jecp.2006.04.003

Brauth, S.E., Hall, W.S., & Dooling, R.J. (Eds.). (1991). *Plasticity of development.* Cambridge, MA: MIT Press.

Brysbaert, M., Stevens, M., Mandera, P., & Keuleers, E. (2016). How many words do we know? Practical estimates of vocabulary size dependent on word definition, the degree of language input and the participant's age. *Frontiers in Psychology, 7*, 1116. doi:10.3389/fpsyg.2016.01116

Bureau of Labor Statistics. (2017). Consumer expenditures – 2016. *Economic News Release* (USDL-17-1175). US Department of Labor. Retrieved from https://www.bls.gov/news.release/cesan.nr0.htm

Cancer, A., Manzoli, S., & Antonietti, A. (2016). The alleged link between creativity and dyslexia: Identifying the specific process in which dyslexic students excel. *Cogent Psychology, 3*: 1190309. Retrieved from http://dx.doi.org/10.1080/23311908.2016.1190309

Chantiluke, K., Christakou, A., Murphy, C.M., Giampietro, V., Daly, E.M.,...Rubia, K. (2014). Disorder-specific functional abnormalities during temporal discounting in youth with Attention Deficit Hyperactivity Disorder (ADHD), autism and comorbid ADHD and autism. *Psychiatry Research: Neuroimaging, 223*, 113-120.

Chen, H., Xu, J., Zhou, Y., Gao, Y., Wang, G., Xia, J. et al. (2015). Association study of stuttering candidate genes GNPTAB, GNPTG and NAGPA with dyslexia in Chinese population. *BMC Genetics, 16*, 1-7. doi:10.1186/s12863-015-0172-5

Chong, S.L., & Siegel, L.S. (2008). Stability of computational deficits in math learning disability from second through fifth grades. *Developmental Neuropsychology, 33*(3), 300-317.

College Board. (2018). Lifetime earnings by education level. *Trends in higher education.* Retrieved from https://trends.collegeboard.org/education-pays/figures tables/lifetime-earnings-education-level#Key%20Points

Cook, B.J. (2004). Inclusive teachers' attitudes toward their students with disabilities: A replication and extension. *The Elementary School Journal, 104*(4), 307-320.

References

Cortese, S., Holtmann, M., Banaschewski, T., Buitelaar, J., Coghill, D.,...Sergeant, J. (2015). Practitioner review: Current best practice in the management of adverse events during treatment with ADHD medications in children and adolescents. *Journal of Child Psychology and Psychiatry, 54*(3), 227–246. doi:10.1111/jcpp.12036

Costa, H.C. et al. (2013). Emergent literacy skills, behavior problems and familial antecedents of reading difficulties: A follow-up study of reading achievement from kindergarten to fifth grade. *Research in Developmental Disabilities, 34*(3), 1018-1035.

Cunningham, D.H. (2015). *The education dollar: A look at spending and funding trends.* Albany, NY: NY State Association of School Business Officials. Retrieved from https://www.nysasbo.org/uploads/files/1442244064_Spending%202015%20%285%29.pdf

Dale, H.S., & Pajares, F. (2009). Self-efficacy theory. In K.R. Wentzel & D.B. Miele (Eds.), *Handbook of motivation at school* (pp. 35-53). New York: Routledge.

Dickerson Mayes, S., Gorman, A.A., Hillwig-Garcia, J., & Syed, E. (2013). Suicide ideation and attempts in children with autism. *Research in Autism Spectrum Disorders, 7*(1), 109-119. Retrieved from https://doi.org/10.1016/j.rasd.2012.07.009

Dinsmore, D.L., Alexander, P.A., & Loughlin, S.M. (2008). Focusing the conceptual lens on metacognition, self-regulation, and self-regulated learning. *Educational Psychology Review, 20*(4), 391-409. doi:10.1007/s10648-008-9083-6

Duranovic, M., Dedeic, M., & Gavric, M. (2015). Dyslexia and visual-spatial talents. *Current Psychology, 34*(2), 207-222.

Eckert, M. (2004). Neuroanatomical markers for dyslexia: A review of dyslexia structural imaging studies. *Neuroscientist, 10*(3), 1–10.

Eide, B.L., & Eide, F.F. (2011). *The dyslexic advantage: Unlocking the hidden potential of the dyslexic brain.* New York, NY: Penguin.

Ellerson, N. (2017). *School budgets 101.* Alexandria, VA: American Association of School Administrators.

Retrieved from https://www.aasa.org/uploadedFiles/Policy_ and_Advocacy/files/SchoolBudgetBriefFINAL.pdf

Elliott, J.G., & Grigorenko, E.L. (2014). *The dyslexia debate*. New York: Cambridge University Press.

Elman, J.L., Bates, E.A., Johnson, M.H., Karmiloff-Smith, A., Parisi, D., & Plunkett, K. (1999). *Rethinking innateness*. Cambridge, MA: MIT Press.

Feldman, H.M., Lee, E.S., Yeatman, J.D., & Yeom, K.W. (2012). Language and reading skills in school-aged children and adolescents born preterm are associated with white matter properties on diffusion tensor imaging. *Neuropsychologia, 50*, 3348-3362. Retrieved from https://doi.org/10.1016/j.neuropsychologia.2012.10.014

Fletcher, J.M., Stuebing, K.K., Barth, A.E., Denton, C.A., Cirino, P.T., Francis, D.J.,...Vaughn, S. (2011). Cognitive correlates of inadequate response to reading intervention. *School Psychology Review, 40*, 3-22.

Fuchs, D., Compton, D.L., Fuchs, L.S., Bryant, V.J., Hamlett, C.L., & Lambert, W. (2012). First-grade cognitive abilities as long-term predictors of reading comprehension and disability status. *Journal of Learning Disabilities, 45*(3), 217–231. doi: 10.1177/0022219412442154

Fuchs, D., McMaster, K.L., Fuchs, L.S., & Al Otaiba, S. (2013). Data-based individualization as a means of providing intensive instruction to students with serious learning disorders. In H.L. Swanson, K.R. Harris, & S. Graham (Eds.). *Handbook of learning disabilities* (pp. 526-544). New York: Guilford Press.

Geary, D.C. (1993). Mathematical disabilities: Cognitive, neuropsychological, and genetic components. *Psychological Bulletin, 114*(2), 345–362.

Geary, D.C. (2013). Learning disabilities in mathematics: Recent advances. In H.L. Swanson, K.R. Harris, & S. Graham (Eds.), *Handbook of learning disabilities* (2nd ed., pp. 239–255). New York: Guilford Press.

Genizi, J., Gordon, S., Kerem, N.C., Srugo, I., Shahar, E., & Ravid, S. (2013). Primary headaches, attention deficit disorder and learning disabilities in children and adolescents. *Journal of Headache Pain, 14*(1), 54.

doi:10.1186/1129-2377-14-54

Germanó, E., Gagliano, A., & Curatolo, P. (2010). Comorbidity of ADHD and dyslexia. *Developmental Neuropsychology, 35*(5) 475-493.

Gilger, J.W., Allen, K., & Castillo, A. (2016). Reading disability and enhanced dynamic spatial reasoning: A review of the literature. *Brain and Cognition, 105,* 55–65.

Gillingham, A., & Stillman, B.W. (1997). *The Gillingham Manual: Remedial training for children with specific disability in reading, spelling, and penmanship* (8th ed.). Cambridge, MA: Educators Publishing Service.

Givón, T. (1995). *Functionalism and grammar.* Amsterdam: John Benjamins.

Gladwell, M. (2013). *David and Goliath.* New York: Little, Brown and Company.

Goswami, U., Mead, N., Foster, T., Huss, M., Barnes, L., & Leong, V. (2013). Impaired perception of syllable stress in children with dyslexia: A longitudinal study. *Journal of Memory and Language, 69*(1), 1-17. Retrieved from https://doi.org/10.1016/j.jml.2013.03.001

Gunning, T. (2003). The role of readability in today's classroom. *Topics in Language Disorders, 23*(3), 175-185.

Heath, S.M., Hogben, J.H., & Clark, C.D. (1999). Auditory temporal processing in disabled readers with and without oral language delay. *Journal of Child Psychology and Psychiatry, 40,* 637-647. doi:10.1017/S0021963099003947

Hinshaw, S.P., & Scheffler, R.M. (2014). *ADHD explosion: Myths, medication, money, and today's push for performance.* New York: Oxford University Press.

Hoh, P.-S. (Spring 2005). The linguistic advantage of the intellectually gifted child: An empirical study of spontaneous speech. *Roeper Review, 27*(3), 178-185.

Hoh, P.-S. (2008). Cognitive characteristics of the gifted. In J. Plucker & C. Callahan (Eds.), *Critical issues and practices in gifted education: What the research says* (pp. 57-83). Austin, TX: Prufrock.

Holm, A., Farrier, F., & Dodd, B. (2008). Phonological awareness, reading accuracy and spelling ability of children with inconsistent phonological disorder. *International Journal of Language and Communication Disorders, 43*, 300–322.

Hommer, R.E., & Swedo, S.E. (2015). Schizophrenia and autism-related disorders. *Schizophrenia Bulletin, 41*(2), 313-314. doi: 10.1093/schbul/sbu188

Hopkins, T., Clegg, J., & Stackhouse, J. (2016). Young offenders' perspectives on their literacy and communication skills. *International Journal of Language & Communication Disorders, 51*(1), 95–109.

Hulme, C., Nash, H.M., Gooch, D., Lervåg, A., & Snowling, M.J. (2015). The foundations of literacy development in children at familial risk of dyslexia. *Psychological Science, 26*, 1877–1886.

Ibrahim, K., & Donyai, P. (2015). Drug holidays from ADHD medication: International experience over the past four decades. *Journal of Attention Disorders, 19*(7), 551-568. doi:10.1177/1087054714548035

Institute of Education Sciences. (2013). *Common guidelines for education research and development: A report from the Institute of Education Sciences, US Department of Education and the National Science Foundation.* Retrieved from http://www.nsf.gov/pubs/2013/nsf13126/nsf13126.pdf

Jahromi, L.B., Meek, S.E., & Ober-Reynolds, S. (2012). Emotion regulation in the context of frustration in children with high functioning autism and their typical peers. *Journal of Child Psychology and Psychiatry, 53*, 1250–1258. doi:10.1111/j.1469-7610.2012.02560.x

Johnson, E.S., Humphrey, M., Mellard, D.F., Woods, K., & Swanson, H.L. (2010). Cognitive processing deficits and students with specific learning disabilities: A selective meta-analysis of the literature. *Learning Disability Quarterly, 33*, 3-18.

Johnson, P.E., Pennington, B.F., Lowenstein, J.H., Nittrouer, S. (2011). Sensitivity to structure in the speech signal by children with speech sound disorder and reading disability. *Journal of Communication Disorders, 44*(3), 294-314. Retrieved from https://doi.org/10.1016/j.jcomdis.2011.01.001

References

Kennedy, M., Kreppner, J., Knights, N., Kumsta, R., Maughan, B.,...Sonuga-Barke, E.J.S. (2016). Early severe institutional deprivation is associated with a persistent variant of adult attention-deficit/hyperactivity disorder: Clinical presentation, developmental continuities and life circumstances in the English and Romanian Adoptees study. *Journal of Child Psychology and Psychiatry, 57*(10), 1113–1125. doi:10.1111/jcpp.12576

Kida, A.S.B., de Ávila, C.R.B., & Capellini, S.A. (2016). Reading comprehension assessment through retelling: Performance profiles of children with dyslexia and language-based learning disability. *Frontiers in Psychology, 7*, 787. doi:10.3389/fpsyg.2016.00787

Krafnick, A.J., Flowers, D.L., Napoliello, E.M., & Eden, G.F. (2011). Gray matter volume changes following reading intervention in dyslexic children. *NeuroImage, 57*(3), 733-741. doi:10.1016/j.neuroimage.2010.10.062

Krutetskii, V.A. (1976). *The psychology of mathematical abilities in schoolchildren.* Chicago: University of Chicago Press.

Landi, N., & Perfetti, C.A. (2007). An electrophysiological investigation of semantic and phonological processing in skilled and less-skilled comprehenders. *Brain and Language, 102*, 30–45. doi:10.1016/j.bandl.2006.11.001

Lewis, B.A., Avrich, A.A., Freebairn, L.A., Hansen, A.J., Sucheston, L.E., Lara, E. et al. (2011). Literacy outcomes of children with early childhood speech sound disorders: Impact of endophenotypes. *Journal of Speech, Language and Hearing Research, 54*, 1628-1643.

MacWhinney, B. (Ed.). (1999). *The emergence of language.* Mahwah, NJ: Lawrence Erlbaum.

Mather, N., & Wendling, B.J. (2012). *Essentials of dyslexia assessment and intervention.* Hoboken, NJ: John Wiley & Sons.

Mazefsky, C.A., Pelphrey, K.A., & Dahl, R.E. (2012). The need for a broader approach to emotion regulation research in autism. *Child Development Perspectives, 6*(1), 92-97. doi:10.1111/j.1750-8606.2011.00229.x

Mel'čuk, I., & Beck, D. (2016). *Language: From meaning to text.* Moscow: Academic Studies Press.

Minshawi, N.F., Hurwitz, S., Fodstad, J.C., Biebl, S., Morriss, D.H., & McDougle, C.J. (2014). The association between self-injurious behaviors and autism spectrum disorders. *Psychology Research and Behavior Management, 7*, 125–136. Retrieved from https://doi.org/10.2147/PRBM.S44635

Mishna, F. (2003). Learning disabilities and bullying: Double jeopardy. *Journal of Learning Disabilities, 36*(4), 336-47.

Morgan, P.L., Farkas, G., Tufis, P.A., & Sperling, R.A. (2008). Are reading and behavior problems risk factors for each other? *Journal of Learning Disabilities, 41*(5), 417-436.

National Center for Education Statistics. (1994). *Literacy behind prison walls*. US Department of Education, Office of Educational Research and Improvement.

National Center for Education Statistics. (2015). Children and youth with disabilities. *The condition of education*. US Department of Education, Institute of Education Sciences. Retrieved from https://nces.ed.gov/programs/coe/indicator_cgg.asp

National Center for Education Statistics. (2017). Annual earnings of young adults. *The Condition of Education 2017* (NCES 2017-144). US Department of Education. Retrieved from https://nces.ed.gov/fastfacts/display.asp?id=77

National Center for Education Statistics. (2017). How did U.S. students perform on the most recent assessments? *The National Assessment of Educational Progress* (NAEP). US Department of Education, Institute of Education Sciences. Retrieved from https://www.nationsreportcard.gov/

National Education Association. (2017). *Background of Special Education and the Individuals with Disabilities Education Act (IDEA)*. Retrieved from http://www.nea.org/home/19029.htm

National Mathematics Advisory Panel (NMAP). (2008). *Foundations for success: Final report of the national math advisory panel*. Washington, DC: US Department of Education.

National Reading Panel. (2000). *Teaching children to read: An evidence-based assessment of the scientific literature on reading and its implications for reading instruction*. Bethesda,

MD: National Institute of Child Health and Human Development.

O'Connor, K. (2012). Auditory processing in autism spectrum disorder: A review. *Neuroscience & Biobehavioral Reviews, 36*(2), 836-854. Retrieved from https://doi.org/10.1016/j.neubiorev.2011.11.008

Office of Special Education and Rehabilitative Services, Office of Special Education Programs. (2014). *36th Annual Report to Congress on the Implementation of the Individuals with Disabilities Education Act, 2014*. Washington, DC: US Department of Education.

Office of Special Education and Rehabilitative Services, Office of Special Education Programs. (2016). *38th Annual Report to Congress on the Implementation of the Individuals with Disabilities Education Act, 2016*. Washington, DC: US Department of Education.

Ozernov-Palchik, O., & Gaab, N. (2016). Tackling the early identification of dyslexia with the help of neuroimaging. *Perspectives on Language and Literacy, 42*(1), 11-17.

Pennington, B.F. (2009). *Diagnosing learning disorders: A neurological framework* (2nd ed.). New York: Guilford Press.

Pennington, B.F. (2011). Controversial therapies for dyslexia. *Perspectives on Language and Literacy, 37*(1), 7-8.

Pennington, B.F., Cardoso-Martins, C., Green, P.A., & Lefly, D.L. (2001). Comparing the phonological and double deficit hypotheses for developmental dyslexia. *Reading and Writing: An Interdisciplinary Journal, 14,* 707–755.

Pennington, B.F., & Olson, R.K. (2005). Genetics of dyslexia. In M.J. Snowling & C. Hulme (Eds.), *The science of reading: A handbook* (pp. 453–472). Oxford: Blackwell.

Plucker, J., & Callahan, C. (Eds.). (2013). *Critical issues and practices in gifted education: What the research says.* Waco, TX: Prufrock.

Radford, A., Atkinson, M., Britain, D., Clahsen, H., & Spencer, A. (2009). *Linguistics: An introduction.* Cambridge: Cambridge University Press.

Ramnaraine, L.D., Rahmani, M., Khurshid, K.A. (2016). Sleep problems and disorders in children and adolescents with attention-deficit/hyperactivity disorder. *Psychiatric Annals, 46*(7), 401-407.

Rello-Sanchez, M.L., & Ballesteros, M. (2017). *US Patent Application No. US 2017/0308654 A1*. Alexandria, VA: United States Patent and Trademark Office.

Reynolds, S., & Lane, S.J. (2009). Sensory overresponsivity and anxiety in children with ADHD. *The American Journal of Occupational Therapy, 63*(4), 433-440.

Robinson, S., Howlin, P., & Russell, A. (2017). Personality traits, autobiographical memory and knowledge of self and others: A comparative study in young people with autism spectrum disorder. *Autism, 21*(3), 357-367. doi:10.1177/1362361316645429

Rommelse, N.N.J., Altink, M.E., Fliers, E.A., Martin, N.C., Buschgens, C.J.M.,...Oosterlaan, J. (2009). Comorbid problems in ADHD: Degree of association, shared endophenotypes, and formation of distinct subtypes. Implications for a future *DSM. Journal of Abnormal Child Psychology, 37*, 793-804.

Rose, J. (2009). *Identifying and teaching children and young people with dyslexia and literacy difficulties. (The Rose Report)*. Nottingham, UK: DCSF Publications.

Rose, T., & Zirkel, P. (2007). Orton-Gillingham methodology for students with reading disabilities: 30 years of case law. *The Journal of Special Education, 41*(3), 171-185.

Rhodes, S.M., Park, J., Seth, S., & Coghill, D.R. (2012). A comprehensive investigation of memory impairment in attention deficit hyperactivity disorder and oppositional defiant disorder. *Journal of Child Psychology and Psychiatry and Allied Disciplines, 53*(2), 128-137. doi:10.1111/j.1469-7610.2011.02436.x

Sackerman, R.T., Jr., & Sackerman, S.A. (2016, November 10). *Completing the Picture of Dyslexia: Twice-Exceptional Students*. Paper presented at the New Jersey Education Association Convention, Atlantic City, NJ.

Sanger, D., Moore-Brown, B.J., Montgomery, J., Rezac, C., & Keller, H. (2003). Female incarcerated adolescents with language problems talk about their own communication behaviours and learning. *Journal of Communication Disorders, 36*, 465–486.

Sanger, D., Scheffler, M., Drake, B., Hilgert, K., Cresswell, J.W., & Hansen, D.J. (2000). Maltreated female delinquents speak about their communication behaviours. *Communication Disorders Quarterly, 21*, 176–187.

Schwarz, A. (2016). *ADHD nation*. New York: Scribner.

Shanahan, M. A. et al. (2006). Processing speed deficits in attention deficit/hyperactivity disorder and reading disability. *Journal of Abnormal Child Psychology, 34*, 585-602.

Shaywitz, S.E. (2003). *Overcoming dyslexia*. New York: Knopf.

Smith, L.O., & Elder, J.H. (2010). Siblings and family environments of persons with autism spectrum disorder: A review of the literature. *Journal of Child and Adolescent Psychiatric Nursing, 23*(3), 189-195.

Snowling, M.J. (2000). *Dyslexia*. Oxford, UK: Blackwell.

Snowling, M.J. (2008) Specific disorders and broader phenotypes: The case of dyslexia. *The Quarterly Journal of Experimental Psychology, 61*(1), 142-156. doi:10.1080/17470210701508830

Snowling, M. J., Adams, J. W., Bowyer-Crane, C., & Tobin, V. (2000). Levels of literacy among juvenile offenders: The incidence of specific reading difficulties. *Criminal Behaviour and Mental Health, 10*(4), 229-241.

Snowling, M.J., Melby-Lervåg, M. (2016). Oral language deficits in familial dyslexia: A meta-analysis and review. *Psychological Bulletin, 142*, 498-545.

Staff, J., Whichard, C., Siennick, S.E., & Maggs, J. (2015). Early life risks, antisocial tendencies, and preteen delinquency. *Criminology, 53*(4), 677-701. doi:10.1111/1745-9125.12093

Sternberg, R.J., & Grigorenko, E.L. (1999). *Our labeled children: What every parent and teacher needs to know about learning disabilities*. Cambridge, MA: Perseus.

Styhre, A. (2011). Practice and intuitive thinking. *International Journal of Organizational Analysis, 19*(2), 109-126. doi:10.1108/19348831111135065

Suler, J. (2004). The online disinhibition effect. *CyberPsychology & Behavior, 7*(3), 321-6. doi:10.1089/1094931041291295

Tallal, P. (2012). Improving neural response to sound improves reading. *PNAS, 109*, 16406-16407.

The Center for the Study of Learning, Georgetown University Medical Center. (nd). *Frequently asked questions about dyslexia.* Retrieved from http://csl.georgetown.edu/dyslexia/faqs.shtml

Torgesen, J.K., Alexander, A.W., Wagner, R.K., Rashotte, C.A., et al. (2001). Intensive remedial instruction for children with severe reading disabilities: Immediate and long-term outcomes from two instructional approaches. *Journal of Learning Disabilities, 34*(1), 33-58.

US Department of Education. (2016). *Fiscal year 2016 budget summary and background information.* Retrieved from https://www2.ed.gov/about/overview/budget/budget16/summary/16summary.pdf

US Department of Education. (2017). *Fiscal year 2017 budget summary and background information.* Retrieved from https://www2.ed.gov/about/overview/budget/budget17/summary/17summary.pdf

Vacca, J. (2004). Educated prisoners are less likely to return to prison. *Journal of Correctional Education, 55*(4), 297–305.

Vacca, J.S. (2008). Crime can be prevented if schools teach juvenile offenders to read. *Children and Youth Services Review, 30*(9), 1055-1062. Retrieved from https://doi.org/10.1016/j.childyouth.2008.01.013

Valicenti-McDermott, M., Lawson, K., Hottinger, K., Seijo, R., Schechtman, M.,...Shinnar, S. (2015). Parental stress in families of children with autism and other developmental disabilities. *Journal of Child Neurology, 30*, 1728-1735. doi:10.1177/0883073815579705

Van Cauwenberge, V., Sonuga-Barke, E.J.S., Hoppenbrouwers, K., Van Leeuwen, H.K., & Wiersema, J.R. (2017). Regulation of emotion in ADHD: Can children with ADHD override the natural tendency to approach positive and avoid negative pictures? *Journal of Neural Transmission, 124*(3), 397-406.

Vaughn, S., Cirino, P.T., Wanzek, J., Wexler, J., Fletcher, J.M., Denton, C.D.,...Francis, D.J. (2010). Response to intervention for middle school students with reading difficulties: Effects of a primary and secondary intervention. *School Psychology Review, 39*(1), 3-21.

Vaughn, S., & Linan-Thompson, S. (2003). What is special about special education for students with learning disabilities? *Journal of Special Education, 37*, 140-147.

Vellutino, F.R., Fletcher, J.M., Snowling, M.J., & Scanlon, D.M. (2004). Specific reading disability (dyslexia): What have we learned in the past four decades? *Journal of Child Psychology & Psychiatry, 45*, 2-40.

Vellutino, F.R., Scanlon, D.M., Zhang, H., & Schatschneider, C. (2008). Using response to kindergarten and first grade intervention to identify children at-risk for long-term reading difficulties. *Reading and Writing, 21*, 437-480.

Victorio, M. (2014). EHMTI-0290. Headaches in patients with autism spectrum disorder. *The Journal of Headache and Pain, 15*(Suppl 1):B37. doi:10.1186/1129-2377-15-S1-B37

Wanzek, J., & Roberts, G. (2012). Reading interventions with varying instructional emphases for fourth graders with reading difficulties. *Learning Disability Quarterly, 35*(2), 90-101.

Weinstein, A., & Lejoyeux, M. (2010). Internet addiction or excessive Internet use. *The American Journal of Drug and Alcohol Abuse, 36*, 277–283. doi:10.3109/00952990.2010.491880

Wender, P.H. (2001). *ADHD: Attention-deficit hyperactivity disorder in children, adolescents, and adults.* New York: Oxford University Press.

Wentzel, K.R., & Miele, D.B. (2009). *Handbook of motivation at school.* New York: Routledge.

Werfel, K.L., & Krimm, H. (2017). A preliminary comparison of reading subtypes in a clinical sample of children with specific language impairment. *Journal of Speech, Language and Hearing Research, 60,* 2680-2686.

Williams, D. (2010). Theory of own mind in autism: Evidence of a specific deficit in self-awareness? *Autism, 14*(5), 474–494. doi:10.1177/1362361310366314

Yeguez, C.E., Hill, R.M., Buitron, V., & Pettit, J.W. (2018). Stress accounts for the association between ADHD symptoms and suicide ideation when stress-reactive rumination is high. *Cognitive Therapy and Research, 42*(4), 461–467. Retrieved from https://doi.org/10.1007/s10608-018-9910-0

Index

504 Plan, 76

A

Academic Intervention Services (AIS), 4, 48, 258, 298, 371, 471
acquisition of written vocabulary—*see* spelling acquisition
adaptive programs, 325, 461, 463
ADHD, ADD, AD/HD
    cognitive overload in, 271, 274, 290, 506
    correcting, 271, 275, 290
    diagnosis of, 275, 290, 506
    dyslexia coexisting with, 36, 39, 240, 271, 273
    emotion regulation in, 173, 192, 277
    hyperactivity—*see also* restlessness, 191, 268, 271, 290, 360, 501, 506
    impulsivity, 6, 50, 63, 163, 384
    language difficulties and, 268-9, 271-2, 274
    physical agitation—*see also* physical discomfort, 292
    quantified measures for, 275, 506
    sleep disturbance, 172, 484
    symptoms, 63, 172, 180, 262, 271, 277, 290, 506
ADHD medication
    controversy, 187, 277, 284
    drug holidays, 172, 287
    effects on appetite, 157, 185, 192
aggression and learning disabilities, 63, 388
Annals of Dyslexia, 418
anxiety, 173, 202, 208, 383, 385, 392, 484, 501
artificial intelligence—*see also* Dysolve-artificial intelligence system, 343
assessment of special needs, 33-34, 375, 420, 466, 475, 487, 497
assistive technologies, 422
attention span, 240-1, 247
attitude change, 62, 67, 90, 195-6, 198, 218, 226, 247
auditory processing deficits/disorder, 113, 240-2, 247, 508
autism spectrum disorder
    ADHD and, 161, 167, 175, 177
    anxiety in, 173, 202, 208

auditory and visual hallucinations in, 197
auditory processing in, 197
introspection in, 200, 202
language processing and, 507
pain insensitivity in, 192
self-awareness in, 202, 208
self-injurious behaviors in, 191, 392, 484
sibling relations and, 162, 175-6
social interaction in, 168, 197
speech/language impairment and, 187-9, 193
avoidance behavior/strategies, 67, 276, 292

B

Barton Reading and Spelling System, 404, 417
b/d reversal errors, 77, 268, 278, 490, 512
behavior issues—*see also* delinquency, 78-9, 169
below grade-level reading/outcomes—*see also* Orton-Gillingham, *and* compensatory methods, 107, 115, 159, 224, 345, 350, 354, 366, 494
Berlin, R., 416
blends, 435, 446-9
brain plasticity—*see* neuroplasticity
brain reorganization, 247, 253
bridge program, 159, 173
bullying, peer victimization, 63, 78, 87, 90, 144, 167

C

Centers for the Study of Learning and Attention, 419
classification for special services, 491
cognitive impairment, 28, 39, 131
cognitive overload, 133, 176, 188, 197, 234, 246, 248, 253, 271, 274, 290, 292, 449, 501, 506
Committee on Special Education (CSE), 25
comorbid/coexisting/co-occurring conditions—*see under* dyslexia
compensatory methods—*see also* Orton-Gillingham
  cost comparisons of, 405-8
  high costs of, 401-4
  limited results with, 69, 107, 125-6, 281-2, 404-5
  long-term costs of, 405-7
Comprehensive Test of Phonological Processing (CTOPP), 108,

119
Computational Linguistics, 453-4
Computational Microlinguistics, 431, 433, 453-5
computational problem of dyslexia, 450-4, 507
computer expert system—*see under* Dysolve
condition defined, 492
congenital word-blindness, 424, 431
consonant cluster reduction, 311
contextual cues in reading, 75
copying tasks, 427-8
Coral Method®, 109, 111, 119, 128, 149, 310, 327, 337, 339, 340, 390, 454
co-teaching classes, 10, 16, 19

D

decoding words, 75, 129, 233-4, 308, 425-7
defeatism, 90, 137, 253, 392, 480, 484, 517
defiance, defiant behavior—*see also* oppositional defiant disorder, 154, 161, 175, 208-9, 274, 382, 471
deficits
    orthographic/spelling, 35, 41, 127, 129, 278
    phonological/sound, 38, 77, 104, 245, 369, 420
    semantic/meaning, 426
delayed speech, 18, 79, 85, 100
delinquency, juvenile delinquency—*see also* youth offenders, 63, 388, 409
developmental delay, 9, 85
developmental dyslexia—*see also* dyslexia, 416
developmental milestones, 85
Diagnostic and Statistical Manual of Mental Disorders – 5th Ed. (DSM-5), 75, 115, 368, 420, 513
dialect, dialectal features, 306-8
disability defined, 491
disattention, 274
discrepancies—*see also* paradoxical behaviors
    IQ and reading achievement—*see under* dyslexia diagnosis
    listening and reading comprehension, 53
    oral and written vocabularies, 85
    reading and writing abilities, 382
    text reading and comprehension, 17, 75, 217

disorder defined, 491
distractibility, 177, 247, 274
dyscalculia
    definition of, 26, 38
    dyslexia and, 38, 416
    effect of Dysolve on, 470
    effectiveness of traditional interventions on, 26
dysgraphia, 381, 429, 438, 490
dyslexia
    affective/emotional factors in, 125, 353
    anatomical basis of, 419, 424, 435
    chronic condition of, 133, 286, 390, 422, 489, 495
    comorbid/coexisting/co-occurring conditions, 38, 39, 175, 343, 385, 418, 437, 514
    confusion with term and concept, 425-31
    creativity and, 137
    definition of, 429-30
    deprived learning environments, 309, 426, 438, 511
    diagnosis of—*see* dyslexia diagnosis
    economics of, 401-9
    environment and—*see* dyslexia-deprived learning environments
    excelling with, 502-3
    genetics and, 113
    history of, 415-23
    morphological awareness in, 33, 41, 420
    multiple deficits, 420, 430, 438, 441
    myths about, 419, 490
    neurological disorder, 38, 425, 432, 511
    orthographic awareness in, 35, 129, 278, 420
    outgrowing dyslexia, 503
    phonemic awareness in, 66, 128, 420, 499
    phonological awareness in, 40, 128, 245, 369, 420
    problem behaviors and—*see* ADHD, *and* problem behaviors
    psychological effects of—*see also* defeatism, 81, 86, 142-5, 389
    root cause of, 108, 112, 118, 122, 126, 226, 247, 361, 364, 389-90, 429-32, 490, 507
    second language learning and, 110, 120, 427

Index

    symptoms of, 77, 288, 508
    testing in schools on, 14, 285, 368
dyslexia diagnosis
    Diagnostic and Statistical Manual of Mental Disorders – 5th Edition (DSM-5), 75, 115-6, 368, 420, 513
    Dysolve and—*see also* dyslexia-root cause of, 501-2, 507-8
    IQ-reading achievement discrepancy, 116, 420-1
    medical field and—*see Diagnostic and Statistical Manual of Mental Disorders*
    neuroanatomical differences, 419, 424
    neuroimaging technology in—*see also* functional magnetic resonance imaging, 433
    neuropsychological evaluations/assessment for, 96, 103, 115-6, 119, 125, 132, 286, 362-3, 368, 407, 420-1, 469, 501-2, 508
    normative data used in, 119, 469, 475
    problems with remediation not linked to— *see Diagnostic and Statistical Manual of Mental Disorders, and* neuropsychological evaluations
    qualifying threshold in, 286
    school standards for, 160, 224, 282-3, 402
    signs of dyslexia—*see* dyslexia-symptoms of
dyslexia schools, 105-7, 132-3, 407
dyslexic advantage, 492, 512
Dysolve
    analytics—*see* Dysolve-data analytics
    artificial intelligence system—*see also* Dysolve-computer expert system, 343-4, 364, 462-4, 469, 474, 504
    automated program—*see also* Dysolve-computer expert system *and* artificial intelligence system, 131, 246, 406-7, 460, 494
    best age for, 243-4, 503-4
    cloud computing, 344, 399, 459
    computer expert system, 183, 343, 390, 460-4
    continuous capture of data in, 462, 469
    continuous evaluation/assessment, 407, 423, 461, 495-8
    corrective training, 109, 184, 228, 250-1, 318, 339-40, 342, 353, 465-6, 469, 482, 493-6, 498
    cost comparisons with other methods, 405-6

data analytics, 86, 183, 390, 406, 481, 499-500
Dysolve.com, 77, 85, 173, 279, 344, 349, 389, 461, 482, 493, 500, 502
Dysolve Dyslexia, 85, 114, 120, 138, 173, 224-6, 288, 396, 493, 500
Dysolve® Sounds and Spelling Manual, 36, 188
Dysolve® Word Frequency List, 62
ecosystem of human support, 86, 225, 246, 286, 460, 474
fees, subscriptions, payment plans, 369-70, 407, 412, 481, 504
games, gamification of, 237-43, 247, 254, 326, 339, 353, 461-2, 467, 509
human requirements, 460
hybrid program, 61, 187-9, 240-2, 263
improvements in reading, 36-7, 61-2, 110-1, 128-30, 233, 348-50, 502
indices in—*see also* Dysolve-measures in, 65, 262, 279, 290, 340
individuated programs, 423, 465
initial screening, 107, 340, 347, 353
intelligent system—*see also* intelligent program, 339, 454, 465, 467
latent changes during training, 56-8, 241
learning analytics, 467, 470
measures in, 57, 119, 275, 430, 433, 487, 499, 506
nanosecond response time capability, 460
personality changes, 67, 137
predictive analytics, 246, 467, 470
registration for, 353
results of, 5, 37, 49, 59, 95, 130, 153, 213, 242, 259, 299, 335, 341, 359, 470-2
reward system, 123, 353
solving dyslexia problem, 337, 430, 441
support system—*see* Dysolve-ecosystem of human support
system requirements, 459-60
training interruptions, 124, 131, 238, 341, 502
training period, 280, 340
training time, 228

Index

E
early childhood deprivation and language processing, 382-4
early screening for dyslexia, 249, 288, 482
Elliott, J., 422, 487
emotion dysfunction, 277
emotion regulation—*see under* ADHD
emotional factors and dyslexia—*see* dyslexia-affective factors
empowering students with learning disabilities, 29, 64, 90, 301, 318
English as a second language (ESL), 306-7, 352
errors, error rates
    orthographic/spelling, 35, 129, 269, 278-9
    reading—*see* misreadings
    syntactic, 234, 269, 278
evidence-based methods—*see also* reading clinics, 440, 448-50
exceptional, exceptionality—*see also* twice-exceptional, 52-3, 64, 81, 107
expertise of
    dyslexia expert, 107, 327, 338, 342, 343, 462, 466
    dyslexia/reading tutors, 217, 229, 432—*see also* compensatory methods
    dyslexia specialists, 417, 487-8
    teachers in dealing with learning disabilities, 319-21

F
family life and dyslexia, 219, 227, 305, 394
FastForword program, 422
Fernald, G., 418
fidelity of implementation, 498
foreign language learning and dyslexia, 110, 120
forgetfulness—*see also* memory, 36, 245, 375
free appropriate education (FAPE), 403
functional approach to dyslexia, 432-3
functional magnetic resonance imaging (fMRI), MRI studies, 419, 433, 435

G
gender differences and dyslexia, 39, 254, 276
genetics and dyslexia—*see under* dyslexia
giftedness—*see also* exceptional, *and* twice-exceptional
    education, 63

intellectual, 64
masking of learning disability, 64, 320, 347
perfectionism and, 82, 86
traits, 76, 495
witticism and, 52, 208
Gillingham, A., 417
Gillingham Manual, The, 126
grade retention, 185, 229, 233
Grigorenko, E., 422, 487

H

headaches, recurrent headaches, 225, 277-8, 295, 343, 390, 449, 492, 503
helplessness, 158, 248, 388
high school dropout rates, 325, 404
Hinshelwood, J., 416-7
holistic approach to dyslexia, 34
homework for those with dyslexia
    assistance from caretakers, 10, 13, 69-70, 72, 80, 107, 110
    issues, 60, 69-72, 80, 88, 90, 103, 107, 110, 185-9, 205, 231, 250-1, 264, 281, 345, 350, 371, 382
    struggles, 10-3, 60, 103, 107, 231, 281
    time spent, 12-3, 57, 88, 107, 250-1, 382
hyperactivity—*see under* ADHD

I

inattention, 6, 63, 274, 384
independent reading/learning, 32, 146, 186, 232, 234, 373
individual-based programs, 461, 463
Individualized Education Program/Plan (IEP), 25, 104, 174, 188, 316, 373
individualized programs/approaches, 222, 228, 320, 325, 461, 463, 465
individual-specific program, 116, 119, 228, 337, 339, 390
Individuals with Disabilities Education Act (IDEA), 314, 324, 403
individuated programs—*see under* Dysolve
innate language assumption, 431, 424
Institute of Education Sciences, 498, 510
instructional approaches for reading remediation—*see* reading remediation

Index

intelligence, high intelligence, 81, 146-7, 189, 208, 218, 236, 292, 495, 503
intelligent program—*see also* Dysolve-intelligent system, 183-4, 328, 472
intelligibility in writing, 35, 101
International Dyslexia Association (IDA), 418, 425
Internet "addiction", 162-3, 172
intervention programs, 18, 34, 127-8, 415, 466
intervention services—*see also* Academic Intervention Services, 118, 301, 371, 471
IQ criterion for dyslexia—*see under* dyslexia diagnosis
J
Johns Hopkins Center for Talented Youth, 53
L
language acquisition—*see also* snowballing effect, 276, 391-2, 427
language-based conditions, 369, 429, 490-2, 497-9
language-based learning disabilities/difference, 17, 412
language functions, 61, 381, 429, 508
language in society, language and society, 311
language modalities, 62, 453
language-processing deficits/problems, underlying deficits, 6, 429-33, 489-90
language variation, 311
latent changes during training—*see under* Dysolve
learning difference and dyslexia, 226, 253, 394, 491
learning disabilities—*see* specific learning disability
learning problems
    emotional disturbance and—*see also* anxiety, 392, 385, 491, 501
    environmental/economic disadvantage and, 309, 384, 491, 511
    intellectual disabilities and, 491
    physical disabilities and, 491
letter reversals—*see also* b/d reversal errors, 419, 435
lexical storage and retrieval, 124, 133, 271, 438, 450
lexical/word structure, 33, 58, 420, 426
lexile, reading lexile, 324
Lindamood-Bell, 436

linguistic-cognitive tasks, 247, 292
linguistic milestones—*see* developmental milestones
Linguistics, 368, 424, 439, 446
listening comprehension—*see under* discrepancies
literacy levels
    incarcerated population's, 16, 387, 405, 409
    juvenile/youth offenders', 387-8

M

maladaptive behaviors, 175, 484
math disability—*see* dyscalculia
math talent—*see also* visual/visuo-spatial talents, 253
MathCounts, 31, 328
meltdowns in autism, 158, 162-4, 176, 187
memory
    short-term memory, 16-7, 371
    superior memory, 71, 76, 82
    working memory, 16-7, 191
mental lexicon, 450-6
metacognitive awareness, metacognition, 64, 310, 495
metalinguistic awareness, 310
metaphors, 265, 276-7
metathesis, 35
microfeatures, 455, 469
Micro Linguistics, 454-5
micropatterns, 455
misreadings, 61, 77, 308
misspellings—*see* spelling errors
mixed expressive and receptive language disorder, 94, 116
motivation, self-motivation, 65, 240-4, 248, 375
MRI and dyslexia diagnosis—*see* functional magnetic resonance imaging
multisensory instruction—*see also* Orton-Gillingham, 117, 316, 320, 417-8, 469, 475, 499

N

Nation's Report Card, The, 85
National Reading Panel, 510
natural language, 444, 456
natural language processing, 454
negative behaviors—*see also* ADHD, *and* autism, 503

Index

neuroplasticity, 318, 325, 424-5
neuropsychological evaluations/assessments—*see under* dyslexia diagnosis

O

occupational therapy, 380
oppositional defiant disorder, 154, 161, 471
optimism in students who once had dyslexia, 90, 227, 248
oral comprehension in dyslexia—*see under* discrepancies
orthography—*see* spelling
Orton Dyslexia Society, 418
Orton, S., 417
Orton-Gillingham—*see also* compensatory methods, *and* multisensory instruction, *and* structured literacy, 75-6, 105-6, 117, 126, 286, 417, 432, 471, 483, 498
other health impairment (OHI), 380

P

paradoxical behaviors—*see also* discrepancies, 247, 384
parent/special education advocate, 22, 25, 121
parsing of sentence, 33, 40
perceptual sensitivity, 67
Perspectives on Language and Literacy, 418
phoneme-grapheme correspondences, 61
phonemic awareness—*see under* dyslexia
phonetic features, 442
phonics approach, 418
phonological awareness—*see under* dyslexia
phonological disorder, 94
phonological representations, 245
phonotactic constraints, 451
physical discomfort, 234, 274
physical posture changes, 101, 198, 223, 245, 253, 270
poor readers, 309, 312, 438
precocious development, 76, 276
premature birth and language deficits, 9, 16, 18, 37
problem behaviors—*see also* ADHD
    aggression, 63, 388
    avoidance of work—*see* avoidance behavior
    impulsivity—*see under* ADHD
    negativity—*see* negative behaviors

opposition—*see* oppositional defiant disorder
problem-complex of dyslexia, 187, 446-50, 470
processing speed, 40, 61-2, 227, 353
psychological counseling, 152, 192, 225, 380
psychosocial issues, 86, 176, 249, 389
Q
quantified measures—*see under* ADHD, *and* Dysolve-measures
R
reading
    accuracy—*see also* misreadings, 75, 425
    assessment results, 85, 260, 397
    clinics, 132, 233
    comprehension, 17, 53, 75, 85, 425-6
    errors—*see* misreadings
    fiction, 120, 348
    fluency, 128-9, 427
    grade-level competence, 69, 174, 233, 343, 350-1, 367, 390, 406, 471-2, 478, 494
    nonfiction, 120
    problems, 25, 175, 331, 419, 421, 424, 503
    progress—*see also* independent reading, 233
Reading and Writing, 418
reading disability—*see also* dyslexia
    classification of—*see also* specific learning disability, 17, 309, 490-1
    declassification of, 109, 126
    definition of, 427, 437
    high school dropouts and—*see own heading*
    prison inmates with—*see under* literacy levels
reading errors—*see* misreadings
reading remediation/intervention
    alternative therapies, 422
    auditory interventions, 422
    biofeedback, 488
    evidence-/research-based methods—*see* evidence-based methods
    individualized, personalized, individual-based, adaptive, 325, 461-3
    ineffectiveness by junior high, 320, 325, 499

instructional approaches of—*see* compensatory methods
lack of expertise in, 132, 233, 415, 421
low responders, nonresponders to, 405, 415
motor training, 488
multisensory instruction—*see own heading*
poor outcomes in, 404-5
structured literacy—*see own heading*
visual interventions, 488
reading statistics—*see* The Nation's Report Card
research-based methods, 478, 499
resilience, self-resilience, 63, 67, 91, 227, 387
resource room, 104, 116, 144-6
resource teacher, 83, 86
Response to Intervention (RTI), 372, 375, 421, 436, 474, 535
responsive intelligence technology—*see also* artificial intelligence, 454, 459, 463-7, 470, 473, 507
restlessness—*see also* ADHD-hyperactivity, 63, 240, 248, 266, 274, 276
role model to other students, 110, 273, 515

S

schema, 272, 280
segmentation hypothesis, 114, 245
self-consciousness, 320, 326
self-discipline, 55, 65, 91
self-efficacy, 227, 287, 525
self-esteem, 162, 311, 347, 352, 388, 504
semantic features, 443, 450
semantic-syntactic interface, 445
sign language, 18, 99, 135
signs/symptoms of dyslexia—*see* dyslexia-symptoms of
snowballing effect in language acquisition, 85, 391-2
Sociolinguistics—*see* language in society
sound-letter correspondences—*see* phoneme-grapheme correspondences
special education
    expenses, 401-5, 407, 412, 432, 500, 522
    federal and state spending, 234, 401, 403, 410
    outcomes, 324, 411, 483, 512-3
    services, 25, 76, 104, 116, 149, 160, 174, 224, 283, 368, 381,

410, 434, 496, 521, 531
teacher preparation, 313-7, 324
specific learning disability/disorder, 75, 353, 409, 425, 434, 490, 528
speech impairment, speech (sound) disorders, 25, 66, 113, 528-9
speech therapy, 4, 10, 19-21, 94, 102-3, 115, 149
spelling
    acquisition, 36, 67, 120, 243, 412
    errors in dyslexic and typical, 35, 41, 253, 268, 523
standardized reading test results, 62, 95, 124-5, 223, 259-260, 286, 359, 393-4, 482
standardized testing for dyslexia diagnosis—*see* dyslexia diagnosis
stress levels and children with learning disabilities, 39, 64, 118, 172, 175, 223, 246, 278, 293, 534, 536
structure-complex of natural language, 441-6
structured literacy—*see also* Orton-Gillingham, 418, 432, 495
students with learning disabilities
    high school graduation rates, 11, 325, 521
    college enrollment, 233-4, 238, 243, 317, 405
stuttering, 34, 40, 372, 524
suicide ideation, suicidal thoughts, 172, 202, 392, 484, 525, 536
summer reading programs, 117, 126
support system—*see* Dysolve-ecosystem of human support
syllabification, 35, 469
syllable structure, 58, 450, 456
syntactic analysis, 33, 234

T

talent development, 492
talents—*see also* exceptionality
    art, 105, 111, 196
    math, 110-1, 114, 137, 250, 293, 471
    music, 192
    sports, 72, 87, 192
    writing, 273, 470-1
Tallal, P., 422, 436, 534
teachers' attitudes toward students with learning disabilities, 44, 141-2, 209, 223, 252, 524
text comprehension, 17, 137, 191

twice-exceptional, twice-exceptionality—*see also* exceptional, and giftedness, 53, 63, 81-2, 90-1, 199, 495, 503, 505

U
Understood, 427, 437-438

V
victimization—*see* bullying
vision therapy, 21, 417
visual processing, 77, 490
visual/visuo-spatial talents, 114, 131, 492
vocabulary—*see also* discrepancies-oral and written vocabularies, 67, 80, 109, 120, 188, 273, 280, 426, 456, 497

W
WebMD, 428, 438
Wechsler Individual Achievement Test – 3rd Ed. (WIAT-III), 64, 375
whole-word approach, 418
Wilson Reading System, 281-2, 286, 404, 417
writing acquisition—*see* spelling acquisition
writing disability/disorder—*see* dysgraphia

Y
Yale Center for Dyslexia and Creativity, 427, 437
Yale longitudinal study on dyslexia, 419
youth offenders, 387-8

Acknowledgments

Critical decisions on a child's education that can determine her future are often made with great anxiety. Which path is the right one? What have others done in this situation? We speak for the many families out there who are grateful to the 10 cases in this book for the candid revelations on their own experiences. These cases courageously consented to disclose their school records so that others can compare results in a meaningful way to make their own decisions.

We thank as well our other contributors, especially Laura DiStefano and Stephanie and Richard Sackerman, for enabling a balanced view of the challenges faced by teachers and schools. Gloria Reyes deserves full credit for the structure of the case stories, for setting scenes and anchoring each chapter with the children's own words.

Given a project with no playbook, our reviewers helpfully stepped in to offer insightful critiques—Frances Gomes, Kevin Gaugler, Debbie Furman, Ryan Zaccaro, Julie Brooks and Jeanne Sullivan-Jones. Special thanks go to Chan Man Loon for his review from an engineering perspective.

As always, our family's steadfast assistance guided this project to fruition: Kieran Haruta, Charisse Haruta and Kyoichi Haruta. Lee Chi Hur's and Brent Kessler's strategic advice helped us decide on the final shape of this book. We are grateful to Hoh Ngai Hou and Hoh Ngai Seng for their unwavering support whenever we needed it.

Lastly, we thank Tony DiMarco and all who cheered us on and continue to spread the word.

Made in United States
Troutdale, OR
01/22/2025